OLD LONDON
Belgravia, Chelsea & Kensin

THE
'VILLAGE LONDON'
SERIES
from
THE VILLAGE PRESS

THE VILLAGE LONDON SERIES

Other titles already published in hardback are:

VILLAGE LONDON Volume I
VILLAGE LONDON Volume II
LONDON RECOLLECTED Volume I
LONDON RECOLLECTED Volume II
LONDON RECOLLECTED Volume III
LONDON RECOLLECTED Volume IV
LONDON RECOLLECTED Volume V
LONDON RECOLLECTED Volume VI
VILLAGE LONDON ATLAS

Other titles already published in paperback:

VILLAGE LONDON Pt. 1 West and North
VILLAGE LONDON Pt. 2 North and East
VILLAGE LONDON Pt. 3 South-East
VILLAGE LONDON Pt. 4 South-West

OLD FLEET STREET
CHEAPSIDE AND ST. PAUL'S
THE TOWER AND EAST END
SHOREDITCH to SMITHFIELD
CHARTERHOUSE to HOLBORN
STRAND to SOHO
COVENT GARDEN and the THAMES to WHITEHALL
WESTMINSTER to ST. JAMES'S
HAYMARKET to MAYFAIR
HYDE PARK to BLOOMSBURY
BELGRAVIA, CHELSEA & KENSINGTON
PADDINGTON GREEN TO SEVEN SISTERS
HIGHGATE & HAMPSTEAD TO THE LEA

The above thirteen titles are extracts from the hardback edition of London Recollected.

OLD LONDON

Belgravia, Chelsea & Kensington
by
EDWARD WALFORD

THE VILLAGE PRESS

British Library Cataloguing in Publication Data

Walford, Edward, *1823–1897*
  Old London: Belgravia, Chelsea and Kensington
  I. Title   II. Walford, Edward, *1823–1897*
942.1

ISBN 1-85540-016-2

This edition published 1989

The Village Press Ltd.,
7d Keats Parade
Church Street,
Edmonton,
London N9 9DP

Printed and bound in Great Britain
by Biddles Ltd. Guildford, Surrey

CONTENTS.

CHAPTER I.

BELGRAVIA.

CHAPTER II.

KNIGHTSBRIDGE.

CHAPTER III.

THE GREAT EXHIBITION OF 1851.

CHAPTER IV.

PIMLICO.

CHAPTER V.

CHELSEA.

CONTENTS.

CONTENTS.

LIST OF ILLUSTRATIONS.

THE ALBERT MEMORIAL.

THE CHELSEA EMBANKMENT.

HOLLAND HOUSE.

KENSINGTON PALACE.

SWAIN SC

LONDON.

THE WESTERN SUBURBS.

—◆—

CHAPTER I.

BELGRAVIA.

"'Tis hard to say—such space the city wins—
Where country ends and where the town begins."
"Prolusiones Paulinæ," 1876.

Prefatory Remarks—The Building of the District—De Moret, and his Flying-machine—Nature of the Soil of Belgravia—"Slender Billy"—The Spanish Monkey "Mukako" and Tom Cribb's Fighting Dogs—The Grosvenor Family—Enormous Rent-rolls—Belgravia and Bethnal Green compared—Lanesborough House—St. George's Hospital—Old "Tattersall's"—St. George's Place—Liston, the Comedian—Pope's School-days—The Alexandra Hotel—The Old Toll-gate at Hyde Park Corner—Grosvenor Place—The "Feathers" Tavern," and how George Prince of Wales was made an Odd Fellow there—Arabella Row—A Witty Lord Chancellor—The "Bag o' Nails"—The "Three Compasses"—Belgrave Square—"Gentleman Jones"—Eccleston Street—Sir Francis Chantrey—St. Paul's Church, Wilton Place—The Pantechnicon—Halkin Street—Upper and Lower Belgrave Streets—Suicide of Lord Munster—Eaton Square—Chester Square—Ebury Street—Lowndes Square—Cadogan Place—William Wilberforce—The Locality in Former Times.

AVING, in the previous volume, completed our peregrination of what may be called the *interior gyrus*—the innermost circle—of the great metropolis, we may now venture on a somewhat wider journey afield, and roam over that portion of the next circle—but still far from the outermost of all—which, not above half a century ago, certainly was *not* London, but as certainly now forms part of it. We hope, at all events, to find much that will be interesting to our readers even in modern "Belgravia;" but Knightsbridge and Paddington, Chelsea and Kensington, are each and all old enough to have histories of their own; and the two last-named villages have played a conspicuous part in the annals of the Court under our Hanoverian sovereigns, and in those of the aristocracy for even a longer period.

We purpose, therefore, to traverse in turn the fashionable area which has its centre fixed about Eaton and Belgrave Squares; then the undefined region of Knightsbridge, and that portion of Hyde Park which lies to the south of the Serpentine, and formed the site of the first Great Exhibition of 1851. Then across Pimlico to Chelsea, rich in its memories of Sir Hans Sloane and Nell Gwynne; to look in upon the household of good Sir Thomas More; and to speak of Chelsea's famous bun-house, and its ancient china-ware. Next we shall visit Brompton, the "Montpelier" of the metropolis; and then be off to the "old Court suburb" of Kensington, familiar to all Englishmen and Englishwomen as the home of William III., and of most of our Hanoverian sovereigns, and dear to them as the birthplace of Queen Victoria. We shall linger for a time under the shade of the trees which compose its pleasant gardens, and call up the royal memories of nearly two centuries. Then, bearing westwards, we shall look in upon the long galleries of Holland House, and see the chamber in which Addison died, and the rooms in which Charles James Fox and the leading Whigs of the last three reigns talked politics and fashionable news; thence to Percy Cross, and Walham Green and Parsons' Green, and to Fulham, for a thousand years the country seat of the Bishops of London both before and since the Reformation. Then we will saunter about the quaint old suburban village of Hammersmith, with its red-brick cottages and cedar-planted lawns, and so work our way round by way of Shepherd's Bush and Notting Hill —two names of truly rural sound—to Paddington and St. John's Wood—once the property of the Knights of St. John—and so to Kilburn, Hampstead, and Highgate, and Camden and Kentish Towns, till we once more arrive at St. Pancras.

With these few words by way of preface to the present volume, we again take our staff in hand, and turning our back on the "congestion" of traffic at Hyde Park Corner, which has lately been an object of legislation in Parliament, we turn our faces westward, and prepare to go on our way.

The name of "Belgravia" was originally applied as a *sobriquet* to Belgrave and Eaton Squares and the streets radiating immediately from them, but is now received as a collective popular appellation of that "City of Palaces" which lies to the southwest of Hyde Park Corner, stretching away towards Pimlico and Chelsea. The district was first laid out and built by Messrs. Cubitt, under a special Act of Parliament, passed in 1826, empowering Lord Grosvenor to drain the site, raise the level, and erect bars, &c. "During the late reign—that of George IV.," observes a writer in 1831—"Lord Grosvenor has built a new and elegant town on the site of fields of no healthy aspect, thus connecting London and Chelsea, and improving the western entrance to the metropolis, at a great expense."

Where now rise Belgrave and Eaton Squares, the most fashionable in the metropolis, there was, down to about the year above mentioned, an open and rural space, known as the "Five Fields." It was infested, as recently as the beginning of the present century, by footpads and robbers. These fields formed the scene of one of the first, but unsuccessful, attempts at ballooning in London. De Moret, a Frenchman, and a bit of an adventurer, proposed, in 1784, to ascend from some tea-gardens in this place, having attached to his balloon a car, not unlike some of the unwieldy summer-houses which may be seen in suburban gardens, and even provided with wheels, so that, if needful, it could be used as a travelling carriage. "Whether," says Chambers, in his "Book of Days," "M. Moret ever really intended to attempt an ascent in such an unwieldy machine, has never been clearly ascertained. . . . However, having collected a considerable sum of money, he was preparing for his ascent, on the 10th of August in that year, when his machine caught fire and was burnt; the unruly mob avenging their disappointment by destroying the adjoining property. The adventurer himself made a timely escape; and a caricature of the day represents him flying off to Ostend with a bag of British guineas, leaving the Stockwell Ghost, the Bottle Conjurer, Elizabeth Canning, Mary Toft, and other cheats, enveloped in the smoke of his burning balloon."

There was a time, and not so very distant in the lapse of ages, when much of Belgravia, and other parts of the valley bordering upon London, was a "lagoon of the Thames;" * indeed, the clayey swamp in this particular region retained so much water that no one would build there. At length, Mr. Thomas Cubitt found the strata to consist of gravel and clay, of inconsiderable depth. The clay

* In this lagoon there were many islands, as Chels*ey*, Bermonds*ey*, &c.

he removed and burned into bricks, and by building upon the substratum of gravel, he converted this spot from the most unhealthy to one of the most healthy in the metropolis, in spite of the fact that its surface is but a few feet above the level of the river Thames at high water, during spring-tides.

This mine of wealth—the present suburb, or rather city, of Belgravia, for such it has become—passed into the possession of the Grosvenor family in 1656, when the daughter and sole heiress of Alexander Davies, Esq., of Ebury Farm, married Sir Thomas Grosvenor, the ancestor of the present Duke of Westminster. This Mr. Davies died in 1663, three years after the Restoration, little conscious of the future value of his five pasturing fields. "In Queen Elizabeth's time," observes a writer in the *Belgravia* magazine, "this sumptuous property was only plain Eabury, or Ebury Farm, a plot of 430 acres, meadow and pasture, let on lease to a troublesome 'untoward' person named Wharle; and he, to her farthingaled Majesty's infinite annoyance, had let out the same to various other scurvy fellows, who insisted on enclosing the arable land, driving out the ploughs, and laying down grass, to the hindrance of all pleasant hawking and coursing parties. Nor was this all the large-hearted queen alone cared about; she had a feeling for the poor, and she saw how these enclosures were just so much sheer stark robbery of the poor man's right of common after Lammas-tide. In the Regency, when Belgrave Square was a ground for hanging out clothes, all the space between Westminster and Vauxhall Bridge was known as 'Tothill Fields,' or 'The Downs.' It was a dreary tract of stunted, dusty, trodden grass, beloved by bull-baiters, badger-drawers, and dog-fighters. Beyond this Campus Martius of prize-fighting days loomed a garden region of cabbage-beds, stagnant ditches fringed with pollard withes. There was then no Penitentiary at Millbank, no Vauxhall Bridge, but a haunted house half-way to Chelsea, and a halfpenny hatch, that led through a cabbage-plot to a tavern known by the agreeable name of 'The Monster.' Beyond this came an embankment called the Willow Walk (a convenient place for quiet murder); and at one end of this lived that eminent public character, Mr. William Aberfield, generally known to the sporting peers, thieves, and dog-fanciers of the Regency as 'Slender Billy.' Mr. Grantley Berkeley once had the honour of making this gentleman's acquaintance, and visited his house to see the great Spanish monkey 'Mukako' ('Muchacho') fight Tom Cribb's dogs, and cut their throats one after the other—apparently, at least—for the 'gentleman' who really bled the dogs and the peers was Mr.

Cribb himself, who had a lancet hidden in his hand, with which, under the pretence of rendering the bitten and bruised dogs help, he contrived, in a frank and friendly way, to open the jugular vein. A good many of the Prince Regent's friends were Slender Billy's also. Mr. Slender Billy died, however, much more regretted than the Regent, being a most useful and trusty member of a gang of forgers."

The Grosvenors, as already mentioned by us,* are one of the most ancient of the untitled English aristocracy, their ancestor having been the chief hunter (*Le Gros veneur*) to the Dukes of Normandy before the Conquest. It was not till a century ago that they condescended to bear a title, but since that time their growth to the very foremost rank in the peerage has been steady and well-earned, if personal worth and high honour, combined with immense wealth, are to be reckoned as any claim to a coronet.

The chief wealth of the Grosvenors, prior to the marriage of their head with Miss Davies, of Ebury Farm, was drawn out of the bowels of the earth in the north of England. Hence Pope writes—

" All Townshend's turnips, and all Grosvenor's mines."

There can be little doubt that, in right of his Manor of Ebury, the Duke of Westminster enjoys one of the largest rent-rolls, if not the very largest, in the kingdom. The current rumour of the day sets it down at £1,000 a day, or £365,000 a year. Other noblemen, especially the Dukes of Sutherland, Buccleuch, and Northumberland, are thought to approach very nearly to a like rental. As far back as the year 1819, the head of the Grosvenors was returned to the property-tax commissioners as one of the four richest noblemen in the kingdom, the three others being the Duke of Northumberland, the Marquis of Stafford (afterwards Duke of Sutherland), and the Earl of Bridgewater, the annual income in each case being in excess of £100,000. No other peers exceeded that sum at that time; but now, owing to the increased value of land in London, and the steady growth of the productiveness of the agricultural and mining industries, the owners of the above properties have much larger rent-rolls; and the probability is that there are ten or, perhaps, a dozen other peers whose incomes would reach the above-mentioned standard. A very different state of things, it must be said, from that which prevailed when Charles II. was on the throne, if Macaulay may be trusted when he writes of the year 1683 :—
" The greatest estates in the kingdom then very

little exceeded twenty thousand a year. The Duke of Ormond had twenty-two thousand a year. The Duke of Buckingham, before his extravagance had impaired his great property, had nineteen thousand six hundred a year. George Monk, Duke of Albemarle, who had been rewarded for his eminent services with immense grants of crown land, and who had been notorious both for covetousness and for parsimony, left fifteen thousand a year of real estate, and sixty thousand pounds in money, which probably yielded seven per cent. These three dukes were supposed to be three of the very richest subjects in England." The building of this great city of Belgravia, for such we are compelled to call it, fully justified William IV. in bestowing on his lordship the territorial title of "Marquis of Westminster," which has blossomed into a dukedom under Queen Victoria.

Viewing the great metropolis as a world in itself, as Addison and Dr. Johnson, and, indeed, all observant and thoughtful persons for these two centuries past have done, Belgravia and Bethnal Green become, both morally and physically, the opposite poles of the sphere of London—the frigid zones, so to speak, of the capital : the former, icy cold, from its stiff and unbending habit of fashion, form, and ceremony ; the other, wrapped in a perpetual winter of never-ending poverty and squalor.

But it is now time for us to proceed with our perambulation. Close by Hyde Park Corner, at the north end of Grosvenor Place, stands St. George's Hospital. It was built upon the site of a pleasant suburban residence of the first Lord Lanesborough, who died in 1723. Here he was out of the sound of the noisy streets, and could enjoy in private his favourite amusement of dancing. The reader will not forget the line of Pope, in which he is immortalised as—

" Sober Lanesborough, dancing with the gout."

Mr. Jesse writes : "So paramount is said to have been his lordship's passion for dancing, that when Queen Anne lost her Consort, Prince George of Denmark, he seriously advised her Majesty to dispel her grief by applying to his favourite exercise." But this may be possibly a piece of scandal and a *canard* of the day. Lord Lanesborough's house was beyond the turnpike gate, and Pennant says it was his lordship's "country house."

In 1733, Lanesborough House was converted into an infirmary by some seceding governors of Westminster Hospital. The old house for many years formed the central part of the hospital, two wings having been added to it when it was converted to its new purposes. A report of the governors for the year 1734, for which we are indebted to Maitland, tells us that "the hospital is now fitted up, and made much more complete than could have been expected out of a dwelling-house. It will at present contain sixty patients ; but, as the boundaries of their grounds will admit of new buildings for several spacious and airy wards, the subscribers propose to erect such buildings as soon as their circumstances shall enable them." These extra wards have since been supplied at a considerable expense, and in process of time the entire building has been reconstructed. From its commencement the hospital has been mainly dependent upon voluntary contributions, not being richly endowed like Guy's, St. Bartholomew's, and St. Thomas's. Fifty years after its foundation, the subscriptions amounted to a little over £2,000 a year. The hospital was aided by one-third of the proceeds of musical entertainments in the Abbey. In its first half century it had numbered 150,000 patients. The present edifice was commenced towards the end of the reign of George IV., by William Wilkins, R.A., the architect of the National Gallery, University College in Gower Street, and other important buildings ; but several additions have since been made to the original design, the latest being the erection of a new wing on the south-west side, in Grosvenor Crescent, which was completed about the year 1868.

The principal front of the hospital, facing the Green Park, is now nearly 200 feet in length, and forms a rather handsome elevation. The building contains a lecture theatre and an anatomical museum. The expenses of the institution are defrayed by voluntary contributions, and by the interest of funded property arising from legacies. In the year 1880, including some special gifts, its income amounted to upwards of £23,000 ; and the number of persons benefited during the year was above 20,000.

Mr. John Timbs, in his "Curiosities of London," mentions an "ingenious telegraph," which has been devised here for the transmission of orders through the different wards. "In the hall," he writes, "is a column three feet high, with a dial of engraved signals, and on the walls of the different wards are corresponding dials ; so that when the pointer to the hall dial is moved to any signal, all the others move accordingly, and a little hammer strikes a bell, by which means about fifty signals are transmitted daily to each ward, without the possibility of error or the least noise."

The Atkinson Morley Convalescent Home at Wimbledon is connected with this hospital, and there is also a medical school in connection with the institution. Of the many celebrated men whose names are more or less intimately associated with St. George's Hospital, may be mentioned those of Dr. Baily, Dr. W. Hunter, and his brother, John Hunter (who died here suddenly, having been violently excited by a quarrel in the board-room, while suffering under disease of the heart), Sir Benjamin Brodie, Sir Everard Home, and Dr. James Hope, the author of "A Treatise on the Diseases of the Heart," and on "Morbid Anatomy," who was chiefly instrumental in overcoming the prejudice that formerly existed in England, and especially at this hospital, against the use of the stethoscope in the examination of diseases of the chest.

In June, 1876, a curious accident occurred here. Through the bursting of a large tank on the roof, several tons of water suddenly broke through and deluged the lower floors, injuring some of the patients and the medical students, and causing the death of two or three of the patients. It need scarcely be added that, in the sanitary arrangements of the hospital, and also more especially in the important matter of ventilation, recourse has been had to the latest scientific improvements and discoveries.

Like other London hospitals, St. George's draws its patients very largely from the most unfriended classes in its vicinity, very much from the poor of all parts of London, and in no small degree from the poor of all parts of England. In 1870, an inquiry showed that there were above 330 in-patients. Of these, 100 resided within a mile of the hospital; 150 beyond that radius, but within four miles of Charing Cross; while the remainder came from all parts of the country.

At the south-eastern corner of St. George's Hospital, where now is Grosvenor Crescent, was formerly the entrance to Tattersall's celebrated auction-mart, "so renowned through all the breadth and length of horse-loving, horse-breeding, horse-racing Europe," which from all parts sends hither its representatives, when the more important sales are going on, and, with a confidence justified by the known character of the house, commissions the proprietor himself to procure for the nobles and gentry of the Continent fresh supplies for their studs of the finest English horses. The building itself, at the back, occupied part of the grounds of Lanesborough House. The entry was through an arched passage and down an inclined "drive," at the bottom of which was a public-house or "tap," designated "The Turf," for the accommodation of the throngs of grooms, jockeys, and poorer horse-dealers

and horse-fanciers. On the left, an open gateway led into a garden-like enclosure, with a single tree in the centre rising from the middle of a grass-plot, surrounded by a circular path of yellow sand or gravel. Immediately beyond the gateway was the subscription-room; this building, though small, was admirably adapted for the purposes for which it was designed, and it contained merely a set of desks arranged in an octagonal form in the centre, where bets were recorded, and money paid over. On the right of the passage, a covered gateway led into the court-yard, where the principal business of the place was carried on; this was surrounded on three sides by a covered way, and at the extremity of one side stood the auctioneer's rostrum, overlooking the whole area. The stables, where the horses to be sold were kept in the interim, were close at hand, and admirably arranged for light and ventilation. In the centre of the enclosure was a domed structure to an humble but important appendage—a pump, and the structure itself was crowned by a bust of George IV. About the year 1864, "Tattersall's"—as this celebrated auction-mart was familiarly called throughout Europe—was removed further westward to Knightsbridge, where we shall come to it shortly.

The public days at old "Tattersall's" were the Mondays in each week through the year, with the addition of Thursday during the height of the season. The horses of the chief sale, that of the Monday, arrived on the Friday previous. "When the settling-times arrive," observes a writer in the *Penny Magazine* for 1831, "great is the bustle and excitement that prevails throughout Tattersall's. Vehicles of all kinds dash to and fro in incessant motion, or linger altogether inactive in rows about the neighbourhood, while their masters are bidding for a good hunter or a pair of carriage-horses. A more motley assemblage than the buyers or lookers-on at such times it would be impossible to find. Noblemen and ambitious costermongers, bishops and blacklegs, horse-breeders, grooms, jockeys, mingling promiscuously with the man of retired and studious habits fond of riding and breeding the wherewithal to ride; tradesmen about to set up their little pleasure-chaise or business-cart; and commercial travellers, whose calling has inoculated them with a passion for dabbling in horseflesh, and who, in their inns on the road, talk with great gusto and decision of all that pertains to Tattersall's, on the strength of some occasional half-hour's experience in the court-yard."

Richard Tattersall, the founder of the above establishment, was training-groom to the last Duke of Kingston, brother of Lady Mary Wortley Montagu, and husband of the notorious duchess. On the death of his patron, in 1773, he appears to have opened his auction-mart; but the foundation of his fortune was laid by his purchase of the racehorse "Highflyer," for the enormous sum of £2,500, and, it is supposed, on credit—an evidence of the high character for integrity which he must have already acquired. "Of his personal qualities," it has been observed, "perhaps the establishment itself is the best testimony; what Tattersall's is now, it seems to

and extended as far as the Alexandra Hotel. Here Dr. Parr used to stay when he came up to London from his parsonage at Hatton. Here, too, lived for some years John Liston, the comedian, who had removed hither after his retirement from the stage. "He had long outlived the use of his faculties," writes Leigh Hunt, "and used to stand at his window at 'the Corner' sadly gazing at the tide of human existence which was going by, and which he had once helped to enliven." Mr.

ENTRANCE TO OLD "TATTERSALL'S." (*See page* 5.)

have essentially been from the very outset—a place where men of honour might congregate without breathing, or, at all events, in but a greatly lessened degree, the pestilential vapour that usually but too often surrounds the stable; where men of taste might enjoy the glimpses afforded of the most beautiful specimens of an exquisitely beautiful race, without being perpetually disgusted with the worst of all things—that of the jockey or horse-dealer." We shall have more to say of "Tattersall's," however, when we come to Knightsbridge.

St. George's Place, or Terrace, now a series of princely mansions, was, till lately, a long row of low brick houses, of only one or two storeys, on the west side of the hospital, fronting Hyde Park,

Planché, who was one of his most intimate friends, writes thus of this singular monomaniac: "His sole occupation was sitting all day long at the window of his residence, timing the omnibuses, and expressing the greatest distress and displeasure if any of them happened to be late. This had become a sort of monomania; his spirits had completely forsaken him. He never smiled or entered into conversation, and eventually he sunk into a lethargy, from which he woke no more in this world."

In this terrace, probably, was the school to which Pope was sent at ten or eleven years of age, and where, as he tells us, he forgot nearly all that he had learnt from his first instructor, a worthy priest;

ST. GEORGE'S HOSPITAL, 1745. (*See page 4.*)

and it is to his stay at this school that the poet thus refers later in life :—

> " Soon as I enter at my country door,
> My mind resumes the thread it dropt before ;
> Thoughts, which at Hyde Park Corner I forgot,
> Meet and rejoin me in my pensive grot."

The Alexandra Hotel, which covers the ground formerly occupied by some half-dozen of the houses in St. George's Place, is one of the most important and largest hotels in the metropolis. It was built shortly after the marriage of the Prince of Wales with the Princess Alexandra of Denmark, after whom it is named. The hotel is largely patronised by families of distinction from the country, and also by foreign notabilities, who, during their stay in London, desire to be within easy reach of the Court and the principal quarters of the West End. A few short yards westward beyond the Alexandra Hotel the roadway enters Knightsbridge, which we shall deal with in the next chapter.

The old toll-gate at Hyde Park Corner, between Piccadilly and Knightsbridge, considerably narrowed the entrance into Piccadilly at its western end ; and its removal, as we have mentioned in our account of that thoroughfare,* was a great improvement not only to Piccadilly itself, but to Knightsbridge as well. Our illustration (see page 10) shows the auctioneer in the act of brandishing his hammer, and exclaiming, *de more*, "Once, twice, thrice ! Going, going, gone !" to the great satisfaction, no doubt, of the speculative contractor who purchased the old materials in order to mend the roads.

Grosvenor Place forms the eastern boundary of Belgravia, extending southward from St. George's Hospital, and overlooking the gardens of Buckingham Palace, of which we have already spoken. It was till recently described as "a pleasant row of houses," mostly built during the Grenville Administration, in the early part of the present century. "When George III. was adding a portion of the Green Park to the new garden at Buckingham House," says Mr. Peter Cunningham, quoting from Walpole's "George III.," " the fields on the opposite side of the road were to be sold, at the price of £20,000. This sum Grenville refused to issue from the Treasury. The ground was consequently leased to builders, and a new row of houses, overlooking the king in his private walks, was erected, to his great annoyance."

Lord Hatherton removed, in 1830, from Portman Square to a house in Grosvenor Place, which Macaulay terms a palace. Macaulay tells about

this neighbourhood a good story, which would not gratify the pride of the head of the house of Grosvenor. "When Lord Hatherton changed his residence his servants gave him warning, as they could not, they said, go into such an unheard-of part of the world as Grosvenor Place. I can only say that I have never been in a finer house." Verily there is as much truth to-day, as there was two thousand years ago, in the old Roman satirist's line—

" Maxima quæque domus servis est plena superbis."

Lord Hatherton continued to reside here for many years. He had a choice gallery of paintings, which are mentioned, in some detail, by Dr. Waagen, in his work on " Art and Artists in England."

During the years 1873-76 the appearance of a great part of this street was totally changed. In place of some dozen or so houses of ordinary appearance, which formerly stood at the north end, five princely mansions have been erected, in the most ornate Italian style ; one of these is occupied by the Duke of Grafton, and another by the Duke of Northumberland, since his expulsion from Charing Cross. Lower down is the residence of the head of the Rothschild family. In the adjoining house lived for some time the late Earl Stanhope (better known by his courtesy title of Lord Mahon), the historian and essayist, author of a "History of the War of the Succession in Spain," "A History of England, from the Peace of Utrecht," and other works. Lord Stanhope, who was many years President of the Society of Antiquaries, was grandson of the inventor of the Stanhope printing-press.

At the southern end, in Hobart Place, formerly Grosvenor Street West, was an inn called "The Feathers," about which a good story is told by Mr. J. Larwood in his "History of Sign-boards :"— "A lodge of Odd Fellows was held at this house, into the private chamber of which George Prince of Wales one night intruded very abruptly, with a roystering friend. The society at that moment was celebrating some of its awful mysteries, which no uninitiated eye might behold, and these were witnessed by the profane intruders. The only way to repair the sacrilege was to make the Prince and his companion 'Odd Fellows'—a title which they certainly deserved as richly as any members of the club. The initiatory rites were quickly gone through, and the Prince was chairman for the remainder of the evening. In 1851 the old public-house was pulled down, and a new gin-palace built on its site, in the parlour of which," adds Mr. Larwood, "the chair used by the distinguished 'Odd Fellow' is still preserved, along with a portrait of his Royal High-

---

* See Vol. IV., p. 290.

ness in the robes of the order." Another public-house in Grosvenor Street perpetuated, writes Mr. J. Larwood, the well-known fable of the "Wolf and the Lamb," which was pictured by a sign representing a lion and a kid. The house was known as the "Lion and Goat."

At the bottom of Grosvenor Place, and reaching to Buckingham Palace Road, is a large triangular piece of ground, intersected by a part of Ebury Street, and covered with lofty and handsomely-constructed houses, known respectively as Grosvenor Gardens and Belgrave Mansions. On the east side of this triangular plot is Arabella Row, one side of which is occupied by the royal stables of Buckingham Palace, which we have already described.* This row was once, not so very long ago, well tenanted. Among others, here lived Lord Erskine, after he had ceased to hold the seals as Lord Chancellor. His lordship, who held them only a year, was not only an orator, but a wit, as the following anecdote will show :—Captain Parry was once at dinner in his company, when Lord Erskine asked him what he and his crew lived upon in the Frozen Sea. Parry said that they lived upon seals. "And capital things, too, seals are, if you only keep them long enough," was the reply. One of the houses in Arabella Row is the official residence of the Queen's Librarian at Windsor Castle.

At the corner of Arabella Row and Buckingham Palace Road, is a public-house, rejoicing in the once common sign of the "Bag o' Nails"—a perversion of "The Bacchanals" of Ben Jonson. "About fifty years ago," writes the author of "Tavern Anecdotes," in 1825, "the original sign might have been seen at the front of the house; it was a Satyr of the Woods, with a group of 'jolly dogs,' ycleped Bacchanals. But the Satyr having been painted black, and with cloven feet, it was called by the common people 'The Devil;' while the Bacchanalian revellers were transmuted, by a comic process, into the 'Bag of Nails.'"

In Grosvenor Row, a thoroughfare which has disappeared in the march of modern improvements that have recently taken place in this neighbourhood, was another inn, "The Three Compasses," well known as a starting-point for the Pimlico omnibuses. It was generally known as the "Goat and Compasses"—possibly a corruption of the text, "God encompasseth us;" though Mr. P. Cunningham sees in it a reproduction of the arms of the Wine Coopers' Company, as they appear on a vault in the Church of S. Maria di Capitolo, at Cologne—a shield, with a pair of compasses, an axe, and a dray, or truck, with goats for supporters. "In a country like England, dealing so much at one time in Rhenish wine, a more likely origin," he observes, "could hardly be imagined." Mr. Larwood, however, points out that possibly the "Goat" was the original sign, and that the host afterwards added the Masonic "Compasses," as is often done now.

Belgrave Square, into which we now pass, was so named after the Viscountcy of Belgrave, the second title of Earl Grosvenor before he was raised to his superior titles. It was built in the year 1825, and covers an area of about ten acres. It was designed by George Basevi, the detached mansions at the angles being the work of Hardwick, Kendall, and others. It is nearly 700 feet in length by a little over 600. The houses are uniform, except the large detached mansions at the angles. Those in the sides are adorned with Corinthian columns and capitals.

Belgrave Square has always been occupied by the heads of the highest titled nobility, and by many foreigners of distinction. Lord Ellesmere lived here till he built Bridgewater House. Among other notabilities who have resided here may be named the first Lord Combermere, Sir Roderick Murchison, the geologist, Sir Charles Wood, afterwards Lord Halifax, and General Sir George Murray, who acted as Quartermaster-General to the British army during the Peninsular War. At the south-west corner lived for some years another distinguished General, Lord Hill, the hero of Almarez. In this square the Count de Chambord and his mother held their court, during a short visit which they paid to England in 1843. The Austrian Embassy has been for several years located in this square.

In Chapel Street, which runs from the south-east corner of Belgrave Square into Grosvenor Place, resided Mr. Richard Jones, a teacher of elocution, generally known as "Gentleman Jones," who is mentioned by Lord William Lennox, and by nearly all the writers of modern London anecdote. Here he used to have scores of pupils practising for the pulpit, the bar, or the senate. "Under his able tuition," says Lord W. Lennox, "many a reverend gentleman, who mumbled over the service, became a shining light; many an embryo lawyer, who spoke as if he had a ball of worsted in his mouth, became a great orator; and many a member of Parliament, who 'hummed and hawed,' and was unintelligible in the gallery, turned out a distinguished speaker."

Eccleston Street derives its name from Eccleston,

---

* See Vol. IV., p. 69.

in Cheshire, where the Grosvenors own a property. The large house at the corner of this street was for many years the residence of Sir Francis Chantrey, the sculptor. He was born at Norton, near Sheffield, in 1781, and, as a boy, used to ride a donkey, carrying milk into the town. "On a certain day, when returning home upon his donkey, Chantrey was observed by a gentleman to be very intently engaged in cutting a stick with

There is, or was, in it a small gallery with a lanthorn, by Sir John Soane. Sir F. Chantrey was pronounced by the "Foreigner," who is known as the author of "An Historical and Literary Tour in England," to be the only English sculptor of his age who was distinguished by true originality, though still young in reputation.

Macaulay tells a good story of him, and one most creditable to his magnanimity, which kept him

SALE OF HYDE PARK TURNPIKE.   (*See page* 8.)

his penknife. Excited by his curiosity, he asked the lad what he was doing, when, with great simplicity of manner, but with courtesy, the lad replied, 'I am cutting *old Foxe's head.*' Foxe was the schoolmaster of the village. On this, the gentleman asked to see what he had done, pronounced it to be an excellent likeness, and presented the youth with *sixpence;* and this may, perhaps, be reckoned the first money which Chantrey ever obtained for his ingenuity."

He took up his residence here shortly after his marriage in 1809. The house was then two separate residences—Nos. 29 and 30, Lower Belgrave Place—but Chantrey threw the two houses into one, and named them anew as part of Eccleston Street. In the studios at the back, all his best works—his bust of Sir Walter Scott, his "Sleeping Children," and his statue of Watt—were executed.

from being ashamed of his early struggles in life. When Chantrey dined with Rogers, he took particular notice of a certain vase, and of the table on which it stood, and asked Rogers who made the latter. "A common carpenter," said Rogers. "Do you remember the making of it?" asked Chantrey. "Certainly," replied Rogers, in some surprise; "I was in the room while it was finished with the chisel, and gave the workmen directions about placing it." "Yes," said Chantrey. "I was the carpenter; I remember the room well, and all the circumstances." Chantrey died at the close of the year 1841: he expired whilst sitting in an easy-chair in his drawing-room. By his will Sir Francis left a considerable sum to the Royal Academy, to be devoted to endowing the Presidentship of that institution, and in other ways to "the encouragement of British Fine Art in Painting and Sculpture," the bequest to take effect on the death or second marriage of his wife. Lady Chantrey died in 1875, when the above legacy, which had gone on accumulating, became available for the purposes to which it was to be devoted.

On the north-west side of Belgrave Square are Wilton Crescent and Wilton Place. In the latter, which opens into Knightsbridge Road, a little westward of the Alexandra Hotel, is St. Paul's Church, which is deserving of notice, from the fact of its clergy having always been prominent leaders of the Ritualistic or extreme "high church" party. The first incumbent was the Rev. W. J. E. Bennett, who was succeeded by the Hon. and Rev. Robert Liddell, and he by Lord Russell's son-in-law, Mr. Villiers. The church, which was consecrated in 1843, is built in the Early Perpendicular style, and was erected at a cost of £11,000. It consists only of a nave and chancel, and a lofty tower crowned with eight pinnacles; the windows are filled with stained glass, and the interior is rich in ornamentation. This church has been the scene of many a strong conflict between the parishioners and the incumbent respecting the ceremonials carried on here, which culminated in one of the vestrymen, more courageous than the rest—a Mr. Westerton— bringing the matter in dispute before the courts of law.

Between Motcomb, Lowndes, and Kinnerton Streets, all of which are on the western side of the square, is a large building, called the Pantechnicon, used of late years for storing furniture, carriages, works of art, &c. It was originally built about the year 1834, as a bazaar, and was established principally for the sale of carriages and household furniture. There was also a "wine department," consisting of a range of dry vaults for the reception and display of wines; and the bazaar contained likewise a "toy department." The building, which covered about two acres, was burnt to the ground in 1874, when a large quantity of valuable property was destroyed. The work of rebuilding was soon afterwards commenced, the new structure being erected on detached blocks, and of fire-proof materials, so that the chances of the building being again destroyed in a similar way are considerably reduced.

Halkin Street, on the northern side of the square, was so called from Halkin Castle, in Flintshire, one of the seats of the ducal owner. In this street is a chapel, which has been since 1866 used by the Presbyterian body. The building is somewhat singular in shape, neither square nor oblong, the end opposite the entrance being considerably wider than the other.

Connecting the south-east corner of Belgrave Square with Ebury Street, and skirting the east ends of Eaton and Chester Squares, are Upper and Lower Belgrave Streets. In the former, in 1842, the Earl of Munster committed suicide. He was the eldest son of William IV. by Mrs. Jordan. He married Miss Wyndham, one of the natural daughters of Lord Egremont, with whom he had a fortune of £40,000 or £50,000. He had the place of Constable of Windsor Castle, which was continued to him by the Queen, and he had just been appointed to the command of the troops at Plymouth, with which he was much pleased. Mr. Raikes, in his "Journal," speaks of him as "a very amiable man in private life, not without some talent, and given to study Eastern languages." As Colonel Fitz-Clarence, he had shown great bravery and energy in arresting the leaders of the Cato Street conspiracy. He was raised to a peerage on his father's accession to the throne.

Eaton Square was designed and built by Messrs. Cubitt in 1827. It was named after Eaton Hall, in Cheshire, the principal seat of the Duke of Westminster. It occupies an oblong piece of ground, and the centre is divided by roadways into six separate enclosures. No. 71 was for some time, during the rebuilding of the Houses of Parliament, the official residence of the Speaker of the House of Commons. Most of the mansions, in fact, have at different times been occupied by members of one or other division of the Legislature. No. 75 was for many years the residence of the late Mr. Ralph Bernal, M.P. for Rochester, and Chairman of Committees in the House of Commons. He was a distinguished antiquary and connoisseur, and made here his superb collection of works of art, including china, armour, articles of *virtu*, and antiquities of every description, the sale of which, occupying thirty-two days, was one of the "events" of the season of 1855.

At No. 83 lived, during the closing years of his life, the late Lord Truro. The son of an attorney on College Hill, in London, Thomas Wilde began life in his father's office; but having afterwards studied for the higher branch of the profession, he was, at the age of thirty-five, called to the bar at the Inner Temple. In 1820 he was engaged as one of the counsel for Queen Caroline on her "trial" in the House of Lords, which, doubtless, brought him a handsome fee; and he is said to have had a retaining fee of 3,000 guineas in the case of the British Iron Company against Mr. John Attwood. Before his accession to the Upper House on being made Lord Chancellor, he sat in the House of Commons as member for Newark.

and also for the City of Worcester. He died in 1855, immensely rich, having married, as his second wife, a daughter of the late Duke of Sussex.

At the east end of the square is St. Peter's Church, an Ionic building designed by Hakewill, western end of the square, was erected in 1844, the foundation-stone being laid by Earl Grosvenor, father of the present Duke of Westminster; and it was built from the designs of Mr. Thomas Cundy in the Decorated style of the fourteenth century.

INTERIOR OF THE COURT-YARD OF OLD "TATTERSALL'S." (*See page* 5.)

and consecrated in 1827. The altar-piece, "Christ crowned with thorns," was painted by W. Hilton, R.A., and presented to the church by the British Institution.

Chester Square, which almost abuts upon the north side of Eaton Square, was commenced about the year 1840, and was so called after the City of Chester, near which place Eaton Hall is situated. The picturesque Gothic church of St. Michael, which stands in a commanding position at the

Its principal external feature is the tower, with a lofty spire, which, till some additions to the body of the church were made in 1874, appeared to be somewhat out of proportion to the remainder of the fabric.

Ebury Street and Ebury Square were so called from Ebury or Eabery Farm, which stood on this site. The farm embraced upwards of 400 acres, meadow and pasture, and was let on lease by Queen Elizabeth for the sum of £21 per annum, to a person named Whashe, by whom, as Strype tells us, "the same was let to divers persons, who, for their private commodity, did inclose the same and had made pastures of arable land; thereby not only annoying her Majesty in her walks and passages, but to the hindrance of her game, and great injury to the common, which at Lammas was wont to be laid open." In Ebury Street there was formerly an open-air skating-rink and club-house,

Chesham, in Buckinghamshire, the ground landlord, a descendant of William Lowndes, Secretary to the Treasury in the reign of Queen Anne." "The site of this square," as Mr. John Timbs informs us, "was once a coppice, which supplied the Abbot and Convent of Westminster with wood for fuel."

Lowndes Square has numbered among its residents at different times men who have distinguished themselves in their several walks of life. Of them

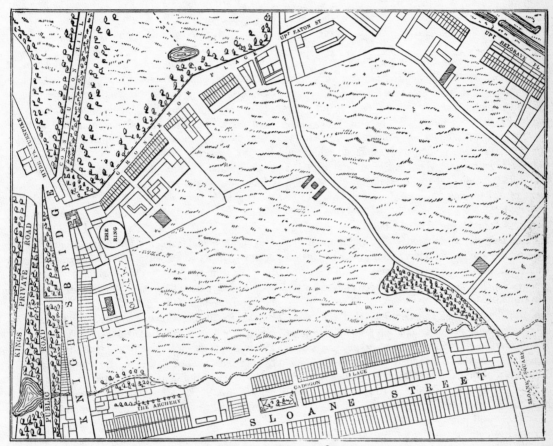

MAP OF BELGRAVIA, 1814.

called the "Belgravia." Its career, however, was but of short duration, as the skating-rink mania soon passed away. The Manor House of the Eabury Estate stood between Hobart Place and the bottom of Grosvenor Place.

The western limits of Belgravia are Lowndes Square, Cadogan Place, and the few connecting streets on the east side of Sloane Street. Lowndes Square itself dates from about the year 1838, when it was built on a vacant piece of ground, described in Rocque's "Map of London and its Environs," engraved in 1746, as then belonging to "—Lowndes, Esq.;" and it was so called, says Mr. Peter Cunningham, "after Mr. Lowndes, of The Bury, near

we may mention Sir John Rennie, the architect of New London Bridge; Sir William Tite, another distinguished architect, and some time M.P. for Bath; General Lord Airey; Thomas Brassey, the engineer; and the Right Hon. Robert Lowe, M.P. for London University.

At the corner of Lowndes Square and Cadogan Place, we quit the Duke of Westminster's estate. Cadogan Place, which occupies an extensive area of ground, is open on the west side to Sloane Street. It is called after the family of Lord Cadogan, into whose hands the manor of Chelsea came, by the marriage of the first Lord Cadogan with the heiress of Sir Hans Sloane.

Here lived Mr. and Mrs. Zachary Macaulay from about 1818 to 1823, when they removed to Great Ormond Street, as already stated. From Cadogan Place, the young Macaulays used to walk on a Sunday—or, as they were taught to call the day, the " Sabbath "—across the " Five Fields," now Belgrave Square, to the Lock Chapel, then situated in Grosvenor Place.

In a house in Cadogan Place, on the 29th of July, 1833, died William Wilberforce, the eminent philanthropist, many years M.P. for Yorkshire, who is best known for his devotion to the abolition of the slave-trade. There is something peculiarly touching in the fact that Wilberforce died—*felix opportunitate mortis*—just as the abolition of the slave-trade was in the act of being carried through Parliament, and the last fetters struck from the slaves' hands and feet. His funeral took place on the 3rd of August, in Westminster Abbey. On that day, his friend's son, Thomas Babington Macaulay, writes :—" We have laid him side by side with Canning, at the feet of Pitt, and within two steps of Fox and Grattan. He died with the promised land full in view." Before the end of the next month the British Parliament formally abolished slavery throughout the dominions of the Crown, and the last touch was put to the work that had consumed so many pure and noble lives. It was agreed that he should have been buried in the grave of his friends the Stephens, at Stoke Newington, but the voice of the country ruled otherwise. A subscription was immediately opened among Mr. Wilberforce's friends in London, and his statue has been placed in Westminster Abbey. At York, a County Asylum for the Blind has been founded in honour of him, while his townsmen of Hull have raised a column to his memory. Great part of our coloured population in the West Indies went into mourning at the news of his death ; and the same was the case at New York, where also an eulogium was pronounced upon him by a person publicly selected for the task.

In Cadogan Place lived Sir Herbert Taylor, the Private Secretary and attached friend of King William IV. Here, too, was the last London residence of the celebrated actress, Mrs. Jordan. Another resident in Cadogan Place, in more recent times, was Mr. Wynn Ellis, of Tankerton Castle, Whitstable, formerly M.P. for Leicester. He had for many years a mania for collecting pictures, chiefly the works of the old masters, of which he was an excellent connoisseur. Dr. Waagen (1835), in his " Art and Artists in England," mentions a visit paid by him to Mr. Wynn Ellis's gallery :— " He possesses, besides many good old pictures, the best copy of Wilson's celebrated landscape, together with the ' Children of Niobe,' formerly in the possession of the Duke of Gloucester."

Mr. Wynn Ellis died in 1875, having by his will left to the nation, for exhibition in the National Gallery, his large collection of the works of the old masters. These alone number some four or five hundred. The mere mention of the names of certain of the artists tell their own tale ; for among the collection there are more than one painting, in some cases several, from the brushes of Raphael, Rubens, Murillo, Claude, Van der Velde, Hobbima, Holbein, Guido, Leonardo da Vinci, the Poussins, and a score of others. Mr. Ellis's collection of works by modern artists was brought to the hammer at Christie's, and the sale formed one of the events of the season. Mr. Ellis began life as a warehouseman on Ludgate Hill, and accumulated a large fortune, many thousands of which he left to different charities.

Of Sloane Square, at the south end of Cadogan Place, we shall speak in a future chapter, when dealing with Sloane Street.

In a map of London and its neighbourhood, published in 1804, the whole of the site of Belgravia, between Grosvenor Place and Sloane Street, appears still covered with fields. They are crossed by " the King's private road," which is now occupied by Hobart Place, the roadway in the centre of Eaton Square, and Westbourne Place, terminating in Sloane Square. About the centre of Grosvenor Place, at that time, stood the Lock Hospital or Asylum, which was founded in 1787 by the Rev. Thomas Scott, the commentator ; a little to the south, at the corner of the " King's private road," was the Duke's Hospital. What is now Ebury Street was then an open roadway, called Ranelagh Street, having a few houses on one side only. Twenty years later the whole character of this locality was considerably changed. Belgrave Square and Wilton Crescent had sprung into existence, as also had Cadogan Square and Cadogan Place, together with a few connecting streets. Sir Richard Phillips, in his " Walk from London to Kew," published in 1817, speaks of the creeks which at that time ran from the Thames " in the swamps opposite Belgrave Place," and adds that they " once joined the canal in St. James's Park, and, passing through Whitehall, formed by their circuit the ancient isle of St. Peter's. Their course," he continues, " has been filled up between the wharf of the water-works and the end of the canal in St. James's Park, and the isle of St. Peter's is no longer to be traced." The cut on the preceding page shows the locality in 1814.

CHAPTER II.

KNIGHTSBRIDGE.

" Cubat hic in colle Quirini,
Hic extremo in Aventino ; visendus uterque :
Intervalla vides humanè commoda."—*Horace*.

Derivation ot the Name of Knightsbridge—Early History of the Locality—The Old Bridge—Insecurity of the Roads, and Bad Reputation of the Innkeepers—Historical Events connected with Knightsbridge—The Old " Swan " Inn—Electioneering Riots—An Eccentric Old Lady—The " Spring Garden " and the " World's End "—Knightsbridge Grove—Mrs. Cornelys as a Vendor of Asses' Milk—Albert Gate—The " Fox and Bull "—The French Embassy—George Hudson, the " Railway King "—The Cannon Brewery—Dunn's Chinese Gallery—Trinity Chapel and the Lazar House—" Irregular " Marriages—Knightsbridge Barracks—Smith and Barber's Floor-cloth Manufactory—Edward Stirling, the " Thunderer " of the *Times*—Kent House—Kingston House—Rutland Gate—Ennismore Place—Brompton Oratory—Brompton Church—Count Rumford and other Distinguished Residents—New " Tattersall's "—The Green—Chalker House—The " Rose and Crown " Inn—The " Rising Sun "—Knightsbridge Cattle Market.

In the early Saxon days, when " Chelsey," and " Kensing town," and " Charing " were country villages, there lay between all three a sort of " No Man's Land," which in process of time came to be called " Knightsbridge," although it never assumed, or even claimed, parochial honours, nor indeed could be said to have had a recognised existence. It was a district of uncertain extent and limits ; but it is, nevertheless, our purpose to try and " beat the bounds " on behalf of its former inhabitants.

The name of Knightsbridge, then, must be taken as indicating, not a parish, nor yet a manor, but only a certain locality adjoining a bridge which formerly stood on the road between London and far distant Kensington. There is much difficulty as to the derivation of the name, for in the time of Edward the Confessor, if old records are correctly deciphered, it was called " Kyngesburig;" while some hundred years or so later we find it spoken of as " Knightsbrigg," in a charter of Herbert, Abbot of Westminster. A local legend, recorded by Mr. Davis, in his " History of Knightsbridge," says that : " In ancient time certain knights had occasion to go from London to wage war for some holy purpose. Light in heart, if heavy in arms, they passed through this district on their way to receive the blessing awarded to the faithful by the Bishop of London at Fulham. For some cause or other, however, a quarrel ensued between two of the band, and a combat was determined upon to decide the dispute. They fought on the bridge which spanned the stream of the Westbourne, whilst from its banks the struggle was watched by their partisans. Both fell, if the legend may be trusted ; and the place was ever after called Knightsbridge, in remembrance of their fatal feud."

Another possible derivation of the name is quoted from Norden, the topographer, by the Rev. M. Walcott, in his " Memorials of Westminster : "—" Kingsbridge, commonly called Stonebridge, near Hyde Park Corner, [is a place] where

I wish no true man to walk too late without good guard, as did Sir H. Knyvett, Knight, who valiantly defended himself, there being assaulted, and slew the master thief with his own hands." However, in all probability the name is of older date than either of the above events ; therefore we may be content to leave the question for the solution ot future topographers, merely remarking that whether it was originally " Knightsbrigg," or " Kyngesbrigg," King Edward the Confessor held lands here, and possibly may have built a bridge for the use of the monks of Westminster, to whom he devised a portion of his acres. That such was the case we learn from a charter preserved in the British Museum, which conveyed to the monks of Westminster, along with the manor of Chelsea, " every third tree, and every horse-load of fruit grown in an adjacent wood at Kyngesbyrig, as heretofore by law accustomed."

" Knightsbridge," observes Mr. Davis, in his " History," " is not mentioned in Domesday Book, neither are Westbourne, or Hyde, or Paddington, these places being probably included in the surrounding manors." Moreover, we read that " Knightsbridge lies in the manor of Eia or Ea, formerly a portion of Cealcyth (Chelcheth or Chelsey), and now known as Eabury or Ebury." The manor of Ea, as confirmed to the Abbey of Westminster by the Conqueror, seems to have included all the lands lying between the Westbourne on the west, and the Tyburn on the east, from the great road which ran from Tyburn towards Uxbridge down to the Thames. Yet, curiously enough, as Mr. Davis tells us, though given thus early to the Abbey, the manor was not included in the franchise of the city of Westminster, though Knightsbridge, which lay partly, at least, beyond it, was so included. The fact is the more strange, as a large part of Knightsbridge belonged for many centuries, and indeed still in theory belongs, to the parish of St. Margaret, Westminster.

In the course of time the monks of Westminster

appear to have claimed and exercised further rights over this district, including the holding of market and a fair, the erection of a gallows-tree, and those of imprisoning evil-doers, and of seizing the goods of condemned persons and run-aways. They further appropriated sundry lay fees in "Knythbrigg, Padyngton, Eya, and Westbourne, without licence of the king." In 1222 the Tyburn stream was laid down as the west boundary of that parish, excepting the hamlet of Knightsbridge, which lay beyond it.

The manor of Ea, or Eabury, was afterwards included in St. Martin's-in-the-Fields, when the latter was cut off from St. Margaret's; but when St. George's, Hanover Square, was carved out of St. Martin's, in 1724, both Knightsbridge and Eabury were assigned to the parish of St. George's. The rivulet, however, being made the western boundary between St. George's parish and Chelsea, it came about that Knightsbridge stands partly in all the three parishes above mentioned. When the bounds of St. Margaret's and other parishes were beaten, the parochial authorities passed through one part or other of the hamlet; and we may be sure that many a Knightsbridge urchin was whipped at the frontiers in order to impress the exact limits indelibly on his memory. Indeed, in the parish books of St. Margaret's there are several entries of sums spent by the beadles, &c., at Knightsbridge, on the "perambulation." Knightsbridge was, at all events, cut off, at a very early date, from St. Margaret's parish. It would appear, therefore, that only a portion of the hamlet was within the manor of Ea, including, as nearly as possible, all that now forms the parish of St. George's, Hanover Square. In Domesday Book it is given as ten hides; it was afterwards divided into three manors —viz., Neyte, Eabury, and Hyde. The first-named manor was near the Thames; and Hyde, with certain lands taken from Knightsbridge, formed Hyde Park. All these manors belonged to the Abbey till the Reformation, when they "escheated to"—i.e., were seized by—the king. They were afterwards exchanged by his most gracious and rapacious majesty for the dissolved Priory of Hurley, in Berkshire.

Somehow or other, however, though the time and the way are not known, Knightsbridge reverted to its former owners, the Abbey of Westminster, in whose hands it has since remained, with the ex-ception of the few years of the Puritan Protectorate, though the outlying lands about Kensington Gore passed into lay hands, as also did the manor of Eabury, in which it would seem that there was abundance of game, and large portions of waste land laid open to them for the pasturage of their cattle. Be this as it may, however, the manor passed into the hands first of the Whashes, or Walshes, and then into those of a family named Davis, the last male of whom, Alexander Davis, left an only daughter and heiress, Mary, who, in 1676, was married, at St. Clement Danes' Church, to Sir Thomas Grosvenor, into whose hands she carried the manor, as already stated. Her lineal descendants, it is almost needless to state, are the present Duke of Westminster and Lord Ebury.

The bridge which spanned the Westbourne, and gave its name to the hamlet of Knightsbridge, is described by Strype as of stone, and probably is the same which lasted down to our own day. It stood where now is Albert Gate, and probably portions of it are still embedded in the high road a few yards south of that entrance, and opposite to Lowndes Square. The stream is now little more than the surplus water of the Serpentine, which passes here in a covered drain under the high road; but Mr. Davis tells us that, as lately as 1809, it overflowed its banks so much that the "neighbour-hood became a lake, and that foot-passengers were for several days rowed from Chelsea by Thames boatmen."

As far back as the reign of Edward III. (1361), we find Knightsbridge spoken of as "a town;" for during the plague in that reign a royal edict was issued from the Palace at Westminster, to the effect "that all bulls, oxen, hogs, and other grass crea-tures to be slain for the sustenance of the people, be led as far as the town of Stratford on the one side of London, *and the town of Knightsbridge* on the other, to be slain."

In Thornton's "Survey of London," published in 1780, Knightsbridge is described as "a village a little to the east of Kensington, with many public-houses and several new buildings lately erected, but none of them sufficiently remarkable to admit of particular description." Indeed, it was not till quite the end of the last century, or, perhaps, early in the present, that Knightsbridge became fairly joined on to the metropolis. A letter, in 1783, describes the place as "quite out of London." And so it must have been, for as late as that date, writes Mr. Davis, "the stream ran open, the streets were unpaved and unlighted, and a May-pole was still on the village green. It is not ten years [he wrote in 1854] since the hawthorn hedge has disappeared entirely from the Gore, and the blackbird and starling might still be heard. . . . . Few persons imagine, perhaps, that within the recollection of some who have not long passed from us, snipes and woodcocks might occasionally be found. Forty years since there was neither a draper's nor a butcher's shop between Hyde Park Corner and Sloane Street, and only one in the whole locality where a newspaper or writing-paper could be bought. There was no conveyance to London but a kind of stage-coach; the roads were dimly lighted by oil; and the modern paving to be seen only along Knightsbridge Terrace. Till about 1835 a watch-house and pound remained at the east end of Middle Row; and the stocks were to be seen, as late as 1805, at the end of Park-side, almost opposite the Conduit."

The high road which led through Knightsbridge towards Kensington, and so on to Brentford, was, two centuries ago, very badly kept and maintained, as regards both its repairs and the security of those who passed along it. There was no lack of inns about Knightsbridge; but the reputation of their keepers would not bear much inquiry, as it is almost certain that they were in league with the highwaymen who infested the road. As a proof of the former part of our assertion, it may be mentioned that when Sir Thomas Wyatt brought up his forces to attack London, this was the route by which they came. "The state of the road," we are told, "materially added to their discomfiture, and so great was the delay thereby occasioned that the Queen's party were able to make every preparation, and when Wyatt's men reached London, their jaded appearance gained them the name of ' Draggle-tails.' " In this condition, however, things remained for more than a century and a half; for, in 1736, when the Court had resided at Kensington for nearly fifty years, Lord Hervey writes to his mother thus, under date November 27th :—" The road between this place (Kensington) and London is grown so infamously bad, that we live here in the same solitude we should do if cast on a rock in the middle of the ocean; and all the Londoners tell us there is between them and us a great impassable gulf of mud. There are two roads through the park; but the new one is so convex, and the old one so concave, that by this extreme of faults they agree in the common one of being, like the high road, impassable."

As to the danger from footpads to which travellers were exposed on the high road between Kensington and London, we will quote the following proofs. In the register of burials at Kensington is the following entry, which speaks for itself: —" 1687, 25th November.—Thomas Ridge, of Portsmouth, who was killed by thieves almost at Knightsbridge." John Evelyn, too, writes in his "Diary," November 25th, 1699:—"This week robberies were committed between the many lights

which were fixed between London and Kensington on both sides, and while coaches and travellers were passing." Lady Cowper, too, has the following entry in her "Diary," in October, 1715:— " I was at Kensington, where I intended to stay as long as the camp was in Hyde Park, the roads being so secure by it that we might come from London at any time of the night without danger, which I did very often."

It is clear, from the *Gentleman's Magazine* for April, 1740, that about a quarter of a century later matters were as bad as ever. "The Bristol mail," writes Sylvanus Urban, "was robbed, a little beyond Knightsbridge, by a man on foot, who took the Bath and Bristol bags, and, mounting the postboy's horse, rode off towards London." Four years later three men were executed for highway robberies committed here; and in another attempted highway robbery, a little westward of the bridge at Knightsbridge, we read of a footpad being shot dead.

This being the case, we need not be surprised to find, from the *Morning Chronicle* of May 23, 1799, that it was necessary at the close of last century to order a party of light horse to patrol every night the road from Hyde Park Corner to Kensington; and Mr. Davis, in his work already quoted, states that persons then (1854) alive well remembered when "pedestrians walked to and from Kensington in bands sufficient to ensure mutual protection, starting on their journey only at known intervals, of which a bell gave due warning." It would, however, be unfair to suppose that Knightsbridge, in this respect, was worse than any other suburb of London at that time, as we have already shown in our accounts of Marylebone, Tottenham Court Road, and other parts.

In proof of the bad character of the innkeepers of Knightsbridge, we may mention that Sheffield, Duke of Buckingham, tells us that when about to be engaged in a duel with the Earl of Rochester, he and his second "lay over-night at Knightsbridge privately, to avoid being secured at London upon any suspicion;" adding, that he and his friend "had the appearance of highwaymen, for which the people of the house liked us all the better." So also in *The Rehearsal*, written to satirise Dryden, we find the following dialogue, the drift of which is obvious :—

Smith : But pray, Mr. Bayes, is not this a little difficult, that you were saying e'en now, to keep an army thus concealed in Knightsbridge?

Bayes : In Knightsbridge? No, not if the innkeeper be his friends.

The "wood at Kyngesbrigg," of which we have

spoken, and which modern topographers identify with the spot where now stands Lowndes Square, may give us some clue to the character of the neighbourhood six or seven hundred years ago. No doubt, it formed a portion of that forest with which, as we learn from Fitz-Stephen, London was surrounded on almost every side. "It owned no lord," says Mr. Davis, "and the few inhabitants enjoyed free chase and other rights in it. It was

every reason to believe, both from local tradition, and also from the helmets, swords, &c., which from time to time have been dug up in the neighbourhood, that it was the scene of more than one encounter between the Royal and Parliamentary forces in the time of Charles I. Here, too, was the house occupied by the "infamous" Lord Howard, of Escrick, by whose perjured evidence so noble a patriot as Algernon Sidney was sent to

THE SPRING GARDEN, "WORLD'S END." *From a Drawing in the Crace Collection.* (*See page* 21.)

disafforested by order of Henry III.; and in the reign of his son, Edward I., if we may trust Mr. Lysons, Knightsbridge was a manor belonging to the Abbey. To their lands here, in the course of the next half century or so, the monks added others at Westbourne, and both were jointly erected into a manor—that of 'Knightsbridge and Westbourne'—a name still retained in legal documents." Mr. Davis adds that "the whole of the isolated parts of St. Margaret's parish—including a part of Kensington, its palace, and gardens—are included in this manor."

As we have already related, Knightsbridge was the last halting-place of Sir Thomas Wyatt and his Kentish followers, before his foolish assault on London in the reign of Queen Mary; and there is

the block. Roger North, in his "Examen," tells us that when the Rye House Plot became known, the king commanded that Howard should be arrested, and that accordingly his house was searched by the Serjeant-at-Arms, to whom he surrendered at discretion. He saved his own life by despicably turning round upon the partners of his guilt. Many allusions to his conduct on this occasion will be found in the satires and ballads of the day, of which the following may be taken as an average specimen :—

"Was it not a d—— thing
That Russell and Hampden
Should serve all the projects of hot-headed Tory?
But much more untoward
To appoint my Lord Howard
Of his own purse and credit to ra'se men and money?

THE NORTH SIDE OF KNIGHTSBRIDGE IN 1829, FROM THE CANNON BREWERY TO HYDE PARK CORNER.
(*From a Drawing in the Crace Collection.*)

Who at Knightsbridge did hide
Those brisk boys unspy'd,
That at Shaftesbury's whistle were ready to follow
But when aid he should bring,
Like a true Brentford king,
He was here with a whoop and there with a hollo ! "

Through Knightsbridge passed the corpse of Henry VIII., on its way to its last resting-place at Windsor. The fact is thus recorded in the parish books of St. Margaret's :—" Paid to the poor men that did bere the copis (copes) and other necessaries to Knightsbridge, when that the King was brought to his buryal to Wynsor, and to the men that did ring the bells, 3 shillings."

The next historical event connected with this neighbourhood is the intended assassination of William III. by two Jacobite gentlemen—curiously enough, named Barclay and Perkins—in 1694. Their plan was to waylay the king on his return to Kensington from some hunting expedition, and to shoot him. The plot, however, was revealed by one of their accomplices, who met at the " Swan Inn," Knightsbridge, to arrange the time and place; and the two principals were hung at Tyburn, though they never carried their plot into execution.

The " Swan," two centuries ago, was an inn of so bad a reputation, as to be the terror of jealous husbands and anxious fathers, and is often alluded to as such in some of the comedies of the time; as, for instance, in Otway's *Soldier of Fortune*, where Sir David Dance says : " I have surely lost her (my daughter), and shall never see her more ; she promised me strictly to stay at home till I came back again. . . . For aught I know, she may be taking the air as far as Knightsbridge, with some smooth-faced rogue or another. 'Tis a bad house, that Swan ; the Swan at Knightsbridge is a confounded house." The house has also the honour, such as it is, of being mentioned by Tom Brown in his " School Days," and also by Peter Pindar.

More recently, Knightsbridge has gained some celebrity, as the scene of one or two passing riots, as, for instance, in the year 1768, on the election of Wilkes for Middlesex. " It was customary," writes Mr. Davis, " for a London mob to meet the Brentford mob in or about Knightsbridge; and as Wilkes' opponent was riding through with a body of his supporters, one of them hoisted a flag, on which was inscribed 'No Blasphemer,' and terrible violence instantly ensued." Again, in 1803, another election riot, in which one or two lives were lost, took place in the High Street, Sir Francis Burdett being the popular favourite. Another riot took place here in 1821, at the funeral of two men who had been shot by the soldiers at the funeral of Queen Caroline.

It should, perhaps, be mentioned here, in illustration of the strongly-marked character of the inhabitants of the locality, that in the days of Burdett, when politics ran high, the people of Knightsbridge were mostly " Radicals of the first water." At that time " Old Glory," as Sir Francis Burdett was called before his conversion to Toryism, was in every respect the man of their choice as member for Westminster. And it was in compliment to the inhabitants of Knightsbridge, and in acknowledgment of their support, that he and his colleague, Sir John Hobhouse, on one occasion, when " chaired," chose to make their start from the corner of Sloane Street.

From a chance allusion in Butler's " Hudibras " to this place, it may be inferred that in the Puritan times it formed the head-quarters of one of the hundred-and-one sects into which the " religious world " of that day was divided ; for the dominant faction are there accused of having—

" Filled Bedlam with predestination
And Knightsbridge with illumination."

As stated in the previous chapter, the commencement of the Knightsbridge Road is about fifty yards west of the Alexandra Hotel. Here, at the corner of the main road and of Wilton Place, stood formerly a tobacconist's shop, which very much narrowed the thoroughfare, and was not removed till about the year 1840. It was occupied by an eccentric old woman, a Mrs. Dowell, who was so extremely partial to the Duke of Wellington, that she was constantly devising some new plan by which to show her regard for him. She sent him from time to time patties, cakes, and other delicacies of the like kind ; and as it was found impossible to defeat the old woman's pertinacity, the duke's servants took in her presents. To such a pitch did she carry her mania, that she is said to have laid a knife and fork regularly for him at her own table day by day, constantly expecting that the duke would sooner or later do her the honour of dropping in and " taking pot luck " with her. In this hope, however, we believe we may safely assert that she was doomed to disappointment to the last.

At the back of the above-mentioned house was in former times one of the most noted suburban retreats in the neighbourhood of London, called the " Spring Garden," a place of amusement formed in the grounds of an old mansion which stood on the north side of what is now Lowndes Square. Dr. King, of Oxford, mentions it in his diary as " an excellent spring garden ;" and among the entries of the Virtuosi, or St. Luke's Club, founded by Vandyck, is the following item :—" Paid—Spent at Spring Gardens, by Knightsbridge, forfeiture, £3 15s." Pepys also, no doubt, refers to these same gardens in his " Diary," when he writes :—" I lay in my drawers and stockings and waistcoat [at Kensington] till five of the clock, and so up ; and being well pleased with our frolic, walked to Knightsbridge, and there ate a mess of cream ; and so on to St. James's." Again, too, on another occasion :—" From the town, and away out of the Park, to Knightsbridge, and there ate and drank in the coach ; and so home." It is probable that the sign of the house in this Spring Garden was the " World's End," for the following entry in Mr. Pepys' " Diary " can hardly refer to any other place but this :—" Forth to Hyde Park, but was too soon to go in ; so went on to Knightsbridge, and there ate and drank at the ' World's End,' where we had good things ; and then back to the Park, and there till night, being fine weather, and much company." And again, the very last entry in his " Diary," under date of May 31st, 1669 :—" To the Park, Mary Botelier and a Dutch gentleman, a friend of hers, being with us. Thence to the ' World's End,' a drinking-house by the Park, and there merry, and so home late."

Whether the tavern attached to this Spring Garden enjoyed the doubtful reputation of the " World's End " at Chelsea is not quite certain.

The house to which this garden was attached, having been successively occupied as a museum of anatomy, an auction-room, and a carpenter's workshop, was pulled down about the year 1826, in order to lay out the ground for building. Lowndes Square, however, was not begun till about 1838, or completed till 1848 or 1849. The stream which ran along the west side of Spring Gardens had along its banks a path leading down to Bloody Bridge, and thence to Ranelagh. On grand gala nights this path was protected by a patrol, or by the more able of the Chelsea pensioners. It only remains to add that various relics of the Civil War have been discovered upon this site, such as swords, spurs, and bits, and other relics telling of more modern and more prosaic encounters, such as staves and handcuffs, tokens of successful or unsuccessful struggles between footpads and constables.

A little west of Wilton Place, a narrow roadway, called Porter's Lane, led into some fields, in which stood an old mansion, known as Knightsbridge Grove, and approached from the highway by an avenue of fine trees. This is the house which, about 1790, was taken by the celebrated Mrs.

Cornelys, under the assumed name of Mrs. Smith, as a place for company to drink new asses' milk. After the failure of all her plans and schemes to secure the support of the world of fashion for her masquerades and concerts at Carlisle House, in Soho Square, as we have already seen,* and not cast down by the decree of the Court of Chancery, under which her house and furniture were sold by auction in 1785, here she fitted up a suite of rooms for the reception of visitors who wished to breakfast in public. But the manners of the age were changed, and her taste had not adapted itself to the varieties of fashion. After much expense incurred in the gaudy embellishment of her rooms after the foreign fashion, she was obliged to abandon her scheme, and to seek a refuge from her merciless creditors. A former queen—or rather empress—of fashion, she closed her eccentric and varied career a prisoner for debt in the Fleet Prison, in August, 1797. The house was afterwards kept by a sporting character, named Hicks, under whom it was frequently visited by George, Prince Regent, and his friends.

The entrance into Hyde Park, opposite Lowndes Square, is named Albert Gate, after the late Prince Consort ; the houses which compose it stand as nearly as possible on the site of the old bridge over the Westbourne, which gave its name to the locality. We gave a view of this old bridge in our last volume, page 402. Mr. Davis, in his " Memorials of Knightsbridge," tells us that there was also another bridge across this brook, just inside the park to the north, erected in 1734. At the west end of the former bridge stood, at one time, a celebrated inn, known as the " Fox and Bull," traditionally said to have been founded in the reign of Elizabeth, and to have been used by her on her visits to Lord Burleigh at Brompton. The house is referred to in the *Tatler*, No. 259, and it is said to be the only inn that bore that sign. " At the ' Fox and Bull,' " writes Mr. Davis, " for a long while was maintained that Queen Anne style of society where persons of ' parts ' and reputation were to be met with in rooms open to all. A Captain Corbet was for a long time its head ; a Mr. Shaw, of the War Office, supplied the *London Gazette*, and W. Harris, of Covent Garden Theatre, his play-bills." Among its visitors may be named George Morland, and his patron, Sir W. W. Wynn, and occasionally Sir Joshua Reynolds, who painted its sign, which was blown down in a storm in 1807. The " Fox and Bull," it may be added, served for some years as a receiving-house

* See Vol. III., p. 188.

of the Royal Humane Society, in Hyde Park. Hither was brought the body of the first wife of the poet Shelley, after she had drowned herself in the Serpentine ; and here the judicial business of the locality was conducted, a magistrate sitting once a week for that purpose. The old house was Elizabethan in structure, and contained rooms and ceilings panelled and carved in the style of her day, and with large fire-places and fire-dogs. The house stood till the year 1835. The skeletons of several men were found beneath it in the course of some excavations in the early part of the present century, these were supposed to have been those of soldiers killed here in the Civil War.

On the east side of the old bridge was a low court of very old houses, named after the "White Hart Inn," but these were swept away about 1841. The stags on the side pedestals of the gate, we learn from the "Memorials of Knightsbridge," were modelled from a pair of prints by Bartolozzi, and formerly kept watch and ward in Piccadilly, at the entrance to the Ranger's Lodge in the Green Park.*

When this entrance was first formed, the late Mr. Thomas Cubitt designed and built two very lofty mansions on either side, which were sneeringly styled the "Two Gibraltars," because it was prophesied that they never would or could be "taken." Taken, however, they were ; that on the eastern side was the town residence of the "Railway King," George Hudson, before his fall ; it has since been occupied as the French Embassy. Queen Victoria paid a visit to the Embassy in state in 1854, and the Emperor Louis Napoleon held a levée here, on his visit to London, in the summer of the following year.

"The career of George Hudson, ridiculously styled the 'Railway King,'" writes Mr. J. Timbs, in his "Romance of London," "was one of the *ignes fatui* of the railway mania of 1844-5. He was born in a lowly house in College Street, York, in 1800 ; here he served his apprenticeship to a linendraper, and subsequently carried on the business as principal, amassing considerable wealth. His fortune was next increased by a bequest from a distant relative, which sum he invested in North-Midland Railway shares. Mr. Smiles describes Hudson as a man of some local repute when the line between Leeds and York was projected. His views as to railways were then extremely moderate, and his main object in joining the undertaking was to secure for York the advantages of the best railway communication. . . . The grand test

by which the shareholders judged him was the dividends which he paid, although subsequent events proved that these dividends were, in many cases, delusive, intended only to make things pleasant. The policy, however, had its effect. The shares in all the lines of which he was chairman went to a premium ; and then arose the temptation to create new shares in branch and extension lines, often worthless, which were issued at a premium also. Thus he shortly found himself chairman of nearly 600 miles of railways, extending from Rugby to Newcastle, and at the head of numerous new projects, by means of which paper wealth could be created, as it were, at pleasure. He held in his own hands almost the entire administrative power of chairman, board, manager, and all. Mr. Hudson was voted praises, testimonials, and surplus shares alike liberally, and scarcely a word against him could find a hearing.

"The Hudson testimonial was a taking thing, for Mr. Hudson had it in his power to allot shares (selling at a premium) to the subscribers to the testimonial. With this fund he bought of Mr. Thomas Cubitt, for £15,000, the lofty house on the east of Albert Gate, Hyde Park. There he lived sumptuously, and went his round of visits among the peerage.

"Mr. Hudson's brief reign soon drew to a close. The speculation of 1845 was followed by a sudden reaction. Shares went down faster than they had gone up : the holders of them hastened to sell in order to avoid payment of the calls ; and many found themselves ruined. Then came repentance, and a sudden return to virtue. The golden calf was found to be of brass, and hurled down, Hudson's own toadies and sycophants eagerly joining in the chorus of popular indignation ; and the bubbles having burst, the railway mania came to a sudden and ignominious end."

The rest of the site now covered by Albert Gate was occupied by the Cannon Brewery—so called from a cannon which surmounted it—and was surrounded by low and filthy courts with open cellars. The celebrated Chinese collection of Mr. Dunn was located here in the interval between the removal of the brewery and the erection of the present sumptuous edifices.

It is not a little singular that among all the changes as to the limits of parishes, it should have been forgotten that, from time immemorial, there was a chapel in the main street of Knightsbridge which could very easily, at any time, have been made parochial. This edifice, known as Trinity Chapel, still stands, though much altered, between the north side of the main street and

---

* See Vol. IV., p. 180.

the park; it was, in ancient times, attached to a lazar-house, of the early history of which little or nothing is known. No doubt it was formed before the Reformation, though the earliest notice of it in writing is in a grant of James I., to be seen in the British Museum, ordering "the hospital for sick, lame, or impotent people at Knightsbridge" to be supplied with water by an underground pipe, laid on from the conduit in Hyde Park. Lysons, however, tells us, in his "Environs of London," that there is among the records of the Chapter of Westminster a short MS. statement of the condition of the hospital in the latter part of Elizabeth's reign, from which it appears that it generally had about thirty-five inmates, and that it was supported by the contributions of charitable persons, being quite unendowed. The patients, it appears from this document, attended prayers mornings and evenings in the chapel, the neighbours also being admitted to the services on Sunday. The inmates dined on "warm meat and porrege," and each one had assigned to him, or her, a separate "dish, platter, and tankard, to kepe the broken for the whole."

A few notes on the disbursement made on behalf of the poor inmates, taken from the parish books of St. Margaret's, will be found in Mr. Nichols' "Illustrations of the Manners and Experiences of Ancient Times." The latter history of the hospital is almost as uncertain as its earlier chapters. We know even the names of a few of the "cripples," and other inmates—mostly wayfarers —who were discharged from it, after having been relieved; but although it was certainly in existence when Newcourt was collecting materials for his "Repertorium," in the reign of George I., no further trace of its existence or of its demolition can be found. It is traditionally asserted, however, that in the time of the Great Plague of 1665, the lazar-house was used as a hospital for those stricken by that disorder, and that such as died within its walls were buried in the enclosed triangular plot of ground which was once part of Knightsbridge Green. A writer in the first volume of *Notes and Queries* states that in the case of leprosy arising in London, the infected persons were taken off speedily into one of the lazar-houses in the suburbs. "The law was strictly carried out, and where resistance was made the sufferers were tied to horses, and dragged thither by force."

The chapel, being "very old and ruinous," was rebuilt by a subscription among the inhabitants of Knightsbridge, and opened as a chapel of ease by the authority of Laud, then Bishop of London, who licensed a minister to perform service in it. During the Commonwealth it was served by a minister appointed by the Parliament, and afterwards passed into lay hands. In the end, however, it was given back to the Dean and Chapter of Westminster; this body still appoints the incumbent, who is supported by a small endowment and the pew-rents.

The present chapel, now called the Church of Holy Trinity, was entirely restored and remodelled in 1861, from the designs of Messrs. Brandon and Eyton. It is a handsome Gothic building, with accommodation for about 650 worshippers, and was erected at a cost of about £3,300. The principal peculiarity about it is the roof, which is so constructed as to have a continuous range of clerestory lights the whole length of the church. These are accessible from the outside, so as to regulate the ventilation.

The chapel possesses some good communion plate. In the list of its ministers occur no names of note, unless it be worth while to record that of the Rev. Dr. Symons, who read the funeral service over Sir John Moore at Corunna.

In the registers of the chapel is recorded only one burial, under date 1667. It is probable that those who died in this hamlet were buried at St. Margaret's, Westminster, or at Chelsea, or Kensington. Mr. Davis, however, mentions a tradition that the enclosure on Knightsbridge Green was formerly used as a burying-ground. If this be so, the records of the fact have long since been lost. The statement, however, may have reference to the victims of the plague, as stated above.

The registers of baptisms are still in existence, and so are those of the marriages solemnised here —some of them, as might be expected, rather irregular, especially before the passing of Lord Hardwicke's Marriage Act in 1753, which seems to have put an extinguisher on such scandals. With reference to these irregular or "stolen" marriages, a writer in the *Saturday Review* observes:— "This was one of the places where irregular marriages were solemnised, and it is accordingly often noticed by the old dramatists. Thus in Shadwell's *Sullen Lovers*, Lovell is made to say, 'Let's dally no longer; there is a person in Knightsbridge that pokes all stray people together. We'll to him; he'll dispatch us presently, and send us away as lovingly as any two fools that ever yet were condemned to marriage.' Some of the entries in this marriage register are suspicious enough—'secrecy for life,' or 'great secrecy,' or 'secret for fourteen years,' being appended to the names. Mr. Davis, in his 'Memorials of Knightsbridge,' was the first to exhume from this document the name of the adventuress, 'Mrs. Mary Ayliss,' whom Sir Samuel Morland married as his fourth wife, in 1687. The readers of Pepys will remember how pathetically Morland wrote, eighteen days after the wedding, that, when he had expected to marry an heiress, 'I was, about a fortnight since, led as a fool to the stocks, and married a coachman's daughter not worth a shilling.' In 1699, an entry mentions one

before her marriage as Lady Mary Tudor; and lastly, the great Sir Robert Walpole, to a daughter of the Lord Mayor of London, by whom he became the father of Horace Walpole. Many of the marriages here solemnised were runaway matches, and, as such, are marked in the registers with the words "private" and "secresy."

Of the barracks at Knightsbridge, facing the Park, usually occupied by one of the regiments of

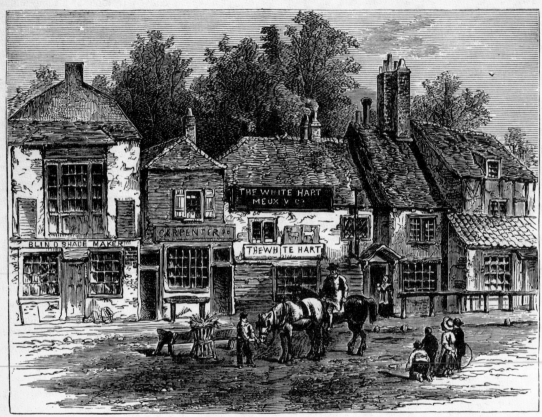

THE "WHITE HART," KNIGHTSBRIDGE, 1820. *(See page 22.)*

'Storey at yᵉ Park Gate.' This worthy it was who gave his name to what is now known as Storey's Gate. He was keeper of the aviary to Charles II., whence was derived the name of the Birdcage Walk. In the same year, Cornelius Van der Velde, limner, was married here to Bernada Van der Hagen. This was a brother of the famous William Van der Velde, the elder, and himself a painter of nautical pictures, in the employment of Charles II."

Among those who were married here, with more or less of secrecy or privacy, not mentioned in the above extract, were Sir John Lenthall, son of the Speaker of the House of Commons under Cromwell; the widow of the second Earl of Derwentwater— this lady was the youngest natural daughter of Charles II., by the actress, Mrs. Davis, known

the Guards, there is little to say, except that they are badly placed, and were long an eyesore to the neighbourhood. They originally consisted of a range of dull heavy brick buildings, erected in 1794-5. In the centre of the building is an oblong parade-ground, around which are apartments for the private soldiers, placed over the stables. At the west-end is a riding-school, and a wing cut up into residences for the officers. New barracks were erected here in 1879-80, and are said to be the best of the kind in Europe. They form an extensive quadrangle, and there are reading-rooms for both the non-commissioned officers and privates.

At the corner of South Place and Hill Street, nearly opposite the barracks, stands the celebrated floor-cloth manufactory of Messrs. Smith and

Barber. It was established as far back as the year 1754, and is said to be the oldest manufactory of the kind in London. The first block used for patterns was cut by its founder, Mr. Abraham Smith, and is still preserved in the factory. An illustration of it is given in Dodd's "British Manufactures," where the process of the manufacture will be found minutely described. In the adjoining house, No. 2, lived the Rev. Mr. Gamble, one of the incumbents

temporaries of Lord Chancellor Clarendon"), who married as her second husband Sir George C. Lewis, M.P., some time Chancellor of the Exchequer. He died here in 1863. Next door to it is Stratheden House, so named after the wife of Lord Chancellor Campbell, who wrote here his "Lives of the Chancellors." He died here suddenly in June, 1861. The mansion had previously been owned by Lord De Dunstanville.

KINGSTON HOUSE, KNIGHTSBRIDGE.

of Knightsbridge Chapel; and after him Mr. Edward Stirling, known as the "Thunderer" of the *Times*, from whom it passed to his son, the gifted and amiable John Stirling, whose early death was so much lamented. There he used to receive among his visitors Professor Maurice, John Stuart Mill, and Thomas Carlyle; and here Sir Colin Campbell took up his residence for a time between his Crimean and his last Indian campaign.

Kent House, so called after the late Duke of Kent, who for a short time resided in it, and added considerably to its size, stands only a few yards to the west of South Place. It was for many years the residence of a brother of the late Earl of Clarendon, and afterwards of his widow, Lady Theresa Villiers (author of "The Friends and Co-

It was at Kingston House—situated some little distance westward of Kent House—that, on the 26th of September, 1842, the eminent statesman, the Marquis Wellesley, died, at the age of eighty-two. He was the elder brother of the "great" Duke of Wellington. Mr. Raikes tells us, in his "Journal:" "He had in his time filled various offices in the State at home, had been Governor-General of India, and twice Lord-Lieutenant of Ireland. He was a man of considerable talent and acquirements, particularly in the Latin and Greek languages. His first wife was a French lady—a Madame Roland —formerly his mistress. His second wife was an American—Mrs. Patterson."

Rutland Gate, a row of houses standing a little westward of the barracks, on the south side of the road, was built about 1840, and was so called from a large mansion which formerly stood on the site, belonging to the Dukes of Rutland. Here was the picture-gallery of Mr. John Sheepshanks, bequeathed by him to the nation, and now housed in the Sheepshanks Gallery at the South Kensington Museum. It was rich in works by Mulready, Leslie, and Landseer.

Ennismore Place, close by Prince's Gate, is so called from the second title of the Earl of Listowel, to whom the ground on which it stands belongs or belonged.

Brompton Road is the name given to a row of houses built about the year 1840, on what was a garden a century ago. At a house here, then numbered 45, Brompton Row, but now 168, Brompton Road, lived the celebrated philanthropist and philosopher, Count Rumford, and afterwards his daughter Sarah, Countess Rumford. The count had come to England as an exiled loyalist from America, and having risen to high employ in England, had been sent, in 1798, as Ambassador to London from Bavaria. Here he entertained Sir William Pepperell, and other American loyalists. Owing to George III.'s opposition to his appointment as a diplomatic representative of Bavaria, he lived in a private capacity. He died in France in 1814. The house is minutely described, in 1801, by M. Pictet, an intimate friend of the count, in a life of Count Rumford, published in 1876. It is still full, from top to bottom, of all sorts of cleverly-contrived cupboards, writing-desks, &c., fixed in the walls, and with fireplaces on a plan unlike those in the adjoining dwellings. It remains very much in the same state as in the count's time, though a stucco front appears to have been added. "The house had been let by Count Rumford to the Rev. William Beloe, the translator of Herodotus, who quitted possession of it in 1810. The countess, his daughter, lived in it and let it alternately, among her tenants being Sir Richard Phillips and Mr. Wilberforce. She disposed of the lease in 1837 to its present owners."

On the south side of Ennismore Place is Brompton Square, which consists of houses open at the south end to the Brompton Road, and terminating at the northern end with a semi-circular sweep, with a gateway leading to Prince's Terrace and Ennismore Gardens. At No. 22 in this square died, in 1836, George Colman "the Younger," the author of *John Bull*. Here also lived Mr. Luttrell, the friend of Sam Rogers, and the most brilliant of conversationalists *temp.* George IV. In consequence of the salubrity of the air in this neighbourhood, Brompton Square has long been a

favourite abode for singers and actors. Behind the west side stands Brompton Church, a poor semi-Gothic structure, dating from about 1830. It was built from the designs of Professor Donaldson, and has a lofty tower and stained-glass windows of ancient design and colour. The church is approached by a fine avenue of lime-trees, and its churchyard contains a very large number of tombs ; all, however, are modern, and few are of interest to the antiquary. John Reeve, the comic actor, who died in 1838, is buried here. Adjoining the parish church stands a building in the Italian style, known as the Oratory of St. Philip Neri, consisting of a large chapel, very secular in appearance, and a fine residence in the Italian style. They cover the site of a country house standing in its own grounds, which as lately as the year 1851 was used as a school. The clergy attached to the Oratory are secular priests, living voluntarily in a community, but not tied by religious vows. The first rector, and indeed the founder of this community in London, was the Rev. Frederick William Faber, formerly of University College, Oxford, and well known as the author of "The Cherwell Water-Lily," and other poems. He died in 1863.

Knightsbridge, however, has in its time numbered many other distinguished residents. Among them, Lady Anne Hamilton, the faithful friend and attendant of the Princess Caroline of Brunswick ; the artist Chalon ; Paul Bedford, the actor ; McCarthy, the sculptor ; and Ozias Humfrey, the Royal Academician (the friend of Reynolds, Dr. Johnson, and Romney), who is thus celebrated by the poet Hayley, when abandoning miniatures for oil portraits :—

> "Thy graces, Humfrey, and thy colours clear,
> From miniature's small circle disappear ;
> May thy distinguished merit still prevail,
> And shine with lustre on a larger scale."

Here died, in 1805, at the age of upwards of eighty, Arthur Murphy, the author, who was a friend of Johnson, Reynolds, Burke, and others. Boswell thus relates the manner in which an acquaintance first commenced between Dr. Johnson and Mr. Murphy :—"During the publication of the *Gray's Inn Journal*, a periodical paper which was successfully carried on by Mr. Murphy alone, when a very young man, he happened to be in the country with Mr. Foote ; and having mentioned that he was obliged to go to London in order to get ready for the press one of the numbers of that journal, Foote said to him, 'You need not go on that account. Here is a French magazine, in which you will find a very pretty Oriental tale ; translate that, and send it to your printer.' Mr. Murphy having read the tale, was highly pleased with it, and followed Foote's advice. When he returned to town, this tale was pointed out to him in the *Rambler*, from whence it had been translated into the French magazine. Mr. Murphy then waited upon Johnson, to explain this curious incident. His talents, literature, and gentleman-like manners were soon perceived by Johnson, and a friendship was formed which was never broken."

Here, at a farm-house which supplied the royal family with milk, the fair Quakeress, Hannah Lightfoot, is said to have resided, after she had captivated the susceptible heart of George III., in the first year of his reign; but the story is discredited.

At the junction of Brompton Road with the main road through Knightsbridge, and near to Albert Gate, stands the great sporting rendezvous and auction-mart for horses, "Tattersall's." It was removed to this spot in 1865 from Grosvenor Place, where, as we have seen in the preceding chapter, it was originally established. The building occupies a site previously of comparatively little value, and has before its entrance a small triangular space planted with evergreens. The building in itself is arranged upon much the same plan as that of its predecessor, which we have already described. Immediately on the right of the entrance is the subscription-room and counting-house, both of which are well designed to meet their requirements; whilst beyond is a spacious covered court-yard, with a small circular structure in the centre, in which is a pump, surmounted by the figure of a fox; the dome which covers it bears a bust of George IV. The fox, it is presumed, belongs to the poetry of Tattersall's, suggesting, as it does, breezy rides over hill and dale and far-stretching moorlands. The royal bust above refers to more specific facts of which the establishment can boast; it is a type of the lofty patronage that has been acceded to the house from its earliest days. The bust represents the "first gentleman of Europe," as he has been, absurdly enough, called, in his eighteenth year, when the prince was a constant attendant at Tattersall's. The yard itself is surrounded by stabling for the horses, and galleries for carriages which may be there offered for sale. The great public horse auction is on Mondays throughout the year, with the addition of Thursdays in the height of the season. The subscription to the "Rooms," which is regulated by the Jockey Club, is two guineas annually; and the betting at Tattersall's, we need scarcely add, regulates the betting throughout the country.

The Green, as the triangular plot of ground in front of Tattersall's, mentioned above, is called, was once really a village-green, and it had its village may-pole, at all events, down to the end of the last century. It was larger in its extent in former days, several encroachments having been made upon its area. At its east end there stood, till 1834, a watch-house and pound, to which Addison refers in a very amusing paper in the *Spectator* (No. 142). Pretending, by way of jest, to satisfy by home news the craving for foreign intelligence which the late war had created in 1712, he writes: "By my last advices from Knightsbridge, I hear that a horse was clapped into the pound there on the 3rd inst., and that he was not recovered when the letters came away." A large part of what once was the Green is now covered by some inferior cottages, styled Middle Row; on the north side was an old inn, which rejoiced in the sign of the "Marquis of Granby," with reference to which we may be pardoned for quoting Byron's lines:—

"Vernon, the 'Butcher' Cumberland, Wolfe, Hawke,
    Prince Ferdinand, Granby, Burgoyne, Keppel, Howe,
  Evil and good, have had their tithe of talk,
    And filled the sign-posts then as Wellesley now."

The small portion on the north side, fenced in by rails, is probably the old burial-ground belonging to the Lazar House, already mentioned.

Of Knightsbridge Terrace, now a row of shops, old inhabitants tell us that, when Her Majesty came to the throne, it consisted wholly of private houses. Here was Mr. Telfair's College for the Deaf and Dumb, and here lived Maurice Morgan, one of the secretaries to Lord Shelburne when the latter was Premier, and honourably mentioned by Boswell in his "Life of Johnson." Close to the corner of Sloane Street, too, lived Rodwell, the composer.

Among the oldest dwellings in this hamlet are some of the irregular houses on the south side of the road, between the Green and Rutland Gate. Mr. Davis, writing in the year 1859, in his "History of Knightsbridge," mentions Chalker House, built in 1688, now a broker's, and for many years a boarding-house. "Three doors beyond it," he continues, "is an ancient inn, now known as the 'Rose and Crown,' but formerly as the 'Oliver Cromwell,' but which has borne a licence for above three hundred years. It is the oldest house in Knightsbridge, and was formerly its largest inn, and not improbably was the house which sheltered Wyatt, while his unfortunate Kentish followers rested on the adjacent green. A tradition, told by all old inhabitants of the locality, that Cromwell's body-guard was once quartered here, is still very prevalent: an inscription to that effect was till lately painted on the front of the house; and on an ornamental piece of plaster-work was formerly emblazoned the great Lord Protector's coat of arms." Mr. Davis does not guarantee the literal truth of this tradition, though he holds that nothing is more certain than that Knightsbridge was the scene of frequent skirmishes during the Civil War. This was natural enough, considering that the hamlet was the first place on the great western road from London. We know for certain that the army of the Parliament was encamped about the neighbourhood in 1647, and that the head-quarters of Fairfax were at Holland House; and the same was the case just before and after the fight at Brentford. It was on the strength of this, and other traditions, that Mr. E. H. Corbould made this inn the subject of a painting, "The Old Hostelrie at Knightsbridge," exhibited in 1849. "He laid the scene as early as 1497. Opposite the inn is a well, surmounted by a figure of St. George; while beyond is the spacious green, the meandering stream, and the bridge over it, surmounted by an embattled tower; further off appears the old hospital and chapel. . . . . . The house of late," continues Mr. Davis, "has been much modernised, and in 1853 had a narrow escape from destruction by fire; but enough still remains, in its peculiar chimneys, oval-shaped windows, its low rooms, its large yard and extensive stabling, with galleries above and office-like places beneath, to testify to its antiquity and former importance." It was pulled down about the year 1865. Another hostelry in the main street was

the "Rising Sun;" though a wooden inn, it was an ancient house, and its staircase and the panelling of its walls were handsomely carved. On the spot now occupied by the Duke of Wellington's stables, there was also, in former times, an inn known as the "Life Guardsman," and previously as the "Nag's Head."

We may mention that a market for cattle was held at Knightsbridge every Thursday till an early year in the present century, and that the last pen posts were not removed till 1850.

The air of this neighbourhood has always been regarded as pure and healthy. Swift brought his friend Harrison to it for the benefit of pure air; and half a century later it maintained the same character, for we read that Lady Hester Stanhope sent a faithful servant thither, with the same object in view. In sooth, "Constitution" Hill at one end, and "Montpelier" Square at the other, both derive their names from this peculiarity. The fact is that the main street of Knightsbridge stands on a well-defined terrace of the London clay, between the gravel of Hyde Park and that of Pimlico, resting on thick layers of sand, which cause the soil to be porous, and rapidly to absorb the surface-water.

The water-supply of Knightsbridge has always been remarkably good, being drawn from several conduits in and about Park-side and to the south of Rotten Row. One of these, known as St. James's, for the Receiving Conduit, supplied the royal palaces and the Abbey with water.

CHAPTER III.

THE GREAT EXHIBITION OF 1851.

"Anon, out of the earth a fabric huge
Rose like an exhalation."—Milton.

Previous Exhibitions of a somewhat similar Character—The Marquis d'Aveze's projected Exhibition—Various French Expositions—Competitive Exhibitions in England—Prince Albert's Proposal for holding an Industrial Exhibition of All Nations—His Royal Highness becomes Chairman of the Royal Commission—Banquet at the Mansion House—Lecturers and Agents sent all over the Country, to Explain the Objects of the Exhibition—Reception of Plans and Designs—Mr. Paxton's Design accepted—Realisation of one of the Earliest Poetical Dreams in the English Language—General Description of the Building—Opening of the Exhibition by Her Majesty—Number of Visitors—Removal of the Building—The National Albert Memorial.

THAT portion of Hyde Park, between Prince's Gate and the Serpentine, running parallel with the main road through Knightsbridge and Kensington, is memorable as having been the site of the great Industrial Exhibition of 1851, wherein were brought together, for the first time, under one spacious roof, for the purposes of competition, the various productions of the inventive genius and industry of nearly all the nations of the earth.

Before proceeding with a description of the building and an epitome of its principal contents, it may not be out of place to take a brief glance at some previous exhibitions of a similar character, which had been held in France, at various times, within the preceding hundred years. As far back as the year 1756—about the same time that our Royal Academy opened to the public its galleries of painting, engraving, and sculpture—the productions of art and skill were collected and displayed in London, for the purpose of stimulating public industry and inventiveness; and although these exhibitions were, to a certain extent, nothing more than would now be termed "bazaars," they were found to answer so successfully the ends for which they were instituted, that the plan was adopted in France, and there continued, with the happiest results, even long after it had been abandoned in England. When the first French Revolution was at its height, the Marquis d'Aveze projected an exhibition of tapestry and porcelain, as a means of raising funds for relieving the distress then existing among the workers in those trades. Before, however, he could complete his arrangements, he was denounced, and on the very day on which his exhibition was to have been opened, he was compelled to fly from the vengeance of the Directory. So firm a hold, however, had the idea taken on the public mind, that it was not allowed to die out. A few years afterwards, on his return to Paris, the marquis resumed his labours, and in 1798 actually succeeded in opening a National Exposition in the house and gardens of the Maison d'Orsay. The people flocked in great numbers to view the show, which altogether proved a complete success. In that same year, too, the French Government organised its first official Exposition of national manufacture and the works of industry. It was held on the Champ de Mars, in a building constructed for the purpose, called the Temple of Industry. Three years later a second Exposition took place, and more than two hundred exhibitors competed for the prizes offered for excellence. In the following year a third Exposition was held on the same spot, the number of exhibitors increasing to upwards of four hundred. So great was the success of these several shows, that out of them arose an institution similar to our Society of Arts, called the *Société d'Encouragement*, a society to which the working classes of France are largely indebted for the taste which they have acquired for the beautiful in art, and for the cultivation of science as a handmaid to industry. In 1806 the fourth French Exposition was held in a building erected in front of the Hôpital des Invalides; this was even more successful than its predecessors; for while the previous Expositions had each remained open only about a week, this one was kept open for twenty-four days, and was visited by many thousands of people. The number of exhibitors rose from about five hundred to nearly fifteen hundred, and nearly every department of French industry was represented. At different periods between the years 1819 and 1849, seven other Expositions were held in France, the last of which was restricted to national products. The Industrial Show of 1855, however, was, like our own Great Exhibition of 1851, international.

During all this time there had grown up in England exhibitions, consisting chiefly of agricultural implements and cattle, together with local exhibitions of arts and manufactures. In Birmingham, Leeds, Manchester, Dublin, and other great centres of industry, bazaars, after the French pattern, had been successfully held from time to time. The one which most nearly approached the idea of the French Exposition, in the variety and extent of the national productions displayed, was the Free Trade Bazaar, held for twelve days, in 1845, in Covent Garden Theatre—an exhibition which excited considerable public interest, and doubtless did much to make the London public acquainted with many arts and manufactures of which they had hitherto had but a very confused and imperfect knowledge.

Roused from their remissness by the success that had attended the various French Expositions, the English people, during the years 1847 and 1848, re-opened their exhibitions, chiefly at the instigation and by the aid of the Society of Arts, by whom the plan had been revived. So great was now the importance of these industrial displays, that they became a subject of national consideration; but it was felt that something more was necessary than France or England had as yet attempted to give them their proper development and effect.

At this point, an idea was entertained by the late Prince Consort of gathering together into one place the best specimens of contemporary art and skill, and the natural productions of every soil and climate, instead of the mere local or national productions of France and England. "It was to be a whole world of nature and art collected at the call of the queen of cities—a competition in which every country might have a place, and every variety of intellect its claim and chance of distinction. Nothing great, or beautiful, or useful, be its native home where it might; not a discovery or invention, however humble or obscure; not a candidate, however lowly his rank, but would obtain admission, and be estimated to the full amount of genuine worth. It was to be to the nineteenth what the tournament had been to the fourteenth and fifteenth centuries—a challenge at once and welcome to all comers, and to which every land could send, not its brightest dame and bravest lance, as of yore, but its best produce and happiest device for the promotion of universal happiness and brotherhood."[*]

---

[*] "Comprehensive History of England," vol. iv., p. 798.

The undertaking received Her Majesty's royal sanction on the 3rd of January, 1850 ; on the 11th of the same month the Royal Commissioners held their first meeting; and on the 14th of February Prince Albert sat as Chairman of the Commission. On the 21st of March the Lord Mayor of London invited the mayors of nearly all the cities, boroughs, and towns of the United Kingdom to a banquet at the Mansion House to meet the Prince, and upon

At first, many manufacturers and merchants in foreign countries were exceedingly averse to the proposed Exhibition ; but, as was the case with those at home, discussion and better information led to more enlightened views. Prince Albert, in his speech at a banquet held at York, said, in the name of the Royal Commission :—" Although we perceive in some countries an apprehension that the advantages to be derived from the Exhibition

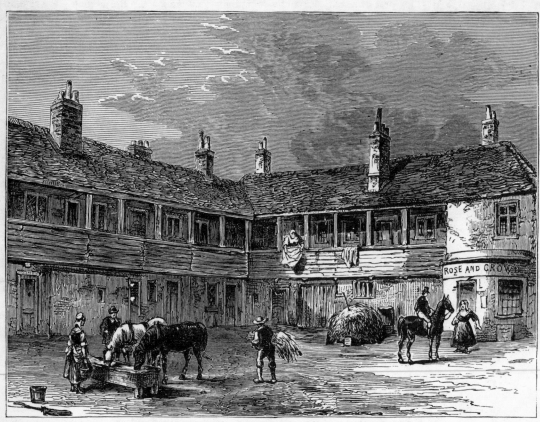

COURTYARD OF THE "ROSE AND CROWN," 1820. (*See page 27.*)

that occasion his Royal Highness lucidly explained the object of the proposed undertaking.

The Exhibition, it was announced, was to belong exclusively to the people themselves of every nation, instead of being supported and controlled by their respective governments ; and in order that nothing might be wanting in its character as a great competitive trial, the sum of £20,000 was set apart for the expense of prizes, which were to be awarded to the successful competitors. At first, the real magnitude and the great difficulties of the project were not fully perceived ; and the proposal was scarcely made public by the Society of Arts, of which Prince Albert was at the head, before impediments began to rise up in their way, and for more than a year they were beset with difficulties.

will be mainly reaped by England, and a consequent distrust in the effects of our scheme upon their own interests, we must, at the same time, freely and gratefully acknowledge, that our invitation has been received by all nations, with whom communication was possible, in that spirit of liberality and friendship in which it was tendered, and that they are making great exertions, and incurring great expenses, in order to meet our plans." Upon the same occasion, Lord Carlisle, one of the most enlightened men of the age, expressed a hope that " the promoters of this Exhibition were giving a new impulse to civilisation, and bestowing an additional reward upon industry, and supplying a fresh guarantee to the amity of nations. Yes, the nations were stirring

EXTERIOR OF THE GREAT EXHIBITION OF 1851.

at their call, but not as the trumpet sounds to battle; they were summoning them to the peaceful field of a nobler competition; not to build the superiority or predominance of one country on the depression and prostration of another, but where all might strive who could do most to embellish, improve, and elevate their common humanity."

At a meeting held in Birmingham, Mr. Cobden, in speaking of the advantages that might be expected to flow from this Exhibition, said, "We shall by that means break down the barriers that have separated the people of different nations, and witness one universal republic; the year 1851 will be a memorable one, indeed: it will witness a triumph of industry instead of a triumph of arms. We shall not witness the reception of the allied sovereigns after some fearful conflict, men bowing their heads in submission; but, instead, thousands and tens of thousands will cross the Channel, to whom we will give the right hand of fellowship, with the fullest conviction that war, rather than a national aggrandisement, has been the curse and the evil which has retarded the progress of liberty and of virtue; and we shall show to them that the people of England—not a section of them, but hundreds of thousands—are ready to sign a treaty of amity with all the nations on the face of the earth."

Lecturers and competent agents were now sent throughout the country to explain the objects of the Exhibition, and the advantages likely to arise from it; besides which, the subject had been proclaimed in every country far and wide—in fact, a challenge had been given, such as men had never heard, to an enterprise in which every nation might hope to be the victor. It was arranged that the great competition should be opened in London on the 1st of May, 1851; but as yet a place for the accommodation of the specimens and the spectators had to be erected. The directors of the Exhibition were for a time perplexed, for they found, on calculation, that no building on earth would be sufficiently large to contain a tithe of its contents. After many expedients had been proposed and rejected, Mr. (afterwards Sir Joseph) Paxton, the celebrated horticulturist at Chatsworth, came forward with a simple plan, which effectually solved all the difficulty.

The number of plans and designs sent in to the Committee appointed by the Royal Commission amounted to nearly two hundred and fifty, including several foreigners; but none of these appeared to be satisfactory. Accordingly, the Committee set to work and perfected a design for themselves, from the various suggestions afforded by the competing architects, adding, as a contribution "entirely their own," a dome of gigantic proportions. This dome at once became so unpopular with the public, and the contest about its site grew so fierce, that the whole scheme of the Exhibition seemed at one time likely to have collapsed. At "the eleventh hour," however, Mr. Paxton, as we have stated above, came forward with a plan, which he considered would meet all the requirements of the Committee, and avoid all the objections of the public. "It was not," said Mr. Paxton himself, at a meeting of the Derby Institute, "until one morning, when I was present with my friend, Mr. Ellis, at an early sitting in the House of Commons, that the idea of sending in a design occurred to me. A conversation took place between us, with reference to the construction of the new House of Commons, in the course of which I observed, that I was afraid they would also commit a blunder in the building for the Industrial Exhibition; I told him that I had a notion in my head, and that if he would accompany me to the Board of Trade I would ascertain whether it was too late to send in a design. I asked the Executive Committee whether they were so far committed to the plans as to be precluded from receiving another; the reply was, 'Certainly not; the specifications will be out in a fortnight, but there is no reason why a clause should not be introduced, allowing of the reception of another design.' I said, 'Well, if you will introduce such a clause, I will go home, and, in nine days hence, I will bring you my plans all complete.' No doubt the Executive thought me a conceited fellow, and that what I had said was nearer akin to romance than to common sense. Well, this was on Friday, the 11th of June. From London I went to the Menai Straits, to see the third tube of the Britannia Bridge placed, and on my return to Derby I had to attend to some business at the Board Room, during which time, however, my whole mind was devoted to this project; and whilst the business proceeded, I sketched the outline of my design on a large sheet of blotting-paper. Well, having sketched this design, I sat up all night, until I had worked it out to my own satisfaction; and, by the aid of my friend Mr. Barlow, on the 15th, I was enabled to complete the whole of the plans by the Saturday following, on which day I left Rowsley for London. On arriving at the Derby station, I met Mr. Robert Stephenson, a member of the Building Committee, who was also on his way to the metropolis. Mr. Stephenson minutely examined the plans, and became thoroughly engrossed with them, until at length he exclaimed that the design was just the thing, and he only wished it had been submitted to the Committee in time. Mr. Stephenson, however, laid the plans before the Committee, and at first the idea was rather pooh-poohed; but the plans gradually grew in favour, and by publishing the design in the *Illustrated London News*, and showing the advantage of such an erection over one composed of fifteen millions of bricks and other materials, which would have to be removed at a great loss, the Committee did, in the end, reject the abortion of a child of their own, and unanimously recommended my bantling. I am bound to say that I have been treated by the Committee with great fairness. Mr. Brunel, the author of the great dome, I believe, was at first so wedded to his own plan that he would hardly look at mine. But Mr. Brunel was a gentleman and a man of fairness, and listened with every attention to all that could be urged in favour of my plans. As an instance of that gentleman's very creditable conduct, I will mention that a difficulty presented itself to the Committee as to what was to be done with the large trees, and it was gravely suggested that they should be walled in. I remarked that I could cover the trees without any difficulty; when Mr. Brunel asked, 'Do you know their height?' I acknowledged that I did not. On the following morning Mr. Brunel called at Devonshire House, and gave me the measurement of the trees, which he had taken early in the morning, adding— 'Although I mean to try to win with my own plan, I will give you all the information I can.' Having given this preliminary explanation of the origin and execution of my design, I will pass over the question of merit, leaving that to be discussed and decided by others when the whole shall have been completed."

Notwithstanding that Sir Robert Peel and Prince Albert strongly favoured Mr. Paxton's scheme, it was at first but coldly received by the Building Committee, who still clung to their own plan. Nothing daunted, Mr. Paxton appealed to the British public; and this he did by the aid of the woodcuts and pages of the *Illustrated London News*. Everybody but the Committee was at once convinced of the practicability, simplicity, and beauty of Mr. Paxton's plan, which, in fact, was but a vast expansion of a conservatory design, built by him at Chatsworth for the flowering of the Victoria Lily. The people and the Prince were heartily with him; and, thus encouraged, Mr. Paxton resolved to make another effort with the Building Committee. It happened that the Committee had invited candidates for raising their edifice to suggest any improvements in it that might occur to them. This opened a crevice for the tender of Mr. Paxton's plan as an "improvement" on that of the Committee. After some discussion, the result was that the glazed "palace" was chosen unanimously, not only by the Building Committee, but by the Royal Commissioners also. Mr. Paxton's design, as everybody knows, was that of a huge building in the style of a garden conservatory, in which iron and glass should be almost the sole materials, wood being introduced only in the fittings. This method was at once adopted, and the result was a building in Hyde Park, nearly twice the breadth and fully four times the length of St. Paul's Cathedral. The edifice —which was appropriately called the "Crystal Palace"—covered nearly twenty acres of ground, and contained eight miles of tables. It was erected and finished in the short space of seven months. "With its iron framework, that rose towards the sky in dark slender lines, and its walls of glittering crystal, that seemed to float in mid-air like a vapour, it appeared, indeed, an exhalation which a breath of wind might disperse— a *fata morgana* that would disappear with a sudden shift of sunshine. But on looking more nearly it was seen to be a solid edifice, the iron pillars of which were rooted deep in the earth; while within the combination of light and lofty arches, with ribs forming a graceful metallic net-work, gave strength and security to the edifice." It is a curious fact that the edifice realised the conceptions of one of the earliest poetical dreams in the English language; and one would almost believe that when Chaucer, four centuries and a half ago, wrote the following lines in his "House of Fame," he was endowed with a prophetic as well as a poetic faculty :—

> "I dreamt I was
> Within a *temple made of glass*,
> In which there were more images
> Of *gold* standing in sundry stages,
> In more rich tabernacles,
> And with *jewels*, more pinnacles,
> And more curious *portraitures*,
> And quaint manner of figures
> Of gold-work than I saw ever.
> *   *   *   *   ⚬
> "Then saw I stand on either side
> Straight down to the doors wide
> *From the daïs many a pillar*
> *Of metal* that shone out full clear.
> *   *   *   *   ⚰
> "Then gan I look about and see
> That there came ent'ring in the hall,
> A right great company withal,
> *And that of sundry regions*

Of all kinds of conditions,
That dwell in earth beneath the moon,
Poor and rich.

*   *   *   *   *

" Such a great congregation
Of folks as I saw roam about,
Some within and some without,
Was never seen or shall be more!"

The superintendence of the construction of the building was entrusted to Mr. (afterwards Sir) Matthew Digby Wyatt, and the construction itself was undertaken by Messrs. Fox, Henderson, and Co., of Birmingham. The ground-plan of the building was a parallelogram, 1,851 feet long—a fact worthy of mention, seeing that the number corresponds with the date of the year in which the Exhibition was held—by 456 feet wide in the broadest part, with a transept upwards of 400 feet long and 72 feet wide intersecting the building at right angles in the middle. The side walls rose in three stages: the outer wall rising from the ground twenty-four feet, the second twenty feet higher, and the third twenty feet higher still, or sixty-four feet from the bottom of its supporting pillars, giving within the building a great central avenue or nave seventy-two feet wide, and on each side of it three avenues twenty-four feet wide, and two of forty-eight feet; the transept, having a semi-circular roof, being 108 feet high, to give ample room for three or four trees in the Park which remained enclosed under it. The edifice was a trifle longer than Portland Place. "I walked out one evening," says Sir Charles Fox, "and there setting out the 1,848 feet upon the pavement, found it the same length within a few yards; and then considered that the Great Exhibition building would be three times the width of that fine street, and the nave as high as the houses on either side."

As no brick and mortar were used, and all the proportions of the building depended upon its iron pillars and girders, nearly all the materials arrived on the spot ready to be placed and secured in their destined positions. Yet vast operations were necessary even then in its construction, and called forth the most admirable display of scientific ingenuity, systematic arrangements, and great energy. Hardly any scaffolding was used, the columns, as they were set up, answering their purpose. Machines for performing all the preparatory operations required to be done on the spot were introduced in the building, and some of them invented for the occasion; such, for instance, as the sash-bar machine, gutter-machine, mortising-machine, painting-machine, glazing-machine, and other ingenious contrivances for economising labour.

Throughout the progress of the building it was visited by many of the most distinguished persons in the country; and the contractors finding that the numbers who flocked to it impeded in some degree their operations, determined to make a charge of five shillings for admission, the proceeds of which were to constitute an accident-relief fund for the workmen. A very considerable sum was thus raised, though the number of accidents was very small, and the nature of the accidents not at all serious. During the months of December and January upwards of 2,000 persons were employed upon the building.

Whatever wonders the Exhibition was to contain, the building itself, when completed, was looked upon as the greatest wonder of all. Shortly before it was opened to the public, the *Times* observed that, "Not the least wonderful part of the Exhibition will be the edifice within which the specimens of the industry of all nations are to be collected. Its magnitude, the celerity with which it is to be constructed, and the materials of which it is to be composed, all combine to ensure for it a large share of that attention which the Exhibition is likely to attract, and to render its progress a matter of great public interest. A building designed to cover 753,984 superficial feet, and to have an exhibiting surface of about twenty-one acres, to be roofed in, and handed over to the Commissioners within little more than three months from its commencement; to be constructed almost entirely of glass and iron, the most fragile and the strongest of working materials; to combine the lightness of a conservatory with the stability of our most permanent structures—such a building will naturally excite much curiosity as to the mode in which the works connected with it are conducted, and the advances which are made towards its completion. Enchanted palaces that grow up in a night are confined to fairy-land, and in this material world of ours the labours of the bricklayer and the carpenter are notoriously never-ending. It took 300 years to build St. Peter's at Rome, and thirty-five to complete our own St. Paul's. The New Palace of Westminster has already been fifteen years in hand, and still is unfinished. We run up houses, it is true, quickly enough in this country; but if there be a touch of magic in the time occupied, there is none in the appearance of so much stucco and brick-work as our streets exhibit. Something very different from this was promised for the great edifice in Hyde Park. Not only was it to rise with extraordinary rapidity, but in every other respect is to be suggestive of 'Arabian Nights' remembrances."

The decoration of the building, both in design and in execution, was entrusted to Mr. Owen Jones, about 500 painters being employed upon the work. The under sides of the girders were painted red, the round portions of the columns yellow, and the hollows of the capitals blue, in due proportions. All the stalls were covered with red cloth, or pink calico; by which means not only was the unsightly woodwork concealed, but a warmth of colouring was given to the whole ground area of the building, which, combined with the mass of blue overhead, and the yellow stripes of the columns, produced a most harmonious effect, which was further softened by covering the roof and south side with unbleached calico, to prevent the glare of light which would necessarily take place in a building whose roof and sides were chiefly of glass. Mr. Jones also displayed great knowledge in his profession by the judicious distribution of various large articles and groups of articles, with a view to their effect upon the general internal aspect of the Exhibition.

The first column of the edifice was fixed on the 26th of September, 1850, and by the middle of January, 1851, notwithstanding various alterations in some of the details of the plan, little of the exterior of the vast structure remained to be finished, and by the 1st of May everything was complete; the contributions from all nations were in their places; and the Exhibition was opened by Her Majesty Queen Victoria in person, attended by her Royal Consort, the Archbishop of Canterbury, Her Majesty's ministers and great officers of state, the foreign ambassadors and ministers, the Royal Commissioners, &c. The opening ceremony took place with a punctuality which was the source of much congratulation. A chair of state had been placed upon a daïs of three steps, on the north of the centre facing the south transept, and over it was suspended, by invisible rods, a canopy of blue and silver. In front, in the centre of the transept, was a large glass fountain, and on either side, a little in the rear, were equestrian statues of Her Majesty and the Prince Consort. The doors of the "Crystal Palace" were opened on the morning of that eventful day at nine o'clock for the admission of the purchasers of season tickets, of which about 20,000 had been sold. The visitors were so judiciously sprinkled over the different parts of the building, by the tickets assigning to every person the staircase or section he was to repair to, that there was nothing like crushing in any part of the building, with one temporary exception of a rush of persons beyond the barriers before the platform, which was soon set right by a party of sappers. The following particulars of the opening ceremony we here quote from the *Gentleman's Magazine*:—" The Queen left Buckingham Palace in state at twenty minutes before twelve, accompanied by Prince Albert and their two eldest children, the Prince and Princess of Prussia, Prince Frederick William of Prussia, and their respective suites. They were conveyed in nine carriages. Some time before Her Majesty entered, the heralds in their tabards, the officers of state, Her Majesty's ministers, the foreign ambassadors, and the officers of the household troops, in their full costumes, with the Executive Committee and other functionaries of the Exhibition, the architect and contractors in court dresses, and the Lord Mayor and Aldermen in their robes, had assembled round the platform, and the 'beef-eaters' were ranged behind. At length a flourish of trumpets announced the Queen's arrival at the north door of the building, and Her Majesty and her Royal Consort, leading by the hand the Prince of Wales and the Princess Royal, appeared before the vast assemblage of her subjects, and 'the crystal bow' rang with enthusiastic shouts, overpowering the sound of the cannon discharged on the other side of the Serpentine. It was a moment of intense excitement. In the midst of the grandest temple ever raised to the peaceful arts, surrounded by thousands of her subjects and men of all nations, was the ruler of this realm and its vast dependencies, herself the centre of the great undertaking. Her emotions, as she gracefully and repeatedly acknowledged her people's gratulations, were very evident. The Prince Consort having conducted Her Majesty to the throne, the National Anthem was sung by a choir of near a thousand voices, accompanied by the organ of Messrs. Gray and Davidson." Prince Albert then quitted the Queen's side, and, advancing at the head of the Royal Commissioners, over whose deliberations he had indefatigably presided, delivered in an emphatic tone of voice the report of the completion of their labours, from which it appears that the number of exhibitors whose productions it had been found possible to accommodate was about 15,000, of whom nearly one-half were British. The remainder represented the productions of more than forty foreign countries, comprising almost the whole of the civilised nations of the globe. In arranging the space allotted to each, the report stated that the Commissioners had taken into consideration both the nature of its productions and the facilities of access to this country afforded by its geographical position. The productions of Great Britain and her dependencies were arranged in the western portion of the building, and those of foreign countries in the eastern. The Exhibition was divided into four great classes, viz. :—1. Raw Materials ; 2. Machinery ; 3. Manufactures ; 4. Sculpture and the Fine Arts. With regard to the rewards would be assigned. Her Majesty's reply to the address was followed by a prayer, offered up by the Archbishop of Canterbury ; and that finished, the majestic "Hallelujah Chorus" burst forth, its strains reverberating through the arched transept and "long-drawn aisles" of the building.

NAVE OF THE GREAT EXHIBITION OF 1851.

distribution of rewards to deserving exhibitors, the report went on to state that the Commissioner had decided that they should be given in the form of medals, not with reference to merely individual competition, but as rewards for excellence, in whatever shape it might present itself. The selection of the persons to be so rewarded was entrusted to juries, composed equally of British subjects and of foreigners, many of whose names were a guarantee of the impartiality with which the "The state procession was then formed, and passed down the northern avenue of the west nave. The spectators were arranged on either side, and as Her Majesty passed along, the cheers were taken up in succession by the whole of the long array, and seconded with waving of hats and handkerchiefs from the galleries. Her Majesty and the Prince acknowledged these gratulations by continual bowing. The various objects of interest around were for a time almost disregarded, but the effect of the whole upon the eye, as the Sovereign and her attendants threaded their way between the living throng, and the lines of statuary and other works of art, and the rich assemblage

Master-General of the Ordnance), united arm-in-arm in this triumph of peace, were the objects of much attraction. When the procession reached the west end, the magnificent organ by Mr. Willis,

THE ALBERT MEMORIAL. (*See page* 38.)

of the products of industry, was exceedingly impressive; and the ovation of industry far outshone all the splendours of old Rome, with no fettered captives in the rear, or wailing widows and orphans at home to dim its lustre. The Duke of Wellington and the Marquis of Anglesey (who joined the procession as Commander-in-Chief and

with its 4,700 pipes, commenced playing the National Anthem, which was heard to the remotest end of the building. The procession returned by the south side to the transept, round the southern part of which it passed, amidst the cheers of the people, the peals of two organs, and the voices of 700 choristers, to the eastern or foreign division of the nave, where the French organ took up the strain, and the delicate lady, whose tempered sway is owned by a hundred millions of men, pursued her course amongst the contributions of all the civilised world. As she passed the gigantic equestrian figure of Godfrey de Bouillon, by the Belgian sculptor, Simonis, which seems the very impersonation of physical strength, we could not but be struck by the contrast, and by the reflection how far the prowess of the crusader is transcended by the power of well-defined liberty and constitutional law. The brilliant train having at length made the complete circuit of the building, Her Majesty again ascended the throne, and pronounced the Exhibition opened. The announcement was repeated by the Marquis of Breadalbane as Lord Steward, followed immediately by a burst of acclamations, the bray of trumpets, and a royal salute across the Serpentine. The royal party then withdrew; the National Anthem was again repeated; and the visitors dispersed themselves through the building, to gratify their curiosity without restraint."

It would be impossible, and indeed superfluous, within the space at our command, to attempt to give anything even like a *résumé* of the multifarious articles here brought together; suffice it to say, that the Exhibition comprised most of the best productions in the different branches of art, manufactures, &c., from all parts of the civilised globe, and that it became properly enough called the "World's Fair," for it attracted visitors from all parts of the world. We have already mentioned the glass fountain in the transept; that object, from its central position, was invariably fixed upon as the rendezvous, or meeting-place, by family groups or parties of visitors, in case of their losing sight of one another in the labyrinth of tables and articles which thronged the building. Another object, which we cannot well pass over, was the famous Koh-i-noor, or "Mountain of Light," which had been specially lent by Her Majesty. This royal gem—the value of which has been variously stated at from £1,500,000 to £3,000,000—appeared to be one of the greatest curiosities of the Exhibition, judging from the numbers congregated around it during the day. The Exhibition was open for 144 days, being closed on the 11th of October. The entire number of visitors was above 6,170,000, averaging 43,536 per day. The largest number of visitors in one day was 109,760, on the 8th of October; and at two o'clock on the previous day 93,000 persons were present at one time. The entire money drawn for tickets of admission amounted to £506,100; and after all expenses

were defrayed, a balance of £213,300 was left over, to be applied to the promotion of industrial art.

At the time when the Exhibition was over, so firm a hold had the fairy-like palace obtained upon the good opinion of the public, that a general desire for its preservation sprung up. Application was made to Government that it should be purchased and become the property of the nation; but it was ruled otherwise. The building was, however, not doomed to disappear altogether, for a few enterprising gentlemen having stepped forward, it was rescued from destruction. It was decided that the building should be removed to some convenient place within an easy distance of London, and accordingly it was transferred to Sydenham, where a fine estate of three hundred acres had been purchased, on which the edifice was raised again in increased grandeur and beauty, and where, under the name of the Crystal Palace, it soon became one of the most popular places of recreation in or near the metropolis.

The whole building was removed from Hyde Park before the close of 1852; and in the following year it was proposed to place upon the site a memorial of the Exhibition, to include a statue of Prince Albert—the originator of this display of the industry of all nations. The spot ultimately chosen for the memorial, however, is somewhat to the west of the ground covered by the Exhibition building; in fact, it is just within the southeastern enclosure of Kensington Gardens, directly opposite the centre of the Horticultural Gardens, and looking upon the South Kensington establishments, in the promotion of which the Prince Consort always took so deep an interest. The memorial, which took upwards of twenty years before it was completed, and cost upwards of £130,000, was erected from the designs of Sir Gilbert Scott. It consists of a lofty and widespreading pyramid of three quadrangular ranges of steps, forming, as it were, the base of the monument, which may be described as a colossal statue of the Prince, placed beneath a vast and gorgeous Gothic canopy, about thirty feet square, supported at the angles by groups of columns of polished granite, and "surrounded by works of sculpture, illustrating those arts and sciences which he fostered, and the great undertakings which he originated." The memorial partakes somewhat, in the richness of its colours, decorations, and mosaics, of the Renaissance Gothic style; and its whole height from the roadway is 176 feet. The first flight of granite steps, forming the basement, is 212 feet wide, with massive abutments of solid granite. At the four corners of the second flight of steps are gigantic square masses of carved granite, occupied with colossal groups of marble statuary, emblematical of Europe, Asia, Africa, and America, and executed respectively by Messrs. Macdowell, Foley, Theed, and Bell. Above the topmost flight of steps rises the memorial itself, the podium or pedestal of which is carved with nearly 200 figures, life-size, and all more or less in high relief. They are all portrait-statues of celebrities in the different walks of art, literature, science, &c. At the four corners of this, again, as on the base below, are allegorical groups of statuary—one of Commerce, by Thornycroft; one of Manufactures, by Weekes; one of Agriculture, by Marshall; and one of Engineering, by Lawlor. The statue of the Prince—which was not completed till early in the year 1876—is richly gilt, and rests upon a pedestal fifteen feet high; it represents the Prince sitting on a chair of state, and attired in his regal-looking robes as a Knight of the Garter. This great work was entrusted to Mr. Foley. The roof of the canopy is decorated with mosaics, representing the royal arms and those of the Prince on a ground of blue and gold. At the angles of the four arches above the canopy are marble figures, life-size. The spandrils of the arches above the trefoil are filled in with rich and elaborate glass mosaics on a gilt ground, portraying Poetry, Painting, Sculpture, and Architecture. One of the main features of the whole design is the beautiful spire, in which every portion of the metal surface is covered with ornament; the surface in many parts is coated with colours in enamel, with coloured marbles and imitation gem-work; and up to the very cross itself, which surmounts the whole, there is the same amount of extraordinary detail and finish, as if each part were meant for the most minute and close inspection.

CHAPTER IV.

PIMLICO.

"I'll have thee, Captain Gilthead, and march up
And take in Pimlico."—*Old Play*.

Etymology of Pimlico—The Locality Half a Century Ago—Warwick Square—Vauxhall Bridge Road—The Army Clothing Depôt—St. George's Square—The Church of St. James the Less—Victoria Railway Station—New Chelsea Bridge—The Western Pumping Station, and Metropolitan Main-Drainage Works—St. Barnabas Church—St. Barnabas Mission House and Orphanage—Bramah, the Engineer and Locksmith—Thomas Cubitt, the Builder—The "Monster" Tavern—The "Gun," the "Star and Garter," and the "Orange" Tea-Gardens—"Jenny's Whim"—Tart Hall—Stafford Row—St. Peter's Chapel and Dr. Dodd—Richard Heber and his famous Library.

THE name Pimlico is clearly of foreign derivation, and it has not a little puzzled topographers. Gifford, in a note in his edition of Ben Jonson, tells us that "Pimlico is sometimes spoken of as a person, and may not improbably have been the master of a house once famous for ale of a particular description;" and we know, from Dodsley's "Old Plays," and from Ben Jonson's writings, that there was another Pimlico at Hoxton, or (as the place was then termed) Hogsdon, where, indeed, to the present day there is a "Pimlico Walk." It is evident, from a reference to *The Alchemist* of Ben Jonson, that the place so named at "Hogsdon" was a place of resort of no very good repute, and constantly frequented by all sorts of people, from knights, ladies, and gentlewomen, down to oyster-wenches :—

"Gallants, men, and women,
And of all sorts, tag-rag, been seen to flock here,
In these ten weeks, as to a second Hogsdon,
In days of Pimlico."

In another play of about the same period a worthy knight is represented as sending his daughter to Pimlico "to fetch a draught of Derby ale." It is antecedently probable, therefore, that the district lying between Chelsea and St. James's Park should have got the name from an accidental resemblance to its antipodes at Hoxton. And this supposition is confirmed by Isaac Reed, who tells us, in Dodsley's "Old Plays," how that "a place near Chelsey is still called Pimlico, and was resorted to within these few years on the same account as the former at Hogsdon." It may be added that Pimlico is still celebrated for its ales, and also that the district is not mentioned by the name of Pimlico in any existing document prior to the year 1626.

"At this time"—*i.e.* the reign of Charles I., writes Mr. Peter Cunningham—"Pimlico was quite uninhabited, nor is it introduced into the rate-books of St. Martin's (to which it belonged) until the year 1680, when the Earl of Arlington — previously rated as residing in the Mulberry Gardens—is rated, though still living in the same house, under the head of Pimlico. In 1687, seven years later, four people are described as living in what was then called Pimlico—the Duke of Grafton, Lady Stafford, Thomas Wilkins, and Dr. Crispin. The Duke of Grafton, having married the only child of the Earl of Arlington, was residing in Arlington House; and Lady Stafford in what was then and long before known as Tart Hall." Arlington House, as we have seen,* was ultimately developed into Buckingham Palace.

The district of Pimlico may be regarded as embracing the whole of Belgravia, which we have already dealt with in a previous chapter, as well as the locality extending from Buckingham Palace Road to the Thames, and stretching away westward to Chelsea. This latter portion includes the Grosvenor Road and the Eccleston sub-district of squares, terraces, and streets, nearly all of which have sprung up within the last half-century.

In the map appended to Coghlan's "Picture of London," published in the year 1834, the whole of this division of Pimlico, between Vauxhall Bridge Road and Chelsea (now Buckingham Palace) Road, appears unbuilt upon, with the exception of a few stray cottages here and there, and a few blocks of houses near the river; the rest of the space is marked out as gardens and waste land, intersected by the Grosvenor Canal, the head of which, forming an immense basin, is now entirely covered by the Victoria Railway Station. Its rustic character at the above date may be inferred from the fact, that a considerable portion of the space between the two roads above mentioned is described as "osier beds," whilst a straight thoroughfare connecting the two roads is called Willow Walk. These osier beds are now covered by Eccleston Square and a number of small streets adjacent to it; whilst "Willow Walk" has been transformed into shops and places of business, and is now known as Warwick Street. On the north side of Warwick Street, covering part of the "old Neat House" Gardens, to which we have already referred,† is Warwick Square, which is bounded on the north-east by Belgrave Road, and on the south-west by St. George's Road. In Warwick Square stands St. Gabriel's Church, a large building of Early English architecture, erected from the designs of Mr. Thomas Cundy, who was also the architect of St. Saviour's Church, in St. George's Square, close by. Vauxhall Bridge Road, which dates from the erection of the bridge, about the year 1816, is a broad and well-built thoroughfare, opening up a direct communication, by way of Grosvenor Place, between Hyde Park Corner and Vauxhall Bridge, and so on to Kennington and the southern suburbs of London. Of Vauxhall Bridge, and of Trinity Church, in Bessborough Gardens, close by, we have already spoken.‡

Not far from St. George's Square stands an extensive range of buildings, known as, the Army Clothing Depôt—one of the largest institutions that has ever been established for the organisation and utilisation of women's work. "Previous to the year 1857," observes a writer in the *Queen* newspaper, "all the clothes for the British army were made by contractors, whose first thought seemed to be how to amass a fortune at the expense of the makers and the wearers of the clothes primarily, and of the British public indirectly. But in that year the Army Clothing Depôt was established, somewhat experimentally, in Blomberg Terrace, Vauxhall Road; the experiment answering so well, that an extension of the premises became imperative. In 1859 the present depôt was opened, although since then it has largely increased, and has not yet, apparently, come to the full stage of its development. The whole of the premises occupy about seven acres, the long block of buildings on the one side being used as the Government stores, while the corresponding block consists of the factory. The main feature of the latter is a large glass-roofed central hall of three storeys, with spacious galleries all round on each storey. The ventilation is ensured by louvres, so that the whole atmosphere can be renewed in the space of five minutes or so; the temperature is kept at an average of 60° to 63°, and each operative enjoys 1,200 cubic feet of air, so that we have at the outset the three requirements of light, air, and warmth, in strongly-marked contrast to the crowded rooms of the contractor, or the more wretched chamber of the home-worker. Five hundred and twenty-seven women are at present working in the central hall, and five hundred in the side rooms, which also accommodate about two hundred men. This forms the working staff of the factory, which comprises, therefore, what may be called the pick of the sewing-machine population in London. It may well be imagined that the prospect of so comfortable an abiding place would attract great numbers of workpeople; and, indeed, this has been so much the case that very rigorous rules have been obliged to be made to guard against unworthy admissions. 'The good of the public service' is the motto of the factory, and everything else must yield to that; so that, both for in-door and out-door hands, all candidates must first of

---

all appear before a committee, consisting of the matron, the foreman cutter, the foreman viewer, and the instructor, who are held responsible for the selection of proper persons. In-door candidates as needlewomen must be healthy and strong, and, if single, between the ages of seventeen and thirty; if married or widows, they must have no children at home young enough to demand their care. These points being settled, the candidates are examined as to any previous training or fitness for army work, and are required to show what they can do. If all these requirements are satisfactory, the matron inquires into their character, and finally they are examined by the doctor, who certifies to their fitness, after which they are placed in a trial division in the factory for further report and promotion."

St. George's Square, with its trees and shrubs, presents a healthful and cheering aspect, almost bordering on the Thames, just above Vauxhall Bridge. It covers a considerable space of ground, and is bounded on the north side by Lupus Street—a thoroughfare so called after a favourite Christian name in the Grosvenor family, perpetuating the memory of Hugh Lupus, Earl of Chester after the Norman Conquest. St. Saviour's Church, which was built in 1865, is in the Decorated style of Gothic architecture, and with its elegant tower and spire forms a striking object, as seen from the river.

In Upper Garden Street, which runs parallel with Vauxhall Bridge Road, is the Church of St. James the Less, built in 1861, from the designs of Mr. G. E. Street, R.A. The edifice was founded by the daughters of the late Bishop of Gloucester and Bristol (Dr. Monk) as a memorial to their father, who was also a Canon of Westminster. It is constructed of brick, with dressings of stone, marble, and alabaster; and it consists of a nave, side aisles, a semi-circular apse, and a lofty tower and spire. The roof of the chancel is groined, and is a combination of brick and stone. A very considerable amount of elaborate detail pervades the interior. The chancel is surrounded by screens of brass and iron, and over the chancel-arch is a well-executed fresco painting, by Mr. G. F. Watts, R.A., of "Our Saviour attended by Angels." Some of the windows are filled with stained glass. The building, including the decorations, cost upwards of £9,000.

The Victoria Railway Station, situated at the northern end of Vauxhall Bridge Road, covers, as we have stated above, a considerable portion of the basin of the old Grosvenor Canal; it unites the West-end of London with the lines terminating at London Bridge and Holborn Viaduct, and also serves as the joint terminus of the Brighton Railway and of the London, Chatham, and Dover Railway. Like the stations at Charing Cross and Cannon Street, which we have already described, the Victoria Railway Station has a "monster" hotel—"The Grosvenor"—built in connection with it. The lines of railway, soon after leaving the station, are carried across the Thames by an iron bridge of four arches, called the Victoria Bridge, and then diverge.

On the western side of the railway bridge is a handsome new bridge, which now connects this populous and increasing neighbourhood with Battersea and Vauxhall. The railway bridge somewhat mars the structural beauty of the one under notice; but when looked at from the embankment on either side, "above bridge," or, better still, from a boat in the middle of the river, the bridge appears like a fairy structure, with its towers gilded and painted to resemble light-coloured bronze, and crowned with large globular lamps. The bridge, which is constructed on the suspension principle, is built of iron, and rests upon piers of English elm and concrete enclosed within iron casings. The two piers are each nearly ninety feet in length by twenty in width, with curved cut-waters. The roadway on the bridge is formed by two wrought-iron longitudinal girders, upwards of 1,400 feet, which extend the whole length of the bridge, and are suspended by rods from the chains. At either end of the bridge are picturesque lodge-houses, for the use of the toll-collectors. The bridge was built from the designs of Mr. Page, and finished in 1857, at a cost of £88,000.

Nearly the whole of the river-side between Vauxhall Bridge and Chelsea Bridge forms a broad promenade and thoroughfare, very similar in its construction to the Victoria Embankment, which we have already described, and of which it is, so to speak, a continuation—the only break in the line of roadway being about a quarter of a mile between Millbank and the Houses of Parliament, where the river is not embanked on the north side. This roadway is known partly as Thames Bank, or Thames Parade, and partly as the Grosvenor Road. One of the principal buildings erected upon it is the Western Pumping Station, which was finished in 1874-5, completing the main-drainage system of the metropolis. The foundation-stone of the structure was laid in 1873, and the works cost about £183,000. This station provides pumping power to lift the sewage and a part of the rainfall contributed by the district, together estimated at 38,000 gallons per minute. a height of eighteen feet in the Low Level Sewer, which extends from Pimlico to the Abbey Mills Pumping Station, near Barking, in Essex. The requisite power is obtained from four high-pressure condensing beam-engines of an aggregate of 360-horse power. Supplementary power, to be used in case of accident to the principal engines, or on any similar emergency, is provided by an additional high-pressure, non-condensing engine of 120-horse

below the entablature which surmounts the shaft. Altogether, this chimney really makes a most conspicuous and beautiful object as one comes down the river. The foundations of this great pile of brickwork are carried down into the London clay, and even then bedded in a mass of concrete cement 35 feet square.

The system of the main-drainage of London, which has been carried out by the Metropolitan

THE "MONSTER" TEA GARDENS, 1820. (*See page* 45.)

power, supplied from two boilers similar to those for the principal engines. This engine and its boilers are erected in a separate building to the rear of the main buildings, near the canal. The works further comprise coal vaults, settling pond, and reservoirs for condensing water, repairing-shops, stores, and dwelling-houses for the workmen and superintendent in charge of the works. In all they cover nearly four acres. The principal engine-house is situate facing the main road and river, and the height of this building rises to upwards of seventy-one feet. But all this is dwarfed by the chimney-shaft, which is very nearly the height of the Monument, being only ten feet short of it. The shaft is square, and the sides are relieved by three recessed panels, arched over a short distance

Board of Works, comprises 117 square miles of sewers, and, as each was concluded, it added to the health and comfort of the inhabitants of the metropolis. The main sewers are eighty-two miles long, and cost about £4,607,000; and the local boards and vestries assisted in completing the work, which comprised 635 miles of sewers.

At the western extremity of Buckingham Palace Road, near Ebury Square, stands a handsome Gothic church, built in the severest Early English style, which has acquired some celebrity as "St. Barnabas, Pimlico." It was built in 1848-50, as a chapel of ease to St. Paul's, Knightsbridge, under the auspices of its then incumbent, the Rev. W. J. E. Bennett. Attached to it are large schools, a presbytery or college for the officiating clergy,

"JENNY'S WHIM" BRIDGE, 1750. (*See page* 45.)

who must almost of necessity be celibates. The church gained some notoriety during the earlier part of the Ritualistic movement, and, indeed, the services were not allowed to be carried on without sundry popular outbursts of indignation. Of late, however, this church has ceased to occupy the public attention, having been fairly eclipsed by other churches, which are marked by a still more "advanced" Ritual. The church is a portion of a college founded on St. Barnabas' Day, 1846, and is built upon ground presented by the first Marquis of Westminster. The fabric has a Caen-stone tower and spire, 170 feet high, with a peal of ten bells, the gifts of as many parishioners. The windows throughout are filled with stained glass, with subjects from the life of St. Barnabas. An oak screen, richly carved, separates the nave from the chancel; the open roof is splendidly painted, and the superb altar-plate, the font, the illuminated "office" books, and other costly ornaments, were the gifts of private individuals.

In Blomfield Place, close by St. Barnabas' Church, are two or three useful institutions, of modern growth, which must not be overlooked. One of these is St. John's School for girls, which was established in 1859, under the auspices of the Sisterhood of St. John, and with the sanction of the Bishop of London. The school is "specially adapted for the children of clergymen, professional men; for those whose parents are abroad, who need home-training and care; also for young ladies desirous of improving their education, or to be fitted for governesses." Adjoining the school-house is St. Barnabas' Mission House, and also the St. Barnabas' Orphanage. The latter institution was established in 1860, and is supported by ladies living in the immediate neighbourhood. It is also placed under the care of the "sisters" of St. John.

In 1815, according to the "Beauties of England and Wales," the "chief ornament of this neighbourhood" was the "amazingly extensive and interesting manufactory of Mr. Bramah, the engineer, lock-smith, and engine-maker. . . . These works have been deemed worthy the inspection of royalty, and have excited the admiration of the most powerful emperor of Christendom, Alexander of Russia." John Joseph Bramah, the founder of these engineering works, was nephew of Joseph Bramah, "a many-sided mechanist, one who did the world large service, and who, aided by a good business faculty in buying and selling, did himself and his heirs service also;" whose bust, modelled by Chantrey, was destroyed (but for what reason does not appear) by Lady Chantrey, after the

sculptor's death. The younger Bramah inherited the business faculty of his uncle, and his love for mechanism, if not his inventive skill. He it was who here gathered together a huge business in railway plant, with the aid and help of the two Stephensons, George and Robert, and subsequently transferred it to Smethwick, near Birmingham, as the "London Works," joining with himself Charles Fox and John Henderson as his partners; and out of their works finally grew up the original Crystal Palace, as we have shown in the last chapter.

Another large establishment, which flourished for many years at Thames Bank, was that of Mr. Thomas Cubitt, the founder of the well-known firm in Gray's Inn Road which bears his name. The large engagements which resulted in the laying-out and erection of Belgrave Square were commenced by Mr. Cubitt, in 1825. Mr. Cubitt died towards the close of 1855. "Through life," observes a writer in the *Builder*, "he had been the real friend of the working man; and among his own people he did much to promote their social, intellectual, and moral progress. He established a workman's library; school-room for workmen's children; and by an arrangement to supply generally to his work-men soup and cocoa at the smallest rate at which these could be produced, assisted in establishing a habit of temperance, and superseding, to a great extent, the dram-drinking which previously existed among them. Although his kindness was appreciated by many, yet at times his motives have been misconstrued, and unkind remarks have been made. In alluding to these, he has often said to one who was about him and possessed his confidence, 'If you wait till people thank you for doing anything for them, you will never do anything. It is right for me to do it, whether they are thankful for it or not.' To those under him, and holding responsible situations, he was most liberal and kind. He was a liberal benefactor at all times to churches, schools, and charities, in those places with which he was connected, and always valued, in a peculiar degree, the advantages resulting to the poor from the London hospitals." Mr. Cubitt was a man of unassuming demeanour, and bore his great prosperity with becoming modesty. One instance of his equanimity occurred when his premises were unfortunately burnt down, in the year before his death. He was in the country at the time, and was immediately tele-graphed for to town. The shock to most minds, on seeing the great destruction which occurred, attended with pecuniary loss to the amount of £30,000, would have been overpowering. Mr. Cubitt's first words on entering the premises, however, were, "Tell the men they shall be at work within a week, and I will subscribe £600 towards buying them new tools."

So late as 1763, Buckingham House enjoyed an uninterrupted prospect south and west to the river, there being only a few scattered cottages and the "Stag" Brewery between it and the Thames. Lying as it did at the distance of only a short walk from London, and on the way to rural Chelsea, this locality was always a great place for taverns and tea-gardens. The "Monster" Tavern, at one period an inn of popular resort, at the corner of St. George's Row and Buckingham Palace Road, and for many years the starting-point of the "Monster" line of omnibuses, is probably a corruption, perhaps an intentional one, of the "Monastery." Mr. Larwood writes thus, in his "History of Sign-boards:"—"Robert de Heyle, in 1368, leased the whole of the Manor of Chelsea to the Abbot and Monastery or Convent of Westminster for the term of his own life, for which they were to pay him the sum of £20 a year, to provide him every day with two white loaves, two flagons of convent ale, and once a year a robe of esquire's silk. At this period, or shortly after, the sign of the 'Monastery' may have been set up, to be handed down from generation to generation, until the meaning and proper pronunciation were alike forgotten, and it became the 'Monster.' . . This tavern," he adds, "I believe, is the only one with such a sign."

We have already spoken of the Mulberry Gardens, which occupied the site of Buckingham Palace.* Here also were the "Gun" Tavern and Tea-gardens, with convenient "arbours and costume figures." These gardens were removed to make way for improvements at Buckingham Gate. Then there was the "Star and Garter" Tavern, at the end of Five-Fields' Row, which was at one time famous for its fireworks, dancing, and equestrianism; and the "Orange," as nearly as possible upon the site of St. Barnabas' Church.

Another tavern or place of public entertainment in this neighbourhood, in former times, was "Jenny's Whim." This establishment, which bore the name down to the beginning of the present century, occupied the site now covered by St. George's Row, near to Ebury Bridge, which spanned the canal at the north end of the Commercial Road. This bridge was formerly known as the "Wooden Bridge," and also as "Jenny's Whim Bridge" (see page 43); and down to about the year 1825, a turnpike close by bore the same lady's name.

A hundred years ago, as is clear from allusions to it in the *Connoisseur* and other periodicals, "Jenny's Whim" was a very favourite place of amusement for the middle classes. At a somewhat earlier date, it would appear to have been frequented alike by high and low, by lords and gay ladies, and by City apprentices; and indeed was generally looked upon as a very favourite place of recreation. The derivation of the name is a little uncertain; but Mr. Davis, in his "History of Knightsbridge," thus attempts to solve it:—"I never could unearth the origin of its name, but I presume the tradition told me by an old inhabitant of the neighbourhood is correct, namely, that it was so called after its first landlady, who caused the gardens round her house to be laid out in so fantastic a manner, as to cause the expressive little noun to be affixed to the pretty and familiar Christian name that she bore."

In the "Reminiscences" of Angelo, however, it is said that the founder of "Jenny's Whim" was not a lady at all, but a celebrated pyrotechnist, who lived in the reign of George I. If so, this assertion carries back the existence of the "Whim" as a place of amusement to a very respectable antiquity. Angelo states that it was "much frequented from its novelty, being an inducement to allure the curious to it by its amusing deceptions." "Here," he adds, "was a large garden; in different parts were recesses; and by treading on a spring—taking you by surprise—up started different figures, some ugly enough to frighten you outright—a harlequin, a Mother Shipton, or some terrific animal." Something of the same kind, it may here be remarked, was to be seen in the days of Charles I., in the Spring Garden near Charing Cross.† "In a large piece of water facing the tea alcoves," adds Mr. Angelo, "large fish or mermaids were showing themselves above the surface." Horace Walpole, in his letters, occasionally alludes to "Jenny's Whim," in terms which imply that he was among "the quality" who visited it. In one of his epistles to his friend Montagu, he writes, rather spitefully and maliciously, it must be owned, to the effect that at Vauxhall he and his party picked up Lord Granby, who had arrived very drunk from "Jenny's Whim." In 1755, a satirical tract was published, entitled, "Jenny's Whim; or a Sure Guide to the Nobility, Gentry, and other Eminent Persons in this Metropolis." "Jenny's Whim" has occasionally served the novelist for an illustration of the manners of the age. Let us take the following passage from "Maids of Honour," a tale *temp.* George I.:—

---

* See Vol. IV., p. 62.   † See Vol. IV., p. 77.

"Attached to the place there were gardens and a bowling-green," writes the author ; "and parties were frequently made, composed of ladies and gentlemen, to enjoy a day's amusement there in eating strawberries and cream, cake, syllabub, and taking other refreshments, of which a great variety could be procured, with cider, perry, ale, wine, and other liquors in abundance. The gentlemen played at bowls—some employed themselves at skittles ; whilst the ladies amused themselves with a swing, or walked about the garden, admiring the sunflower and hollyhocks, and the Duke of Marlborough cut out of a filbert-tree, and the roses and daisies, currants and gooseberries, that spread their alluring charms in every part."

No doubt, therefore, we may conclude that a century, or a century and a half ago, "Jenny's Whim" was a favourite meeting-place for lovers in the happy courting seasons, and that a day's pleasure near Ebury Bridge was considered by the fair damsels of Westminster and Knightsbridge one of the most attractive amusements that could be offered to them by their beaux ; and many a heart which was obdurate elsewhere, gave way to gentle pressure beneath the influence of its attractions, aided by the *genius loci*, who is always most complaisant and benignant on such occasions. "Sometimes," writes Mr. Davis, "all its chambers were filled, and its gardens were constantly thronged by gay and sentimental visitors." We may be sure, therefore, that always during the season—in other words, from Easter-tide till the end of St. Martin's summer, when the long evenings drew on—"Jenny's Whim" was largely frequented by the young people of either sex, and that its "arbours" and "alcoves" witnessed and overheard many a tale of love. It is well perhaps that garden walls have not tongues as well as ears. But, in any case, it is perhaps a little singular that a place, once so well known and so popular, should have passed away, clean forgotten from the public memory.

All that appears to be known in detail about the house is, that it contained a large room for parties to breakfast in ; and that the grounds, though not large, were fairly diversified, as they contained a bowling-green, several alcoves and arbours, and straight, prim flower-beds, with a fish-pond in the centre, where the paths met at right angles. There was also a "cock-pit" in the garden, and in a pond adjoining the brutal sport of duck-hunting was carried on. This feature of the garden is specially mentioned in a short and slight sketch of the place to be found in the *Connoisseur* of March 15th, 1775 :—"The lower part of the people have their Ranelaghs and Vauxhalls as well as 'the quality.'

Perrott's inimitable grotto may be seen for only calling for a pint of beer ; and the royal diversion of duck-hunting may be had into the bargain, together with a decanter of Dorchester [ale] for your sixpence at 'Jenny's Whim.'"

Mr. Davis states, in his work above quoted, that the house was still partly standing in 1859, when his book was published, and might be easily identified by its "red brick and lattice-work."

Notwithstanding all the attractions which the district of Pimlico thus afforded to the Londoners, to betake themselves thither in order to enjoy the good things provided for their entertainment, access to it must have been somewhat difficult and dangerous in the last century—a state of things, as we have more than once remarked, that seems to have been pretty similar in all the suburbs of the metropolis ; for we read in the *London Magazine* that, as lately as 1773, two persons were sentenced to death for a highway robbery in "Chelsea Fields," as that part of Pimlico bordering the Chelsea Road was then called. It is also not a matter of tradition, but of personal remembrance, that for the first twenty years of the present century persons who resided in the "suburb" of Pimlico rarely thought of venturing into London at night, so slight was the protection afforded them by the watchmen and "Charlies," aided by the faint glimmer of oil lamps, few and far between.

Not far from the Mulberry Gardens, on the west side of what is now James Street, as we have stated in the previous volume,* stood a mansion, called Tart Hall, which was built, or, at all events, extensively altered and enlarged, in the reign of Charles I., for the wife of Thomas, "the magnificent Earl of Arundel." On her death it passed into the hands of her second son, William, Lord Stafford, one of the victims of the plot of the infamous Titus Oates, in 1680, and whose memory is still kept up in the names of Stafford Place and Stafford Row. Strange to say, that John Evelyn himself, usually so circumstantial in all matters of detail, dismisses this legal murder without a single remark, beyond the dry entry in his "Diary," under December 20th, 1680: "The Viscount Stafford was beheaded on Tower Hill." It is said that the old gateway, which stood till early in the last century, was never opened after the condemned nobleman passed through it for the last time.

The building is described in the "New View of London" (1708), as being "near the way leading out of the Park to Chelsea ;" and its

---

* See Vol. IV., p 25.

site is marked in Faithorne's Map of London, published in 1658.

In his " Morning's Walk from London to Kew" (1817), Sir Richard Phillips writes :—" The name of Stafford Row reminded me of the ancient distinction of Tart Hall, once the rival in size and splendour of its more fortunate neighbour, Buckingham House. . . . It faced the Park, on the present site of James Street ; its garden-wall standing where Stafford Row is now built, and the extensive livery-stables being once the stables of its residents."

The origin of Tart Hall is unknown ; but the name is probably a corruption or abridgment of a longer word. It is noted, as to situation, in "Walpole's Anecdotes," as " without the gate of St. James's Park, near Buckingham House," and is described by him as " very large, and having a very venerable appearance."

After the removal of the Arundel marbles and other treasures from Arundel House, in the neighbourhood of the Strand,* the remainder of the collection, as Walpole tells us, was kept at Tart Hall ; but they were sold in 1720, and the house was subsequently pulled down. From the same authority we learn that some carved seats, by Inigo Jones, purchased at this sale, were placed by Lord Burlington in his villa at Chiswick. In the Harleian MSS., in the British Museum, is to be seen "A Memorial of all the Roomes at Tart Hall, and an Inventory of all the household stuffs and goods there, except of six Roomes at the North end of the ould Building (which the Right Honourable the Countess hath reserved unto her peculiar use), and Mr. Thomas Howard's Closett, &c.," dated September, 1641. The memorial is curious as giving a catalogue, not only of the picture-gallery, but of the carpets and decorations of this once magnificent palace. It is, however, too long in its details to be reprinted here.

In Stafford Row, which lies immediately at the back of Buckingham Palace Hotel, lived, in the year 1767, William Wynne Ryland, the engraver, who was executed for forgery in 1783 ; here, too, during the early part of the present century, died Mrs. Radcliffe, the author of " The Mysteries of Udolpho." Richard Yates, the actor, who was famous in the last century for his delineation of " old men," died at his residence in this Row in 1796. The following singular story of the ill fortune which attended the actor and his family is told by Peter Cunningham, in his " Hand-book of London :"—" Yates had ordered eels for dinner,

and died the same day of rage and disappointment, because his housekeeper was unable to obtain them. The actor's great-nephew was, a few months afterwards—August 22nd, 1796—killed while endeavouring to effect an entrance into the house from the back garden. The great-nephew, whose name was Yates, claimed a right to the house, as did also a Miss Jones, and both lived in the house for some months after Yates' death. Yates, while strolling in the garden, was bolted out after an early dinner, and, while forcing his way in, was wounded by a ball from a pistol, which caused his death. The parties were acquitted."

St. Peter's Chapel, on the west side of Charlotte Street, which runs southwards out of Buckingham Palace Road, just opposite to the Palace, and skirts the west end of Stafford Place, enjoys a melancholy celebrity, as having been the scene of the ministrations of Dr. Dodd, of whose execution for a forgery on Lord Chesterfield we shall have to make fuller mention when we come to speak of "Tyburn Tree." The following account of the life of Dr. Dodd is said to have been sketched by himself while lying in Newgate, awaiting his execution, and to have been finished by Dr. Johnson :—" I entered very young on public life, very innocent—very ignorant—and very ingenuous. I lived many happy years at West Ham, in an uninterrupted and successful discharge of my duty. A disappointment in the living of that parish obliged me to exert myself, and I engaged for a chapel near Buckingham Gate. Great success attended the undertaking ; it pleased and elated me. At the same time Lord Chesterfield, to whom I was personally unknown, offered me the care of his heir, Mr. Stanhope. By the advice of my dear friend, now in heaven, Dr. Squire, I engaged, under promises which were not performed. Such a distinction, too, you must know, served to increase a young man's vanity. I was naturally led into more extensive and important connections, and, of course, with greater expenses and more dissipations. Indeed, before I never dissipated at all—for many, many years, never seeing a playhouse, or any public place, but living entirely in Christian duties. Thus brought to town, and introduced to gay life, I fell into its snares. Ambition and vanity led me on. My temper, naturally cheerful, was pleased with company ; naturally generous, it knew not the use of money ; it was a stranger to the useful science of economy and frugality ; nor could it withhold from distress what it too much (often) wanted itself.

" Besides this, the habit of uniform, regular,

sober piety, and of watchfulness and devotion, wearing off, amidst this unavoidable scene of dissipation, I was not, as at West Ham, the innocent man that I lived there. I committed offences against my God, which yet, I bless Him, were always, on reflection. detestable to me.

"But my greatest evil was expense. To supply it, I fell into the dreadful and ruinous mode of raising money by annuities. The annuities other publications prove. I can say, too, with pleasure, that I studiously employed my interest, through the connections I had, for the good of others. I never forgot or neglected the cause of the distressed; many, if need were, could bear me witness. Let it suffice to say, that during this period I instituted the Charity for the Discharge of Debtors."

Close by Charlotte Street, in a small gloomy

THE "GUN TAVERN," 1820. (*See page* 45.)

devoured me. Still, I exerted myself by every means to do what I thought right, and built my hopes of perfect extrication from all my difficulties when my young and beloved pupil should come of age. But, alas! during this interval, which was not very long, I declare with solemn truth that I never varied from the steady belief of the Christian doctrines. I preached them with all my power, and kept back nothing from my congregations which I thought might tend to their best welfare; and I was very successful in this way during the time. Nor, though I spent in dissipation many hours which I ought not, but to which my connections inevitably led, was I idle during this period; as my 'Commentary on the Bible,' my 'Sermons to Young Men,' and several house, inside the gates of Messrs. Elliot's Brewery, between Brewer Street, Pimlico, and York Street, Westminster, lived Richard Heber, some time M.P. for the University of Oxford, and the owner of one of the finest private libraries in the world. Here he kept a portion of his library; a second part occupying an entire house in James Street, Buckingham Gate; a third portion, from kitchen to attics, was at his country seat at Hodnet, in Shropshire; and a fourth at Paris. "Nobody," he used to say, "could do without three copies of a book—one for show at his country house, one for personal use, and the third to lend to his friends." And this library, as we learn from "A Century of Anecdote," had but a small beginning —the accidental purchase of a chance volume picked up for a few pence at a bookstall, and about which Mr. Heber was for some time in doubt whether to buy it or not. The catalogue of Mr. Heber's library was bound up in five thick octavo volumes. Dr. Dibdin once addressed to him a letter entitled " Bibliomania ; " but he was no bibliomaniac, but a ripe and accomplished scholar. Mr. Heber took an active part in founding the Athenæum Club, and he was also a member

drawing the courtiers from Portland Place and Portman Square to the splendid mansions built by Messrs. Basevi and Cubitt, in what was known at that time, and long before, as the 'Five Fields.' It seems but the other day," he adds, "that the writer of this brief notice of the place played at cricket in the Five Fields, 'where robbers lie in wait,' or pulled bulrushes in the 'cuts' of the Willow Walk, in Pimlico."

THE OLD CHELSEA MANOR HOUSE. (*See page* 52.)

of several other literary societies ; indeed, to use the phrase of Dr. Johnson, " He was an excellent clubber." He was the half-brother of Reginald Heber, Bishop of Calcutta, and died a bachelor in 1833, in the sixtieth year of his age. His extensive library was dispersed by auction in London. The sale commenced upon the 10th of April, 1834, and occupied *two hundred and two days*, and extended through a period of more than *two years*. The catalogue of this remarkable sale filled more than two thousand printed octavo pages, and contained no less than 52,672 lots.

Mr. Peter Cunningham, in noticing the growth of this locality in his " Hand-book of London," says : " George IV. began the great alterations in Pimlico by rebuilding Buckingham House, and

As might be naturally expected, the removal of King William and his Court from St. James's to Buckingham Palace, on his accession to the throne in 1830, gave a considerable impetus to the improvement of Pimlico, although a town of palaces had already been commenced upon the " Five Fields," as that dreary region had been formerly called. The ground landlord of a considerable portion of the land thus benefited by these metropolitan improvements was Lord Grosvenor, who, in the year 1831, was created Marquis of Westminster, and who, as we have already stated in our description of Grosvenor House in a former chapter, was grandfather of the present ducal owner.*

* See Vol. IV., p. 371.

CHAPTER V.

CHELSEA.

"The sands of Chelsey Fields."—Ben Jonson.

Boundary of the Parish—Etymology of its Name—Charles II. and Colonel Blood—Chelsea Fields—The "Dwarf's Tavern"—Chapels of French Huguenot Refugees—Gardens and Nurseries—Appearance of Chelsea from the River—Chelsea in the Last Century—A Stag Hunt in Chelsea—History of the Manor—The Old Manor House and its Eminent Residents—Lord Cremorne's Farm at Chelsea—Lady Cremorne—Lindsey House—The Moravians—The Duchess of Mazarine—Sir Robert Walpole's House—Shrewsbury House—Winchester House—Beaufort House and the "Good" Sir Thomas More—Anecdotes of Sir Thomas More—The Old and New Parish Churches.

FEW, if any, of the suburban districts of the metropolis can lay claim to greater interest, biographical as well as topographical, than the locality upon which we have now entered. In Faulkner's "History of Chelsea," we read that the parish is "bounded on the north by the Fulham Road, which separates it from Kensington; on the east by a rivulet, which divides it from St. George's, Hanover Square, and which enters the Thames near Ranelagh; on the west a brook, which rises near Wormholt Scrubs, and falls into the Thames facing Battersea Church, divides this parish from that of Fulham; and on the south it is bounded by the Thames." Lysons observes that the most ancient record in which he has seen the name of this place mentioned is a charter of Edward the Confessor, in which it is written "Cealchylle."* The name seems to have puzzled the Norman scribes, for in Domesday Book it is written both "Cercehede" and "Chelched;" and in certain documents of a later date it is called "Chelcheth," or "Chelcith." "The word 'Chelsey,'" observes Mr. Norris Brewer, in the "Beauties of England and Wales," "was first adopted in the sixteenth century, and the present mode of spelling the name appears to have grown into use about a century back." It may here be remarked that the name of Chelsea has been derived by some writers from "Shelves" of sand, and "ey," or "ea," land situated near the water. But Lysons prefers the etymology of Norden, who says that "it is so called from the nature of the place, its strand being like the chesel [*ceosel*, or *cesol*], which the sea casteth up of sand and pebble stones, thereof called Chevelsey, briefly Chelsey." In like manner it may be added that the beach of pebbles thrown up by the action of the sea outside Weymouth harbour, is styled the Chesil bank. Perhaps it is the same word at bottom as Selsey, the name of a peninsula of pebbles on the Sussex coast, near Chichester.

As a symbol of infinity, Ben Jonson, in his "Forest," speaks of

"All the grass that Romney yields,
    Or the sands of Chelsey Fields."

Macaulay reminds us that, at the end of the reign of Charles II., Chelsea was a "quiet country village, with about a thousand inhabitants; the baptisms averaging little more than forty in the year." At that time the Thames was sufficiently clear and pure for bathing above Westminster. We are told that, on one occasion, Charles II. was bathing at Chelsea, when the notorious Colonel Blood lay hid among the reeds at Battersea, in order to shoot him. Notwithstanding its remoteness from the metropolis, however, Chelsea does not appear to have escaped the ravages of the "Great Plague," for it raged here as well as in other suburbs of London, as Pepys informs us, in his "Diary," under date of April 9th, 1666:—"Thinking to have been merry at Chelsey; but, being almost come to the house by coach, near the waterside, a house alone, I think the 'Swan,' a gentleman walking by called out to us that the house was shut up because of the sickness."

Chelsea Fields must have been quite a rustic spot even to a yet later date, for Gay thus addresses his friend Pulteney:—

"When the sweet-breathing spring unfolds the buds,
Love flies the dusty town for shady woods;
Then . . . .
. . . Chelsea's meads o'erhear perfidious vows,
And the press'd grass defrauds the grazing cows."

In "Chelsea Fields" was formerly a tavern, known as "The Dwarf's," kept by John Coan, a diminutive manikin from Norfolk. "It seems to have been a place of some attraction," says Mr. Larwood, "since it was honoured by the repeated visits of an Indian king." Thus the *Daily Advertiser* of July 12, 1762, says: "On Friday last the Cherokee king and his two chiefs were so greatly pleased with the curiosities of the Dwarf's Tavern, in Chelsea Fields, that they were there again on Sunday, at seven in the evening, to drink tea, and will be there again in a few days." The reputation of the tavern, under its pygmean proprietor, was but brief, as the "unparalleled" Coan, as he is styled, died within two years from the above date.

---

* "Environs of London," vol. ii., p. 70.

In the reign of William III., the French Huguenot refugees had two chapels in Chelsea : the one in "Cook's Grounds," now used by the Congregationalists, and another at Little Chelsea, not far from Kensington.

"Chelsea," observes a writer in the *Mirror*, in 1833, "though now proverbial for its dulness, was formerly a place of great gaiety. Thousands flocked to Salter's—or, as it was dubbed, 'Don Saltero's'—coffee-house in Cheyne Walk ; the Chelsea buns were eaten by princesses ; and the public were allowed to walk in thirteen acres of avenues of limes and chestnut-trees in the gardens adjoining the College. This privilege was disallowed in 1806 ; but within the last few weeks these grounds have been again thrown open to the public." The ground round about Chelsea and its neighbourhood, like that of Bermondsey, and other low-lying districts bordering upon the Thames, is peculiarly adapted for the growth of vegetables, fruits, and flowers ; indeed, Chelsea has long been remarkable for its gardens and nurseries. Dr. Mackay, in his " Extraordinary Popular Delusions," tells us that about the time of Her Majesty's accession, there was a gardener in the King's Road, Chelsea, in whose catalogue a single tulip was marked at two hundred guineas —a remnant, perhaps, of the tulip-mania, which, two centuries before, had ruined half of the merchants of Holland, and threatened to prove as disastrous here as the "South Sea Bubble." It may be added, too, that the first red geranium seen in England is said to have been raised by a Mr. Davis here, about the year 1822.

Chelsea, which was once a rustic and retired village, has been gradually absorbed into the metropolis by the advance of the army of bricklayers and mortar-layers, and now forms fairly a portion of London, Pimlico and Belgravia having supplied the connecting link. Environed though it is by the growing suburbs, the place has still an old-fashioned look about it, which the modern, trimly-laid-out flower-gardens on the new embankment only tend to increase. Looked at from the Battersea side of the river, with the barges floating lazily along past the solid red-brick houses, screened by sheltering trees, Chelsea presents such a picture as the old Dutch " masters " would have revelled in, especially as the Thames here widens into a fine "reach," well known to oarsmen for the rough "seas" which they encounter there on those occasions when the wind meets the tide ; in fact, the river is wider at this particular spot than anywhere "above bridge." In the reign of Charles II. it was such a fashionable rendezvous

that it was frequently called " Hyde Park on the Thames."

Bowack thus writes, in an account of Chelsea, published in 1705 :—"The situation of it upon the Thames is very pleasant, and standing in a small bay, or angle, made by the meeting of Chelsea and Battersea Reaches, it has a most delightful prospect on that river for near four miles, as far as Vauxhall eastward, and as Wandsworth to the west."

In the last century, Chelsea being, in fact, quite a suburban place, had its own society ; "its many honourable and worthy inhabitants," as we are told by Bowack, " being not more remarkable for their titles, estates, and employments, than for their civility and condescension, and their kind and facetious tempers, living in a perfect amity among themselves, and having a general meeting every day at a coffee-house near the church, well known for a pretty collection of varieties in nature and art, some of which are very curious." The coffee-house here mentioned was the renowned Don Saltero's, of which we shall have more to say in the next chapter.

Mr. Peter Cunningham speaks of Chelsea as "at one time the Islington of the West-end," and thus enumerates the articles for which it has from time to time been famous :—Its manor house, its college, its botanic garden, its hospital, its amusements at Ranelagh, its waterworks, its buns, its china, and its custards.

"About the year 1796," writes Faulkner, in his " History of Chelsea," " I was present at a stag-hunt in Chelsea. The animal swam across the river from Battersea, and made for Lord Cremorne's grounds. Upon being driven from thence, he ran along the water-side as far as the church, and turning up Church Lane, at last took refuge in Mrs. Hutchins's barn, where he was taken alive."

The connection of Chelsea with Westminster, already stated in our account* of the " Monster " Tavern, Pimlico, is probably of very old standing, for even during the rule of our Norman kings it appears to have been one of the manors belonging to the abbey of St. Peter. Little, however, is known with certainty of the history of this now extensive parish till the time of Henry VII., when the manor was held by Sir Reginald Bray, from whom it descended to Margaret, only child of his next brother, John, who married William, Lord Sandys. From Lord Sandys the manor passed, in exchange for other lands, to that rapacious king, Henry VIII., by whom it was assigned to Katharine

---

* See above, p. 45.

Parr, as part of her marriage jointure. Faulkner, in his work above quoted, says that "Henry was probably induced to possess this manor from having observed, in his frequent visits to Sir Thomas More, the pleasantness of the situation on the bank of the Thames; and, from the salubrity of the air, deeming it a fit residence for his infant daughter, the Princess Elizabeth, then between three and four years of age. But after having obtained it, finding that the manor house was ancient, and at that time in the possession of the Lawrence family, he erected a new manor house, on the eastern side of the spot where Winchester House lately stood, and supplied it with water from a spring at Kensington." The manor was subsequently held by John Dudley, Duke of Northumberland; by Anne, Duchess of Somerset, widow of the "Protector;" by John, first Lord Stanhope, of Harrington; by Katharine, Lady Howard, wife of the Lord Admiral; by James, first Duke of Hamilton; by Charles, Viscount Cheyne; and by Sir Hans Sloane, the celebrated physician, who purchased it in 1712 from the Cheyne family, and from whom it passed by marriage to Charles, second Lord Cadogan, of Oakley, through which alliance the manor of Chelsea became vested in the Cadogans, with whom it still remains.

The old manor house stood near the church, and was sold by Henry VIII. to the Lawrence family, after whom Lawrence Street derives its name. The new manor house stood on that part of Cheyne Walk fronting the Thames, between the Pier Hotel and the house formerly known as "Don Saltero's Coffee-house." The building, of which a view of the north front is engraved in Faulkner's "History of Chelsea" (see page 49), was of a quadrangular form, enclosing a spacious court, and was partly embattled. The mansion was pulled down shortly after the death of Sir Hans Sloane, in the middle of the last century, and a row of houses erected on the site.

Like Kensington, Chelsea has been from time to time the residence of many individuals of high rank, who were attracted to it on account of its nearness to the Court, and its easiness of access at a time when the roads of the suburbs were bad, and the Thames was the "silent highway" to families who could afford to keep their barge. So far as rank and station are concerned, perhaps the first and foremost of its residents was the Princess (afterwards Queen) Elizabeth. After her father's death, Miss Lucy Aikin tells us, in her "Memoirs of the Court" of that sovereign, the princess "had been consigned to the care and protection of the Queen Dowager (Katharine Parr), with whom she usually made her abode at one or other of her jointure houses at Chelsea, or at Hanworth, near Hounslow."

In the reign of Elizabeth, the Lord High Admiral, the Earl of Effingham, was among the residents of this place; and we are told by Bishop Goodman that, in her "progresses" from Richmond to Whitehall, the "Virgin Queen" would often dine with his lordship at Chelsea, and afterwards set out thence towards London, late at night, by torchlight, in order that the Lord Mayor and aldermen, and the other loyal citizens, might not see those wrinkles and that ugly throat of hers, with which Horace Walpole has made us familiar in his representation of a coin struck shortly before her death.

Thomas Beauchamp, Earl of Warwick, who acquired high renown at the battles of Cressy and Poictiers, appears to have occasionally resided at Chelsea. It is supposed that he occupied a house and premises which afterwards belonged to Richard Beauchamp, Bishop of Salisbury, and which were granted by Richard III. to Elizabeth, widow of Thomas Mowbray, Duke of Norfolk, for life, "to be held by the service of a red rose." The site of this mansion, however, is now unknown, as also is the spot once occupied by a house in Chelsea which was possessed by William, Marquis of Berkeley, an adherent of the Earl of Richmond (afterwards Henry VII.).

In April, 1663, we find Lord Sandwich at his Chelsea lodging, eating cakes made by the mistress of the house, and, it may be added, the mother of his own mistress—cakes so good that, says Pepys, "they were fit to present to my Lady Castlemaine"—a curious parody of the lines of the old nursery rhyme:—

> "Now was not that a dainty dish
> To set before a king?"

Among the residents of Chelsea in the last century was Lord Cremorne, who occupied a house called Chelsea Farm, which was situated at a short distance from the bridge on the site long covered by Cremorne Gardens. Lady Cremorne is celebrated in the "Percy Anecdotes" as the best mistress of a household that ever lived. She had a servant, Elizabeth Palfrey, who had lived with her for forty-eight years, during the latter half of the time as housekeeper, and who so regulated affairs that in all that long time not one of the female servants was known to have left her place, except in order to be married. Such mistresses are rare now, and probably were not common even in her day. As late as 1826, the name of Viscountess Cremorne appears in the "Royal Blue Book," with

"Chelsea Farm" as her country residence. The edifice, which was built of brick, overlooked the river, from which it was separated by a lawn, pleasantly shaded by stately trees. The house had a somewhat irregular appearance externally, and little to boast of in the way of architecture; but the interior was commodious, and the best suite of rooms well adapted to the use of a distinguished family. Here was a small but judicious collection of pictures, formed by Viscount Cremorne, among which were some by noted Flemish and Italian masters.

Lindsey Row and Lindsey Place, facing the river immediately westward of Battersea Bridge, mark the site of Lindsey House, the residence of the Berties, Earls of Lindsey. About the middle of the last century the mansion was purchased by Count Zinzendorf, a leader of the peculiar sect known as Moravians, for the purpose of establishing a settlement of that society in Chelsea; but the project failed; the building was again sold, and subsequently demolished, or cut up into private tenements.

In a small house in Chelsea, rented from Lord Cheyne, died, in difficulties, the beautiful Duchess of Mazarine, one of the frail beauties of the Court of Charles II.

In Lyson's "Environs," we read that about the year 1722 Sir Robert Walpole, the well-known prime minister of George II., "became possessed of a house and garden in the stable-yard at Chelsea." The house was "next the college," adjoining Gough House. Sir Robert frequently resided there, improved and added to the house, and considerably enlarged the gardens by a purchase of some land from the Gough family; he erected an octagonal summer-house at the head of the terrace, and a large green-house, where he had a fine collection of exotics. A good story is told about Queen Caroline, when dining one day here with Lady Walpole. Sir Paul Methuen, who was one of the company, was remarkable for his love of romances. The queen asked him what he had been reading of late in his own way. "Nothing, madam," said Sir Paul; "I have now commenced, instead of romances, a very foolish study, 'The History of the Kings and Queens of England.'" Horace Walpole informs us that he remembered La Belle Jennings (afterwards Duchess of Marlborough) coming to his parents' house to solicit a pension.

Shrewsbury House, or, as it was sometimes called, Alston House, in Cheyne Walk, near the waterside, if we may trust Priscilla Wakefield's "Perambulations in London," was a paper manufactory at the time of its demolition in 1814. It was an irregular brick building, forming three sides of a quadrangle. The principal room was upwards of 100 feet long, and was originally wainscoted with carved oak. One of the rooms was painted in imitation of marble, and others were ornamented with certain "curious portraits on panel." Leading from the premises towards the King's Road was a subterranean passage, which is traditionally said to have communicated with a cave, or dungeon, situated at some distance from the house.

Winchester House, the Palace of the Bishops of Winchester from about the middle of the seventeenth down to the commencement of the present century, stood on the spot now occupied by the Pier Hotel, and its gardens adjoined Shrewsbury House. It was a heavy brick building, of low proportions, and quite devoid of any architectural ornament. The interior was fairly commodious, and "much enriched by the collection of antiques and specimens of natural history" placed there by Bishop North, the last prelate who occupied it. Bishop Hoadley, who died here in 1761, was so lax in his ideas of Church authority, that some free-thinking Christians were wittily styled by Archbishop Secker, "Christians secundum usum Winton," in allusion to the customary title of books printed "for the use of the Winchester scholars."

The chief interest of Chelsea, however, not only to the antiquary, but to the educated Englishman, must lie in the fact that it was the much-loved home of that great man whose memory English history will never allow to die, Sir Thomas More. Here he resided, surrounded by his family, in a house about midway between the Thames and the King's Road, on the site of what is now Beaufort Street. In Aubrey's "Letters from the Bodleian," we read:—"His country house was at Chelsey, in Middlesex, where Sir John Danvers built his house. The chimney-piece, of marble, in Sir John's chamber, was the chimney-piece of Sir Thomas More's chamber, as Sir John himself told me. Where the gate is now, adorned with two noble pyramids, there stood anciently a gate-house, which was flatt on the top, leaded, from whence was a most pleasant prospect of the Thames and the fields beyond; on this place the Lord Chancellor More was wont to recreate himself and contemplate."

Erasmus—himself one of the most cherished friends of Sir Thomas—describes the house as "neither mean nor subject to envy, yet magnificent and commodious enough." The building, which was erected early in the sixteenth century, was successively called Buckingham House and Beaufort House, and was pulled down about the middle of the last century. At the end of the garden Sir Thomas erected a pile of buildings, consisting of a chapel, gallery, and library, all being designed for his own retirement. His piety, staunch and firm

retired to the new buildings, where he spent the whole day in prayer and meditation."

Sir Thomas usually attended Divine service on Sundays at Chelsea Church, and very often assisted at the celebration of mass. The Duke of Norfolk

CHELSEA FARM, 1829. (*See page* 53.)

as was his adherence to the Roman Catholic creed, is acknowledged even by Protestant writers. Wood, in his "Ecclesiastical Antiquities," says :—"More rose early, and assembled his family morning and evening in the chapel, when certain prayers and Psalms were recited. He heard mass daily himself, and expected all his household to do so on Sundays and festivals ; whilst, on the eves of great feasts, all watched till matins. Every Friday, as was also his custom on some other occasions, he

coming one day to dine with him during his chancellorship, found him in church with a surplice on, and singing in the choir. "God's body, my Lord Chancellor !" said the duke, as they returned to his house. "What ! a parish clerk ! a parish clerk ! you dishonour the king and his office." "Nay," said Sir Thomas, "you may not think your master and mine will be offended with me for serving God, his master, or thereby count his office dishonoured."

OLD MANSIONS IN CHELSEA. (*From Faulkner's "Chelsea."*)

1. Church Place, 1641.   2. Gough House, 1760.   3. Shrewsbury House, 1540.   4. Beaufort House, 1628.   5. Winchester House.

In later years the chapel in More's house appears to have been free to the public, for in various marriage licences, granted towards the commencement of the last century, persons were to be married "in the parish church, in the chapel of Chelsea College, or the chapel of Beaufort House." The only fragment of the house remaining down to the present century was a portion of the cellars, which existed beneath the house No. 17, forming one of the line of dwellings now known by the name of Beaufort Row. An avenue, with a high wall on each side, constituted the chief approach to the house, or that from the river-side; and fronting the entrance of this avenue were the stairs used by Sir Thomas More when descending to his barge. A terrace-walk, which stretched from the house towards the east, is described in the legal writings of the estate as being so much raised that it was ascended by several steps. After the demolition of the house a portion of the ground was occupied as a burial-place for the Moravian Society, and the remains of the stables were converted into public schools.

The most important circumstances in the life of Sir Thomas More are too well known to need repetition in these pages. His domestic life at Chelsea has been described by Erasmus in the following words:—"There he converses with his wife, his son, his daughter-in-law, his three daughters and their husbands, with eleven grandchildren. There is not any man living so affectionate as he, and he loveth his old wife as well as if she was a young maid. You would say there was in that place Plato's Academy; but I do his house an injury in comparing it to Plato's Academy, where there were only disputations of numbers and geometrical figures, and sometimes of moral virtues. I should rather call his house a school, or university of Christian religion, for though there is none therein but readeth or studieth the liberal sciences, their special care is piety and virtue; there is no quarrelling or intemperate words heard; none seen idle; that worthy gentleman doth not govern with proud and lofty words, but with well-timed and courteous benevolence; everybody performeth his duty, yet is there always alacrity; neither is sober mirth anything wanting."

Erasmus was the correspondent of Sir Thomas More long before he was personally acquainted with his illustrious friend; and although strongly dissimilar in religious opinions, when the great reformer and scholar visited England he was the frequent guest of Sir Thomas at Chelsea. The house of More was, indeed, the resort of all who were conspicuous for learning and taste. Collet,

Linacre, and Tunstall often partook of the hospitality of his table. Here Sir Thomas often entertained "Master John Heywood," the early English playwright, and cracked with him many a joke. It is said that it was through Sir Thomas More that he was introduced to the Lady Mary, and so was brought under the notice of Henry VIII., who appointed him the Court jester. Those were, indeed, strange days, when a buffoon dared to laugh in the face of a sovereign who could send to the scaffold so venerable, so grave and learned a scholar, and so loyal a subject of the Crown. The wit of Sir Thomas More was almost boundless, and he was also no mean actor. It is related of him that when an interlude was performed he would "make one among the players, occasionally coming upon them by surprise, and without rehearsal fall into a character, and support the part by his extemporaneous invention, and acquit himself with credit." It was probably by his intercourse with Heywood that the latent dramatic powers of the great Lord Chancellor were called out.

Henry VIII., to whom More owed his rise and fall, frequently came to Chelsea, and spent whole days in the most familiar manner with his learned friend; and "it is supposed," says Faulkner, in his "History of Chelsea," "that the king's answer to Luther was prepared and arranged for the public eye, with the assistance of Sir Thomas, during these visits." Notwithstanding all this familiarity, Sir Thomas understood the temper of his royal master very well, as the following anecdote sufficiently testifies:—"One day the king came unexpectedly to Chelsea, and dined with him, and after dinner walked in his garden for the space of an hour, holding his arm about his neck. As soon as his Majesty was gone, Sir Thomas's son-in-law observed to him how happy he was, since the king had treated him with that familiarity he had never used to any person before, except Cardinal Wolsey, with whom he once saw his Majesty walk arm-in-arm." "I thank our Lord," answered Sir Thomas, "I find his grace my very good lord indeed; and I believe he doth as singularly love me as any subject within this realm; however, son Roper, I may tell thee I have no cause to be proud thereof, for if my head would win him a castle in France, it should not fail to go off."

Sir Thomas More is said to have converted one part of his house into a prison for the restraint of heretics; and according to a passage in "Foxe's Book of Martyrs," he here kept in prison, and whipped in his garden, one John Baynham, a lawyer, who was suspected of holding the doctrines of Wycliffe, and who was ultimately burnt at Smithfield. But it must be remembered that he lived in an age when religious persecution was practised by all parties, and when, as Byron writes—

"Christians did burn each other, quite persuaded
That all th' Apostles would have done as they did."

More's fondness for animals is an interesting and curious peculiarity. Erasmus tells us, that watching their growth, development, and dispositions, was one of his chief pleasures. "At Chelsea may be seen many varieties of birds, and an ape, a fox, a weasel, and a ferret. Moreover, if anything foreign, or otherwise remarkable, comes in his way, he greedily buys it up, and he has his house completely furnished with these objects; so that, as you enter, there is everywhere something to catch the eye, and he renews his own pleasure as often as he becomes a witness to the delight of others." With one of his favourite dogs, Sir Thomas would frequently sit in fine weather on the top of the gate-house, in order to enjoy the agreeable prospect. A curious story is told in the "Percy Anecdotes," which will bear repeating :—"It happened one day that a 'Tom o' Bedlam,' a maniac vagrant, got upstairs while Sir Thomas was there, and coming up to him, cried out, 'Leap, Tom, leap!' at the same time, attempting to throw his lordship over the battlements. Sir Thomas, who was a feeble old man, and incapable of much resistance, had the presence of mind to say, 'Let us first throw this little dog over.' The maniac threw the dog down immediately. 'Pretty sport,' said the Lord Chancellor; 'now go down and bring him up; then we'll try again.' While the poor madman went down for the dog, his lordship made fast the door of the stairs, and, calling for help, saved his life."

Sir Thomas More is to be remembered also with gratitude on quite another score, and on higher grounds; for he was the generous patron of Holbein, the Court painter, who occupied rooms in his house for three years, and was employed in drawing portraits of his patron and his family.

Hoddesdon, in his "History of More," says :—"He seldom used to feast noble men, but his poor neighbours often, whom he would visit in their houses, and bestow upon them his large liberality —not groats, but crowns of gold—even more than according to their wants. He hired a house also for many aged people in Chelsea, whom he daily relieved, and it was his daughter Margaret's charge to see them want nothing; and when he was a private lawyer he would take no fees of poor folks, widows, nor pupils."

By indefatigable application Sir Thomas More cleared the Court of Chancery of all its causes. One day, having ended a cause, he called for the next,

and was told that "there was no other depending in the court." He was delighted to hear it, and ordered it to be inserted in the records of the court. This gave rise to the epigram—not the worst in the English language—which we have already quoted in our account of Lincoln's Inn.* After having held the Great Seal for two years and a half, Sir Thomas, on being pressed by the king to hasten on his divorce from Catherine of Arragon, resigned his office in May, 1532. He retired cheerfully to the privacy of domestic life, and to the studies which he was not long to enjoy. On the day after he resigned the chancellorship, Sir Thomas went to church, as usual, with his wife and family, none of whom he had yet informed of his resignation. During the service, as was his custom, he sat in the choir in a surplice. After the service it was usual for one of his attendants to go to her ladyship's pew and say, "My lord is gone before." But this day the ex-Chancellor came himself, and, making a low bow said, "Madam, my lord is gone." Then, on their way home, we are told, "to her great mortification, he unriddled his mournful pleasantry, by telling her his lordship was gone, in the loss of his official dignities." He was included in the bill of attainder introduced into Parliament to punish Elizabeth Barton—"the holy maid of Kent"—and her accomplices; but on his disclaiming any surviving faith in the nun, or any share in her treasonable designs, his name was ultimately struck out of the bill. On the passing of the Act of Succession, which declared the king's marriage with Catherine invalid, and fixed the succession in the children of Anne Boleyn, More declined to accept it, and refused to take the oath. A few days afterwards he was committed to the Tower, and in the space of a few short months, as is known to every reader of English history, was placed on his trial for high treason, found guilty, and executed on Tower Hill. More retained his mild and characteristic jocularity to the last. "Going up the scaffold, which was so weak that it was ready to fall," we read in Roper's "Life of More," "he said hurriedly to the lieutenant, 'I pray you, Master Lieutenant, see me safe up; and for my coming down, let me shift for myself.' When the axe of the executioner was about to fall, he asked for a moment's delay while he moved aside his beard. 'Pity that should be cut,' he murmured; '*that* surely has not committed treason.'"

"Thou art the cause of this man's death," said Henry VIII. to Anne Boleyn when the news of his execution was brought to the guilty couple; and the king rose, left his paramour, and shut himself up in his chamber "in great perturbation of spirit." At that perturbation we need not wonder—the greatest man of the realm had been beheaded as a victim to the royal lust. It may be truly said that during the reign of Henry VIII. there lived and moved, in a prominent position, but one man whose memory is held in high esteem by all parties, and that man was Sir Thomas More. Protestants as well as Roman Catholics alike venerated his name, while they held his life up as a model for all time, and even the more extreme Protestants had less to say in his disfavour than about any other leading son of the Church. Risen through his own exertions from comparative obscurity, Sir Thomas More held the highest lay position in the land, bore off the palm in learning as in probity, was faithful to his God as well as to his king and to his own lofty principles, and died because he would not and could not make his conscience truckle to the lewd desires of his earthly master. A grand lawyer, a great statesman, a profound politician, an example of domesticity for all generations, a deep student of the things of the spiritual as well as of the temporal life, and a Catholic of Catholics—Sir Thomas More earned and commanded, and will continue to command, the profoundest respect of all high-minded Englishmen. Sir Thomas More, indeed, was justly called by Thomson, in his "Seasons"—

"A dauntless soul erect, who smiled on death."

Sir Thomas More's house appears to have become afterwards the residence of royalty. Anne of Cleves died here in 1557; and Katharine Parr occupied it after her re-marriage with Admiral Seymour, having charge of the Princess Elizabeth, then a child of thirteen.

The old parish church of Chelsea, dedicated to St. Luke, stands parallel with the river. It is constructed chiefly of brick, and is by no means conspicuous for beauty. It appears to have been erected piecemeal at different periods, and the builders do not seem to have aimed in the slightest degree at architectural arrangement; nevertheless, though the building is sadly incongruous and much barbarised, its interior is still picturesque. The chancel and a part of the north aisle are the only portions which can lay claim to antiquity; the former was rebuilt shortly before the Reformation. The eastern end of the north aisle is the chapel of the Lawrence family, which was probably founded in the fourteenth century. The southern aisle was erected at the cost of good Sir Thomas More, who also gave the communion plate. With a forecast of the coming troubles, he remarked, "Good men

give these things, and bad men will soon take them away." At the commencement of the present century modern windows, with frames of woodwork, were introduced. These, it need hardly be said, in no way improved the already mean appearance of the fabric. More's chapel, which was an absolute freehold, and beyond the control of the bishop, was allowed to fall into a very dilapidated condition; but it has recently been purchased by a Mr. R. H. Davies, who has transferred it to the rector, churchwardens, and trustees of the new church of St. Luke, under whose charge the old parish church is placed; and it has since been partially restored. The church was considerably enlarged in the middle of the seventeenth century, at which time the heavy brick tower at the west end was erected. The interior consists of a nave, chancel, and two aisles, comprehending the two chapels above mentioned. The roof of the chancel is arched, and it is separated from the nave by a semi-circular arch, above which hang several escutcheons and banners; the latter, very faded and tattered, are said to have been the needlework of Queen Charlotte, by whom they were presented to the Royal Volunteers. They were deposited here on the disbandment of the regiment. Near the south-west corner of the church, resting upon a window-sill, is an ancient book-case and desk, on which are displayed a chained Bible, a Book of Homilies, and some other works, including "Foxe's Book of Martyrs." In the porch, placed upon brackets on the wall, is a bell, which was presented to the church by the Hon. William Ashburnham, in 1679, in commemoration of his escape from drowning. It appears, from a tablet on the wall, that Mr. Ashburnham was walking on the bank of the Thames at Chelsea one very dark night in winter, apparently in a meditative mood, and had strayed into the river, when he was suddenly brought to a sense of his situation by hearing the church clock strike nine. Mr. Ashburnham left a sum of money to the parish to pay for the ringing of the bell every evening at nine o'clock, but the custom was discontinued in 1825. The bell, after lying neglected for many years in the clock-room, was placed in its present position after a silence of thirty years.

The monuments in the church are both numerous and interesting. On the north side of the chancel is an ancient altar-tomb without any inscription, but supposed to belong to the family of Bray, of Eaton. On the south wall of the chancel is a tablet of black marble, surmounted by a flat Gothic arch, in memory of Sir Thomas More. It was originally erected by himself, in 1532, some three years before his death; but being much worn, it was restored, at the expense of Sir John Lawrence, of Chelsea, in the reign of Charles I., and again by subscription, in 1833.

The Latin inscription was written by More himself; but an allusion to "heretics," which it contained, is stated to have been purposely omitted when the monument was restored. A blank space is left for the word. Although More's first wife lies buried here, the place of interment of Sir Thomas himself is somewhat doubtful. Weever and Anthony Wood say that his daughter, Margaret Roper, removed his body to Chelsea. Earlier writers, however, differ as to the precise spot of his burial, some saying that he was interred in the belfry, and others near the vestry of the chapel of St. Peter, in the Tower. It is recorded that his daughter took thither the body of Bishop Fisher, that it might lie near her father's, and, therefore, it is probable that the Tower still contains his ashes. The head of Sir Thomas More is deposited in St. Dunstan's Church at Canterbury, where it is preserved in a niche in the wall, secured by an iron grate, near the coffin of Margaret Roper.

In the south aisle is a fine monument to Lord and Lady Dacre, dated 1594. It was this Lady Dacre who erected the almshouses in Westminster which bore her name.* She was sister to Thomas Sackville, Earl of Dorset, the poet. In the north aisle is the monument of Lady Jane Cheyne, daughter of William Cavendish, Duke of Newcastle, and wife of Charles Cheyne, after whom Cheyne Row is named. The monument is the work of Bernini, and is said to have cost £500. Here is buried Adam Littleton, Prebendary of Westminster and Rector of Chelsea, the author of a once celebrated Latin Dictionary. He was at one time "usher" of Westminster School; and after the Restoration

he took pupils at Chelsea. He wrote the preface to Cicero's Works, as edited by Gale, and was a perfect master of the Latin style. Collier says of him that his erudition gained for him the title of "the Great Dictator of Learning." In the churchyard is a monument to Sir Hans Sloane, the physician. It consists of an inscribed pedestal, upon which is placed a large vase of white marble, entwined with serpents, and the whole is surmounted by a portico supported by four pillars.

In the old burial-ground lie Andrew Millar, the eminent London bookseller, and John B. Cipriani, one of the earliest members of the Royal Academy.†

The new church of St. Luke, situated between King's Road and Fulham Road, was built by James Savage, in 1820, in imitation of the style of the fourteenth and fifteenth centuries, and has a pinnacled tower, nearly 150 feet high. It is, however, a poor specimen of modern Gothic. The most remarkable feature of the building is the roof of the nave, which is vaulted with stone, with a clear height of sixty feet from the pavement to the crown of the vault. The porch extends the whole width of the west front, and is divided by piers and arches into five bays, the central one of which forms the lower storey of the tower. The large east window is filled with stained glass, and beneath it is a fine altar-screen of antique design. Immediately over the altar is a painting, "The Entombing of Christ," said to be by Northcote. The church will seat about 2,000 persons, and was erected at a cost of about £40,000—the first stone being laid by the Duke of Wellington. The first two rectors of the new church were Dr. Gerard V. Wellesley (whose name is still retained in Wellesley Street), brother of the Duke of Wellington, and the Rev. Charles Kingsley, father of Charles Kingsley, Canon of Westminster, and author of "Alton Locke," &c.

CHAPTER VI.

CHELSEA (*continued*).

"Then, farewell, my trim-built wherry;
Oars, and coat, and badge, farewell!
Never more at Chelsea Ferry
Shall your Thomas take a spell."—*Dibdin.*

Cheyne Walk—An Eccentric Miser—Dominicetti, an Italian Quack—Don Saltero's Coffee House and Museum—Catalogue of Rarities in the Museum—Thomas Carlyle—Chelsea Embankment—Albert Bridge—The Mulberry Garden—The "Swan" Inn—The Rowing Matches for Doggett's Coat and Badge—The Botanic Gardens—The Old Bun-house.

VISITORS to Chelsea by water, landing at the Cadogan Pier, will not fail to be struck by the antique appearance of the long terrace of houses

stretching away eastward, overlooking the river, and screened by a row of trees. This is Cheyne Walk, so named after Lord Cheyne, who owned the

* See Vol. IV., p 12.   † See Faulkner's "History of Chelsea," vol. ii., p 38.

manor of Chelsea near the close of the seventeenth century. The houses are mostly of dark-red brick, with heavy window-frames, and they have about them altogether an old-fashioned look, such as we are accustomed to find in buildings of the time of Queen Anne. The place, from its air of repose of the same for her sole use and benefit, and that of her heirs." He was buried at North Marston, near Aylesbury, where he held a landed property, and where the Queen ordered a painted window to be put up to his memory. A sketch of the career of this modern rival of John Elwes will

CHEYNE WALK AND CADOGAN PIER, 1860.

and seclusion, has always reckoned among its inhabitants a large number of successful artists and literary celebrities.

Here, in a large house very scantily furnished, lived during the latter portion of his existence—we can scarcely call it life—Mr. John Camden Neild, the eccentric miser, who, at his decease in August, 1852, left his scrapings and savings, amounting to half a million sterling, to the Queen, "begging Her Majesty's most gracious acceptance be found in Chambers' "Book of Days." Here, too, lived Dominicetti, an Italian quack, who made a great noise in his day by the introduction of medicated baths, which he established in Cheyne Walk, in 1765. It is thus immortalised in Boswell's "Life of Johnson:"—"There was a pretty large circle this evening. Dr. Johnson was in very good humour, lively, and ready to talk upon all subjects. Dominicetti being mentioned, he would not allow him any merit. 'There is nothing in all this boasted system. No, sir; medicated baths can be no better than warm water; their only effect can be that of tepid moisture.' One of the company took the other side, maintaining that medicines of various sorts, and some, too, of most powerful effect, are introduced into the human fumigated; but be sure that the steam be directed to thy head, for *that* is the *peccant part.*' This produced a triumphant roar of laughter from the motley assembly of philosophers, printers, and dependents, male and female." Dominicetti is said to have had under his care upwards of 16,000 persons,

CARLYLE'S HOUSE, GREAT CHEYNE ROW. (*See page* 64.)

frame by the medium of the pores; and therefore, when warm water is impregnated with salutiferous substances, it may produce great effects as a bath. The Doctor, determined to be master of the field, had recourse to the device which Goldsmith imputed to him in the witty words of one of Cibber's comedies, 'There is no arguing with Johnson; for when his pistol misses fire, he knocks you down with the butt-end of it.' He turned to the gentleman: 'Well, sir, go to Dominicetti, and get thyself

including Edward, Duke of York. He spent some £37,000 on his establishment, but became bankrupt in 1782, when he disappeared.

In the middle of Cheyne Walk is, or was till recently (for it was doomed to destruction in 1866), the house known to readers of anecdote biography as "Don Saltero's Coffee House," celebrated not only as a place of entertainment, but also as a repository of natural and other curiosities. John Salter, its founder, was an old and trusty servant of

Sir Hans Sloane, who, from time to time, gave him all sorts of curiosities. With these he adorned the house, which he opened as a suburban coffee-house, about the year 1690. The earliest notice of Salter's Museum is to be found in the thirty-fourth number of the *Tatler*, published in June, 1709, in which its owner figures as "Don Saltero," and several of its curious contents are specified by the writer, Sir Richard Steele. Beside the donations of Sir Hans Sloane, at the head of the "Complete List of Benefactors to Don Saltero's Coffee-room of Curiosities," printed in 1739, figure the names of Sir John Cope, Baronet, and his son, "the first generous benefactors." There is an account of the exhibition in the *Gentleman's Magazine* for 1799, where it is stated that Rear-Admiral Sir John Munden, and other officers who had been much upon the coasts of Spain, enriched it with many curiosities, and gave its owner the name of "Don Saltero;" but the list of donors does not include the admiral, though the name of "Mr. Munden" occurs in the list subjoined to the nineteenth edition of the catalogue. The title by which Salter was so well known in his own day may be accounted for even at this distance of time by the notice of him and his collection, as immortalised in the pages of Sir Richard Steele. "When I came into the coffee-house," he says, "I had not time to salute the company before my eye was diverted by ten thousand gimcracks, round the room and on the ceiling." The Don was famous for his punch, and his skill on the fiddle. "Indeed," says Steele, "I think he does play the 'Merry Christ-Church Bells' pretty justly; but he confessed to me he did it rather to show he was orthodox than that he valued himself upon the music itself." This description is probably faithful, as well as humorous, since he continues, "When my first astonishment was over, there comes to me a sage, of a thin and meagre countenance, which aspect made me doubtful whether reading or fretting had made it so philosophic."

In the *Weekly Journal* of Saturday, June 22nd, 1723, we read the following poetical announcement of the treasures to be seen at this coffee-house, which may be regarded as authentic and literally true, since it is sanctioned by the signature of the proprietor himself :—

"SIR,
　　Fifty years since to Chelsea great,
　　　From Rodman, on the Irish main,
　　I strolled, with maggots in my pate,
　　　Where, much improved, they still remain.

"Through various employs I've passed—
　　A scraper, virtuoso, projector,

Tooth-drawer, trimmer, and at last,
　　I'm now a gimcrack whim collector.

"Monsters of all sorts here are seen,
　　Strange things in nature as they grow so,
Some relicks of the Sheba queen,
　　And fragments of the famed Bob Crusoe.

"Knicknacks, too, dangle round the wall,
　　Some in glass cases, some on shelf;
But what's the rarest sight of all,
　　Your humble servant shows himself.

"On this my chiefest hope depends—
　　Now if you will my cause espouse,
In journals pray direct your friends
　　To my Museum Coffee-house;

"And, in requital for the timely favour,
　　I'll gratis bleed, draw teeth, and be your shaver:
Nay, that your pate may with my noddle tally,
And you shine bright as I do—marry! shall ye
Freely consult your revelation, Molly;
Nor shall one jealous thought create a huff,
For she has taught me manners long enough."
　　　　　　　　　　　　　　　　"DON SALTERO.

"*Chelsea Knackatory.*"

The date of Salter's death does not appear to be known precisely, but the museum was continued by his daughter, a Mrs. Hall, until about the accession of George III. We know little of the subsequent history of the house until January, 1799, when the whole place, with the museum of curiosities, was sold by auction by Mr. Harwood. They are described in the catalogue as follows :— "A substantial and well-erected dwelling-house and premises, delightfully situate, facing the river Thames, commanding beautiful views of the Surrey hills and the adjacent country, in excellent repair, held for a term of thirty-nine years from Christmas last, at a ground-rent of £3 10s. per annum. Also the valuable collection of curiosities, comprising a curious model of our Saviour's sepulchre, a Roman bishop's crosier, antique coins and medals, minerals, fossils, antique fire-arms, curious birds, fishes, and other productions of nature, and a large collection of various antiquities and curiosities, glass-cases, &c. N.B. The curiosities will be sold the last day. May be viewed six days preceding the sale. Catalogues at sixpence each." The number of lots was a hundred and twenty-one; and the entire produce of the sale appears to have been little more than £50. The highest price given for a single lot was £1 16s.—lot 98, consisting of "a very curious model of our Blessed Saviour's sepulchre at Jerusalem, very neatly inlaid with mother of pearl."

"It is not improbable," writes Mr. Smith in his "Historical and Literary Curiosities," "that this very celebrated collection was not preserved either entire or genuine until the time of its dispersion;

since the gift of John Pennant, of Chelsea, the great-uncle of Thomas Pennant, the topographical writer, appears to have been wanting in the forty-seventh edition of the catalogue of the museum. This donation consisted of a part of a root of a tree, shaped like a swine, and sometimes called 'a lignified hog;' but the several editions of the catalogue differ considerably in the insertion or omission of various articles. The exhibition was contained chiefly in glass cases ranged on the tables, placed in the front room of the first floor of the building; but the walls also were covered with curiosities, and the entrance passage displayed an alligator suspended from the ceiling, with a variety of ancient and foreign weapons hung at the sides."

Perhaps, however, the most novel and interesting particulars which can now be given concerning this museum may be gleaned from the "Exhibition Catalogue" itself, which shows that it consisted rather of strange and wonderful, than of really valuable specimens. The title is "A Catalogue of Rarities, to be seen at Don Salter's Coffee-house in Chelsea; to which is added a complete list of the donors thereof. Price 2d.

" 'O Rare!' "

In the *first glass* were contained the model of the holy sepulchre, and a variety of curiosities of a similar character: such as "painted ribbands from Jerusalem, with a pillar to which our Saviour was tied when scourged, with a motto on each;" "boxes of relicks from Jerusalem;" "a piece of a saint's bone in nun's work;" several pieces of the holy cross in a frame, glazed; a rose of Jericho; dice of the Knights Templars; an Israelitish shekel; and the Lord's Prayer in an ivory frame, glazed. There were also several specimens of carving on cherry-stones, representing the heads of the four Evangelists and effigies of saints; with some cups and baskets made out of the same minute materials. The same case also contained a number of fine coins and medals, both British and foreign, and "a model of Governor Pitt's great diamond," which was taken out of the sale. There were also a few natural curiosities, as "a bone of an angel-fish; a sea-horse; a petrified crab from China; a small pair of horns, and several legs of guinea-deer; a handkerchief made of the asbestus rock, which fire cannot consume; a piece of rotten wood not to be consumed by fire; the rattle of a rattlesnake with twenty-seven joints; a large worm that eats into the keels of ships in the West Indies; serpents' tongues; the bark of a tree, which when drawn out appears like fine lace; a salamander; a fairy's or elf's arrow; a little skull, very curious." The most

remarkable artificial rarities contained in the *second glass* were "a piece of Solomon's temple; Queen Katherine's wedding shoes; King Charles the Second's band which he wore in disguise; and a piece of a coat of mail one hundred and fifty times doubled." Of foreign productions this case contained "a Turkish almanack; a book in Chinese characters; letters in the Malabar language; the effigies and hand of an Egyptian mummy; forty-eight cups, one in another; and an Indian hatchet used by them before iron was invented." The natural curiosities included "a little whale; a giant's tooth; a curious ball of fish-bones found near Plymouth; Job's tears that grow on a tree, wherewith they make anodyne necklaces; a nut of the sand-box tree; several petrified plumes and olives; a young frog in a tobacco-stopper; and a piece of the caul of an elephant." The *third glass* comprised "black and white scorpions; animals in embryo; the worm that eats into the piles in Holland; the tarantula; a nest of snakes; the horns of a shamway; the back-bone of a rattlesnake."

The *fourth glass* consisted of artificial curiosities, and included "a nun's whip; a pair of garters from South Carolina; a Chinese dodgin, which they weigh their gold in; a little Sultaness; an Indian spoon of equal weight with gold; a Chinese nun, very curious; Dr. Durham's paper made of nettles." The *fifth glass* contained "a Muscovy snuff-box, made of an elk's hoof; a humming-bird's nest, with two young ones in it; a starved swallow; the head of an Egyptian; a lock of hair of a Goa goat; belts of wampum; Indian money; the fruit of the horn-tree."

The following curiosities were also disposed in various parts of the coffee-room, with many others less remarkable in their names and appearance—"King James's coronation sword; King William's coronation sword and shoes; Henry VIII.'s coat of mail, gloves, and spurs; Queen Elizabeth's Prayer-book, stirrup, and strawberry dish; the Pope's infallible candle; a set of beads, consecrated by Clement VII., made of the bones of St. Anthony of Padua; a piece of the royal oak; a petrified child, or the figure of death; a curious piece of metal, found in the ruins of Troy; a pair of Saxon stockings; William the Conqueror's family sword; Oliver's broad-sword; the King of Whiddaw's staff; Bistreanier's staff; a wooden shoe, put under the Speaker's chair in James II.'s time; the Emperor of Morocco's tobacco pipe; a curious flea-trap; an Indian prince's crown; a starved cat, found between the walls of Westminster Abbey when the east end was repaired; the jaws of a wild boar that was starved to death by his tusks growing inward;

a frog, fifteen inches long, found in the Isle of Dogs; the Staffordshire almanack, used when the Danes were in England; the lance of Captain Tow-How-Sham, king of the Darien Indians, with which he killed six Spaniards, and took a tooth out of each head, and put in his lance as a trophy of his valour; a coffin of state for a friar's bones; a cockatrice serpent; a large snake, seventeen feet long, taken in a pigeon-house in Sumatra—it had in its belly fifteen fowls and five pigeons; a dolphin with a flying-fish at his mouth; a gargulet, that Indians used to cool their water with; a whistling arrow, which the Indians use when they would treat of peace; a negro boy's cap, made of a rat-skin; Mary Queen of Scots' pin-cushion; a purse made of a spider from Antigua; manna from Canaan; a jaw of a skate, with 500 teeth; the mermaid fish; the wild man of the woods; the flying bull's head; and, last of all, a snake's skin, ten feet and a half long—a most excellent hydrometer." It may be added that, according to Pennant, the ex-Protector, Richard Cromwell, was one of the regular visitors at Don Saltero's coffee-house in its earliest days. The place was one of the exhibitions which Benjamin Franklin went to see when working as a journeyman printer in London.

In Cheyne Walk is the Cheyne Hospital for Sick and Incurable Children. Lindsey House, built about 1660, and named after the Berties, Earls of Lindsey, was afterwards used as a conference hall by the Moravian missionaries, and subsequently cut up into tenements.

At No. 5, Great Cheyne Row, an old-fashioned red-brick house, lived for many years Thomas Carlyle, who so far identified himself with this neighbourhood as to be known to the world in common parlance as "The Philosopher of Chelsea." The house and the habits of its tenant are thus described by a writer who signs himself "Quiz," in the *West Middlesex Advertiser* :—

"The house tenanted by Carlyle has on its front an appearance of antiquity, which would lead us to ascribe it to the days of Queen Anne. In one of his later pamphlets, 'Shooting Niagara,' associated with a hit at modern brick-makers and brick-layers, Carlyle has an allusion to the wall at the end ('head,' as he writes) of his garden, made of bricks burnt in the reign of Henry VIII., and still quite sound, whereas bricks of London manufacture in our day are used up in about sixty years. This wall was, of course, the boundary wall of the old park or garden belonging to Chelsea Manor-house. But this remark only comes incidentally, and we know scarcely anything about Carlyle's house and its belongings from himself. Other people have

reported a variety of particulars, not to be credited without large deductions, concerning his home and personal habits. Thus, an American divine, giving an account of an interview he had with the Chelsea sage, indulges in minutiæ such as the following :— 'We were shown into a plainly-furnished room, on whose walls hung a rugged portrait of Oliver Cromwell. Presently an old man, apparently over threescore years and ten, walked very slowly into the room. He was attired in a long blue woollen gown, reaching down to his feet. His grey hair was in an uncombed mop on his head. His clear blue eye was sharp and piercing. A bright tinge of red was on his thin cheek, and his hand trembled as he took our own. This most singular-looking personage reminded us of an old alchemist, &c.' Much in the Yankee mannerism, certainly, yet it comes as a slight retribution, that one who has been so hard on America should be commented on in true Yankee fashion. Others have given us accounts of rooms in the house heaped up with books, not at all marshalled in the regular order we should have expected, when they belonged to a man so fond of the drill-sergeant. One correspondent of a London paper tells us of a collection of portraits of great men, gathered by degrees from picture-galleries, shops, and book-stalls. As it is rumoured, the contrivances resorted to by some of Carlyle's admirers, at the period of life when most of us are inclined to be enthusiastic in our likings, with the intent of seeing the interior of his house, or coming into personal communication with him, have been both ingenious and ludicrous. Some have, it is said, called at his house, and inquired for an imaginary Jones or Smith, in the hope that they might catch a glimpse at the interior, or see the man himself in the background. Possibly, there have been those who have made friends with the 'dustmen,' so that they may glean up some scraps of MSS. from the miscellaneous contents of his waste-basket. I have not heard, though, whether any one ever went so far as to assume the garb of a policeman, to ensnare the affections of some damsel at 5, Great Cheyne Row, and in this way make discoveries about the philosopher's personal habits.

"Mr. J. C. Hotten, in some notes on Carlyle, states that 'he always walks at night, carrying an enormous stick, and generally with his eyes on the ground.' This is an exaggeration of the stick, and so far from being only out at night, those accustomed to be in the streets of Chelsea know that Carlyle has, for years past, taken a stroll in all weathers in the morning, and in the afternoon he is frequently to be seen wending his way towards

St. James's Park. Hence certain persons have waylaid him in these walks from curiosity, the Chelsea sage himself being supremely unconscious of being watched. He has been seen to conduct a blind man over a crossing, the person being necessarily ignorant as to who was showing him a kindness, and a little knot of human beings will touch his sympathies, and cause him to pause. I saw Carlyle once step up to a shop-window, around which several individuals stood looking at something. This something was a new portrait of himself, as he quickly perceived; but before they were awake to the fact that the original was close by, he had moved off, giving his stick a rather contemptuous twirl."

The connection of Thomas Carlyle with Chelsea is, at all events, of upwards of forty years' duration, as he was a resident there in the early part of 1834; two years previously, when in London, he visited Leigh Hunt, who at that time lived close to Cheyne Row; and, probably, it was at that time that he resolved to make it his fixed abode. The two writers were neighbours here until 1840, when Leigh Hunt removed to Kensington, which he has immortalised under the title of the "Old Court Suburb;" and their friendship continued until Hunt's death.

At Chelsea, it is almost needless to add, Carlyle wrote his history of "The French Revolution," "Past and Present," his "Life of John Stirling," "Oliver Cromwell's Letters and Speeches," and his "Life of Frederick the Great;" in fact, nearly all the works which have made his name famous through the world.

His wife died at Chelsea suddenly in April, 1866, just as she heard of the delivery of his inaugural address as Lord Rector of Edinburgh University. She left a work unfinished. Charles Dickens admired her literary talents very much. He writes to his friend Forster: "It was a terrible shock to me, and poor dear Carlyle has been in my mind ever since. How often have I thought of the unfinished novel! No one now to finish it. None of the writing women come near her at all." Mr. Forster adds: "No one could doubt this who had come within the fascinating influence of that sweet and noble nature. With some of the highest gifts of intellect, and the charm of a most varied knowledge of books and things, there was something beyond. No one who knew Mrs. Carlyle could replace her loss when she had passed away."

On the 4th of December, 1875, Thomas Carlyle completed his eightieth year (having been born in 1795, in the once obscure village of Ecclefechan, in Scotland), on which occasion he received con-

gratulations from a number of the chief *littérateurs* of Germany, and also a present of a gold medal, struck in honour of the day, from a number of English friends and admirers. He died here on the 5th of February, 1881, and was buried at Ecclefechan.

Sir John Goss, who was many years organist at St. Paul's Cathedral, was for some time a resident in Cheyne Row.

The embankment facing Cheyne Walk, extending from Battersea Bridge, close by old Chelsea Church, to the grounds of Chelsea Hospital, a distance of nearly a mile, presents a pleasing contrast to the red-bricked houses of which we have been speaking. Although the proposition to embank the northern shore of the Thames between Chelsea Hospital and Battersea Bridge was first made by the Commissioners of Her Majesty's Woods and Forests in 1839, the practical execution of the idea was not commenced even on a small scale until some twenty years afterwards. These works originally formed a portion of a scheme for which the Commissioners of Woods and Forests obtained an Act of Parliament in 1846, and which embodied the formation of an embankment and roadway between Vauxhall and Battersea bridges, and the construction of a suspension bridge at Chelsea. The funds which it was estimated would be required were procured, but they proved insufficient for the whole of the work, the bridge costing more than was anticipated. A narrow embankment and roadway were therefore constructed as far as the western end of the Chelsea Hospital gardens, where they terminated in a *cul de sac*. In time, however, the necessity arose for making a sewer to intercept the sewage of the district west of Cremorne, and to help it on its way to Barking. But there was no good thoroughfare from Cremorne eastwards along which to construct it; so it was proposed to form a route for the sewer, and at the same time to complete an unfinished work by continuing the embankment and road on to Battersea. Application was made to Government for the return of £38,150, a sum which remained unexpended from the amount originally raised for the bridge and embankment, and which would have assisted in the prosecution of the new work. The application, however, was unsuccessful, and Sir William Tite, who from the first took a very active interest in the matter, appealed to the Metropolitan Board of Works to undertake the work independently of Government assistance. The Board, therefore, made several applications to Parliament for an Act, which they succeeded in obtaining in 1868. The designs for the embankment, roadway, and sewer were at once prepared by Mr. (afterwards Sir James) Bazalgette, the engineer to the Board, and the whole work was completed and opened to the public in 1874.

At its commencement by Battersea Bridge very little land has been reclaimed from the Thames; but a great change has been effected in the appearance of the spot by doing away with the old awkward approach to the steamboat pier under the archway of a private house, the pontoon being and the granite wall. This garden extends nearly to Oakley Street, which the road rises gradually to meet, while the path falls slightly in order to pass under the shore end of the new Albert Bridge. There is another pretty little piece of garden at this part of the route. After this the reclaimed land becomes of yet greater extent as Cheyne Row is reached. From this spot the Embankment and its surroundings can be seen to the best advan-

THE BOTANICAL GARDENS, CHELSEA, 1790. (*See page* 68.

now moored close to the wall. A picturesque block of houses, too, which stood between this spot and Chelsea Church has been entirely removed. They formed a narrow quaint-looking old thoroughfare, called Lombard Street, one part of which was spanned by the upper rooms of an old house. The backs of one side of this thoroughfare overlooked, and here and there overhung, the river; but they have all been cleared away, and the narrow street converted into a broad one, so that one side of it faces the river. After passing the church the road widens out, and as the space between the houses and the embankment wall becomes greater, a piece of land has been laid out as a garden, so that there are two roads, one in front of the shops, the other between the garden tage. The rough hammer-dressed granite wall runs in a straight line from here to where it meets the old roadway formed by the Office of Woods and Forests. In the ground beneath the pavement have been planted trees on both sides of the road, similar to those planted on the Victoria Embankment. But nothing adds so much to the picturesqueness of this part of the Thames-side roadway, and helps to relieve the appearance of newness which is so marked a feature in the Victoria Embankment, as the line of old trees planted on what was formerly the edge of the river, with the background formed by a fine old row of private houses. The trees are now in the garden divided by a gravel walk, which fills up the space between the two roadways. At the end of Cheyne Walk the

Queen's Road branches off to the left, and runs into the bottom of Lower Sloane Street. At the junction of two roads, but where was formerly the diverging point of one from the river-side, stood the "Swan" tavern, famous as the goal of many a hotly-contested aquatic race from its namesake near London Bridge. Not far from this time-

his diary that he saw "at Mr. Gate's a sample of the satin made at Chelsea of English silkworms for the Princess of Wales, very rich and beautiful." But it has long disappeared, owing to the steady progress of bricks and mortar.

As late as 1824, there was to be seen near Chelsea Bridge a sign of "The Cricketers," painted

THOMAS CARLYLE. (*See page* 64.)

honoured inn are the Botanical Gardens of the Society of Apothecaries.

The Albert Bridge, opposite Oakley Street, constructed upon the suspension principle, was opened in 1873; it forms a useful communication between Chelsea and Battersea Park. Cadogan Pier, close to the bridge, serves as a landing-place for passengers on the river steamboats.

Near the river and Cheyne Walk was a large mulberry-garden, one of those established in the suburbs of London by order of James I., about the year 1610. Thoresby, writing in 1723, tells us in

by George Morland. "At the above date," says Mr. Larwood, "this painting by Morland had been removed inside the house, and a copy of it hung up for the sign. Unfortunately, however, the landlord used to travel about with the original, and put it up before his booth at Staines and Egham races, cricket matches, and similar occasions"—all of which removals, it may be presumed, did no great good to it.

The "Old Swan" inn, which was the goal of Doggett's annual rowing match, stood on the east side of the Botanical Gardens, and was long since turned into a brewery, and the race, down to about the year 1873, ended at the new "Swan," higher up the river, as mentioned above.

The "Swan," very naturally, was a favourite sign for inns by the waterside, and Mr. J. T. Smith, in his "Book for a Rainy Day," or rather a waterman who speaks in his pages, enumerates a goodly list of "Swans" between London and Battersea bridges in 1829:—"Why, let me see, master," he writes, "there's the 'Old Swan' at London Bridge—that's one; then there's the 'Swan' in Arundel Street—that's two; then our's here " (at Hungerford Stairs), "three; the 'Swan' at Lambeth—that's down though. Well, then there's the 'Old Swan' at Chelsea, but that has been long turned into a brew-house; though that was where our people" (the watermen) "rowed to formerly, as mentioned in Doggett's will; now they row to the sign of the 'New Swan' beyond the Physic Garden—we'll say that's four. Then there's two 'Swans' at Battersea—six."

We have already spoken at some length of Tom Doggett, the famous comedian,* and of the annual rowing match by Thames watermen for the honour of carrying off the "coat and badge," which, in pursuance of his will, have been competed for on the 1st of August for the last 150 years; suffice it to say, then, that in the year 1873 the old familiar "Swan" inn was demolished to make room for the new embankment. The old "Swan" tavern enjoyed a fair share of public favour for many years. Pepys, in his "Diary," thus mentions it, under date April 9, 1666:—"By coach to Mrs. Pierce's, and with her and Knipp, and Mrs. Pierce's boy and girl abroad, thinking to have been merry at Chelsea; but being come almost to the house by coach, near the waterside, a house alone, I think the 'Swan,' a gentleman walking by called to us to tell us that the house was shut up because of the sickness. So we, with great affright, turned back, being holden to the gentleman, and went away (I, for my part, in great disorder) to Kensington." In 1780 the house was converted into the Swan Brewery; and the landing of the victor in the aquatic contest thenceforth took place, as above stated, at a house bearing the same sign nearer to Cheyne Walk. Since the demolition of this house the race has been ended close to the spot where the old tavern stood. This rowing match—although not to be compared in any way to the great annual aquatic contest between the Universities of Oxford and Cambridge—occasions a very lively scene, the river being covered with boats, and the utmost anxiety evinced by the friends of the contending parties. In former times it was customary for the winner on his arrival to be saluted with shouts of applause by the surrounding spectators, and carried in triumph on the shoulders of his friends into the tavern.

On a vacant space of ground in front of the Swan Brewery stood formerly a mansion, erected in the reign of Queen Anne, which was for many years inhabited by Mrs. Banks, the mother of Sir Joseph Banks.

"The Physic Garden," to which we now come, was originated by Sir Hans Sloane, the celebrated physician, and was handed over in 1721 by him, by deed of gift, to the Apothecaries' Company, who still own and maintain it. The garden, which bears the name of the "Royal Botanic," was presented to the above company on condition that it "should at all times be continued as a physic-garden, for the manifestation of the power, and wisdom, and goodness of God in creation; and that the apprentices might learn to distinguish good and useful plants from hurtful ones." Various additions have been made to the "Physic Garden" at different periods, in the way of greenhouses and hot-houses; and in the centre of the principal walk was erected a statue of Sir Hans Sloane, by Michael Rysbraeck.

"We visited," writes P. Wakefield in 1814, "the 'Physic or Botanic Garden,' commenced by the Company of Apothecaries in 1673, and patronised by Sir Hans Sloane, who granted the freehold of the premises to the company on condition that they should present annually to the Royal Society specimens of fifty new plants till their number should amount to two thousand. From a sense of gratitude they erected in the centre of the garden a marble statue of their benefactor. Above the spacious greenhouse is a library, furnished with a large collection of botanical works, and with numerous specimens of dried plants. We could not quit these gardens without admiring two cedars of great size and beauty."

"At the time the garden was formed," writes the author of "London Exhibited in 1851," "it must have stood entirely in the country, and had every chance of the plants in it maintaining a healthy state. Now, however, it is completely in the town, and but for its being on the side of the river, and lying open on that quarter, it would be altogether surrounded with common streets and houses. As it is, the appearance of the walls, grass, plants, and houses is very much that of most London gardens—dingy, smoky, and, as regards the plants, impoverished and starved. It is, however,

* See Vol. III., p. 308.

interesting for its age, for the few old specimens it contains, for the medical plants, and, especially, because the houses are being gradually renovated, and collections of ornamental plants, as well as those which are useful in medicine, formed and cultivated on the best principles, under the curatorship of Mr. Thomas Moore, one of the editors of the 'Gardener's Magazine of Botany.'" In spite of the disadvantages of its situation, here are still grown very many of the drugs which figure in the "London Pharmacopœia." The two cedars of Lebanon, which have now reached the age of upwards of 150 years, are said to have been presented to the garden by Sir Joseph Banks, the distinguished naturalist, who here studied the first principles of botany. Of Sir Hans Sloane, and of his numerous public benefactions, we have already spoken in our account of the British Museum.* It only remains, therefore, to add that he was a contributor of natural specimens of rocks from the Giant's Causeway to Pope's Grotto at Twickenham; that he attended Queen Anne in her last illness at Kensington; and that he was the first member of the medical profession on whom a baronetcy was conferred.

During the last century, and early in the present, a pleasant walk across green fields, intersected with hedges and ditches, led the pedestrian from Westminster and Millbank to "The Old Bun House" at Chelsea. This far-famed establishment, which possessed a sort of rival museum to Don Saltero's, stood at the end of Jew's Row (now Pimlico Road), not far from Grosvenor Row. The building was a one-storeyed structure, with a colonnade projecting over the foot pavement, and was demolished in 1839, after having enjoyed the favour of the public for more than a century and a half. Chelsea has been famed for its buns since the commencement of the last century. Swift, in his "Journal to Stella," 1712, writes, "Pray are not the fine buns sold here in our town as the rare Chelsea buns? I bought one to-day in my walk," &c. It was for many years the custom of the Royal Family, and the nobility and gentry, to visit the Bun-house in the morning. George II., Queen Caroline, and the princesses frequently honoured the proprietor, Mrs. Hand, with their company, as did also George III. and Queen Charlotte; and her Majesty presented Mrs. Hand with a silver half-gallon mug, with five guineas in it. On Good Friday mornings the Bun-house used to present a scene of great bustle— upwards of 50,000 persons have assembled here, when disturbances often arose among the London

mob; and in one day more than £250 has been taken for buns.

The following curious notice was issued on Wednesday, March 27th, 1793:—"Royal Bun House, Chelsea, Good Friday.—No Cross Buns. Mrs. Hand respectfully informs her friends and the public, that in consequence of the great concourse of people which assembled before her house at a very early hour, on the morning of Good Friday last, by which her neighbours (with whom she has always lived in friendship and repute) have been much alarmed and annoyed; it having also been intimated, that to encourage or countenance a tumultuous assembly at this particular period might be attended with consequences more serious than have hitherto been apprehended; desirous, therefore, of testifying her regard and obedience to those laws by which she is happily protected, she is determined, though much to her loss, not to sell *Cross Buns* on that day to any person whatever, but Chelsea buns as usual."

The Bun-house was much frequented during the palmy days of Ranelagh, after the closing of which the bun trade declined. Notwithstanding this, on Good Friday, April 18th, 1839, upwards of 24,000 buns were sold here. Soon after, the Bun-house was sold and pulled down; and at the same time was dispersed a collection of pictures, models, grotesque figures, and modern antiques, which had for a century added the attractions of a museum to the bun celebrity. Another bun-house was built in its place, but the olden charm of the place had fled, and Chelsea buns are now only matters of history.

Sir Richard Phillips, in his "Morning's Walk from London to Kew," a few years before the demolition of the old Bun-house, after describing his ramble through Pimlico, writes: "I soon turned the corner of a street which took me out of sight of the space on which once stood the gay Ranelagh. . . . Before me appeared the shop so famed for Chelsea buns, which for above thirty years I have never passed without filling my pockets. In the original of these shops—for even of Chelsea buns there are counterfeits—are preserved mementoes of domestic events in the first half of the past century. The bottle-conjuror is exhibited in a toy of his own age; portraits are also displayed of Duke William and other noted personages; a model of a British soldier, in the stiff costume of the same age; and some grotto-works, serve to indicate the taste of a former owner, and were, perhaps, intended to rival the neighbouring exhibition at Don Saltero's. These buns have afforded a competency, and even wealth, to four generations of the same family;

* See Vol. IV., p. 494.

and it is singular that their delicate flavour, light-ness, and richness, have never been successfully imitated."

In the *Mirror* for April 6, 1839, are two views of the old Bun-house, which were taken just before its demolition.

Chelsea would seem at one time to have enjoyed a reputation not only for buns, but for custards, if we may judge from the following allusion to them by Gay, in his " Trivia : "—

" When W—— and G——, mighty names, are dead,
Or but at Chelsea under custards read."

CHAPTER VII.

CHELSEA (*continued*).—THE HOSPITAL, &c.

"Go with old Thames, view Chelsea's glorious pile,
And ask the shattered hero whence his smile."
Rogers's " Pleasures of Memory."

Foundation of the Hospital—The Story of Nell Gwynne and the Wounded Soldier—Chelsea College—Archbishop Bancroft's Legacy—Transference of the College to the Royal Society—The Property sold to Sir Stephen Fox, and afterwards given as a Site for the Hospital—Lord Ranelagh's Mansion—Dr. Monsey—The Chudleigh Family—The Royal Hospital described—Lying in State of the Duke of Wellington—Regulations for the Admission of Pensioners—A few Veritable Centenarians—The " Snow Shoes " Tavern—The Duke of York's School—Ranelagh Gardens, and its Former Glories—The Victoria Hospital for Sick Children.

ON the west side of the Physic Garden, with its lawns and flower-beds stretching almost down to the river, stands a noble hospital, the counterpart of that at Greenwich, still providing an asylum for invalid soldiers—as its rival did, till recently, for sailors worn out in the service of their country.

It is well known that the foundation of this splendid institution was the work of Charles II. John Evelyn has the following entry in his " Diary," under date 27th of January, 1682 :—" This evening Sir Stephen Fox acquainted me againe with his Majesty's resolution of proceeding in the erection of a royal hospital for merited soldiers, on that spot of ground which the Royal Society had sold to his Majesty for £1,300, and that he would settle £5,000 per annum on it, and build to the value of £20,000, for the reliefe and reception of four com-panies—viz., 400 men, to be as in a colledge or monasterie." It appears that Evelyn was largely consulted by the king and Sir Stephen Fox as to the details of the new building, the growth of whose foundations and walls he watched constantly, as he tells us in his " Diary."

It was not without a pang that the British public saw Greenwich "disestablished ; " and, observes a writer in the *Times*, " the parting with the wooden-legged veterans, in their antique garb, and with their garrulous prattle—too often, it is to be feared, apocryphal—about Nelson, Duncan, Jervis, and Collingwood, was like the parting from old friends. The associations connected with Chelsea Hospital," continues the writer, " possess nearly the same his-torical interest with those awakened by Greenwich. Both piles—although that upon the river-bank is by far the more splendid edifice—were built by Sir

Christopher Wren. Chelsea has yet a stronger claim upon our sympathies, since, according to popular tradition, the first idea of converting it into an asylum for broken-down soldiers sprang from the charitable heart of Nell Gwynne, the frail actress, with whom, for all her frailties, the English people can never be angry. As the story goes, a wounded and destitute soldier hobbled up to Nellie's coach-window to ask alms, and the kind-hearted woman was so pained to see a man who had fought for his country begging his bread in the street that she prevailed on Charles II. to establish at Chelsea a permanent home for military invalids. We should like to believe the story ; and, indeed, its veracity may not be incompatible with a far less pleasant report, that the second Charles made a remarkably good thing, in a pecuniary sense, out of Chelsea Hospital."

Before entering upon an account of Chelsea Hos-pital, it may be desirable to notice here a collegiate building which formerly occupied the site of this great national edifice. This college was originated, soon after the commencement of the seventeenth century, by Dr. Matthew Sutcliffe, Dean of Exeter, for the study of polemical divinity. King James I. laid the first stone of the edifice, in May, 1609, and bestowed on it the name of " King James's College at Chelsey." According to the Charter of Incorpora-tion, the number of members was limited to a provost and nineteen fellows, seventeen of whom were required to be in holy orders ; the other two might be either laymen or divines, and they were to be employed in recording the chief historical events of the era. Dr. Sutcliffe was himself the first provost, and Camden and Hayward were the first historians. Archbishop Laud called the institution "Controversy College;" and, according to "Alleyn's Life," "the Papists, in derision, gave it the name of an alehouse."

It is, perhaps, worthy of a passing note that Archbishop Bancroft left the books which formed the nucleus of the library at Lambeth Palace, to his successors in the see of Canterbury, with the condition that if certain stipulations were not complied with, his legacy should go to Chelsea College, if built within six years of his own decease.

From a print of the original design, prefixed to Darley's "Glory of Chelsey College new Revived" (a copy of which is published in Faulkner's "History of Chelsea"), it would appear that the buildings were originally intended to combine two quadrangles, of different, but spacious, dimensions, with a piazza along the four sides of the smaller court. Only one side of the first quadrangle, however, was completed, and the whole collegiate establishment very soon collapsed. Evelyn tells us that the plan of Chelsea College embraced a quadrangle, with accommodation for 440 persons, "after the dimensions of the larger quadrangle at Christchurch, Oxford." Shortly after the death of the third provost, Dr. Slater, which occurred in 1645, suits were commenced in the Court of Chancery respecting the title to the ground on which the college stood, when it was decreed that Dr. Sutcliffe's estates should revert to his rightful heirs, upon their paying to the college a certain sum of money. The college buildings were afterwards devoted to various inappropriate purposes, being at one time used as a receptacle for prisoners of war, and at another as a riding-house.

Its next destination would appear to have been of a higher order; for it appears that the king gave it, or offered it, to the then newly-founded Royal Society. John Evelyn writes, in his "Diary," under date September 24th, 1667:— "Returned to London, where I had orders to deliver the possession of Chelsey Colledge (used as my prison during the warr with Holland, for such as were sent from the Fleete to London) to our Society [the Royal Society], as a gift of his Majesty, our founder." And again, under date September, 14th, 1681, Evelyn writes:—"Din'd with Sir Stephen Fox, who proposed to me the purchasing of Chelsey College, which his Majesty had some time since given to our Society, and would now purchase it again to build a hospital or infirmary for soldiers there, in which he desired my assistance, as one of the council of the Royal Society."

On the failure of the college, the ground escheated to the Crown, by whom, as stated above,

it was afterwards granted to the Royal Society. This body, in turn, sold the property to Sir Stephen Fox, for Charles II., who "generously gave" it as a site for a Royal Hospital for Aged and Disabled Soldiers, but at the same time pocketing Dr. Sutcliffe's endowment, and leaving the building to be erected at the cost of the nation.

On part of the site of the college was erected, towards the close of the seventeenth century, the mansion of the Earls of Ranelagh, whose name was perpetuated in that of the gardens which were ultimately opened to the public on that spot.

We read in the *Weekly Post*, of 1714, a rumour to the effect that "the Duke and Duchess of Marlborough are to have the late Earl of Ranelagh's house at Chelsea College;" but the arrangement does not appear to have been carried out, for in 1730 an Act was passed, vesting the estates of the Earl of Ranelagh in trustees; and a few years later the house and premises were sold in lots, and shortly afterwards opened as a place of public entertainment, of which we shall have more to say presently. Lord Ranelagh's house and gardens are thus described by Bowack, in 1705:—"The house, built with brick and cornered with stone, is not large, but very convenient, and may well be called a cabinet. It stands a good distance from the Thames. In finishing the whole, his lordship has spared neither labour nor cost. The very greenhouses and stables, adorned with festoons and urns, have an air of grandeur not to be seen in many princes' palaces."

Again, in Gibson's "View of the Gardens near London," published in 1691, these grounds are thus described:—"My Lord Ranelagh's garden being but lately made, the plants are but small, but the plats, border, and walks are curiously kept and elegantly designed, having the advantage of opening into Chelsea College walks. The kitchen-garden there lies very fine, with walks and seats; one of which, being large and covered, was then under the hands of a curious painter. The house there is very fine within, all the rooms being wainscoted with Norway oak, and all the chimneys adorned with carving, as in the council-chamber in Chelsea College." The staircase was painted by Noble, who died in 1700.

A portion of the old college seems to have remained standing for many years, and ultimately to have become the residence of Dr. Messenger Monsey, one of Dr. Johnson's literary acquaintances, and many years Physician to the Royal Hospital.

From Boswell's "Life of Johnson" we learn that the character of Dr. Monsey, in point of natural humour, is thought to have borne a near resemblance to that of Dean Swift; and like him, he too will be long remembered for the vivid powers of his mind and the marked peculiarity of his manners. "His classical abilities were indeed enviable, his memory throughout life was wonderfully retentive, and upon a variety of occasions enabled him, with an inexhaustible flow of words, to pour forth the treasures of erudition acquired by reading, study, and experience; insomuch that he was truly allowed

tration, the reversion of his place had been successively promised to several medical friends of the Paymaster-General of the Forces. Looking out of his window one day, and observing a gentleman below examining the college and gardens, who he knew had secured the reversion of his place, the doctor came down stairs, and going out to him, accosted him thus:—'Well, sir, I see you are examining your house and gardens, that *are to be*,

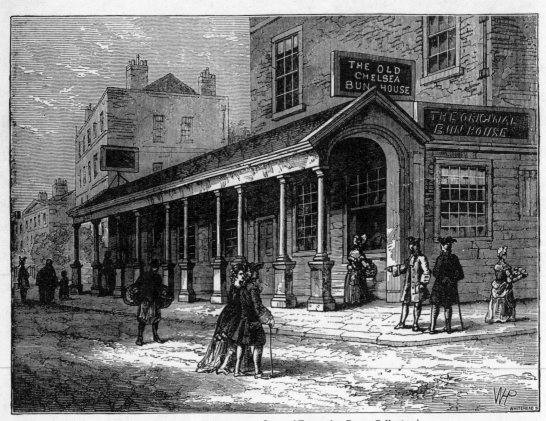

THE CHELSEA BUN-HOUSE, 1810.   (*From the Crace Collection.*)

to be a storehouse of anecdote, a reservoir of curious narrative for all weathers; the living chronicle, in short, of other times. The exuberance of his wit, which, like the web of life, was of a mingled yarn, often rendered his conversation exceedingly entertaining, sometimes indeed alarmingly offensive, and at other times pointedly pathetic and instructive; for, at certain happy intervals, the doctor could lay aside Rabelais and Scarron to think deeply on the most important subjects, and to open a very serious vein." The following anecdote, told in Faulkner's "History of Chelsea," is very characteristic of the doctor's turn of temper, and is said to be well attested:—"He lived so long in his office of Physician to Chelsea Hospital, that, during many changes of adminis-

and I will assure you that they are both very pleasant and very convenient. But I must tell you one circumstance: you are the fifth man that has had the reversion of the place, and I have buried them all. And what is more,' continued he, looking very scientifically at him, 'there is something in your face that tells me I shall bury you too.' The event justified the prediction, for the gentleman died some years after; and what is more extraordinary, at the time of the doctor's death there was not a person who seems to have even solicited the promise of the reversion."

Dr. Monsey's death is recorded as having taken place in December, 1788, "at his apartments in Chelsea College," at the great age of ninety-five. Johnson, though he admired his intellect, disliked

CHELSEA HOSPITAL.

his private character; and Boswell quotes him, saying of old Dr. Monsey, of Chelsea College, that he was " a fellow who swore and talked indecently." Here, as Taylor tells us in his " Recollections," the Doctor " had a large box in his chamber, full of air-holes, for the purpose of carrying his body to his friend, Mr. Forster, in case he should be in a trance when supposed to be dead. It was provided with poles, like a sedan-chair. In his will, which is to be seen in the *Gentleman's Magazine* (vol. 50), he gave instructions that his body should not be buried with any funeral ceremony, but be dissected, and then thrown into the Thames, or wherever the surgeon who operated might please. " It is surprising," observes John Wilson Croker, "that this coarse and crazy humourist should have been an intimate friend and favourite of the elegant and pious Mrs. Montagu." In all probability, however, he knew how to conduct himself in the presence of ladies and bishops, for Dr. Percy, the Bishop of Dromore, says that he never knew him guilty of the vices ascribed to him by Johnson.

The Chudleighs, the father and mother of Elizabeth, Duchess of Kingston,* lived in the College, and the future duchess, as a girl, used to romp and play in its galleries and gardens. They were friends of Sir Robert Walpole, who resided at no great distance.

Here died, in 1833, John Heriot, Comptroller of the Hospital. He was a native of Haddington, in Scotland, and wrote some novels. He was the first editor of the *Sun*, when that paper was started as an evening paper in the interest of Pitt's Administration, and it soon rose to 4,000 a day—a very large circulation for the time, considering the scarcity of educated readers and the heavy stamp-duty then imposed on newspapers.

As we have already observed, a considerable part of the old college grounds, and probably part of the college itself, ultimately became the site of the Royal Hospital for Wounded and Superannuated Soldiers. Dr. Jortin, with his usual sprightliness, observed on this that, "with a very small and easy alteration it was made a receptacle of maimed and discarded soldiers. For if the king's project had been put into execution, the house would most probably have become a house of discord, and 'peace be within thy walls' would have been a fruitless wish, and a prayer bestowed in vain upon it."

King Charles himself laid the first stone of the new building (which had been designed by Wren),

in the presence of the chief nobility and gentry of the kingdom, and the whole structure was finished in 1690, at a cost, it is said, of £150,000. The building is of red brick, with stone quoins, cornices, pediments, and columns; and consists of three courts, two of which are spacious quadrangles; the third, the central one, is open on the south side towards the river, and has its area laid out in gardens and walks. A Latin inscription on the frieze of the large quadrangle tells us that the building was founded by Charles II., augmented by James II., and completed by William and Mary, for the aid and relief of soldiers worn out by old age or by the labours of war. In the central area is a bronze statue of Charles II. in Roman imperial armour, supposed to be the work of Grinling Gibbons; and in the grounds is a granite obelisk erected to the memory of the officers and men who fell in the Indian campaigns. There is also here a statue, by Noble, to Sir J. McGrigor, the Physician-General to the army under Wellington in Spain. In the eastern and western wings of this court are the wards of the pensioners; they are sixteen in number, and are both spacious and airy.

At the extremity of the eastern wing is the governor's house. The ceiling of the principal room is divided into oblong compartments, appropriately ornamented, and the walls are hung with several portraits of royalty, from the time of King Charles II. In the western wing are the apartments of the lieutenant-governor.

The north front is of great extent, and faced by avenues of limes and chestnut-trees. In the centre of the structure is a handsome portico of the Doric order, surmounted by a lofty clock turret in the roof. Beneath are the principal entrances. On the eastern side of the vestibule, a short flight of steps leads to the chapel. This is a lofty apartment, with an arched ceiling; it is rather over 100 feet in length, by about thirty in width, and is paved with black and white marble. The pews for the various officers of the establishment are ranged along the sides, and the pensioners sit in the middle on benches. Over the communion-table is a painting of the Ascension, by Sebastian Ricci. King James II. presented a handsome service of plate, an altar-cloth, pulpit-cloth, several velvet cushions, and four handsomely-bound prayer-books. From the walls on either side of the chapel are suspended a large number of colours captured by the British army, including thirteen " eagles " captured from the French at Barossa, Talavera, and Waterloo. The dining-hall is on the western side of the vestibule, and is of the same dimensions as the chapel.

The furniture of this room is massive and simple. Above the doorway, at the eastern end, is a gallery; the upper end is occupied by a large painting, which was presented by the Earl of Ranelagh. It was designed by Verrio, and finished by Henry Cooke, an artist who studied Salvator Rosa. The chief figure of the composition is King Charles II., mounted on a richly-caparisoned horse; in the background is a perspective view of the Royal Hospital; and fanciful representations of Hercules, Minerva, Peace, and "Father Thames," are introduced, by way of allegory. The sides of the hall are hung with numerous engravings of military subjects, and there is also a large painting of the Battle of Waterloo, and an allegorical picture of the victories of the Duke of Wellington, by James Ward, R.A. A dinner for the pensioners is regularly placed in this hall every day (with the exception of Sunday), at twelve o'clock; but they do not dine in public, as every man is allowed to take his meal in his own apartment in the wards. The hall serves also as a reading-room for the old pensioners, and here they are allowed to sit and smoke—for they are allowed one penny a day for tobacco, which is called "Her Majesty's bounty"— and while away the time with card-playing and other amusements, and also with the perusal of books and newspapers. In this hall the remains of the "great" Duke of Wellington were deposited, in November, 1852, preparatory to the public funeral in St. Paul's Cathedral. Her Majesty, accompanied by Prince Albert, the Prince of Wales, and Princess Royal, visited Chelsea Hospital during part of the ceremony of lying in state; afterwards the veterans of Chelsea were admitted; on one day the admission was restricted to those who were provided with' tickets from the Lord Chamberlain's office; and then, for four days, the public were admitted without tickets, when the crush was so great that several persons were killed in the attempt to gain admission.

The east, or "Light Horse" court, comprises the apartments of many official persons connected with the institution, such as the governor, the deputy-treasurer, secretary, chaplain, apothecary, comptroller, steward, and other officials. The west court is partly occupied by the board-room, used by the commissioners for their meetings, and by the apartments of various officers connected with the establishment. Still further to the west is the stable-yard; and, on the site of the mansion formerly occupied by Sir Robert Walpole is the infirmary, which is admirably adapted for the patients admitted within its walls.

Chelsea Hospital affords a refuge for upwards of 500 inmates. The number of out-pensioners, from whom they are selected, is about 64,000; and of these, on an average, nearly 8,000 are over seventy years of age. Here the veterans, whether wounded, disabled, or merely advanced in years, find a home, and for their accommodation, comfort, and medical treatment, a liberal provision is made. An applicant for admission must be on the permanent pension list, must be of good character, must have no wife or children dependent on him for support, and he must be incapable of supplementing his pension by labour. He must show that he has given good service "by flood and field." A monthly list of applications is kept, in the order in which they are received; and at the end of the month the commissioners, having regard to the number of vacancies and the eligibility of the candidates, according to the terms of the Royal Warrant of 1862, sanction the selection and admission of the most meritorious. All the wants of the inmates are liberally provided for. Their clothing is certainly rather of an antique style; but, nevertheless, it is picturesque. They wear long scarlet coats, lined with blue, and the original three-cornered cocked hat of the last century; but then, as the quartermaster once said to the War Office Committee, "they are old men." Their diet consists of beef on Sundays and mutton on week-days; but, in order to break the monotony, at their own request, bacon has been substituted for mutton on one week-day. A pint of porter daily is the allowance for each man; and there is a fund of about £540 a year, derived from private legacies, which is devoted to maintaining the library and providing extra personal comforts and amusements. The pensioners are divided into six companies, the captains and other officers of each company being responsible for the cleanliness of the ward and the preservation of order.

The expenditure of the hospital is chiefly met by an annual Parliamentary vote; but the institution enjoys a small independent income from property and interest on unclaimed prize-money. With all this liberal provision, however, it appears, from the War Office Committee reports which have been published, that Chelsea Hospital is not popular with soldiers. The inmates, indeed, are contented; but it is admitted that soldiers serving under the colours look forward to out-pensions at the close of their military career, and that the severance of home-ties, the monastic character of the institution, and a certain amount of disciplinary restraint, outweigh the advantages of the hospital, except in the instance of men (perhaps who have earned only small pensions) aged, infirm, and helpless, without family or friends able and willing to support them. Even the very old prefer providing for themselves out of the hospital if they can ; there are only about 230 men in the hospital over seventy—generally fewer than that.

Adjoining the hospital is a burial-ground for the pensioners, wherein repose a few veritable centenarians, if the records of their deaths are to be relied upon. Thomas Asbey, died 1737, aged 112 ; Robert Comming, died 1767, aged 116 ; Peter Dowling, died 1768, aged 102 ; a soldier who fought at the battle of the Boyne, died 1772, aged 111 ; and Peter Bennet, died 1773, aged 107.

In Pimlico Road—or, as it was formerly called, Jew's Row, or Royal Hospital Row—" there is," writes Larwood, in 1866, in his " History of Signboards," " a sign which greatly mystifies the maimed old heroes of Waterloo and the Peninsula, and many others besides. I refer to the 'Snow Shoes.' But this hostelry is historic in its origin. Its sign was set up during the excitement of the American War of Independence, when 'Snow Shoes' formed a leading article in the equipment of the troops sent out to fight the battles of King George, against old Washington and his rebels." John Timbs, in his " Curiosities of London," says that the tradition of the foundation of the hospital being due to the influence of Nell Gwynne is kept in countenance by the head of that royal favourite having been for very many years the sign of a public-house in Grosvenor Row. More than one entry in Evelyn's " Diary," however, proves that Sir Stephen Fox " had not only the whole managing" of the plan, but was himself " a grand benefactor" to it. He was mainly advised by Evelyn, who arranged the offices, " would needes have a library, and mentioned several bookes."

North of the hospital is the Duke of York's School, or Royal Military Asylum. This institution was founded by the late Duke of York, for the support and education of children of soldiers of the regular army, who remain there until of a suitable age, when they are apprenticed, or sent into service. The building is constructed chiefly of brick, with stone dressings and embellishments, and it comprises three sides of a quadrangle. In the centre of the chief front is a stone portico of the Doric order ; four massive pillars support the pediment, the frieze of which is inscribed as follows—" The Royal Military Asylum for the Children of Soldiers of the Regular Army ;" and the whole is surmounted with the royal arms. In this part of the building are the dining-rooms and school-rooms for the children, and also bath-rooms and a committee-room. The north and south wings contain the

dormitories for the boys and girls, and apartments for several officers of the establishment. In the front the ground is laid out in grass plats and gravel walks, and planted with trees ; attached to each wing is a spacious play-ground for exercise, with cloistral arcades for the protection of the children in inclement seasons. The affairs of the Royal Military Asylum are regulated by commissioners appointed by the Government, who have to apply to Parliament for an annual grant for the support of the institution. The commissioners also have the selection of the children, whose admission is regulated in accordance with the following rules : —Orphans, or those whose fathers have been killed, or have died on foreign stations ; those who have lost their mothers, and whose fathers are absent on duty abroad ; those whose fathers are ordered on foreign service, or whose parents have other children to maintain." The children are supported, lodged, and educated, until they are of a suitable age to be disposed of as servants and apprentices. The boys undergo a regular military training ; and it is a pleasing sight to witness them going through their exercises, with their military band of juvenile performers. According to the original intention of the founders of this institution, the number of children admitted into the asylum is not to exceed seven hundred boys and three hundred girls, exclusive of such as, on an exigency, may be admitted to the branch establishment in the Isle of Wight. The boys are clothed in red jackets, blue breeches, blue stockings, and black caps ; and the girls in red gowns, blue petticoats, straw hats, &c. The latter are taught the ordinary branches of needlework and household work.

A considerable part of the grounds lying immediately at the south-east corner of Chelsea Hospital once formed the site of Ranelagh Gardens, as we have already observed. " Ranelagh," writes Mr. Lambert, in his " History of London and its Environs," published in 1806, " was the seat of an Irish nobleman of that title, in whose time the gardens were extensive. On his death the estate was sold, and the principal part of the gardens was converted into fields, though the house remained unaltered. Part of the gardens also was permitted to remain. Some gentlemen and builders having become the purchasers of these, a resolution was taken to convert them into a place of entertainment. Accordingly, Mr. William Jones, architect to the East India Company, drew the plan of the present Rotunda, which is an illustrious monument of his genius and fancy. The chief material employed was wood, and it was erected in 1740." He describes it as " a noble edifice, somewhat resembling the Pantheon at Rome, with a diameter externally of 185 feet, and internally of 150 feet. The entrances," he adds, "are by four Doric porticoes opposite each other, and the first storey is rustic. Round the whole on the outside is a gallery, the stairs to which are at the porticoes; and overhead is a slated covering which projects from the body of the Rotunda. Over the gallery are the windows, sixty in number, and over these the slated roof. The interior is elegantly decorated, and, when well illuminated and full of company, presents a most brilliant spectacle. Indeed, it may be said of Ranelagh that, as a public place of amusement, it is not to be equalled in Europe for beauty, elegance, and grandeur. Before the Act of Parliament passed in 1752, which prohibited all places of entertainment from being opened before a certain hour in the afternoon, the Rotunda was open every day for public breakfasts. It was not, however, a place of much note until it was honoured with the famous masquerades in the late reign, which brought it into vogue. But the immorality so frequently practised at masquerades has lessened their reputation, and they are not now attended, as formerly, by persons of rank and fashion. The entertainments consist of music and singing, and upon particular occasions fireworks also are exhibited; and during the summer season the gardens may be seen in the day-time on payment of a shilling. The price of admittance in the evening is half-a-crown, including tea and coffee, which are the only refreshments allowed; but on extraordinary occasions the price is raised."

Sir Richard Phillips, in his "Modern London," published in 1804, in noticing Ranelagh, writes:— "This place is situated about two miles west of London, in the village of Chelsea. It consists of a splendid Rotunda and gardens. The Rotunda itself, used as a promenade, is very spacious, and brilliantly illuminated, with a neat orchestra. The amusements of Ranelagh, generally speaking, are limited to miscellaneous performances, vocal and instrumental; and in the gardens there are fireworks and illuminations. Masquerades are sometimes given in a very good style; but the genius of the English people seems not well calculated for this species of amusement. Ranelagh has lately been engaged by the 'Pic-Nic Society,' and it is supposed will be appropriated to their entertainments."

Besides the Rotunda there was a small Venetian pavilion in a lake, to which the company were rowed in boats, and the grounds were planted with trees. The decorations of the various buildings were designed by Capon, an eminent scene-painter. In each of the refreshment-boxes was a painting; in the centre of the Rotunda was a heating apparatus, concealed by arches, porticoes, and niches, paintings, &c.; and supporting the ceiling, which was decorated with celestial figures, festoons of flowers, and arabesques, and lighted by circles of chandeliers.

In the *Gentleman's Magazine* for 1742 is the following description of Ranelagh Gardens from a foreigner's point of view:—"I repaired to the rendezvous, which was the park adjoining to the Palace Royal, and which answers to our Tuilleries, where we sauntered, with a handful of fine company, till it was almost twilight—a time, I thought, not a little unseasonable for a tour into the country. We had no sooner quitted the park but we found ourselves in a road full of people, illuminated with lamps on each side; the dust was the only inconvenience; but in less than half an hour we found ourselves at a gate where money was demanded, and paid for our admittance; and immediately my eyes were struck with a large building, of an orbicular figure, with a row of windows round the attic storey, through which it seemed to be liberally illuminated within, and altogether presented to the eye such an image as a man of a whimsical imagination would not scruple to call a giant's lanthorn. Into this enchanted palace we entered, with more haste than ceremony; and at the first glance I, for my part, found myself dumb with surprise and astonishment, in the middle of a vast amphitheatre; for structure, Roman; for decorations of paint and gilding, gay as the Asiatic; four grand portals, in the manner of the ancient triumphal arches, and four times twelve boxes, in a double row, with suitable pilasters between, form the whole interior of this wonderful fabric, save that in the middle a magnificent orchestra rises to the roof, from which descend several large branches, which contain a great number of candles enclosed in crystal glasses, at once to light and adorn this spacious Rotunda. Groups of well-dressed persons were dispersed in the boxes; numbers covered the area; all manner of refreshments were within call; and music of all kinds echoed, though not intelligibly, from every one of those elegant retreats, where Pleasure seemed to beckon her wanton followers. I have acknowledged myself charmed at my entrance; you will wonder, therefore, when I tell you that satiety followed. In five minutes I was familiar with the whole and every part; in the five next indifference took place; in five more my eyes grew dazzled, my head became giddy, and all night I dreamed of Vanity Fair."

The Rotunda was first opened with a public breakfast in April, 1742; and, for a short time, morning concerts were given, consisting of selections from oratorios. Walpole, in a letter to Sir Horace Mann, written during the next month, gives us the following particulars of this once famous place of

years later we find the following record by the same gossiping chronicler :—"Every night constantly I go to Ranelagh, which has totally beat Vauxhall. Nobody goes anywhere else—everybody goes there. My Lord Chesterfield is so fond of it that he

Ranelagh Houfe Thursday—May 15 a Ball.

The Doors to be opened at nine

A CARD OF INVITATION TO RANELAGH.　(*See page* 80.)

amusement :—"There is a vast amphitheatre, finely gilt, painted, and illuminated, into which everybody that loves eating, drinking, staring, or crowding, is admitted for twelve pence. The building and disposition of the gardens cost sixteen thousand pounds. . . . I was there last night, but did not find the joy of it. Vauxhall is a little better, for the garden is pleasanter, and one goes by water." Ranelagh, however, appears soon to have eclipsed its rival on the other side of the water, for two

says he has ordered all his letters to be directed thither." And again, some four years afterwards, he tells us : "Ranelagh is so crowded, that in going there t'other night in a string of coaches, we had a stop of six-and-thirty minutes."

The Jubilee Masquerade, "after the Venetian manner," held here in 1749, about seven years after the gardens were first opened, is thus described by gossiping Horace Walpole :—"It was by far the best understood and prettiest spectacle I ever saw

THE ROTUNDA, RANELAGH GARDENS, IN 1750. (*See page 77.*)

—nothing in a fairy tale ever surpassed it. One of the proprietors, who is a German, and belongs to court, had got my Lady Yarmouth to persuade the king to order it. It began at three o'clock; at about five, people of fashion began to go. When you entered, you found the whole garden filled with marquees and spread with tents, which remained all night very commodely. In one quarter was a May-pole, dressed with garlands, and people dancing round it to a tabour and pipe, and rustic music, all masked, as were all the various bands of music that were disposed in different parts of the garden; some like huntsmen, with French horns; some like peasants; and a troop of harlequins and scaramouches in the little open temple on the mount. On the canal was a sort of gondola, adorned with flags and streamers, and filled with music, rowing about. All round the outside of the amphitheatre were shops, filled with Dresden china, japan, &c., and all the shopkeepers in masks; the amphitheatre was illuminated, and in the middle was a circular bower, composed of all kinds of firs, in tubs, from twenty to thirty feet high; under them orange-trees, with small lamps in each orange, and below them all sorts of auriculas in pots; and festoons of natural flowers hanging from tree to tree. Between the arches, too, were firs, and smaller ones in the balconies above. There were booths for tea and wine, gaming-tables and dancing, and about two thousand persons present. In short, it pleased me more than the finest thing I ever saw."

Not many weeks after this there was another "Subscription Masquerade" here, also described at some length by the same old Court gossip, Walpole:—"The king was well disguised in an old-fashioned English habit, and much pleased with somebody who desired him to hold their cups as they were drinking tea. The Duke [of Cumberland] had a dress of the same kind, but was so immensely corpulent that he looked like 'Cacofoco,' the drunken captain in *Rule a Wife and Have a Wife*. The Duchess of Richmond was a Lady Mayoress of the time of James I.; and Lord De la Warr, Queen Elizabeth's 'Garter,' from a picture in the Guard Chamber at Kensington; they were admirable masks. Lord Rochford, Miss Evelyn, Miss Bishopp, Lady Stafford, and Miss Pitt, were in vast beauty, particularly the last, who had a red veil, which made her look gloriously handsome. I forgot Lady Kildare. Mr. Conway was the 'Duke' in *Don Quixote*, and the finest figure that I ever saw. Miss Chudleigh was 'Iphigenia,' and so lightly clad that you would have taken her for Andromeda. . . . The maids of honour were so offended they would not

speak to her. Pretty Mrs. Pitt looked as if she came from heaven, but was only thither in the habit of a Chanoineness. Lady Betty Smithson (Seymour) had such a pyramid of baubles upon her head that she was exactly the Princess of Babylon in Grammont."

In 1754 the evening amusements here were advertised under the name of Comus's Court; and in 1759 a burlesque ode on St. Cecilia's Day, written by Bonnell Thornton, was performed; and we are told that "among the instruments employed there was a band of marrow-bones and cleavers, whose endeavours were admitted by the *cognoscenti* to have been a great success."

From Boswell we learn that even the sage and grave Dr. Johnson was as fond of Ranelagh as he was of the Pantheon. When somebody said, cynically, that there "was not half a guinea's worth of pleasure in seeing Ranelagh," he replied, "No; but there is half a guinea's worth of inferiority to other people in not having seen it." Indeed, if we may believe the statement of his friend, Dr. Maxwell, some time assistant preacher at the Temple, Dr. Johnson "often went to Ranelagh, which he deemed a place of innocent recreation." But this is rather a proof of Dr. Johnson's own purity than a testimony to the morals of the place, for "to the pure all things are pure." The gardens were constantly visited also by Oliver Goldsmith; even when he was in difficulties, he would take an Irish cousin there, and treat her to the admission. Sometimes poor Oliver would stroll thither with Dr. Johnson and Sir Joshua Reynolds, to see the great world of which he at once knew so much and so little.

The King of Denmark and his suite paid a visit to Ranelagh in 1768, when, we are told, his Majesty "examined the Temple and other buildings, which gave him great satisfaction."

The scene of the finish of the first Regatta on the Thames, in June, 1775, must have been one of the crowning glories of Ranelagh. The admission ticket on the occasion, engraved by Bartolozzi, was long held in high estimation by collectors. Plans of the regatta were sold, from a shilling to a penny each, and songs on the occasion sung, in which "Regatta" was the rhyme for "Ranelagh," and "Royal Family" echoed to "liberty." "On the return of the wager boats," writes Mr. Faulkner, in his "History of Chelsea," "the whole procession moved, in picturesque irregularity, towards Ranelagh. The Thames was now a floating town. The company landed at the stairs about nine o'clock, when they joined the assembly which came by land in the Temple of Neptune a temporary octagon kind of building, erected about twenty yards below the Rotunda, lined with striped linen of the different-coloured flags of the navy, ornamented with streamers of the same kind loosely flowing, and lustres hanging between each. This room discovered great taste. At half after ten the Rotunda was opened for supper, which displayed three circular tables, of different elevations, elegantly set out. The Rotunda was finely illuminated with parti-coloured lamps; the centre was solely appropriated for one of the fullest and finest bands of music, vocal and instrumental, ever collected in these kingdoms, the number being 240, in which were included the first masters, led by Giardini, and the whole directed by Mr. Simpson. . . . . Supper being over, a part of the company retired to the Temple, where they danced without any regard to precedence; while others entertained themselves in the great room. Several temporary structures were erected in the gardens, such as bridges, palm-trees, &c., which were intended to discover something novel in the illumination style, but the badness of the evening prevented their being exhibited."

In 1802 an *afternoon breakfast* was given here, under the auspices of the Pic-Nic Society, at which about two thousand persons of distinction were present. On this occasion M. Garnerin and Captain Snowden made an ascent in a balloon, and alighted at Colchester in less than an hour. "This," as Hone in his "Year-Book" observes, "was the most memorable ascent in England from the time of Lunardi."

In the following year a magnificent ball was held in the Rotunda; it was given by the knights of the Order of the Bath, on the occasion of an "installation," and is said to have been a "gala of uncommon splendour." But even this was surpassed in brilliancy by an entertainment given shortly afterwards by the Spanish Ambassador. "The whole external front of the house," we read, "was illuminated in a novel manner, and the portico immediately leading to the Rotunda was filled on each side with rows of aromatic shrubs. The Rotunda itself, at the first opening to the sight, exhibited a most superb appearance. The lower boxes formed a Spanish camp, striped blue and red, each tent guarded by a boy dressed in the Spanish uniform. The gallery formed a Temple of Flora, lighted by a number of gold baskets containing wax tapers. The queen's box was hung with crimson satin, lined with white, which hung in festoons richly fringed with gold, and at the top was a regal crown. In the orchestra, which was converted into a magnificent pavilion,

a table of eighteen covers was laid for the Royal Family. Opposite to Her Majesty's box was a light temple or stage, on which a Spanish dance was performed by children; at another part were beautiful moving transparencies; and a third was a lottery of valuable trinkets, consisting of six hundred prizes. Women, ornamented with wreaths of flowers, made tea; and one hundred valets, in scarlet and gold, and as many footmen, in sky-blue and silver, waited on the company."

From about the year 1780 down to the close of the last century Ranelagh was in the height of its glory. It was visited by royalty, and all the nobility and gentry. "As no place was ever better calculated for the display of female beauty and elegance," writes Mr. Faulkner, in his work above quoted, "it followed, of course, the greatest belles of the day frequented Ranelagh, at the head of whom was the celebrated and beautiful Duchess of Devonshire, a lady eminent for every grace that could adorn the female, and not a few candidates for admiration were in her train." The Rotunda was subsequently used for late evening concerts, and as an assembly-room, and the gardens for the display of fireworks and other out-door amusements. The place soon ceased to be the attractive promenade it had formerly been, and the brilliant display of beauty it had made for years was no more. The whole of the premises were taken down about the year 1805.

Many persons will remember the description of the ideal "Old Gentleman," in Hone's "Table-Book." "He has been induced to look in at 'Vauxhall' again, but likes it still less than he did years back, and cannot bear it in comparison with Ranelagh! He thinks everything looks poor, flaring, and jaded. 'Ah!' says he, with a sort of triumphant sigh, 'ah! Ranelagh was a noble place! Such taste! such elegance! and such beauty! There was the Duchess of A——, the finest woman in England, sir; and Mrs. B——, a mighty fine creature; and Lady Susan what's-her-name, who had that unfortunate affair with Sir Charles. Yes, indeed, sir, they came swimming by you like swans. Ranelagh for me!'"

Whether it be true or not that ladies of *bon ton* "came swimming by you like swans," there can be no doubt that Ranelagh, in its palmy days, was a favourite haunt of the "upper ten thousand," and that "duchesses" and "Lady Susans" in plenty jostled there against the troops of plebeian City and country dames.

A writer in the *Connoisseur* (No. 22) complains: "The modest excesses of these times [the reign of George II.] are in their nature the same with those which were formerly in vogue. The present races of 'bucks,' 'bloods,' and 'free-thinkers' are but the spawn of the Mohocks and Hell-fire Clubs; and if our modern fine ladies have had their masquerades, their Vauxhalls, their Sunday tea-drinking at Ranelagh, and their morning chocolate in the Haymarket, they have only improved upon the 'Ring,' the Spring Gardens, the New Exchange assignations, and the morning Puppet-show, which enjoyed the attention of their grandmothers. And so, as it is not apparent that our people of fashion are more wicked, so neither are they more wise than their predecessors." The fall of Ranelagh—like other enchanting places of amusement, the description of whose assemblages give us such graphic pictures of the frail beauties of the last century—is thus mournfully set forth in Murphy's "Prologue to Zobeide:"—

> "Adieu, Almack's! Cornelys' masquerade!
>   Sweet Ranelagh!"

The picture of ruin and desolation which the site of Ranelagh presented after the demolition of the Rotunda and the dismantling of its gardens, is ably reproduced by Sir Richard Phillips, in his "Walk from London to Kew." "On entering Chelsea," he writes, "I was naturally led to inquire for the site of the once gay Ranelagh. I passed up the avenue of trees, which I remember often to have seen blocked up with carriages. At its extremity I looked for the Rotunda and its surrounding buildings; but, as I could not see them, I concluded that I had acquired but an imperfect idea of the place in my nocturnal visits! I went forward, on an open space, but still could discern no Ranelagh. At length, on a spot covered with nettles, thistles, and other rank weeds, I met a working man, who, in answer to my inquiries, told me that he could see I was a stranger, or I should have known that Ranelagh had been pulled down, and that I was then standing on the site of the Rotunda! Reader, imagine my feelings, for I cannot analyse them! This vile place, I exclaimed, the site of the once enchanting Ranelagh! It cannot be! The same eyes were never destined to see such a metamorphosis! All was desolation! A few inequalities appeared in the ground, indicative of some former building, and holes filled with muddy water showed the foundation-walls; but the rest of the space, making about two acres, was covered with clusters of tall nettles, thistles, and docks. On a more accurate survey I traced the circular foundation of the Rotunda, and at some distance discovered the broken arches of some cellars, once filled with the choicest wines, but now with dirty water. Further on were marks against a garden wall, indicating that the water-boilers for tea and coffee had once been heated there. I traced, too, the site of the orchestra, where I had often been ravished by the finest performances of vocal and instrumental music. My imagination brought the objects before me; I fancied I could still hear an air of Mara's. I turned my eye aside, and what a contrast appeared! No glittering lights! no brilliant happy company! no peals of laughter from thronged boxes! no chorus of a hundred instruments and voices! All was death-like stillness! Is such, I exclaimed, the end of human splendour? Yes, truly, all is vanity; and here is a striking example. Here are ruins and desolation, even without antiquity! I am not mourning, said I, over the remains of Babylon or Carthage—ruins sanctioned by the unsparing march of time; but here it was all glory and splendour, even yesterday! Here, but seven years have flown away, and I was myself one of three thousand of the gayest mortals ever assembled in one of the gayest scenes which the art of man could devise—ay, on this very spot; yet the whole is now changed into the dismal scene of desolation before me!"

Although not a vestige of the gardens remains, its memory is preserved by naming after it some of the streets, roads, and places which have been built near its site. Mr. Jesse, in his work on "London," published in 1871, tells us that "a single avenue of trees, formerly illuminated by a thousand lamps, and over-canopying the wit, the rank, and the beauty of the last century, now forms an almost solitary memento of the departed glories of Ranelagh. Attached to these trees, the author discovered one or two solitary iron fixtures, from which the variegated lamps were formerly suspended."

According to Mr. John Timbs' "Club Life of London," there was subsequently opened in the neighbourhood a New Ranelagh; but it would appear to have been short-lived, as its memory has quite passed away.

Such, however, was the celebrity of the old Ranelagh, that another Ranelagh, like a second Salamis, was established in the suburbs of Paris; as witness the following extract from a French writer in 1875:—
"The name of Ranelagh Gardens, almost forgotten in England, will soon be equally so in Paris. Or rather, it would be, but for the inscription on the neighbouring street, preserving a title which no revolution need trouble to alter. Some alterations now undertaken by the Parisian authorities in the street recall to mind the chequered fortunes of the French Ranelagh. It was started in the summer

of 1774 by a simple gardener of the Bois de Boulogne as a private speculation, the name, of course, being borrowed from Chelsea. The gardener was patronised by the Prince de Soubise, and the concerts and balls were at first a great success. But the novelty died out, and about nine years afterwards the proprietor was fain to escape ruin by becoming manager to a private club, with a more select *clientèle*. Thenceforth, till the Revolution, the place was a success. Marie Antoinette had been seen there, and the club invitations were much sought after. The Republic, pure and simple, would have been fatal to the gardens had not the Directory come to the rescue. Under its less rigid *régime* came Trénitz, with his troop of Muscadins and Merveil-leuses. Morisart died just before the fall of the Empire, and in time to escape the sight of the Cossacks trampling his pet flower-beds and lawns. From 1816 to 1830 another aristocratic club held its *réunions* at Ranelagh, and under the Orleans dynasty it became again a public place of enter-tainment. At last came M. Thiers' scheme of fortifying Paris, and his ramparts cut the gardens in half. This was in 1840; and twenty years later a decree suppressed for ever the last lingering vestige of gaiety, and consigned the ground to building purposes."

Queen's Road West (formerly called Paradise Row) has been the residence of many of the "nobility and gentry" of Chelsea in former times. In a large mansion adjoining Robinson's Lane, lived the Earl of Radnor in the time of Charles II., and here his lordship entertained the king "most sumptuously" in September, 1660. The parish register contains several entries of baptisms and deaths in the Radnor family.

Sir Francis Windham had a house in this road at the commencement of the last century. After the battle of Worcester he entertained Charles II. at Trent, where the king remained concealed for several days. Dr. Richard Mead, the eminent physician, of whom we have already spoken in our account of Great Ormond Street,* resided in this neighbourhood for some time, as appears by the parish books. Another physician of note who lived here about the same time was Dr. Alexander Blackwell, who resided in a house near the Botanic Garden. Dr. Blackwell became involved in diffi-culties; and after leaving Chelsea he went to Sweden, where he was appointed physician to the king. Subsequently, however, he was found guilty of high treason, "in plotting to overturn the con-stitution of the kingdom, and sentenced to be broken alive on the wheel."

In the Queen's Road, adjoining the Royal Hos-pital, with its gardens stretching down towards the river, and close by the spot where formerly stood the residence of Sir Robert Walpole, is the Victoria Hospital for Sick Children. The building, which was converted to its present use in 1866, was for-merly known as Gough House. It was built by John, Earl of Carberry—one of the "noble authors' mentioned by Horace Walpole—at the commence-ment of the last century. The estate afterwards came into the possession of the Gough family, and the house subsequently was made use of for many years as a school for young ladies. The house has lately been raised a storey, and additional wards have been provided. These improvements were effected at an expense of about £3,000, and the hospital was formally re-opened by the Princess Louise.

At the eastern end of Queen's Road, forming one side of a broad and open thoroughfare, connect-ing Sloane Street with new Chelsea Bridge, stand some fine barracks for the Foot Guards, erected about the year 1863. They are constructed in a substantial manner with light-coloured brick, re-lieved with rustic quoins of red brick, and they consist of several commodious blocks of buildings, the largest of which contains quarters for the officers, &c. They afford accommodation for about 1,000 men. It has been said, perhaps with some truth till lately, that this is the only handsome structure in the way of barracks to be seen in the entire metropolis. If so, the assertion is not very creditable to our character as a nation, considering the duties that we owe to those who defend our homes and our commerce in the field.

In 1809, the Serpentine — which joined the Thames by Ranelagh—rose so high as to overflow its banks, and boats were employed in carrying passengers between the old Bun-house and Chelsea Hospital.

Mr. Larwood, in his "History of Sign-boards," says that there is, or, at all events, was in 1866, in Bridge Row, a public-house bearing the sign of the "Chelsea Water-works." These water-works, after which it was named, were constructed about the year 1724. A canal was dug from the Thames, near Ranelagh to Pimlico, where an engine was placed for the purpose of raising the water into pipes, which conveyed it to Chelsea, Westminster, and other parts of western London. The reservoirs in Hyde Park and the Green Park were supplied by pipes from the Chelsea Waterworks, which, in 1767, yielded daily 1,750 tons of water.

* See Vol. IV., p. 560.

CHELSEA WATER-WORKS, IN 1750. (*See page* 83.)

CHAPTER VIII.

CHELSEA (*continued*).—CREMORNE GARDENS, &c.

"Where smiling Chelsea spreads the cultured lands,
Sacred to Flora, a pavilion stands;
And yet a second temple neighb'ring near
Nurses the fragrance of the various year."—*Anon.*

Chelsea Farm, the Residence of Lord Cremorne—Cremorne Gardens—Attempts at Aërial Navigation—Ashburnham House—The Ashburnham Tournament—The "Captive" Balloon—Turner's Last Home—Noted Residents in Lindsey Row—The King's Road—The Old Burial-ground —St. Mark's College—The "World's End" Tavern—Chelsea Common—Famous Nurseries—Chelsea Park—The "Goat in Boots"—The Queen's Elm—The Jews' Burial-ground—Shaftesbury House—The Workhouse—Sir John Cope—Robert Boyle, the Philosopher and Chemist—The Earl of Orrery—Mr. Adrian Haworth—Dr. Atterbury—Shadwell, the Poet—The "White Horse" Inn—Mr. H. S. Woodfall—The Original of "Strap the Barber" in "Roderick Random"—Danvers Street—Justice Walk—The Old Wesleyan Chapel— Chelsea China—Lawrence Street—Tobias Smollett—Old Chelsea Stage-coaches—Sir Richard Steele and other Noted Residents—The Old Clock-house—The Glaciarium—Hospital for Diseases of Women—Chelsea Vestry Hall, and Literary and Scientific Institution—Congregational Church—Royal Avenue Skating-rink—Sloane Square—Bloody Bridge—Chelsea, Brompton, and Belgrave Dispensary—Royal Court Theatre—Hans Town—Sloane Street—Trinity Church—Sloane Terrace Wesleyan Chapel—Sir C. W. Dilke, Bart.—Ladies' Work Society— Hans Town School of Industry for Girls—"Count Cagliostro"—An Anecdote of Professor Porson—Chelsea House—St. Mary's Roman Catholic Chapel—The "Marlborough Tavern"—Hans Place—Miss Letitia E. Landon—The Pavilion—St. Saviour's Church—Prince's Cricket-ground and Skating-rink—The "South Australian."

A FEW hundred yards to the west of old Battersea Bridge, on the north side of the river, were the celebrated Cremorne Gardens, so named after Thomas Dawson, Lord Cremorne, the site of whose former suburban residence and estate they covered. They proved, to a very great extent, the successors of "Kuper's," Vauxhall, and Ranelagh. In the early part of the present century, Lord Cremorne's mansion, known as Chelsea Farm, was often visited by George III., Queen Charlotte, and the Prince of Wales. In 1825 the house and grounds devolved on Mr. Granville Penn, a cousin of Lady Cremorne, who much improved the estate, but subsequently disposed of it. The natural beauty of the situation soon afterwards led to the grounds being opened to the public as the "Stadium," and a few years later the gardens were laid out with great taste; the tavern adjoining them was enlarged, and the place became the resort of a motley crowd of pleasure-seekers, and generally well attended. To a recent period it retained most of its original features. At night during the summer months the grounds were illuminated with numberless coloured lamps, and there were various ornamental buildings, grottoes, &c., together with a theatre, concert-room, and dining-hall. The amusements provided were of a similar character to those which were presented

Ashburnham House, which stood on the west of the gardens, was built about the middle of the last century by Dr. Benjamin Hoadley, an eminent physician, after whose death it was purchased by Sir Richard Glynn, who sold it to the Earl of Ashburnham, from whom it obtained its present name. It was next in the possession of Dr. Cadogan, and again changing hands at different periods, ultimately became the residence of the Hon Leicester

THE "WORLD'S END," IN 1790. (*See page* 87.)

at Vauxhall Gardens in its palmy days: such as vocal and instrumental concerts, balloon ascents, dancing, fireworks, &c. Several remarkable balloon ascents were made from these grounds, notably among them being that of Mr. Hampton, who, in 1839, ascended with a balloon and parachute, by which he descended from a height of about two miles. More recently an attempt at aerial navigation was made from Cremorne by a foreigner, M. de Groof. The apparatus was suspended beneath the car of a balloon, and when the aeronaut had reached a considerable height, the machine was liberated; but owing to some defect in its construction, it immediately collapsed and fell to the ground with a fearful crash, killing its unfortunate occupant on the spot.

Stanhope, afterwards Earl of Harrington. A strip of waste ground between Ashburnham House and the river, called the "Lots," was for many years "a bone of contention" between the residents in the neighbourhood and the Chelsea Vestry, in consequence of the disgraceful scenes carried on by a large number of "roughs" who were in the habit of meeting there. Here, in 1863, in a large pavilion prettily draped with the flags of all nations and a variety of heraldic trophies and allegorical devices, a sensational entertainment on a scale of great splendour was given, in the shape of a revival of the Eglinton "tournament." A large number of persons took part in it as heralds, seneschals, yeomen, pages, men-at-arms, squires, and banner-bearers, clad in an almost endless variety of shining armour and mediæval costume. In 1869, a monster balloon, nearly 100 feet in diameter, made daily ascents for some time from these grounds. The balloon, appropriately called "The Captive," was secured by a rope about 2,000 feet long, which was let out and wound in by steam power. The Captive balloon, however, one day escaped from its moorings, and the exhibition was discontinued.

In a small house close to Cremorne Pier, Mr. J. M. W. Turner, R.A., resided for some time, under an assumed name, and here, as we have already stated,* he died in 1851. Whilst living here, Turner would not see any person, excepting a very few intimate friends, and, in fact, was too reserved to allow himself to be recognised. This inclination at the close of his life, perhaps, was only natural. Doubtless, Chelsea is proud to add his name to its list of distinguished residents.

Close by, in Lindsey Row, lived Sir Mark Isambard Brunel, the originator and designer of the Thames Tunnel; and Mr. Timothy Bramah, the distinguished locksmith. Here, too, resided Mr. John Martin, R.A. The Rev. A. C. Coxe, in his "Impressions of England," published in 1851, speaking of Chelsea, says :—"We landed not far from this church, and called upon John Martin, whose illustrations of Milton and 'Belshazzar's Feast' have rendered him celebrated as a painter of a certain class of subjects, and in a very peculiar style. He was engaged on a picture of 'The Judgment,' full of his mannerism, and sadly blemished by offences against doctrinal truth, but not devoid of merit or of interest. He asked about Allston and his 'Belshazzar,' and also made inquiries about Morse, of whose claim as the inventor of the electric telegraph he was entirely ignorant."

Mr. Henry Constantine Jennings, an antiquary and virtuoso, settled in Lindsey Row at the close of the last century. His "museum," which comprised a large collection of shells, minerals, preserved birds, quadrupeds, &c., was disposed of by auction in 1820.

Leading from the site of Cremorne Gardens eastward through Chelsea, is a broad thoroughfare, called the King's Road; and by this road we shall now proceed on our way backward towards Sloane Street, picking up such scraps of information respecting the neighbourhood on either side as the records of the district have left for our use. Respecting the King's Road itself, we may state that, prior to the reign of Charles II., it was only a narrow lane through the fields, for the convenience of the farmers and gardeners who had lands in the neigh-

* See Vol. IV., p. 448.

bourhood. Soon after the Restoration, however, it was found that it might be made to serve as a more direct road for the king between St. James's or Whitehall and Hampton Court Palace; and, accordingly, after some discussion between the Government and the parishioners of Chelsea, it was converted into an ordinary coach-road. It continued to be the private road of royalty down to the reign of George III. Pass tickets, admitting passengers along it by sufferance, are still in existence; they bear on the one side a crown and "G. R.," and on the other, as a legend, "The King's Private Road."

Along this road is the burial-ground belonging to the parish of Chelsea, in which lies Andrew Millar, the original publisher of Hume's "History of England," Thomson's "Seasons," and some of Fielding's novels.

The Duke of York was thrown from his horse whilst riding along this road towards Fulham; he had two ribs broken. John Timbs records that, "near the spot where is now the Vestry Hall, the Earl of Peterborough was stopped by highwaymen in what was then a narrow lane; and the robbers, being watched by some soldiers, who formed a part of the guard at Chelsea College, were fired at from behind the hedge. One of these highwaymen turned out to be a student in the Temple, whose father having lost his estate, his son lived by 'play, sharping, and a little on the highway'—the desperate resources of the day."

Nearly opposite Ashburnham House, on the north side of the King's Road, is St. Mark's College, which was established in 1841 by the National Society, as a training institution for schoolmasters. The residence of the principal was formerly known as Stanley House, and was originally built in the reign of Queen Elizabeth, by Sir Arthur Gorges, whose family at that time possessed considerable property in Chelsea. About the middle of the last century it became the property of the Countess of Strathmore, who afterwards married Captain A. R. Bowes, whose barbarity to her drew on him the execration of the country. About the year 1815, Stanley House was sold to Mr. William Hamilton, from whom it subsequently passed to the National Society. The college accommodates about 110 students, and the period of training is for two years, according to the provisions of the Committee of Council on Education. The chapel, which abuts on the Fulham Road, is an unpretending building; but a certain amount of effect is produced in the interior by the stained-glass windows. The buildings of the college form a quadrangle, erected in the Italian style; and there is also in the grounds an octagonal building, used as a practising school. The first Principal of the college, and indeed its joint-founder, the Rev. Derwent Coleridge, a son of the poet, died in 1883.

In the King's Road, near Milman Street, is an inn styled "The World's End." The old tavern, like the "World's End" at Knightsbridge, already described,* was a noted house of entertainment in the reign of Charles II. The tea-gardens and grounds were extensive, and elegantly fitted up. The house was probably called "The World's End" on account of its then considerable distance from London, and the bad state of the roads and pathways leading to it. It figures in a dialogue in Congreve's "Love for Love" in a manner which implies that it bore no very high character.

At the commencement of the present century, the King's Road was a very different place from what it is now. The line of road was almost exclusively occupied by nurserymen and florists, and it became, in consequence, to a certain extent, a fashionable resort for the nobility and gentry. The road, in most parts, was very narrow, and the different grounds were mostly enclosed in wooden palings. At night there were only a few gloomy oil-lamps, and the lives and property of the inhabitants were principally entrusted to a small number of private watchmen. Northward of the King's Road, at no very distant date, a considerable extent of land, stretching away to the Fulham Road, was a vast open heath, known as Chelsea Common. Standing in the central space, which has, singularly enough, been left as a memorial of the old common, and looking at the streets now branching off in various directions, it is not easy to call up visions of the past—say two hundred years ago—when this locality was probably as agreeable a spot as Clapham or Wimbledon Commons in our own time.

Faulkner conjectures that the Fulham Road formed the north boundary of the common, and on the south it reached to some nursery grounds abutting on the King's Road, which said nursery grounds, one may conjecture, had been cut off the common by some party or parties in the days when land boundaries were not always kept with care. Westward, the common must have extended about to the line of Robert and Sydney Streets, and eastward to "Blackland's Lane," as it was first called, afterwards Marlborough Road; or perhaps originally the common was bounded by the road or lane which is now Sloane Street. It is first spoken of as "Chelsea Heath," and it appears to have been covered, at least in part, with heath and furze, therein resembling some of the Surrey commons. One of the earliest records concerning Chelsea Common tells us the fact that the City train-bands used to repair to it for exercise, and that, in the disturbed times of Charles I., reviews of troops were more than once held there.

This common was used in former times as a means of raising money for the benefit of the parish. We have particulars relating to such a usage as far back as the reign of Charles II., when the re-building of the church having been resolved upon, Lord Lindsey, Charles Cheyne, and those interested in the common, agreed to enclose it for twenty-one years, the term commencing in March, 1674. On the expiration in 1695, the ground was again thrown open. Somewhat more than a century later—namely, in 1713—articles were drawn up, Sir Hans Sloane being then lord of the manor, in which, amid sundry other recitals, it is stated that the ground at Chelsea Common having been put to various unlawful uses, the holders decide to let it for three years to one John Hugget. It was stipulated that he was to fence the common "with a good bank and a ditch all around," which it is probable that he did, to the satisfaction of all parties, as he had his term renewed from time to time.

An Act passed in the reign of George I., which empowered the surveyor of the London roads to dig up gravel on any common or waste land convenient to him, gave rise to some disputes in Chelsea. The parties interested in the common were informed that much gravel had been removed from Chelsea, and they objected to this, but the Government paid little heed to the complaint. The agents of the surveyor were warned off, though not expelled by physical force; and they went away for awhile, to come back at the next good opportunity. This matter was not finally settled till 1736; for some years previous to that, however, a regular account was kept of all the gravel removed, and payment demanded (and obtained) from those who kept the roads. It was also in the early part of the eighteenth century that an enterprising individual, probably short of money, set up an experimental turnpike on part of the waste ground on the common near Blackland's Lane. The Chelsea authorities fined him heavily, and his scheme was forthwith abandoned.

It was not until some years after an Act had been obtained for the purpose, that the first streets were formed on what had been Chelsea Common. The earliest building lease appears to bear date in 1790, being to the Hon. George Cadogan. The streets, square, grove (for there is at least one of

* See page 21, ante.

each of these—Marlborough Square and White-head's Grove), and the bye-lanes, display all the variety to be expected under the circumstances, as a number of men took sites of very different sizes, and no general plan was attempted to be carried out.

About the spot now occupied by Pond Place, there were, as may be conjectured, one or more ponds, which supplied water to the cattle grazing on the common. It is worthy of being remembered that William Curtis, the botanist, once lived in Pond Place ; he was originally an apothecary's assistant, but his fondness for botany led him to give himself entirely to its study, as soon as his means allowed him. He was one of the pioneers in the formation of those Natural History Societies which have spread themselves in every part of our islands ; and his "Botanical Magazine," begun in 1787, met with a sale which in that day was looked upon as something remarkable. Curtis at first opened a botanical garden in Lambeth Marsh, and subsequently removed his collection of plants to a nursery-ground at Queen's Elm, Brompton.

Two noted nurseries in the King's Road abutted on Chelsea Common, which were favourite resorts in the reign of George III. and later. Colvill's nursery, at the end of Blackland's Lane, had, at the beginning of the present century, what was considered a large and splendid conservatory, in which the visitor was told there might be counted five hundred species of geranium. Also, there was a green-house, specially arranged so as to show the mode of growth of exotic parasitical plants. The memory of this nursery was kept up by "Colvill Terrace," now extinguished by the uniform numbering of the King's Road. To the west of that ground was Davey's nursery, also fronting the King's Road.

Beyond these nursery-grounds, and also surrounding Chelsea Common on the south side, were large orchards ; but these shared the fate of the waste land, and are now, for the most part, covered with houses. Jubilee Place was built about 1810, and doubtless received its name in memory of the attainment by George III. of the fiftieth year of his sovereignty. King Street, too, in the immediate locality, we may suppose received its name in honour of that particular monarch. Russell Street was originally called Wellesley Street, a name meant to do honour to a family bearing an illustrious name, which, as we have already stated, once furnished Chelsea with a rector. The names of Marlborough, Blenheim, and College Street, applied to some of the streets and places hereabouts, may perhaps lead to the belief that they were so named by persons who have had to do with the Royal Hospital.

Chelsea Park, also situated on the north side of the King's Road, was part of the property of Sir Thomas More. It originally consisted of about thirty acres, and was enclosed with a brick wall, but this has gradually given way to the erection of buildings. Towards the beginning of the last century a manufactory for raw silk was established here, and a number of mulberry-trees were planted for the purpose, but the scheme proved unsuccessful. Park Walk, which now crosses this locality from the King's Road to Fulham Road, appears in old maps as "Lover's Walk," and was planted with trees. The "Goat in Boots" is the sign of a public-house at the end of Park Walk, in the Fulham Road. It is said that the old sign was painted by George Morland, in order to liquidate a bill incurred during a residence here. In old deeds the inn is called simply "The Goat."

A short distance eastward, at the corner of Upper Church Street, is the Queen's Elm Hotel, which keeps in remembrance a story traditionally told respecting the Virgin Queen. The tavern is mentioned in the parish books of Chelsea as far back as 1667, under the name of the Queen's Tree, and the tradition is that it derived its name from the fact of Queen Elizabeth, on her way to or from a visit to Lord Burleigh at Brompton Hall, being caught in a shower of rain, and taking shelter under the branches of a wide-spreading and friendly elm which grew on the spot. The Queen's Elm, it may be added, is mentioned in the parish books of Chelsea as far back as the year 1586, where it is stated that "the tree at the end of Duke's Walk, in Chelsea parish, is called the Queen's Tree," and that "there was an arbour built round it by one Bostocke, at the charge of the parish." There was formerly a turnpike-gate at Queen's Elm ; and "a court of guard" there is mentioned among the defences around London that were ordered to be prepared by the Parliament in 1642.

The Jews' burial-ground, situate at Queen's Elm, was formed, early in the present century, on a piece of land purchased for that purpose. Much of the ground hereabouts, now known as West Brompton, was in former times called the hamlet of Little Chelsea. Towards the end of the seventeenth century, Lord Shaftesbury, the author of "Characteristics," purchased an estate here. He rebuilt the house, and generally resided there during the sitting of Parliament. Locke here wrote part of his "Essay," and Addison several of the "Spectators." Of Lord Shaftesbury's letters there are several extant, dated from Chelsea, in 1708. The mansion was subsequently converted into an additional workhouse for the parish of St. George, Hanover Square.

Mrs. S. Carter Hall, in her "Pilgrimages to English Shrines," gives us the following account of Shaftesbury House:—"The lodge at the entrance, as you see, is peculiar, the gate being of old wrought iron. The porter permitted us to pass in; and while he sought the master, we had leisure to look around us. The stone steps are of old times: they are wide, and much worn; a low wall flanks either side; and on the right, downwards, are steps of narrower dimensions leading to the underground apartments. When we entered, we perceived that the hall is panelled in, so as to form a passage; but this is a modern innovation; there can be no doubt of its having been, in Lord Shaftesbury's time, a good-sized hall; the banisters and supporters of the very handsome staircase are in admirable preservation, delicately rather than richly carved in oak, and not at all injured; the stairs are also of oak. What remains of the old house is chopped up, as it were, into small apartments, but there are rich and varied indications of the 'light of other days' to illumine the whole. Over several of the doors are strips of paintings, which, as well as can be seen through thick varnish, are the productions of no feeble pencil. With a little trouble these old paintings can be made out, but they would seem bitter mockeries, occupied as the house at present is; and yet one of the inmates said, 'She liked to look up at that bit of picture when she was sick a-bed: it took away the notion of a workhouse.' Surely art might be made even a teacher here. Some of the rooms retain an antique air."

In 1733, a workhouse was erected on a piece of ground "near the conduit in the King's Road," which had been given by Sir Hans Sloane. Over the chimney-piece was a picture, by a Flemish painter, of a woman spinning thread, with the legend, "Waste not, want not."

A noted resident in Little Chelsea, at the commencement of the last century, was Sir John Cope, so famous in the rebellion of 1745. His house, having been subsequently used as a private asylum, was pulled down; on its site Odell's Place was erected. Mr. Robert Boyle, the distinguished philosopher and chemist, a son of Richard, Earl of Cork, resided here in 1660. Here he was visited by the learned and eminent of his time—amongst others, by M. de Monconys, who, in his "Travels," after informing us how that, after dinner, he went with his son and Mr. Oldenburg "two miles from London in a stage-coach, for five shillings, to a village called Little Chelsea, to visit Mr. Boyle," gives an account of several experiments which that gentleman made in his presence, and then proceeds: —"He has a very fine laboratory, where he makes all his extracts and other operations, one of which he showed me with salt, which being put in quite dry with gold leaves sixteen times thicker than that used by gilders into a crucible on a slow fire, even over a lighted candle, the salt calcined the gold so perfectly that water afterwards dissolved them both and became impregnated with them, in the same manner as with common salt." Evelyn, in his "Diary," has also recorded a visit to the same place. "I went," he writes, "with that excellent person and philosopher, Sir Robert Murray, to visit Mr. Boyle at Chelsea, and saw divers effects of the Eolipile, for weighing air."

Charles, fourth Earl of Orrery, grand-nephew of Mr. Boyle, was born at Little Chelsea in 1676. He was the improver of an instrument or machine which had been constructed for the purpose of exhibiting the motions of the planets round the sun, and which henceforth was called the Orrery, in his honour; the instrument, which was held in high repute in the last century, is, however, now regarded as little more than an ingenious toy. Edward Hyde, third Earl of Clarendon, died at his house at Little Chelsea in 1723.

Another resident of this part of Chelsea, at the beginning of the present century, was Mr. Adrian Haworth, the eminent entomologist and botanist, author of "Lepidoptera Britannica," "Miscellanea Naturalia," and other important works. He was a native of Hull, lived to a great age, and here he died.

But even greater names are connected with Chelsea. Within only a short distance from where we are now, stood the abodes of Pym, Locke, Addison, Steele, Swift, and Atterbury; and the extinct hamlet of Little Chelsea was gilded by the greater lights of the Augustan age of British literature.

That part of Church Street which lies between the King's Road and the river has in its time had some distinguished residents. The thoroughfare itself appears to have been built at a very early period. Here, for several years, lived Dr. Atterbury, afterwards Bishop of Rochester, whose committal to the Tower on suspicion of being concerned in a plot in favour of the Pretender was one of the principal events at the commencement of the last century. It was whilst living here that Dr. Atterbury became acquainted with Dean Swift, who, in 1711, took up his residence opposite the doctor's house. Previous to becoming a resident at Chelsea,

Swift was a frequenter of its rural scenes. He writes, in May, 1711 :—" I leave my best gown and periwig at Mrs. Van Homrigh's (in Suffolk Street),* then walk up Pall Mall, out at Buckingham House, and so to Chelsea, a little beyond the church.   I

The old "White Horse" inn, in this street, which was burnt down some years since—a new one being substituted for it—was a very ancient structure, built in the Tudor style of architecture.   The house was rich in ancient panelling, together with

CHELSEA CHURCH, 1860.   (See page 58.)

set out about sunset, and get there in something less than an hour; it is two good miles, and just 5,748 steps."

Shadwell, the poet laureate of the seventeenth century, was another inhabitant of Church Street or Church Lane.   He lived in a house which had been previously occupied by Dr. Arbuthnot.

grotesque ornaments and carving, in the form of brackets.   In the principal room, which was large, and consequently well adapted for such a purpose, the old Parochial Guardian Society mostly held its meetings.

Another remarkable old inn in the same street was the "Black Lion," which was situated opposite the rectory garden wall, and was pulled down a few years ago to make room for the present

* See Vol. IV., p. 227.

OLD CHELSEA IN 1750.

1. The Clock House.   2. The Moravian Chapel.   3. The White Horse Inn.

tavern, which still retains the name. It is supposed that the old tavern was in its full glory during the reign of Charles II.; for, in an old house situated at the corner of Danvers Street, coeval with it, was an old pump, which the present proprietor, who has resided there for sixty years, recently pulled down. It bore the date of 1697 on a leaden panel of the pump. The old tea-gardens was, no doubt, the resort of the many fashionable families which lived in the neighbourhood; and attached to it was an extensive bowling-green for those who enjoyed that fashionable game.

At the bottom of Church Lane, close by the old church in Lombard Street, lived, during the last twelve years of his life, Mr. Henry Sampson Woodfall, whose name was brought prominently before the public as the printer of the celebrated " Letters of Junius." He used jocularly to say to his Chelsea friends that he had been *fined* and *confined* by the Court of King's Bench, fined by the Houses of Lords and Commons, and indicted at the Old Bailey.

Mr. W. Lewis, bookbinder, the intimate friend of Dr. Smollett, and his fellow-companion whilst journeying from Edinburgh to London, lived for many years in this street. Lewis figures in the novel of " Roderick Random," under the character of " Strap the Barber." The description of the hero of the novel and of Strap, upon their arrival in London, and of their escapes from dangers and impositions, must be familiar to all who have read that work.

Danvers Street takes its name from Danvers Gardens, on the site of which it was built in the latter end of the seventeenth century. Danvers House adjoined, if it was not actually part of, the property of Sir Thomas More, or that of his son-in-law, Roper. Sir John Danvers, who possessed this property early in the reign of Elizabeth, is said to have first introduced into this country the Italian method of horticulture, of which his garden, as represented by Kip, was a beautiful specimen. Danvers House passed from the Danvers family to the first Marquis of Wharton, in the reign of Queen Anne. The house was pulled down early in the last century.

Justice Walk, which extends from Church Street to Lawrence Street, was so named from a magistrate who lived in it. An avenue of lime-trees formerly adorned it, and rendered it an agreeable promenade for strollers. In this thoroughfare there is a commodious Wesleyan Chapel, built in 1841. The exterior is plain and unpretending; and beneath the chapel is a spacious school-room. The old Wesleyan Chapel of Chelsea was of some anti-

quity, and deserves mention as one of the favourite places of the founder of that community. In its pulpit John Wesley preached for the last time on February 18th, 1791, a fortnight before his death.

Several houses at the corner of Justice Walk and Lawrence Street were formerly used as the show-rooms and manufactory of Chelsea china. The whole of the premises were pulled down towards the close of the last century, and new houses erected on the site. " The manufactory of Chelsea porcelain," says Mr. Faulkner, in his work already quoted, " was set on foot and carried on by a Mr. Spremont, a foreigner. The establishment employed a great number of hands; but the original proprietor, having acquired a large fortune, retired from the concern; and his successors, wanting his enterprise and spirit, did not so well succeed, and in a few years finally abandoned it. Previous to the dissolution of the establishment, the proprietors presented a memorial respecting it to the Government, requesting protection and assistance, in which they stated that 'the manufacture in England has been carried on by great labour and a large expense; it is in many respects to the full as good as the Dresden; and the late Duke of Orleans told Colonel York that the metal or earth had been tried in his furnace, and was found to be the best made in Europe. It is now daily improving, and already employs at least one hundred hands, of which is a nursery of thirty lads, taken from the parishes and charity schools, and bred to designing and painting—arts very much wanted here, and which are of the greatest use in our silk and printed linen manufactories.' Specimens of this porcelain have always been much esteemed, and still retain a great value. At the sale of the effects of Queen Charlotte, the articles in Chelsea china, of which her Majesty had a large collection, brought very high prices." It is recorded that Dr. Johnson had conceived a notion that he was capable of improving on the manufacture of china. He even applied to the directors of the Chelsea China Works, and was allowed to *bake* his compositions in their ovens in Lawrence Street. He was accordingly accustomed to go down with his housekeeper, about twice a week, and stay the whole day, she carrying a basket of provisions with her. The doctor, who was not allowed to enter the *mixing* room, had access to every other part of the premises, and formed his composition in a particular apartment, without being overlooked by any one. He had also free access to the oven, and superintended the whole of the process; but he completely failed, both as to composition and baking, for his materials always yielded to the intensity of the heat, while those of the Company came out of the furnace perfect and complete. Dr. Johnson retired in disgust, but not in despair, for he afterwards gave a dissertation on this very subject in his works.

Chelsea china seems to have been manufactured as far back as the reign of Queen Anne, but was not brought out to anything like perfection till the reign of George II. He and the Duke of Cumberland were the great patrons of the Chelsea China Works, and took much interest in promoting the success of this interesting manufacture. Beaumont painted some of the best landscapes on it; Nollekens' father worked there; and Sir James Thornhill was also employed in designing for it. The clay for the Chelsea china was brought from China by merchant captains, who procured it ostensibly for ballast. The productions of the Chelsea furnaces were thought worthy to vie with those of the celebrated manufactories of Germany. Walpole, in his correspondence with Sir Horace Mann, mentions a service of Chelsea porcelain sent by the King and Queen to the Duke of Mecklenburg, which cost £1,200. Possibly, it was in order to encourage the manufacture that George II. had his coffee-pot of Chelsea china on board the royal yacht. It was evidently *made* for the ship, as it has "ship" burnt in at the bottom. In Mr. Forster's notes to the catalogue of the sale at Stowe, in 1848—where the finest specimens of "rare old china," a pair of small vases, painted with Roman triumphs, sold for £23 10s.—it is stated that George II. brought over artificers from Brunswick and Saxony; whence, probably, M. Brongniart terms Chelsea a "Manufacture Royale." In 1745 the celebrity of Chelsea porcelain was regarded with jealousy by the manufacturers of France, who, therefore, petitioned Louis XV. to concede to them exclusive privileges.

Chelsea ware has always held a high rank among the varieties of English pottery. It reached its perfection about the year 1750; some fifteen years later, owing to the influx of foreign china, and the death of the director of the Chelsea works, Spremont, the workmen were transferred to Derby, where afterwards arose the celebrated Chelsea-Derby manufacture, which marked the first twenty years of the reign of George III., and of which Dr. Johnson remarked that it was "very beautiful, but nearly as dear as silver."

Lawrence Street derives its name from having been erected on the site of the residence of the Lawrence family, which flourished here in the days of bluff King Hal. It is uncertain when this family first settled in Chelsea; but as the "Lawrence Chapel," in the old parish church, is built in the style of architecture which prevailed at the beginning of the fourteenth century, it was probably about that period, or, at all events, some time before they purchased the old manor house. At the "great house" in this street—commonly called Monmouth House—lived Ann, Duchess of Monmouth and Buccleuch, widow of James, Duke of Monmouth. Gay was for some time secretary to the duchess, as stated in Johnson's Life of the poet. Dr. Tobias Smollett afterwards resided in the same house.

A view of the old mansion, which was taken down in 1833, and a fac-simile of an autograph letter, dated thence in 1756, and addressed to Richardson, the actor, are to be seen in Smith's "Historical and Literary Curiosities." The letter is of more than ordinary interest, as Smollett writes thus frankly on a literary subject :—" I was extremely concerned to find myself suspected of a silly, mean insinuation against Mr. Richardson's writings, which appeared some time ago in the *Critical Review;* and I desired my friend, Mr. Millar, to assure you, in my name, that it was inserted without my privity or concurrence." It is pleasant to know that this frank letter was received as kindly as it was intended, and that one of those many " Quarrels of Authors," which have afforded subjects without end to satirists and essayists, was thus avoided. Smollett has immortalised this spot by making it the scene of one of the chapters in his " Humphrey Clinker." Here Smollett wrote his " Adventures of Ferdinand, Count Fathom," the " Reprisals, or the Tars of Old England," and his continuation of Hume's " History of England." He was editor of the *Briton,* a paper set up to support Lord Bute's ministry, and which Wilkes answered by his celebrated *North Briton.*

Between Lawrence Street and Church Street, in former times, was the stabling for the old Chelsea stage-coaches. The fare for inside passengers was 1s. 6d.; outside, 1s.; and no intermediate fare of a lower sum was taken. Such are the changes, however, brought about by the " whirligig of time," that passengers can now go almost from one extremity of London to the other for sixpence, and Chelsea can now be reached by steamboat for the moderate sum of twopence.

Besides the residents in this part of Chelsea in former times, of whom we have already spoken, a few more remain to be mentioned. Sir Richard Steele occupied a house not far from the waterside. In a letter to Lady Steele, dated 14th of February, 1716, Sir Richard writes :—" Mr. Fuller and I came hither to dine in the air, but the mail has been so slow that we are benighted, and chuse to lie here rather than go this road in the dark. I lie at our own house, and my friend at a relation's in the town." Addison, Steele's coadjutor on the *Spectator*, lived for some time close by. Macaulay says that he (Addison) enjoyed nothing so much as the quiet and seclusion of his villa at Chelsea.

At the house of a clergyman here, Mrs. Darby, the mother of Mary Robinson, better known as "Perdita," took up her home, with her children, on being deserted by her husband at Bristol. Soon afterwards she opened a girls' school in the neighbourhood, in which she was aided by her daughter.

In 1823, Mrs. Somerville went to live in Chelsea, her husband being appointed Physician to Chelsea Hospital. She speaks of it as a "dreary and unhealthy situation," and adds that she suffered from sick headaches all the time. Here she numbered among her friends and visitors Lady Noel Byron and her daughter Ada, the Napiers, Maria Edgeworth, Lady Bunbury, and Sir James Mackintosh. Here Gilray, the caricaturist, is supposed to have been born, in 1757. We have already spoken of the unfortunate career of this celebrity in our account of St. James's Street.*

John Pym, a distinguished member of the House of Commons in the seventeenth century, resided here for several years. Count D'Estrades, who came to England to negotiate the sale of Dunkirk, as ambassador from Louis XIV., fixed his abode at Chelsea during the years 1661 and 1662. "It was usual for the foreign ambassadors at that time to make their public entry from the Tower of London, but on this occasion the king sent his own coaches to Chelsea to carry the ambassador, and the count was accompanied by the equipages of the whole of the foreign diplomatic corps at that time in London."†

The Rev. David Williams, the founder of the Royal Literary Fund,‡ lived here for some time, keeping a school. Here he had Franklin for a guest at the time when the American philosopher was subjected to the abuse of Wedderburn before the Privy Council.

Besides its literary celebrities, Chelsea has also had its heroines, of whom mention of one or two will suffice. In the year 1739 was interred, in the College burying-ground, Christian Davies, *alias* Mother Ross, who, according to her own narrative, served in several campaigns under King William and the Duke of Marlborough, and behaved with signal bravery. During the latter portion of her life she resided here, her third husband being a pensioner in the college. At this time she subsisted, as she tells us, principally on the benevolence of "the quality" at Court, whither she went twice a week in a hackney-coach, old age and infirmities having rendered her unable to walk.

The famous Hannah Snell, whose history is recorded in various publications of the year 1750, was actually at that time put upon the out-pensioners' list at Chelsea, on account of the wounds which she received at the siege of Pondicherry. Her singular story excited a considerable share of public attention, and she was engaged to sing and perform the military exercises at various places of public entertainment; some time afterwards she married one Eyles, a carpenter, at Newbury. A lady of fortune, who admired the heroism and eccentricity of her conduct, having honoured her with particular notice, became godmother to her son, and contributed liberally to his education. Mrs. Eyles, to the day of her death, continued to receive her pension, which, in the year 1786, was augmented by a special grant to a shilling a day. In the latter part of her life she discovered symptoms of insanity, and was admitted a patient into Bethlehem Hospital, where she died in 1792.

In Smith Street died, in 1855, Mr. Thomas Faulkner, bookseller, the author of "Histories of Chelsea, Hammersmith, Putney, and Fulham," &c. As a topographer he contributed in the number of his works probably more than any other person to the illustration of the history and antiquities of the western parts of Middlesex, and had his powers of combination and comparison been equal to his industry and perseverance, his labours would have been truly valuable. He began his literary career in 1797, by communications to the *Gentleman's Magazine*, in which, for more than half a century, he occasionally wrote essays and reviews. His contributions also frequently appeared in various volumes of the early series of the *New Monthly Magazine*.

Returning to the King's Road, we may here state that the house adjoining the entrance to the Moravian Chapel and burial-ground, at the north end of Milman's Row, and some few years since pulled down, was for many years in the occupation of the Howard family, of the Society of Friends. The elder Mr. Howard was gardener to Sir Hans Sloane; his brother, having a natural genius for mechanics, became a clockmaker, and made the clock in the old parish church, in 1761, for £50. In front of Howard's house was placed a large clock, and hence the building came to be known as

---

* See Vol. IV., p. 167. † Faulkner's "History of Chelsea."
‡ See Vol. IV., p. 543.

the "Clock-house," a name now applied to what was once the Moravian chapel.

A plot of land behind the old Clock-house formed part of what was formerly Queen Elizabeth's nursery-ground, and on it still exists a mulberry-tree said to have been planted by that queen.

At No. 178, King's Road, was established in 1871 the Chelsea Hospital for Diseases of Women. The institution is open gratuitously to those without means, small fees for medical treatment being required from such as can afford to pay. In 1883 this hospital was removed to a new building near the Queen's Elm, in Fulham Road.

On the south side of the King's Road, nearly opposite Robert Street and the Workhouse, is the Vestry Hall, a handsome and spacious building in the Italian style, constructed of red brick with stone dressings. It was built from the designs of Mr. W. Pocock. A portion of the building is occupied by the Chelsea Literary and Scientific Institution, for the use of which a rental is paid. The whole interior is well arranged and admirably adapted for the requirements of the parish. Adjoining the Vestry Hall are some commodious swimming-baths, which were constructed under the superintendence of Mr. E. Perrett, the designer of the floating-baths at Charing Cross.

In Markham Square, abutting on the King's Road, is the Chelsea Congregational Church. The edifice stands in a very prominent position, and covers a large piece of ground. The form of the building is slightly cruciform, having transepts projecting about five feet from the body of the chapel. The prominent feature of the exterior is a tower and spire, rising from the west side of the southern transept to the height of about 130 feet. The style of the building is in the second period of the Gothic, and the exterior is constructed entirely of stone. There are lofty and spacious school-rooms, with the requisite offices, beneath the chapel.

In the Royal Avenue, a turning on the south side of the road leading towards the Royal Hospital, a skating-rink was formed about 1875, having an area of about 3,000 square yards, laid with Green and King's patent ice.

At the eastern end of the King's Road is Sloane Square, which, together with Sloane Street and Hans Place, all bear testimony to the memory of the eminent physician, Sir Hans Sloane, of whom we have already had occasion to speak.* In 1712 Sir Hans Sloane bought the manor of Chelsea, to which he retired thirty years later, having resigned his public offices and employments. Thither he removed his museum, and there he received the visits of the royal family and persons of high rank, learned foreigners, and distinguished literary and scientific men ; nor did he refuse admittance and advice to either rich or poor who went to consult him respecting their health. At ninety his health began to decline sensibly, and he died here, at the age of ninety-two, in January, 1753.

In the early part of the present century, the houses around Sloane Square were nearly the same in appearance as at the present time ; but the square was an open space, simply enclosed with wooden posts, connected by iron chains. Here Queen Charlotte's Royal Volunteers often assembled, and marched off in military order to Hyde Park, headed by their band. On the eastern side of the square, at that time, was the bridge, of which we have already spoken,† called Bloody Bridge. It was about twelve or fourteen feet wide, and had on either side a wall of sufficient height to protect passengers from falling into the narrow rivulet which it spanned, and which belonged to the Commissioners of Sewers. In old records this structure is called "Blandel Bridge ;" and it probably received its more sanguinary appellation in consequence of the numerous robberies and murders formerly committed on the spot. In more recent times it has assumed the name of "Grosvenor Bridge," from the extensive adjoining property of the Grosvenors.

In 1812 the Chelsea, Brompton, and Belgrave Dispensary was established in Sloane Square, principally through the great exertions of the Rev. George Clark, the then chaplain of the Royal Military Asylum. The objects of the institution, as officially set forth, are "the relief of sick poor (not paupers), the delivery of married women at their own homes, and attention to diseases of women and children." Mr. William Wilberforce, whose name will be for ever associated with the abolition of slavery, took a leading part in the foundation of the dispensary. The earliest annual average of patients relieved at this admirable institution did not exceed 1,200 ; the number benefited yearly amounts now to nearly 7,000.

The Royal Court Theatre, in this square, was opened in January, 1871, for the performance of comedies, farces, and the lighter order of dramas. The building, which was originally erected in the year 1818 as a chapel, replaced a theatre at the beginning, and, singularly enough, the chapel has been replaced by a theatre at its close. The station on the Metropolitan District Railway, close

* See Vol. IV., p. 490.   † See p. 21, ante.

by, doubtless confers great advantages on the surrounding neighbourhood.

At the beginning of the present century considerable addition was made to the parish of Chelsea by the erection of houses in this direction, and most of the new buildings were called Hans Town. Sloane Street is a long and wide thoroughfare, running from north to south, and connecting Knightsbridge with the west part of Pimlico and the east end of

liberality of several beneficent gentlemen, among whom may be named Mr. Joseph Butterworth, who at that time resided principally at Chelsea.

At No. 72, Sloane Street, lived, for many years, Sir Charles Wentworth Dilke, Bart. In early life Sir Charles was associated with the literary labours of his father, who was the chief proprietor, and at one time editor, of the *Athenæum* newspaper. He was one of the earliest promoters of the first Great

THE " BLACK LION," CHURCH STREET, CHELSEA, IN 1820. (*See page* 90.)

Chelsea. On the east side the houses are made to recede, so as to form three sides of a square, called Cadogan Place, of which we have already spoken.* At the south end of Sloane Street, near the square, is Trinity Church, of which the Rev. Henry Blunt was the first incumbent. The edifice, which was consecrated in 1830, is a brick building of Gothic architecture. The western front consists of a centre, flanked by two wide towers rising to a level with the roof, and terminating with lofty octagonal spires. Sittings are provided for about 1,500 worshippers. Sloane Terrace Wesleyan Chapel, which dates from 1811, is a neat and substantial building, and its erection is attributed to the

Exhibition, and, indeed, took a leading share in the work of the Executive Committee. For the ability he displayed in that capacity, the honour of knighthood was offered to him, at the suggestion of the late Prince Consort. This honour, however, he declined, together with all pecuniary remuneration. Mr. Dilke was likewise associated with the second Industrial Exhibition, as one of the five Royal Commissioners appointed by Her Majesty. Almost immediately after the death of the Prince Consort, Her Majesty was pleased to confer a baronetcy on Mr. Dilke, " in recognition of the Prince's friendship and personal regard for him." Sir Charles was M.P. for the borough of Wallingford for a short time, and died in 1869 at St. Petersburg. His son and successor was

* See p. 13, *ante.*

elected in 1868 as one of the first members for the newly-enfranchised constituency of Chelsea. He is the author of a work on "Greater Britain," and of pamphlets on social and political topics, and a member of the Gladstone ministry.

At No. 31 is the Ladies' Work Society, an institution established for the sale of needlework, embroidery, and other articles, the production of ladies in necessitous circumstances. Its president

of the good work it was doing, so that now (1876), under its royal patronage and presidency, the number of members, which at first were 200, have increased to 1,000.

No. 103 is the Hans Town School of Industry for Girls. This institution was founded in the year 1804, and its special object is the training of young girls for servants. A sum of two guineas is charged on admission, and the number of children

THE PAVILION, HANS PLACE, IN 1800. (*See page* 99.)

is her Royal Highness the Princess Louise (Marchioness of Lorne), who herself has designed much of the ornamental work. The institution was established in the year 1871, in North Audley Street, and removed hither in 1875. The members of the society can do their work at home, and send it to Sloane Street for sale—the name of the exhibitors being known only to the ladies who form the committee. An annual subscription of 7s. 6d. constitutes a membership; and when an article is sold at the price set upon it by the exhibitor, a penny in the shilling is deducted towards defraying the necessary expenses of the establishment. In the earlier period of its career the society had a somewhat hard struggle for existence, but it gradually grew in proportion to the publicity given

benefited by this institution amounts to about fifty annually.

In this street the arch-impostor, Count Cagliostro, was living in the year 1786, when he published his celebrated "Letter to the English People," so cruelly criticised by M. de Morande, the editor of the *Courrier de l'Europe*, and thus defended by himself in the *Public Advertiser*, under date September 3rd, 1786 :—"In physics and chemistry, Mr. Joker, arguments go for little and sneers for nothing—experience is all. Permit me, then, to propose a little experiment, which will divert the public, either at your expense or at mine. I invite you to breakfast for the 9th November next, at nine o'clock in the morning : you will furnish the wine and the accessories ; I will furnish one dish in my own style—a little sucking pig, fattened according to my method. Two hours before breakfast I will present him to you alive, fat, and healthy. You will engage to have him killed and cooked, and I will not go near him till the moment when he is put on the table; you shall cut him yourself into four pieces, choose that which attracts you the most, and give me any piece you please. The day after this breakfast one of four things will have happened : either we shall be both dead or both alive, or I shall be dead and you alive, or you dead and I alive. Out of these four chances I give you three, and I bet 5,000 guineas that the day after the breakfast you will be dead and I shall be in good health. You will confess that no fairer offer could be made, and that you must either accept the wager or confess your ignorance, and that you have foolishly and dully cut your jokes upon a subject beyond your knowledge." This characteristic letter failed to persuade M. de Morande to breakfast, and he was fain to back out as best he might, getting well laughed at for his pains.

Count Cagliostro—or, to give him his proper name, Joseph Balsamo—used to advertise in the London newspapers that he was prepared to sell "the Egyptian pill of life at thirty shillings a dram;" doubtless about as efficacious as the preparation called "mummy," which was actually dispensed as a curative for sores, by physicians duly provided with diplomas, so late as the reign of Queen Anne. Cagliostro's doings as a quack of quacks took place just after the "diamond necklace" affair; and through the bursting of that bubble he was temporarily "down on his luck." No legal proceedings were taken against him in England, but subsequently he went to Rome, where he was flung into prison by the Inquisition, not, oddly enough, because he was a charlatan— the Piazza Navona and the Corso swarmed every day with vendors of Elixirs of Life and Love—but because he pretended to be a spirit-rapper. A very different state of things prevails at the present day in our own country.

The following story, having reference to this particular street, we give for what it is worth :— "I had invited Porson," says an English author, "to meet a party of friends in Sloane Street, where I lived; but the eccentric professor had mistaken the day, and made his appearance in full costume the preceding one. We had already dined, and were at our cheese. When he discovered his error, he made his usual exclamation of a *whooe!* as long as my arm, and turning to me, with great gravity, said, 'I advise you in future, sir, when you

ask your friends to dinner, to ask your wife to write your cards. Sir, your penmanship is abominable; it would disgrace a cobbler. I swear that your day is written Thursday, not Friday,' at the same time pulling the invitation out of his pocket. It turned out, however, that he was wrong, which he was obliged to admit."

Towards the commencement of the century, a considerable part of Sloane Street, between the square and Cadogan Place, was laid out as a botanical garden by a Mr. Salisbury. The extent of the grounds was about six acres, and at one time formed an agreeable promenade for company.

At the corner of Cadogan Place and Lowndes Street is Chelsea House, the town residence of Earl Cadogan, whose family formerly had a mansion on the site of the Royal Military Asylum. The house was rebuilt in 1874, from the designs of Mr. W. Young. The principal entrance, in Cadogan Place, is marked by a tetrastyle portico, which is carried up to the first floor as a bay window; another bay window on the same front is carried up two storeys, and finished with balustrades. The front to Lowndes Street has a semi-octagonal bay at each end, carried up the whole height of the building. The ground storey is of rustic stonework, and at the level of the first floor is a stone balcony carried all round the building. The drawing-room windows, which are well studied in proportion and design, have a most imposing effect. The chief rooms are large and lofty, and the principal staircase is of Sicilian marble.

The manor and estate of Chelsea came into the possession of Lord Cadogan's family on the death of Mr. Hans Sloane by his own hand, Charles, second Lord Cadogan, having married Elizabeth, the daughter and co-heir of Sir Hans Sloane. It may be noted here that Horace Walpole was one of the trustees under Sir Hans Sloane's will.

On the west side of the street, in Cadogan Terrace, is the Roman Catholic Chapel of St. Mary's, an unpretending structure, dating from 1811, and one of the oldest of the missionary chapels of that religion. Not far from the chapel are the convent and schools, together with a Roman Catholic burial-ground, with some large vaults and catacombs. The chapel itself was built by M. Voyaux de Franous, one of the French *émigré* clergy. Before its erection, mass was said in a room above a shop. The Duchess of Angoulême was a generous contributor to the building, and laid the first stone. Dr. Poynter, then Vicar-Apostolic of the London district, officiated at the consecration. Poor as the building was, it cost £6,000. It was specially designed for the use of the French veterans confined at Chelsea. Among the assistant clergy here were Cardinal Weld, the late Bishop of Troy, Dr. Cox, Mgr. Eyre, and Bishop Patterson. St. Mary's Church has been lately improved and enlarged.

In Cadogan Street stood formerly an ancient house, which, in its latter days, was known as the "Marlborough Tavern;" the grounds adjoining were used for the purposes of cricket, &c. It is probable that the house was first established as a tavern during the lifetime of the great Duke of Marlborough, who, it is said, at one time resided in Chelsea, though his house is not identified. Marlborough Road, Blenheim Street, &c.—all contiguous in this neighbourhood—doubtless hence received their names. The old "Admiral Keppel" tavern, with its tea-gardens, in Marlborough Road, was demolished in 1856, and on its site a large inn has been erected.

Hans Place, at the north-west corner, between Sloane Street and Brompton Road, is an irregular octagonal space, laid out after the fashion of a London square. Here (at the house No. 25, according to Mr. Peter Cunningham) was born, in August, 1802, Miss Letitia E. Landon, the "L. E. L." of "Annual" celebrity. She went to school three doors off (No. 22), under a Miss Rowden, the same who numbered amongst her pupils Miss Mary R. Mitford. Miss Landon was the daughter of an army agent, and niece of the late Dr. Whittington Landon, Dean of Exeter and Provost of Worcester College, Oxford, who took a sincere interest in the welfare and fame of his relative. Having had the misfortune to lose her father when very young, and her brilliant talents soon becoming manifest, she appeared before the world, while little more than a child, as an enthusiastic and delightful literary labourer. Her first efforts were made in the pages of the *Literary Gazette.* "To her honour, it must be added," says the editor of the *Athenæum,* "that the fruits of her incessant exertion were neither selfishly hoarded nor foolishly trifled away, but applied to the maintenance and advancement of her family." Hans Place is associated with all the earliest recollections of Miss Landon, whose home it was, in fact, until her marriage, in 1838, with Captain George Maclean, Governor of Cape Coast Castle, on the west coast of Africa. She died in October of the same year, universally beloved on account of her amiable and gifted nature, and as simple as a child. Her poems live, and *will* live.

Mr. and Mrs. Alfred Wigan, the popular actor and actress, resided for some time in Hans Place.

Adjoining Hans Place is the Pavilion, formerly the residence of Lady Charlotte Denys, and now of the Earl of Arran. This building was erected in the latter part of the last century by a Mr. Holland, who had taken from Lord Cadogan a lease of one hundred acres of land hereabouts, formerly called "Blacklands," and now Upper Chelsea, for the purpose of forming new streets, &c. Mr. Holland reserved to himself twenty-one acres of land, on which he erected an elegant house for his own residence. The front of the house was originally built as a model for the Pavilion at Brighton, and was ornamented by a colonnade of the Doric order, extending the whole length of the building. The mansion consisted of three sides of a quadrangle, open to the north, and the approach was from Hans Place. The south front of the house faced an extensive and beautifully-planted lawn, gently rising to the level of the colonnade and principal floor. On the west side of the lawn was an ice-house, round which was erected a representation of the ruins of an ancient "priory," in which the appearance of age and decay is said to have been strikingly reproduced. The Gothic stonework was brought from the ancient but now demolished residence of Cardinal Wolsey, at Esher, in Surrey. The lawn was ornamented by a fine sheet of water, besides which the grounds had about them "considerable variety of fanciful intricate paths and scenery, properly ornamented with shrubs, and had a private communication with the house by the walks of the shrubbery."

On the north side of Hans Place, near to Walton Street, is St. Saviour's Church. It was built about the year 1840, and has no particular pretensions to architectural effect. It has no spire, but two dwarf towers flank the entrance facing Walton Place. The interior is perfectly plain. Deep galleries, supported on octagonal pillars and iron girders, extend round three sides. The pillars supporting the front of the galleries are extended upwards, and from their capitals spring pointed arches along each side. In connection with this church there are some excellent schools and charitable societies.

Close by is Prince's Cricket Ground, which was lately one of the principal centres of attraction and conversation during the London "season." The place has always been a cricket-ground of more or less importance, but more than once of late it has been suggested that it would not be bad to transfer to it the "Eton and Harrow Match" from "Lord's." Besides this, there is every accommodation for lawn-tennis, Badminton, and other games. A few years ago a "skating-rink," with artificial ice, for practice at all seasons of the year, was added to the other attractions of "Prince's;" its career, however, was but of short duration. "Prince's" was always rather select and exclusive, but latterly its exclusiveness increased, the price of admission being raised, and all sorts of stringent regulations being introduced by the committee, in order to keep it "select." So "select" indeed had it become, that a cricketing husband, though an old subscriber, might not take his wife into its precincts, nor could a skating wife introduce her husband, or even her daughter. Nay, further, an edict was issued from the despots of "Prince's"—"That no lady was to be admitted at all unless she has been presented at

Court." Of course, therefore, the members became "very select:" no "nobodies" were there; "Lady Clara Vere de Vere" had the skating-rink all to herself, or shared it only with other "daughters of a hundred earls." How delightful! Yes, delightful for Lady Clara and her friend, but not so for the outside public.

The "South Australian" is the sign of a small inn not far from Prince's Grounds. This building tells its own tale, having been put up about the year 1835, when the colony of South Australia was founded, by some one who had a pecuniary interest in it.

CHAPTER IX.

WEST BROMPTON, SOUTH KENSINGTON MUSEUM, &c.

"Uplift a thousand voices, full and sweet,
In this wide hall, with Earth's inventions stored,
And praise th' invisible universal Lord,
Who lets once more in peace the nations meet,
Where Science, Art, and Labour have outpour'd
Their myriad horns of plenty at our feet."—*Tennyson.*

Situation of Brompton—Its Nurseries and Flower-gardens—Cromwell or Hale House—Thistle Grove—The Boltons—Westminster and West London Cemetery—Brompton Hall—St. Michael's Grove—Brompton Grove—John Sidney Hawkins—Gloucester Lodge—The Hospital for Consumption—The Cancer Hospital—Pelham Crescent—Onslow Square—Eagle Lodge—Thurloe Place and Square—Cromwell Road—The International Exhibition of 1862—Annual International Exhibitions—A School of Cookery—Exhibition of Scientific Apparatus—The National Portrait Gallery—The Meyrick Collection of Arms and Armour—The Indian Museum—South Kensington Museum—The Raphael Cartoons—The Sheepshanks, Ellison, and Vernon Galleries—Ancient and Modern Jewellery—The Museum of Patents—The Science and Art Schools—The Royal Albert Hall—The National Training School for Music—Royal Horticultural Gardens—The Fisheries Exhibition.

BROMPTON, which is—or, rather, was till lately—a hamlet to the parish of Kensington, is situated on the north side of Little Chelsea, and on the west of Sloane Street. It has long been celebrated for its soft air, and for its nurseries and flower-gardens; indeed, "Brompton, with its two centuries of nursery-garden fame," writes Mr. John Timbs, "lasted to our times; southward, among 'the groves,' were the 'Florida,' the 'Hoop and Toy,' and other taverns, with tea-gardens attached; there still (1866) remains the 'Swan,' with its bowling-green." At the commencement of the present century the "village" of Brompton was considerably increased by building, and became nominally divided into two parts, termed Old and New Brompton. The latter division of the hamlet chiefly consisted of rows of houses crowded together more closely than was perhaps desirable. "Old Brompton," writes the author of the "Beauties of England and Wales," in 1816, "still retains a similitude of rural aspect, and is yet celebrated for well-cultivated nursery and garden grounds. In this part of the village," continues the writer, "are many handsome detached houses; and here is likewise a domestic building, of comparative antiquity, which requires notice.

This is termed Hale House, but is often called Cromwell House, and is traditionally said to have been the residence of Oliver Cromwell. But for such a tradition there appears no sort of authority. Mr. Lysons* shows that this house was the property of the Methwold family during Cromwell's time; and the same writer observes that 'if there are *any* grounds for the tradition, it may be that *Henry* Cromwell occupied the house before he went out to Ireland the second time.' It appears from the register of this parish that 'Mr. Henry Cromwell and Elizabeth Russell' were married on the 10th of May, 1653; and it may be observed that General Lambert, an eminent supporter of the Cromwell family, is known to have possessed a residence near Earl's Court. Hale House is now divided into two parts, each of which is occupied by a separate family. William Methwold, Esq., who died possessed of the above house in 1652, founded, near his residence, an almshouse for six poor women."

Mr. H. G. Davis, writing on the subject of Cromwell House in *Notes and Queries*, gives the

---

* "Environs of London," vol. ii., p. 507.

following version of the story as that which he had always heard:—"That on some occasion Cromwell's troop was quartered at Knightsbridge, and he one day venturing to stray along the lanes of Brompton, was met by some cavaliers who knew him, and pursued him to this house, where he was sheltered till assistance came from Knightsbridge and liberated him." Faulkner, in his "History of Kensington," describing this house, says: "Over the mantelpiece there is a recess, formed by the curve of the chimney, in which it is said that the Protector used to conceal himself when he visited this house; but why his Highness chose this place for concealment the tradition has not condescended to inform us. This recess is concealed by the wainscot, and is still used as a cupboard." Mr. Faulkner then goes on to state that, though the tradition is "very strong and universal," all documents he has consulted "seem to show that there is not the least foundation for this conjecture;" and presumes "from the marriage of Henry Cromwell having taken place in this parish, that he resided here;" and hence the whole of the story. Mrs. Samuel Carter Hall, mentioning the tradition in her "Pilgrimages to English Shrines," says:— "Upon closer investigation how grieved we have been to discover the truth. . . . We found that Oliver never resided there, but that his son *Richard* had, and *was a ratepayer* to the parish of Kensington some time." Even this latter statement is doubted, for, according to Dr. Rimbault, it is not recorded in the parochial books. Dr. Rimbault, in *Notes and Queries*, states that "the house was known as Hale House in 1596, when a rent-charge of 20s. per annum was laid upon it for the poor of Kensington parish. In 1630 it was purchased by William Methwold, Esq., of the executors of Sir William Blake, who died in that year. This gentleman seems to have been its constant occupant till the period of his death, which occurred in 1652. He is described of Hale House in his will. On May 10, 1653, immediately after his return from Ireland, 'Mr. Henry Cromwell was married to Elizabeth Russell, daughter of Sir Thomas Russell,' at Kensington Church; after which, according to Noble, 'he chiefly resided at Whitehall.' In the following year (1654) he returned to Ireland, and upon his taking leave of that kingdom, he retired to Spinney Abbey, near Soham, in Cambridgeshire, where he died in 1673. The chances of *Henry* Cromwell having resided at Hale House are, therefore, but slender. In 1668 Hale House appears to have been inhabited by the Lawrences, of Shurdington, in Gloucestershire; in 1682 it was in the occupation of Francis Lord Howard of

Effingham, the birth of whose son is thus recorded in the parish registers:—'July 7, 1682. The Honble Thomas Howard, son of the R^t Honourable Francis, Ld Howard, Baron of Effingham, and the Lady Philadelphia, was born at Hale House, in this parish.' Hale House was still the property of the Methwold family, who, in 1754, sold it to John Fleming, Esq., afterwards created a baronet; and in 1790 it was the joint property of the Earl of Harrington and Sir Richard Worsley, Bart., who married his daughters and co-heirs." Such is the brief history of the proprietors and inhabitants of Cromwell House. It was a pleasant rural seat in 1794, when Edmund Burke's only and beloved son died there of a rapid consumption a few days after his election to Parliament. The father's hopes were blasted by the blow, and his own death followed within two years. The house itself was pulled down about the year 1853, to make room for new improvements. The site of its grounds is now marked by part of Cromwell Road.

Brompton is briefly dispatched by Priscilla Wakefield with the remark that "it is a hamlet to Kensington, and has been much recommended to invalids for the softness of the air." An extensive botanical garden, containing also a botanical library, was established here by a Mr. Curtis, in the reign of George III., and was supported by subscriptions for many years.*

What with its nurseries, its groves, and its pleasant detached mansions or cottages, standing apart in their own grounds, this neighbourhood, down to very recent times, presented much of the appearance of a suburban retreat.

Thistle Grove, a turning out of the Fulham Road, nearly opposite the "Queen's Elm" Hotel, covers the site of what was known a century or more ago as "Brompton Heath." Here lived Mr. John Burke, the author of the "Peerage" and the "Commoners" of England. On the west side of Thistle Grove is "The Boltons," a sort of park, comprising two neat-built rows of houses on either side of an oval-shaped inclosure, in which stands St. Mary's Church, a handsome Gothic edifice.

Further westward is the Westminster and West of London Cemetery. It covers about forty acres of ground, and was consecrated in 1840. It has a domed chapel, with semi-circular colonnades of imposing design. In the grounds is a large monument, consisting of an altar-tomb, with athlete figures, and a pompous epitaph, to the memory of Jackson, the prize-fighter, who kept the "Cock"

---

* See page 88, *ante*.

Inn, at Sutton, near Epsom, from which he retired with a fortune, having obtained the patronage of George Prince of Wales and many leaders of the sporting world.   Sir Roderick Murchison, the eminent geologist, lies buried here.

Brompton Hall, the residence of the great Lord Burleigh, which stood near Earl's Court, is described by Faulkner as retaining at that time (1829) some marks of its ancient splendour.   "There was

Mr. J. R. Planché was living in Brompton Crescent about the year 1826; and near him, in Brompton Grove (now covered by the houses of Ovington Square), lived William Jerdan, the editor of the *Literary Gazette* in its palmy days.   At their houses Mr. T. Crofton Croker, Tom Hood, the Rev. Dr. Croly, Miss Landon (the unfortunate "L. E. L."), used to meet constantly, to discuss the last new play or poem, and literary subjects in

ENTRANCE TO BROMPTON CEMETERY.

till lately," adds the author, "a grand porch at the entrance.   The hall, or saloon, is a step lower than the rooms upon the same floor.   The dining-room has a richly-carved ceiling of oak, displaying in the centre the rose and crown, and in its other compartments the fleur-de-lys and portcullis; and on taking down some ancient tapestry a few years since, the arms of Queen Elizabeth, carved in oak, and curiously inlaid with gold, were discovered above the chimney-piece.   There are also in another room the relics of a very curious old wainscot, in small compartments."

In St. Michael's Grove lived Douglas Jerrold; and it was in his house that Charles Dickens first made his acquaintance, in or about 1835, when staying at home invalided.

general.   Jerdan died in June, 1869, at the age of eighty-eight, nearly twenty years after resigning his editorial chair.   His Autobiography, published in four volumes, contains many pleasant notices of his contemporaries.   In Brompton Grove, too, lived Major Shadwell Clarke, the hospitable friend at whose table Theodore Hook was an ever welcome guest, and where he dined the last time that he ever left his house.

In Lower Grove, Brompton, lived and died the antiquary, John Sidney Hawkins, the eldest son of Sir John Hawkins, Dr. Johnson's friend and biographer.   He died about the year 1842, at an advanced age.   He published several works on architectural subjects.

At Gloucester Lodge, was living, in 1809, George

THE CONSUMPTION HOSPITAL, BROMPTON. (*See page* 104.)

Canning, when he fought the duel with his colleague, Lord Castlereagh, and both before and during his premiership. Mr. Rush, in his "Court of London," gives us many accounts of his official interviews with Mr. Canning here, and also of his dinner parties, at which he met all that was illustrious and brilliant in the society of the time. While residing here too, at a later date, Canning's son, the future Governor-General of India, was born ; and here he received several visits from the Princess of Wales, whose cause he so nobly and honourably espoused.

In the Fulham Road, near Pelham Crescent, is the Hospital for Consumption. The original building, on the north side of the road, is a beautiful Elizabethan structure, consisting of a centre and wings, about 200 feet in width. It stands on a square piece of ground, about three acres in extent. The foundation-stone of the hospital was laid by the late Prince Consort in 1841. On the ground floor, the west wing contains physicians' rooms, laboratory, museums, rooms for the resident medical officer and clinical assistants, and servants' hall ; and the east wing contains the apartments of the lady superintendent, store-rooms, secretary's office, board-room, &c. The kitchen and sculleries abut on the north side of the central basement corridor, and are built altogether outside the hospital. The first floor is devoted exclusively to female patients, and the second floor to male patients, the total number of beds being 210. The wards, galleries, and corridors are well lighted, and fitted up with every attention to the comfort and convenience of the patients. The chapel, which stands on the north side of the hospital, parallel with the central portion, was founded in 1849 by the Rev. Sir Henry Foulis, Bart., in memory of a near relative. It is approached from the hospital by a corridor, so that the patients may not be exposed to external air in bad weather. It is fitted up with wide cushioned seats for the patients, and is capable of accommodating the whole of the inmates and a few visitors.

In 1879, the first stone of a new extension building of the hospital was laid on the opposite side of the road. It was built mainly from the proceeds of a bequest of Miss Read, and was completed in 1882. This building is constructed of red brick, and is connected with the parent hospital by a subway. It is about 200 feet in length, and 100 feet high, and besides increasing the accommodation to nearly 350 beds, contains a large out-patient department, lecture theatre, &c.

The Hospital receives patients from all parts of the kingdom, and is almost entirely dependent on voluntary contributions, the expenditure being about £10,000 a year more than the fixed annual income.

On the south side of the road is another of those excellent institutions which minister to the most formidable "ills that flesh is heir to." This is the Cancer Hospital. This building, which was founded in 1851, is constructed of plain white Suffolk bricks, relieved with bands of red bricks, and keystones and cornices of terra-cotta. The principal ground floor, approached by a flight of steps, contains the hall and a handsome stone staircase, apartments for the house surgeon and medical officers, and wards for patients. Apparatus for heating and ventilating the building is provided—everything, in short, that is calculated to add to the comforts and assist the recovery of the patients. The Archbishop of Canterbury, preaching on behalf of the funds of this hospital, observed, " There is no disease more pitiable than that to which this institution is specially devoted. This, therefore, is a case in which I may justly ask your liberal contributions." Chelsea Hospital for Women, a handsome red-brick building in the Fulham Road, was built in 1880.

Large property round about this neighbourhood belongs to Lord Onslow's family ; Onslow Square is so named in consequence, and Cranley Place is so called after the second title of Lord Onslow.

In Pelham Crescent died, in 1869, aged seventy-four, Mr. Robert Keeley, the comic actor. Hard by, in Onslow Square, at No. 36, Thackeray was living in 1858, when he stood his unsuccessful contest for Oxford city, and when he commenced the editorship of the *Cornhill Magazine.*

Eagle Lodge was at one time tenanted by Mr. Bunn, so well known as the lessee of Drury Lane Theatre. Here he used to entertain Malibran, Thalberg, De Beriot, Mr. J. R. Planché, and other friends of music and the drama.

Thurloe Place and Thurloe Square, near the junction of the Fulham, Cromwell, and Brompton Roads, are of too modern a growth to have any historic associations. Cromwell Road, a long and open thoroughfare, extending from Thurloe Square westward to Earl's Court, was doubtless so named after the Cromwellian associations connected with the neighbourhood, as described above. At the eastern end of the road, a considerable space of ground lying between it and the gardens of the Royal Horticultural Society, was the site of the International Exhibition of 1862. The site was purchased by the Royal Commissioners of the Exhibition of 1851, with a portion of the surplus money arising from the receipts of that exhibition. The edifice, which was altogether different from its predecessor in Hyde Park, was built from the designs of Captain Fowke, R.E. It was constructed chiefly of brick, and the ground plan in its general form was that of the letter L, the short limb being the annexe for the machinery in motion. It consisted of a nave and two transepts, each point of intersection at the extremities of the nave being marked by a polygonal hall, surmounted by an immense dome. The southern façade ran along the Cromwell Road, and the building had also a frontage on the east in the Exhibition Road, and on the west in Prince Albert's Road (now Queen's Gate). Between this and the Horticultural Society's boundary was a semi-detached portion of the building, comprising the departments for implements and machinery in motion, extending over an entrance by a covered way or bridge, so that this section was kept entirely separate from the main body of the building. Its entire length was only about 1,150 feet, or 700 feet shorter than its crystal prototype in Hyde Park. The external appearance of the structure was not very striking. It was massive; but its unbroken length left a feeling of painful monotony on the observer, which the enormous domes at either end, 260 feet in height and 160 feet in diameter, failed to vary. Almost in the centre of this mass of brickwork was the grand entrance or portico, built according to an Italian plan. The picture-galleries occupied the first compartment in the front portion of the building, facing the Cromwell Road, and were two in number; they were lighted by clerestory windows in the roof, and formed perhaps the most attractive feature of the Exhibition. The basement storey of this part of the building was devoted to the exhibition of carriages, carts, and other descriptions of road vehicles. Adjoining the picture-gallery, but on the ground floor, was a large space, upwards of 1,000 feet in length, glazed from end to end, which was devoted to manufactures and art productions from every country in the world. Advancing across this court, the nave was reached; this extended the whole length of the building, and was 80 feet in width, or eight feet wider than that of the Crystal Palace of 1851. The nave was 100 feet high, and was crossed at its extremities by two transepts, each 692 feet long by 85 feet in width, and 100 feet high, resembling the nave in the last two respects. At each of the points of their intersection with the nave, rose octagonal halls 160 feet in diameter, each surmounted by a magnificent glass dome 200 feet in height internally, and 250 feet externally, reaching to the top of the pinnacle. These were the largest domes ever built; St. Paul's being only 108 feet in diameter at the base, St. Peter's at Rome being 139 feet, and that of the British Museum reading-room 140 feet. The floors of these dome-covered halls being raised sixteen feet above the floor of the rest of the nave and transepts, afforded an admirable opportunity to the spectator for taking in grand views of the main lines of the building. The extreme ends of the building presented an extraordinary and beautiful appearance when viewed from the floors of these halls. At the angles of these halls were staircases, communicating with the galleries of the main building. On the side walls beneath the roof of the nave and transept were the clerestory windows, twenty-five feet high, of iron and glass, very light and elegant, which, together with the light from the glass domes, brought out in soft relief the architectural and artistic decorations. The nave and transepts were roofed in with wood, coated with felt, meeting in an angle at the centre; this roof was supported by semi-circular arches of timber, springing from iron columns, in pairs, by which the roof was supported at a height of sixty feet from the floor. A very pleasing effect was produced by the combination of the circular ribs and the angular girders carrying the roof; these double columns, girders and ribs, were repeated sixteen times in the nave, and their decorations produced fine polychromatic effects. The *coup d'œil* standing under either of the domes, and looking down the nave, was one of unequalled beauty; the fine proportions of the columns made the immense vista appear as if looking along a kind of iron lace-work. The columns supported on each side of the nave galleries fifty feet in width, one side commanding a view of the nave, and the other looking upon the industrial courts on the ground floor.

The principal entrance, in the Exhibition Road, was situated in the centre of the eastern transept, and led directly to the orchestra erected for the opening ceremony, under the eastern dome, which took place on the 1st of May, 1862. Space will not permit us to do more than notice a few of the most important objects here brought together. In the centre of the nave stood a trophy of small arms by the Birmingham gunmakers, flanked on either side by an Armstrong and a Whitworth gun. The Armstrong was mounted on its carriage of polished wood, and presented in every detail the delicate finish of a trinket. Indeed, the Exhibition seems to have been rich in the display of these marvellous weapons. Elaborate fountains and trophies of a more peaceful kind—such as articles of food, and animal and vegetable substances employed in manufacture, together with others of different manufactured articles—made up the miscellaneous collection. Dividing the British from the foreign portion of the nave was a huge screen in iron-work of elaborate design. At this end of the nave were some noble groups of bronze statues from various countries, and some magnificent candelabra and columns in polished jasper and porphyry from Russia. A very fine collection of Berlin porcelain manufactures was placed on raised counters under the western dome. Sèvres, Vienna, Berlin, and Dresden made great efforts to recover their lost ground in their previous competitions with the English porcelain manufacturers. The attractions of the western dome balanced very fairly the features of interest at the other end of the building. The central object was a circular stand, displaying the Prince of Prussia's collection of China, all of Berlin manufacture, which rivals the richest and most delicate Sèvres. An adjacent parterre was appropriated to the exhibition of the silver objects presented by the City of Berlin to the Princess of Prussia as a wedding gift. The great Koh-i-noor diamond was placed in the English portion of the nave near the jewellery classes, and created, doubtless, as much interest as it occasioned in 1851. Her Majesty's magnificent dessert service of Worcester porcelain was exhibited near here : it is said to eclipse the finest specimen that Sèvres, Dresden, or Vienna have yet produced.

That this second International Exhibition was a success no one will pretend to say ; it is enough to admit that with the first great gathering in 1851 the charm of novelty was worn off, and that even the lapse of eleven years was not sufficient to cause a repetition of that great influx of visitors to London from every part of the civilised world, which we have already noticed.

Although the building was so substantially constructed, it was not destined to remain standing in its entirety long after the closing of the Exhibition in October. Piece by piece it gradually disappeared, till only the inner portion, which had served chiefly as refreshment departments, overlooking the gardens, was left ; and this part has since been made to serve various purposes.

In 1870 it was announced that a series of annual International Exhibitions should be held here, commencing from the following year (1871), under the direction of Her Majesty's Commissioners for the Exhibition of 1851. Hitherto, as we learn from the official announcement of this series of exhibitions, the exhibition of works of Fine Art had been too much limited to the display of pictures and sculpture, dissociated from purposes of utility ; and it might be doubted whether a picture on enamel or on pottery, destined to be applied to a piece of furniture, or a sculpture in wood intended for a picture-frame, however great its merits, would find any place in the Exhibitions of the Royal Academy of London, or in any of the numerous other exhibitions of the works of artists. Still less would a Cashmere shawl or a Persian carpet, the chief excellence of which depended upon its combination of colours, find in any of these exhibitions its proper place. Such a complete separation of artistic work from objects of utility might indeed be said to be only the characteristic of modern times ; for in the ancient and mediæval periods the highest art is to be found in alliance with the meanest materials of manufacture. The Etruscans painted on vases of clay subjects which still charm us by their beauty of composition and skilful drawing ; and the finest works of Raffaele were designed as decorations for hangings to be made of wool. It was intended that these exhibitions should furnish the opportunity of stimulating the revival of the application of the artist's talents to give beauty and refinement to every description of objects of utility, whether domestic or monumental. In these annual Exhibitions it was contended that every work in which Fine Art is a dominant feature would find proper provision made for its display. Painting, on whatever surface, or in any method ; sculpture in every description of material, engravings of all kinds, architectural design as a Fine Art, every description of textile fabric of which Fine Art is a characteristic feature—in short, every work, whether of utility or pleasure, which is entitled to be considered a work of excellence from the artistic point of view, might be displayed in the exhibitions under the division of Fine Art. The industrial portion of these exhibitions was to be confined to educational works and appliances, and new inventions and scientific discoveries. Every artist-workman, moreover, it was stated, would be able to exhibit a work of merit as his own production, and every manufacturer might distinguish himself as a patron of art by his alliance with the artistic talent of the country. In the Fine Art section the artist might exhibit a vase for its beauty of painting, or form, or artistic invention ; whilst a similar vase might appear in its appropriate place among manufactures on account of its cheapness, or the novelty of its material.

It was arranged that these annual Exhibitions should take place in permanent buildings erected on either side of the Horticultural Gardens, connecting that part of the building of 1862 which remained standing with a new and lofty structure, on the north side of the gardens, called the Royal

Albert Hall, of which we shall have more to say presently. On the south side of the Albert Hall, and facing the gardens, is the splendid conservatory of the Royal Horticultural Society, and at each end are long curved arcades, named respectively the East and West Quadrants. Flanking these, and enclosing the gardens, are the buildings in which the principal part of the Exhibition was held. They consist of lower and upper galleries, about 550 feet long and twenty feet wide, with corridors open to the gardens. The lower storeys have side lights; the upper are lighted from the roof. The whole of the Exhibition buildings are in the Decorated Italian style, and harmonise well with the adjacent South Kensington Museum. The mouldings, cornices, and courses are in light-coloured terra-cotta, and red brick is the material used in the construction.

The first of these annual Exhibitions was held in 1871, and in addition to the two permanent features mentioned above, included woollen and worsted manufactures, pottery, and educational apparatus. These were replaced in 1872 by cotton and cotton fabrics; jewellery, including articles worn as personal ornaments, made of precious metals, precious stones, or their imitations; musical instruments of all kinds; acoustic apparatus and experiments; paper, stationery and printing. These various classes comprised also the raw materials, machinery, and processes used in their production.

The third Exhibition of the series, held in 1873, comprehended several classes of subjects not included in the displays of the two previous years. The fine arts, scientific inventions and discoveries, and galleries of painting and sculpture by British and foreign artists, continued as special features of the Exhibition, as before; but this year visitors were enabled to add to the knowledge they had gained of the processes employed in one great department of the textile manufactures which forms so important a part of our national industry, an acquaintance with the mode of producing the beautiful fabrics silk and velvet. Cutlery and edged tools, for which this country has been famous for centuries, were exhibited, Fine-art furniture and decorative work, and stained glass—not entirely absent from the previous Exhibitions, but appearing there in a subordinate position—had now more justice afforded to their claims on our attention.

One novel feature in the Exhibition of 1873 was a School of Cookery, where lectures were delivered and admirably illustrated by the practical experiments of neat-handed cooks. Ladies, naturally, formed a large portion of the audience, and Her Majesty and other members of the Royal Family did not fail to give the sanction of their presence to these novel lectures. The building used for these lectures was subsequently placed at the service of the National Training School for Cookery, by whom the work has since been carried on.

The manufactures selected for the fourth Exhibition, which was opened in the year 1874, were lace, the show of which was magnificent; civil engineering, architecture, and building, including sanitary apparatus and constructions on the one hand, and decorative work on the other; heating by all methods and every kind of fuel, selected in consequence of the high price of coal and the necessity for teaching economy in the combustion of fuel; leather and saddlery, harness, and other articles made of leather; bookbinding; and foreign wines.

Whether these Annual International Exhibitions were successful or not in imparting that knowledge as to the *best* means employed in various arts and trades, and the *best* results achieved, we will not pretend to say. They were not, however, sufficiently attractive to the masses of the people to warrant their continuance year after year, and with the Exhibition of 1874 the series terminated, and the various buildings were set apart for other purposes. In one series of rooms is the National Portrait Gallery, which was originally established in Great George Street, Westminster, in 1859. It is a most interesting collection, from an artistic as well as an historic point of view, and embraces the "counterfeit presentment" of many of England's greatest worthies, whether as sovereigns, statesmen, warriors, poets, authors, &c. Here are the famous Chandos portrait of Shakespeare, several of Queen Elizabeth, and between four and five hundred likenesses of some of the most remarkable men and women in English history, many of them executed by the first painters of the periods. Besides the portraits, there are a few highly interesting casts of effigies from monuments in Westminster Abbey, Canterbury Cathedral, and other places; and also an interesting collection of autographs.

In 1868 was deposited in the building the Meyrick collection of arms and armour, from Goodrich Court, Herefordshire, formed by the late Sir Samuel Meyrick, the author of "A Critical Inquiry into Ancient Armour," and lent to the Museum by its then owner, Colonel Meyrick. It was arranged for exhibition here by Mr. J. R. Planché. The collection of naval models, and of the munitions of war, lent by the War Department, and on view here, contains examples of British ship-building, from the earliest period down to the construction of the turret-ship of the ill-fated Captain Coles.

That portion of the Exhibition galleries overlooking the gardens on the eastern side was made, in 1875, the receptacle of the India Museum. This collection of objects was originally formed by the East India Company, and after its removal from Leadenhall Street, was for a time stowed away in Whitehall Yard, and in various cellars and warerooms, and in the topmost storey of the new India Office. In these rooms were deposited for

Natural History, which was erected to contain the Natural History collections hitherto preserved in the British Museum, where the accommodation for many years past had become too restricted, and the necessity for a larger building keenly felt. The new museum, built from the designs of Mr. A. Waterhouse, fronts the Cromwell Road, and is about 650 feet in length. It is constructed of brick, faced with terra-cotta, of a highly ornamental

THE INTERNATIONAL EXHIBITION OF 1862.

exhibition the numerous costly presents brought from India by the Prince of Wales after his tour in that country in 1875-6.

In 1881 a portion of the buildings on this side the Horticultural Gardens was taken as the site of the Central Institution of the City and Guilds of London, for the purposes of technical education, and to serve as a focus for uniting the different technical schools in the metropolis already in existence, and as a central establishment also to which promising students from the provinces may, by the aid of scholarships, be brought to benefit by the superior instruction which London can command.

The site of the main portion of the Exhibition Buildings is now occupied by the Museum of

character, and consists of three storeys, in addition to the basement. The main part of the building has a tower at each end, and there are also two central towers rising on either side of the entrance. The Mineralogical, Botanical, and Geological collections were removed hither from the British Museum in 1881, and have since been followed by the Zoological specimens.

On the eastern side of the Exhibition Road, and with its principal entrance in Cromwell Road, is the South Kensington Museum, together with the various Science and Art Schools which have been established, under Government, in connection therewith.

This Museum, which now contains upwards of 20,000 rare and choice examples of mediæval and

THE COURT OF THE SOUTH KENSINGTON MUSEUM.

Modern Art workmanship, originated in the year 1852 with a small collection, exhibited in Marlborough House in connection with the Schools of Art. In 1857 the collection was transferred hither to some temporary iron buildings which had been erected for its reception, which, from their material, and from some peculiarities of construction, became popularly known as the " Brompton Boilers." These temporary buildings have been gradually replaced by a permanent edifice. From the year 1853 the Museum has included objects contributed on loan by private owners. In 1862— the year of the second International Exhibition—a special " loan exhibition " of works, chiefly of Mediæval and Renaissance Art, was held here ; and since that time the number of objects on loan has always been considerable. By this means very many of the rarest and most precious examples of art workmanship in this country have been generously permitted by their owners to be seen and leisurely studied by the public. In addition to the "loans," many objects have been acquired by purchase, gift, and bequest ; besides which are reproductions, by the electrotype process and in plaster, of objects in other collections which have been judged to be of special interest and value to the art student.

The plan of the Museum is somewhat irregular, and covers a large space of ground—about twelve acres in extent—acquired by the Government, at a cost of £60,000, being a portion of the estate purchased by Her Majesty's Commissioners for the Exhibition of 1851, out of the surplus proceeds of that undertaking. The buildings, with their courts and galleries, are constructed chiefly of brick, somewhat profusely ornamented with terra-cotta, and were built from the designs of Captain Fowke, R.E. The art collections are chiefly contained in three large courts and a long range of cloisters on the ground floor ; but many rare and valuable objects are shown in the picture-galleries, and also in what is called the Prince Consort Gallery. The visitor, on entering the Museum from the Cromwell Road, passes through a corridor to the New or Architectural Court. This is divided by a central passage and gallery. The majority of the objects it contains are full-size reproductions (in plaster) of architectural works of large dimensions designed for erection in the open air, or in large halls or churches, including the famous Trajan Column at Rome, and the " 'Prentice Pillar " in Roslin Chapel, Scotland ; there is also a full-size copy (by photography) of the Bayeux Tapestry, coloured in imitation of the original needlework.

From this Court we enter the South Court,

a lofty and spacious building, surrounded with galleries, and rich in ornamentation. The upper portion of the walls is divided into thirty-six alcoves, (eighteen on either side), containing portraits, in mosaic, of eminent men of all ages connected with the arts, especially those who have been distinguished as ornamentalists, or as workers in bronze, marble, or pottery. These portraits, which include such men as Phidias, the sculptor of the Elgin marbles, William of Wykeham, Donatello, Torrigiano, Albert Dürer, Michael Angelo, Titian, Hogarth, Sir Joshua Reynolds, and Mulready, are from designs by some of the first artists of the day. This court is divided into two parts by a broad passage which crosses it, above which is the Prince Consort Gallery above mentioned. It would be impossible to give, within the limits at our disposal, a list of the various objects here exhibited, and indeed such a task would be needless, as they are all detailed in the various catalogues sold at the Museum ; suffice it to say that here are deposited the numerous and costly objects comprising the " Loan Collections," together with a miscellaneous assortment of art manufactures. The " Oriental Courts," appropriately decorated by Mr. Owen Jones, contain some examples of the art workmanship of the East Indies, China, Japan, Persia, &c.

The North Court is specially appropriated to the exhibition of Italian sculpture, and architectural models and casts. Many of the most beautiful of these objects are, so to speak, incorporated into the building, the decoration of which is much simpler than that of the South Court. In the east arcade of this court are some textile or woven fabrics, of European origin, including several ecclesiastical vestments and rare fragments of mediæval embroidery. Through the windows of the north arcade is seen the " fernery," which was designed to enable the students in training as art-teachers to draw from plants at all seasons. A considerable portion of the west arcade forms the reading-room of the Art Library. The staircase leading to the galleries is lighted by a large stained-glass window, the subject of which was suggested by a passage in Ecclesiasticus, chapter xxxviii., descriptive of trades. The keramic, or pottery gallery, contains a large collection of Wedgwood's jasper and other wares, and also examples of the porcelain of Bow, Chelsea, Bristol, Plymouth, Worcester, and Derby. Here, too, are represented the great manufacturers of pottery of the present day in Italy, France, and England. The next gallery into which the visitor passes contains a collection of Venetian, German, and other ancient glass vessels. In the Prince

Consort Gallery are placed many of the most interesting and costly possessions of the Museum, in enamel, gold, and silversmith's work, jewellery, watches, clocks, &c. The South Gallery, which we now enter, is filled with cases containing examples of ancient and mediæval ivories. The gallery of the Architectural Court is devoted to examples of art iron-work. From an arched opening at the north end of the Prince Consort Gallery a view of the North Court is obtained. The balcony here is the Singing Gallery from Florence. To the right is the grand fresco of the Industrial Arts as applied to War, by Sir Frederick Leighton, P.R.A. It is a lunette, thirty-five feet long at the base and sixteen feet high. "The scene," observes a writer in the *Athenæum*, "is the entrance to a town or fortress of Italian Gothic architecture; and the figures wear those Italian costumes of the fourteenth century which are dear to artists in designs of the Early Renaissance. The effect of brilliant open daylight has been rendered with peculiar splendour; the colouration is vivid and in a bright, pure key; the treatment is at once severe and elegant, decorative, and monumental, without achaism and without those Mantegnesque affectations of which we have seen much of late. The composition of the figures, not less than that of the chiaroscuro, general colouring, and light and shade, is architectonic; the lines throughout and the arrangement of the groups are adapted to the pedimental form of the lunette; even the shadow of the overhanging arch has been considered in the disposition of the white clouds and buildings in the distance." The companion subject, The Industrial Arts as applied to Peace, is destined to fill the corresponding space on the other side of the north end of the South Court.

Three staircases in different parts of the building lead to the Picture Galleries, which are above the cloisters of the North and South Courts. Several rooms or galleries are devoted to the National Collection of Pictures by British artists. Critical notices of many of the paintings here exhibited will be found in Redgrave's "Century of British Art." In the north gallery are hung the Raphael cartoons. From the authorised "Guide to the Museum" we glean the following particulars concerning these celebrated productions. They are drawn with chalk upon strong paper, and coloured in distemper, and are the original designs, executed by Raphael and his scholars for Pope Leo X., in the year 1513, as copies for tapestry work. Each cartoon is about twelve feet high. They were originally ten, but three are lost—viz., "The Stoning of St. Stephen," the "Conversion of St. Paul," and "St. Paul in

his Dungeon at Philippi." A copy in tapestry of Christ's "Charge to Peter" is hung opposite the original cartoon; and also a tapestry from the Imperial manufactory, the Gobelins, at Paris, a copy of the "Holy Family" by Raphael in the Louvre.

The tapestries, worked in wool, silk, and gold, were hung in the Sistine Chapel at Rome in the year 1519, the year before Raphael died. These are now in the Vatican.

The cartoons remained neglected in the warehouse of the manufacturer at Arras, and were seen there by Rubens, who advised Charles I. to purchase them for the use of a tapestry manufactory which was then established at Mortlake. On the death of Charles I., Cromwell bought them for £300 for the nation. They remained for a long time in a lumber-room at Whitehall, till, by command of William III., Sir Christopher Wren erected a room for them at Hampton Court, in which they hung till Her Majesty permitted them to be removed hither.

Passing through the door at the east end of the gallery, we enter the rooms containing the Sheepshanks' Collection of Paintings. A bust, by Foley, of the late John Sheepshanks, the donor of the pictures, has been placed in this gallery by Miss Sheepshanks. The south-eastern gallery contains the Jones Collection of furniture, Sèvres, and other porcelain, enamelled miniatures, paintings, sculpture, bronzes, &c. It was bequeathed to the Museum in 1882 by Mr. John Jones, of Piccadilly. In five rooms at the south end of the Western Galleries are placed the Dyce and Forster collections. The former collection, bequeathed to the Museum by the Rev. Alexander Dyce, the eminent scholar and editor of Shakespeare, consists of oil paintings, miniatures, drawings, engravings, &c., a few manuscripts, and a library containing upwards of 11,000 volumes. The Forster collection, bequeathed to the Museum in 1876, by Mr. John Forster, the friend and biographer of Charles Dickens, consists of oil and water-colour paintings, drawings, manuscripts, autographs, and a library of 18,000 volumes. Oliver Goldsmith's chair, desk, and walking-cane, bequeathed by Goldsmith to his friend Dr. Hawes, and given to the Museum by Lady Hawes, are exhibited in this gallery. A painting by Maclise, representing "Caxton's Printing-office in the Almonry at Westminster," was bequeathed by Mr. Forster to Lord Lytton, and has been lent by his lordship to the Museum.

The reading-room for the Dyce and Forster libraries is open from 10 a.m. till 5 p.m. daily.

The Historical Collection of British Water-colour Drawings, exhibited in two rooms facing the head of the staircase, is for the most part composed of the gifts of Mrs. Ellison, of Sudbrooke Holme, Lincolnshire, Mr. William Smith, Mrs. Tatlock, Miss Twining, Mr. C. T. Maud, the bequests of the Rev. C. H. Townshend and Mr. J. M. Parsons; examples of Gainsborough, Rooker, Barret, Gilpin, De Loutherbourg, Sandby, Payne, Dayes, Rowlandson, Cerres, and Cipriani; and on a screen several original sketches by the late John Leech.

The Museum of Patents, adjoining the South Court, is a collection illustrative of the progress of national invention, and contains not only models, but several original machines which have been the means of developing our prosperity, and have given new life to the world. As examples may be mentioned the first steam-engine to which James Watt applied his condenser; the first locomotive, " Puffing Billy," and its successor, George Stephenson's " Rocket ;" the first engine ever used in steam navigation, the first Bramah's press, and many other pieces of mechanism of not less historical value.

On the west side of the main buildings of the Museum, facing the Exhibition Road, is a large edifice, containing class-rooms for instruction in various branches of science. This structure was built on the site of the " International Bazaar," a building which was constructed in 1862, and filled with a choice selection of works by persons whose application for space in the Exhibition could not be complied with. The Art Schools extend along the north side of the Museum, and have separate apartments for male and female students.

The Science and Art Department is a division of the Education Department, under the direction of the Lord President of the Council and the Vice-President of the Committee of Council on Education. It was established in 1852. A sum of money is voted annually by Parliament, in aid of local efforts to promote science and art applied to productive industry, such efforts originating with the localities. Payments are made upon results of instruction in science and art, as tested by examination by properly-appointed officials. The National Art Training School was established for the purpose of training art-masters and mistresses for the United Kingdom, and for the instruction of students in designing, &c., to which male and female students are admitted when properly qualified, receiving an allowance in aid of their maintenance, which is proportioned to their attainments, and to their qualification for the duties of teaching required from them. When such

students have obtained certificates of qualification, they may be appointed teachers to the local Schools of Art throughout the United Kingdom. The object of the Science Schools and Classes is to promote instruction in science, especially among the industrial classes, in such subjects as Mathematics, Geometry, Naval Architecture, Mechanics, Chemistry, Botany, and the like. The assistance granted by the Science and Art Department to that end is in the form of public examinations, in which Queen's medals and Queen's prizes are awarded; payments on the results of examination and on attendance; scholarships and exhibitions; building grants; grants towards the purchase of apparatus, &c., and supplementary grants in certain subjects; and special aid to teachers and students. The sum voted by Parliament, for the year 1882-3, for the Science and Art Department, amounted to nearly £351,400. The department, it may be added, has the advantage of the services of gentlemen of the highest standing in their several professions, as examiners both for Science and Art Schools, and as official referees for the purchases made for the collections.

The Royal Albert Hall of Arts and Sciences, to which we now pass, owes its origin to the fund, which was raised in 1862, for the purpose of erecting in Hyde Park the national memorial to the late Prince Consort, which we have already described. With every desire that this recognition of the debt which English art, science, and industry owed to the Prince should be, in every sense of the word, such a memorial as the country itself preferred, the Queen requested a committee of gentlemen to suggest the form which the testimonial should assume. After deliberating upon the matter, the committee recommended the erection of a personal memorial to the Prince Consort in Hyde Park, opposite to what was best known as the Central Hall of Arts and Sciences. Naturally enough, it was expected that large subscriptions would flow in towards the object in view. These expectations were not fully realised, the amount subscribed at that period being less than £70,000. To this sum Parliament added £50,000; and with the £120,000 thus obtained it was resolved to place in Hyde Park the monument of which we have spoken. Further efforts were yet to be made, and in these the Prince of Wales took the initiative. In the year 1865 the Prince of Wales called together a number of gentlemen, who were asked and consented to become vice-patrons of the proposed memorial building. A statement of the intentions of the promoters of the undertaking was issued: the Royal Commissioners of the Exhibition of

1851 gave three acres of land as a site for the building, at the nominal rent of 1s. a year, on a long lease, and subscriptions came in towards the much-cherished object. A provisional committee, consisting of twelve members, was formed, of which the Prince of Wales was president. They held several meetings at Marlborough House; £110,000 was soon subscribed; and there was every prospect of the intentions of the committee being quickly realised, when a sudden stop was put to the efforts of the promoters by the memorable panic of 1866. For a while all further proceedings ceased. In the plans of the proposed hall provision was made for a certain number of sittings; and at the beginning of the year 1867 Messrs. Lucas, the great contractors, came forward, and consented to purchase sittings valued at £38,000, on the understanding that they should receive the contract for the building, the total cost of which was not to exceed £200,000. These terms were agreed to by the provisional committee; the public nobly came forward and subscribed £112,000, the Royal Commissioners of the 1851 Exhibition gave £50,000, Messrs. Lucas' proposition was worth £38,000; and on the 20th of May, 1867, the Queen laid the foundation-stone of the building, the original plans for which came from the late Captain Fowke, R.E.; Colonel Scott, R.E., being the architect. From that time the scheme was successful. A pardonable degree of curiosity was aroused respecting the ultimate destiny of the hall; but this was set aside when it was announced that the new building was intended, amongst other things, to accommodate science congresses, to provide a suitable arena for musical performances, and to serve other equally useful artistic and scientific purposes. For this the building is admirably adapted, from the immense disposable space it offers. Between 6,000 and 7,000 persons can be seated in the hall, and besides this, when the necessity arises, it is possible to place as many as 2,000 spectators in comfortable positions on an inclined staging in the picture-gallery, which runs nearly round the hall.

Guided by the principles upon which the Romans constructed those amphitheatric buildings, the remains of which strike modern spectators with awe and admiration, the designers of the Albert Hall have succeeded in raising a structure of eminently beautiful and attractive proportions. Seen from the Park or the Kensington Road, the hall stands boldly out in all the magnificence which invests a building in the style of Italian Renaissance. The base is of plain red brick, with single-headed windows, the keystone of which is formed of the crown and cushion and the letter "V.," above which the principal floor is divided by terra-cotta pilasters, between which are semicircular-headed windows. An idea of the vast character of the building may be obtained from the knowledge that 70,000 blocks of terra-cotta were used in its construction. The frieze, which is about 800 feet long and about 6 feet wide, was made in sections of 50 feet, of encaustic *tesseræ*, by Messrs. Minton and Co., who employed in its working the female students of the School of Art at Kensington. Above these is the entablature, having a widely-projecting balcony four feet across. Surrounding the building, and high above the balcony, is mosaic work, representing various allegories descriptive of the arts, commerce, and manufactures. These mosaics are from the designs of Messrs. Horsley, Armitage, Yeames, Marks, Poynter, Pickersgill, and Armstead. Round the frieze of the building runs the following inscription in large letters:—"This hall was erected for the advancement of the arts and sciences, and for the works of industry of all nations, in fulfilment of the intentions of Albert, Prince Consort. The site was purchased by the proceeds of the Great Exhibition of the year 1851. The first stone of the hall was laid by Her Majesty Queen Victoria, on the 20th day of May, 1867, and it was opened by Her Majesty the Queen, on the 29th day of March, in the year 1871."

Above the frieze, in terra-cotta, in letters a foot high, is the sacred text: "Thine, O Lord, is the greatness, and the power, and the glory, and the victory, and the majesty: for all that is in the heaven and in the earth is Thine. The wise and their works are in the hand of God. Glory be to God on high, and on earth peace."

In the plan of the interior, it can be seen at once that the architect has taken for his model the old Roman amphitheatre, though with such important modifications as, happily, quite another kind of entertainment, and, unhappily, less genial skies, required. Roman plebeians and aristocrats were mere spectators, looking down on the fierce and bloody spectacles provided for their amusement in the arena. Here it was necessary so to provide that people might both hear and see, but above all things hear. Such a condition gives the key to the arrangement of the interior. Imagine, then, within an outer shell of staircases, corridors, refreshment and retiring rooms, a vast hall, in shape of a graceful oval, of which the southern end is all but filled by the organ and an orchestra rising upwards in tiers of seats. Fronting this orchestra is the auditorium, of horse-shoe form, composed of arena, a level space; the amphitheatre, or, as it might be better termed, the stalls, sloping upwards towards the boxes; three tiers of boxes; above them the balcony; and lastly, above it, what is called the picture-gallery. This gallery is not within the proper limits of the ellipse forming the interior, but is built over the staircases and corridors which form an outer zone to the portions of the auditorium below. It runs, therefore, round the whole of the £100; a *loggia* box, holding eight persons, £800; a box on the grand tier, with ten places, £1,000; and one with five places on the second tier, £500. Thus the unit of £100 is taken as the cost per seat in each case. The subscription season is rather a long one—999 years.

One of the most striking features in the interior is the organ, which stands in the centre of the

THE HORTICULTURAL GARDENS AND EXHIBITION BUILDING.

interior; and the thirty Italian arches, with their scagliola pillars, through which the body of the hall is seen, are really its great ornament.

The boxes and balcony project from the wall into the ellipse, each tier extending three feet beyond that above it. Such an arrangement enables the occupants of each tier to see without much difficulty, and be seen by those above them. One of the most remarkable features of the hall, in fact, is the perfect view of the interior, and of all within it, which can be had from any point. The boxes and stalls were taken by subscription. One of the latter, comprising the right to a revolving chair, like a music stool with arms, in the amphitheatre, cost orchestra, supported by a framework of the lightest and simplest kind, itself its only ornament. It is said to be the largest organ in the world, and was constructed by Mr. Henry Willis, the builder of the organ at St. George's Hall, Liverpool. Some idea of the size of the instrument may be formed when we say that it contains about 120 registers, about 8,000 pipes, distributed over four manuals and a pedal organ. The pipes vary in length from about thirty-four feet to three-quarters of an inch. The only organ in England which approaches it in size is that at the Alexandra Palace, built by the same maker; and it is about double the size of the fine organ of St. Paul's Cathedral. In this organ the builder, for the first time, made use of pneumatic tubes for the connection of the manuals and pedals with pipes at a distance, instead of the old long tracker movement; and it is probable that this invention will, in the course of time, cause important changes in the construction of such gigantic instruments. With its vistas of polished pipes of all sizes, some of them gleaming like silver, the organ arrests the eye at once on entering

feet, the shorter length is 180 feet, and there is a distance of 140 feet between the floor of the arena and the dome.

Since the day of the opening of the hall by Her Majesty, when the orchestra was occupied by 1,200 instrumentalists and vocalists, concerts on a grand and extensive scale have been the chief use to which the building has been put; and it was also used for part of the display in the annual

INTERIOR OF THE ALBERT HALL.

the building; and when one hears that the motive power is supplied by two steam-engines, one might be led to expect such a volume of sound as would almost blow the roof off.

The lighting of the hall is a novelty in itself. Thirty gold-coloured chandeliers, one in each arch, surround the picture-gallery, each having fifteen lights. There is a third ring of sixty chandeliers, with twenty-one lights each; and altogether there are nearly 7,000 gas jets, which can all be lit by electricity in ten seconds.

The spaces over the porches on the east and west sides of the hall have been in each case arranged as a lecture theatre, having a raised floor, with a platform or stage, and holding about 200 people. At its widest part the hall measures 200

industrial Exhibitions of 1871-4. The grandest scenes, perhaps, which have taken place within its walls were on the occasions of the state concerts given in honour of the visits to England of the Shah of Persia, the Czar of Russia, &c.; another brilliant ceremony witnessed here was the installation of the Prince of Wales as Grand Master of the Lodge of Freemasons of England.

Close by the Royal Albert Hall, on a plot of ground granted by the Commissioners of the Exhibition of 1851, is the National Training School for Music, of which the Duke of Edinburgh was the first president. The building was constructed in 1875, at the cost of Sir Charles Freake. The Council of the Society of Arts undertook the supervision of the foundation of scholarships.

The Royal Horticultural Society, whose gardens, as we have already stated, are enclosed by the Exhibition buildings on the south side of the Royal Albert Hall, was established in 1804, and incorporated by royal charter soon afterwards. The society was instituted for the improvement of horticulture in all its branches, and it has an extensive experimental garden at Chiswick, five miles from London, laid out tastefully, and filled with many rare plants. These gardens have acquired great celebrity from their having been established at a period when gardening was in a very low condition in this country, and from having been the means of raising it to its present greatly-improved state. Previously to purchasing the land at Chiswick, the Horticultural Society had temporarily occupied a small piece of ground at Brompton, not far from the gardens which we are about to notice. In 1859 the society obtained (through the late Prince Consort) possession of about twenty acres of land on this site, and new and splendid gardens were laid out. These were opened in the summer of 1862, forming a charming retreat from the bustle of the Exhibition.

Between the Kensington Road and Cromwell Road the ground falls about forty feet, and using this fact in aid of a general effect, the ground has been divided into three principal levels. The entrances to the gardens are on the lower level in Exhibition Road and Queen's Gate, and the central pathway, upwards of seventy-five feet wide, ascending through terraces to the third great level, leads to the winter garden or conservatory. The whole garden is surrounded by Italian arcades, each of the three levels having arcades of a different character. The upper, or north arcade, where the boundary is semi-circular in form, is a modification of the arcades of the Villa Albani at Rome. The central arcade is almost wholly of Milanese brick-work, interspersed with terra-cotta, majolica, &c., while the design for the south arcade has been adapted from the beautiful cloisters of St. John Lateran at Rome. None of these arcades are less than twenty feet wide and twenty-five feet high, and they give a promenade, sheltered from all weathers, more than three-quarters of a mile in length. The arcades and earthworks were executed by the Commissioners for the Exhibition of 1851, at a cost of £50,000, while the laying-out of the gardens and construction of the conservatory were executed by the Horticultural Society, and cost about the same sum. On the upper terrace, in front of the conservatory, and at the head of a lake, stands a memorial of the late Prince Consort, the work of Mr. Joseph Durham, sculptor, originally intended only to com-

memorate the International Exhibition of 1851. The death of the Prince having occurred before the work was completed, the memorial was made into a lasting tribute to the "great founder of the Exhibition." The idea embodied is Britannia (typified by the Prince) supported by the four quarters of the globe—signifying that the Exhibition originated in England, and was supported by all other nations. The monument stands upwards of forty feet in height, and represents the Prince in his robes as Grand Master of the Order of the Bath. The body of the memorial is of grey granite, with columns and panels of red polished Aberdeen granite; the statue of the Prince, and also those of the figures representing each quarter of the globe, being of bronze.

In 1883 a large portion of the gardens of the Horticultural Society was utilised for the purposes of an International Fisheries Exhibition, which was opened by the Prince of Wales on the 12th of May. The exhibition was held in several temporary buildings, covering nearly twelve acres of ground. It was designed with the view of illustrating sea and fresh-water fishing in all its branches, fish-culture, fishing-boats, fish-curing, fishing-tackle and apparatus of all kinds, lifeboats and life-saving apparatus, diving apparatus, indeed, everything immediately relating to and connected with the actual working of all kinds of fishing. Among the more interesting features of the exhibition were the aquaria of sea and fresh water, well stocked with fish, anemones, aquatic plants, &c.; also the fine collection of pictures of marine subjects, and the collection of stuffed and preserved fish, and casts, and drawings; together with specimens and representations illustrative of the relations between extinct and existing fishes. The boat used by Grace Darling and her father, in 1838, in their gallant rescue of nine of the sufferers from the wreck of the *Forfarshire* among the Farne Islands, was exhibited, as also was the old Royal state barge which was built in the reign of James II. Prizes were offered for essays connected with the objects of the Exhibition: on such subjects as the natural history of commercial sea fishes of Great Britain and Ireland, with special reference to such parts of their natural history as bear upon their production and commercial use; as to the effect of the laws for the regulation and protection of fisheries; on improved facilities for the capture and economic distribution of sea fishes; and on improved fishery harbour accommodation. Conferences were also held for reading and discussing papers on subjects connected with the exhibitions; and instruction in cooking fish was given.

OLD GORE HOUSE, IN 1830.

CHAPTER X.

"THE OLD COURT SUBURB."—KENSINGTON.

"When shall we walk to Totnam, or crosse o'er
The water? or take coach to Kensington
Or Paddington? or to some one or other
O' th' City out-leaps for an afternoon?"
Brome's "New Academy" (a play), 1658.

Descent of the Manor—A Parochial Enigma—Derivation of the Name of Kensington—Thackeray's "Esmond"—Leigh Hunt's Reminiscences—Gore House—Mr. Wilberforce, the Philanthropist—Lord Rodney—The Countess of Blessington and her Admirers—An Anecdote of Louis Napoleon—Count D'Orsay's Picture—A Touching Incident—Sale of the Contents of Gore House, and Death of the Countess of Blessington—M. Soyer's "Symposium"—Sale of the Gore House Estate—Park House—Hamilton Lodge, the Residence of John Wilkes—Batty's Hippodrome—St. Stephen's Church—Orford Lodge—Christ Church.

KENSINGTON, which is technically described as a suburb of London, in the Hundred of Ossulston, has long enjoyed distinction from its Palace, in which several successive sovereigns of the Hanoverian line held their court, and which was the birth-place of Queen Victoria. In the time of the Domesday survey the manor of Kensington was owned by the Bishop of Coutances, to whom it was granted by William the Conqueror. It was at that time held by Aubrey de Vere, and subsequently, as history tells us, it became the absolute property of the De Veres, who afterwards gave twenty Earls of Oxford to the English peerage. Aubrey de Vere

was Grand Justiciary of England, and was created Earl of Oxford by the Empress Maud. Upon the attainder of John, Earl of Oxford, who was beheaded during the struggle for power between the houses of York and Lancaster, the manor was bestowed by Edward IV. on his brother Richard, Duke of Gloucester. After passing through the hands of the Marquis of Berkeley and Sir Reginald Bray, the property returned (as is supposed by purchase) to John, Earl of Oxford, son of the attainted nobleman above mentioned. The manor is said to have again passed from that family, probably by sale, in the reign of Elizabeth; and early in the seventeenth century the Earl of Argyll and three other persons joined in a conveyance of the property to Sir Walter Cope, whose daughter conveyed it by marriage to Henry Rich, Earl of Holland. The manor subsequently passed into the hands of Lord Kensington, who was maternally descended from Robert Rich, last Earl of Warwick and Holland, and whose barony, singularly enough, is an Irish one, although the title is derived from this place.

Parochially considered, Kensington is somewhat of an enigma, for it is not only more than Kensington in some places, but it is not Kensington itself in others. In Kensington parish, for instance, are included Earl's Court, Little Chelsea, Old and New Brompton, Kensal Green, and even some of the houses in Sloane Street; while, on the other hand, Kensington Palace and Kensington Gardens are not in Kensington, but in the parish of St. Margaret's, Westminster.

The place, which now forms, as it were, part and parcel of London, was down to comparatively recent times a village, one mile and a half from Hyde Park Corner. The name is stated by some topographers to be derived from Kœnnigston, or from the Saxon *Kyning's*-tun, a term synonymous with King's End Town, and to be the same word as Kennington and Kingston; our monarchs from the earliest date having had residences at all three places. Possibly, however, the " Ken " may be an equivalent to " Kaen," or " Caen," which lies at the root of " Kentish " Town, " Caen-wood," &c.; but we will leave the origin of the name to be discussed by antiquaries, and pass on to a survey of the district in detail.

"Whatever was the origin of its name," writes Leigh Hunt, in the " Old Court Suburb," " there is no doubt that the first inhabited spot of Kensington was an inclosure from the great Middlesex forest which once occupied this side of London, and which extended northwards as far as Barnet." Kensington has been always a favourite, not only with royalty, but with those who more or less bask in the sunshine of princes—poets, painters, &c. The healthfulness and fashion of the place attracted numerous families of distinction; and its importance was completed when William III. bought the house and grounds of the Finch family (Earls of Nottingham), and converted the former into a palace, and the latter into royal gardens. It is emphatically " the old Court suburb," and is familiar to all readers of Thackeray, who has portrayed its features in many of his writings, especially in " Esmond." Leigh Hunt observes that " there is not a step of the way, from its commencement

at Kensington Gore to its termination beyond Holland House, in which you are not greeted with the face of some pleasant memory. Here, to 'minds' eyes' conversant with local biography, stands a beauty looking out of a window; there, a wit talking with other wits at a garden-gate; there, a poet on the green sward, glad to get out of the London smoke and find himself among trees. Here come De Veres of the times of old; Hollands and Davenants, of the Stuart and Cromwell times; Evelyn, peering about him soberly, and Samuel Pepys in a bustle. Here advance Prior, Swift, Arbuthnot, Gay, Sir Isaac Newton; Steele, from visiting Addison; Walpole, from visiting the Foxes; Johnson, from a dinner with Elphinstone; 'Junius,' from a communication with Wilkes. Here, in his carriage, is King William III. going from the palace to open Parliament; Queen Anne, for the same purpose; George I. and George II. (we shall have the pleasure of looking at all these personages a little more closely); and there, from out of Kensington Gardens, comes bursting, as if the whole recorded polite world were in flower at one and the same period, all the fashion of the gayest times of those sovereigns, blooming with chintzes, full-blown with hoop-petticoats, towering with topknots and toupees. Here comes 'Lady Mary,' quizzing everybody; and Lady Suffolk, looking discreet; there, the lovely Bellendens and Lepels; there, Miss Howe, laughing with Nancy Lowther (who made her very grave afterwards); there Chesterfield, Hanbury Williams, Lord Hervey; Miss Chudleigh, not over clothed; the Miss Gunnings, drawing crowds of admirers; and here is George Selwyn, interchanging wit with my Lady Townshend, the ' Lady Bellaston ' (so, at least, it has been said) of ' Tom Jones.' " Probably there is not an old house in Kensington in which some distinguished person has not lived, during the reigns in which the Court resided there; but the houses themselves are, as Leigh Hunt puts it, " but dry bones, unless invested with interests of flesh and blood."

The Royal Albert Hall and the gardens of the Horticultural Society occupy the site of Gore House and grounds. This is probably the estate called the Gara, or the Gare, which Herbert, Abbot of Westminster, gave to the nuns of Kilburn. The spot was, according to John Timbs, anciently called Kyng's Gore. Old Gore House was a low, plain, and unpretending building, painted white, and abutted on the roadway, about 150 yards to the east of the chief public entrance to the Albert Hall. Its external beauty, if it had any, belonged to its southern, or garden side. Standing close to the roadside, it looked as if meant originally for the lodge of some great mansion which had never actually been built : and the row, of which it formed a part, as Leigh Hunt observes, in his "Old Court Suburb," might easily lead one to imagine that it had been divided into apartments for the retainers of the Court, and that either a supernumerary set of maids of honour had lived there, or else that some four or five younger brothers of lords of the bed-chamber had been the occupants, and expecting places in reversion. "The two houses," adds the writer, "seem to be nothing but one large drawing-room. They possess, however, parlours and second storeys at the back, and they have good gardens, so that, what with their flowers behind them, the park in front, and their own neatness and elegance, the miniature aristocracy of their appearance is not ill borne out."

Here, for the best part of half a century, distin-guished statesmen and philanthropists, and after-wards the light and frivolous butterflies of West-end society, used to mix with men of letters and the votaries of science. Here the "lions" of the day were entertained from time to time ; and there were few houses to which the *entrée* was more coveted. At the end of the last century it was little more than a cottage, with a pleasant garden in the rear attached to it, and it was tenanted by a Government contractor, who does not seem to have cared to go to any expense in keeping it in order. Early in the present century it was en-larged on coming into the possession of Mr. Wil-berforce, who soon grew very fond of the spot, and here used to entertain Mr. Pitt, Lord Auckland (who lived hard by), and such eminent philan-thropists as Clarkson, Stephen, Zachary Macaulay, and Romilly ; indeed, it has often been said that the agitation which ended in the abolition of West Indian slavery was commenced in the library of Gore House. Of this place Mr. Wilberforce often speaks in his private correspondence ; and in one place he mentions his *rus in urbe* in the following terms :—"We are just one mile from the turnpike at Hyde Park Corner, having about three acres of pleasure-ground around our house, or rather behind it, and several old trees, walnut and mulberry, of thick foliage. I can sit and read under their shade with as much admiration of the beauties of Nature as if I were down in Yorkshire, or anywhere else 200 miles from the great city." Here, too, his four sons, including the future Bishop of Oxford and of Winchester, were mainly brought up in their childhood and boyhood ; and in the later years of its hospitable owner's life it is on record that "its costliness made him at times uneasy, lest it should force him to curtail his charities," a thing which he was always most anxious to avoid. Mrs. Wilber-force supported in this mansion a school for poor girls, which was under her own personal superin-tendence. At Gore House the gallant admiral, Lord Rodney, was for some time "laid up in port."

Mr. Wilberforce having occupied the house for thirteen years, from 1808 down to 1821, it next passed into the hands of a new meditator, but not so much on the beauties of nature as on those of art and literature—one who was more *spirituelle* in *salons*, that "spiritual" in Wilberforce's sense of the term—the "gorgeous" Countess of Blessington became in turn its proprietor. She lived here during her widowhood, surrounded by a bright and fashionable crowd of aristocratic and literary ad-mirers. Gore House became indeed a centre of attraction to the world of letters ; for besides giving such dinners as Dr. Johnson would have thought "worth being asked to," Lady Blessington prided herself on her success in "bringing people together," in order to please and be pleased in turn. Here were such men of the last generation as Lord Melbourne, the poet Campbell, Samuel Rogers, and many of the *beaux* of "the Regency" and of the reign of George IV., including Count D'Orsay, who married Lady Blessington's daughter, and made the house his home.

"At Gore House," writes Mr. Blanchard Jer-rold, "Prince Louis Napoleon met most of the intellectual society of the time, and became the friend of Count D'Orsay, Sir E. Lytton Bulwer, Sir Henry Holland, Albany Fonblanque, and many others who formed Lady Blessington's circle." The Prince dined at Gore House with a small party of West-end friends and acquaintances, in-cluding Lord Nugent and "Poodle" Byng, on the evening before he started off on his wild and abortive effort to make a descent on Boulogne in August, 1840. "It was the fashion in that day," says Mr. Planché, in his "Recollections," "to wear black satin handkerchiefs for evening dress ; and that of the Prince was fastened by a large spread eagle in diamonds, clutching a thunderbolt of rubies. There was in England at that time but one man who, without the impeachment of coxcombry, could have sported so magnificent a jewel ; and though to my knowledge I had never seen him before, I felt convinced that he could be no other than Prince Louis Napoleon. Such was the fact. . . . There was a general conversation on indifferent matters for some twenty minutes, during which the Prince spoke but little, and then took his departure with Count Montholon. Shortly afterwards, Lord Nugent, Mr. Byng, and I, said good night, and walked townward together. As we went along, one of my companions said to the other, 'What could Louis Napoleon mean by asking us to dine with him at the Tuileries on this day twelve months?' Four days afterwards the question was answered. The news arrived of the abortive landing at Boulogne and the captivity of the Prince." On the first day after his escape from Ham (1846), and his arrival in London, Prince Louis Napoleon again dined here at a party, with

establishments seldom equalled, and still more rarely surpassed, in all the appliances of a state of society brilliant in the highest degree; but, alas! it must be acknowledged, at the same time, a state of splendid misery for a great portion of that time to the mistress of those elegant and luxurious establishments. And now, at the end of that time, we find her forced to abandon that position, to leave all the elegancies and refinements of her

THE OLD TURNPIKE, KENSINGTON, IN 1820.

Lady Blessington, Count D'Orsay, Walter Savage Landor, Mr. John Forster, &c., whom he amused by recounting his recent adventure in detail.

Mr. Madden, in his "Life and Correspondence of the Countess of Blessington," says:—"For nineteen years Lady Blessington had maintained, at first in Seamore Place, and afterwards at Kensington, a position almost queen-like in the world of intellectual distinction, in fashionable literary society, reigning over the best circles of London celebrities, and reckoning among her admiring friends, and the frequenters of her *salons*, the most eminent men of England in every walk of literature, art, and science, in statesmanship, in the military profession, and in every learned pursuit. For nineteen years she had maintained in London

home to become the property of strangers, and in fact to make a departure from the scene of all her former triumphs, with a privacy which must have been most painful and humiliating."

Count D'Orsay painted a large garden view of Gore House, with portraits of the Duke of Wellington, Lords Chesterfield, Douro, and Brougham, Sir E. Landseer, the Miss Powers, and other members of the fashionable circle that gathered there. "In the foreground, to the right," says a description of the picture, "are the great Duke and Lady Blessington; in the centre, Sir E. Landseer, seated, in the act of sketching a fine cow, with a calf by her side; Count D'Orsay himself, with two favourite dogs, is seen on the right of the group, and Lord Chesterfield on the left: nearer the house are the two Miss Powers (nieces of Lady Blessington), reading a letter, a gentleman walking behind. Further to the left are Lord Brougham, Lord Douro, &c., seated under a tree, engaged in conversation."

and Albert Smith and Thackeray, Charles Dickens and William Jerdan, Mr. Monckton Milnes, Mr. A. Baillie Cochrane, Mr. N. P. Willis, the Countess Guiccioli (Byron's *chere amie*), Lords Brougham, Lyndhurst, and Chesterfield, and all the other

THE "HALFWAY HOUSE," KENSINGTON, 1850.

Mr. Madden, in his book above quoted, gives us anecdotes of, or letters from, most of the visitors at Gore House when it was in its prime. Thomas Moore, who sang so touchingly as to unlock the fount of tears in the drawing-room, was often there; so were Horace and James Smith, the authors of the "Rejected Addresses;" so was Sir Henry Lytton Bulwer and his brother, the late Lord Lytton. Walter Savage Landor would repair thither, with his stern eyebrows and kindly heart;

celebrities, who, being added up together into one sum, made up, what Joseph Hume would have styled, the "tottle of the whole" of the Gore House circle. Mr. N. P. Willis thus records an incident during an evening here:—"We all sat round the piano, and, after two or three songs of Lady Blessington's choosing, Moore rambled over the keys awhile, and then sang 'When first I met thee,' with a pathos that beggars description. When the last word had faltered out, he rose and took Lady Blessington's hand, said good-night, and was gone before a word was uttered. . . . I have heard of women fainting at a song of Moore's; and if the burden of it answered by chance to a secret in the bosom of the listener, I should think, from its comparative effect upon so old a stager as myself, that the heart would break with it."

Lady Blessington's "curiosities" and treasures—the contents of the once favourite mansion—were disposed of by auction in the summer of 1849; and she herself went off to Paris, to die in debt, and deserted by her butterfly admirers, but a few weeks afterwards. The contents of the mansion are thus described in the catalogue of the sale:—"Costly and elegant effects: comprising all the magnificent furniture, rare porcelain, sculpture in marble, bronzes, and an assemblage of objects of art and decoration; a casket of valuable jewellery and *bijouterie*, services of rich chased silver and silver-gilt plate, a superbly-fitted silver dressing-case; collection of ancient and modern pictures, including many portraits of distinguished persons, valuable original drawings, and fine engravings, framed and in portfolios; the extensive and interesting library of books, comprising upwards of 5,000 volumes, expensive table services of china and rich cut glass, and an infinity of useful and valuable articles. All the property of the Right Hon. the Countess of Blessington, retiring to the Continent."

In 1851, during the time of the Great Exhibition, Gore House was made a "Symposium," or *restaurant*, by M. Alexis Soyer, whose *cuisine*, whilst *chef* of the Reform Club, enjoyed European fame.* Its walls were once more adorned with a splendour and costliness which it had not known for some years, though, possibly, not with equal taste as that which was so conspicuous under the *régime* of the clever and brilliant lady who had made it a home. Soyer first came to England on a visit to his brother, who was then cook to the Duke of Cambridge; and at Cambridge House he cooked his first dinner in England for the then Prince George. Soyer afterwards entered the service of various noblemen: amongst others, of Lord Ailsa, Lord Panmure, &c. He then was employed by the Reform Club, and the breakfast given by that club, on the occasion of the Queen's coronation, obtained him high commendation. Mr. Mark Boyd, in his "Social Gleanings," tells a good story about M. Soyer. "Meeting him in an omnibus, after his return from the Crimea, I congratulated him on the laurels he had gained with

our army, and was anxious to learn how he had managed this under the privations to which our brave fellows were exposed from short rations, and often from no rations at all! 'Dere is my merit, Monsieur Boyd,' he replied, 'for I did make good dishes out of nothing.'" It is to be feared that his words were literally true.

The Gore House estate, comprising some twenty-one acres, was purchased in 1852 by the Commissioners of the Great Exhibition, out of the surplus fund of that Exhibition, for the sum of £60,000, as a site for a new National Gallery; and the Baron de Villars' estate, adjoining, nearly fifty acres, fronting the Brompton Road, was bought for £153,500, as a site for a Museum of Manufactures; "these localities being recommended for the dryness of the soil, and as the only ground safe for future years amidst the growth of the metropolis." On the latter site, as we have shown in the previous chapter, the South Kensington Museum and the Schools of Art and Science have been erected; but instead of the National Gallery, the ground at Kensington Gore was made to serve as the site for the Albert Hall, &c.

Park House, at the eastern end of the Gore, close by Prince's Gate, indicates the northern boundary of the once famous Kensington or Brompton Park Nursery, which figures in the pages of the *Spectator* as the establishment of Messrs. Loudon and Wise, the most celebrated gardeners of their time. Near to this was Noel House, so called from having been built by one of the Campdens. Hamilton Lodge, Kensington Gore, was the occasional residence of John Wilkes, who here entertained Counts Woronzow and Nesselrode, and Sir Philip Francis. At Palace Gate lives Mr. J. E. Millais, R.A. De Vere Gardens, close by, perpetuate the memory of the Veres, Earls of Oxford.

A little to the west of Kensington Gore, immediately opposite to the broad walk of Kensington Gardens, was, in 1850–1, Batty's Grand National Hippodrome. Its site, which lies at the back of the Prince of Wales' Terrace, covering a considerable space of ground between the two thoroughfares known as Palace Gate and Victoria Road, was for many years used as a riding school, but was ultimately given up for building purposes. Near the old turnpike, which stood a little westward of Gore House, was a small inn known as the halfway house between London and Hammersmith. It was a curious and picturesque structure, but was swept away about the year 1860.

Opposite Queen's Gate Gardens, and adjoining the Gloucester Road, on the west side of the

Horticultural Gardens, is St. Stephen's Church, built in 1866, from the designs of Mr. Joseph Peacock, and is an architectural ornament to the neighbourhood. In this immediate locality was Orford Lodge, built on the site of the "Old Florida Tea Gardens," for the late Duchess of Gloucester, after whom Gloucester Road is named. The Lodge was subsequently tenanted by the Princess Sophia, and also by the Right Hon. George Canning, who was here visited by Queen Caroline. The house was taken down in the year 1852. The thoroughfare which connected Chelsea with the great western road through the village between the Gore and Kensington Square rejoiced in the not very pleasant-sounding name of "Hogmire Lane" —a name, however, suggestive of farm-yards and piggeries, which then, doubtless, were plentiful in the neighbourhood.

Christ Church, in the Victoria Road, is a fine edifice, of Gothic design, dating from the year 1851, and accommodating about 800 persons. All its seats are open. It was built from the designs of Mr. Benjamin Ferrey. The architecture is of the Decorated style, varying from geometrical to flowing. It comprises a nave and chancel, tower and spire. The windows throughout are of flowered quarries; that at the east end is a rich diaper pattern, copied from one in York Minster.

CHAPTER XI.

KENSINGTON (continued).

"Faith, and it's the Old Court Suburb that you spoke of, is it? Sure, an' it's a mighty fine place for the quality."—*Old Play*.

The Old Court Suburb—Pepys at "Kingly Kensington"—The High Street—Thackeray's "Esmond"—Palace Gate—Colby House—Singular Death—Kensington House: its Early History—Famous Inhabitants—Old Kensington Bedlam—The New House—Young Street—Kensington Square—Famous Inhabitants—Talleyrand—An Aged Waltzer—Macaulay's Description of Talleyrand—The New Parish Church—The Old Building—The Monuments—The Bells—The Parish Registers—The Charity School—Campden House—"The Dogs"—Sir James South's Observatory—A Singular Sale—Other Noted Residents at Kensington—Insecurity of the Kensington Road—A Remarkable Dramatic Performance—A Ghost Story—The Crippled Boys' Home—Scarsdale House—The Roman Catholic University College—Roman Catholic Chapels—The Pro-Cathedral—The "Adam and Eve."

HITHERTO, since leaving the side of the river at Chelsea, we have been mostly passing over modern ground, which a century ago was scantily dotted with private residences, and which, therefore, can scarcely be expected as yet to have much of a past history. But now, as we look round the "Old Court Suburb" of Kensington, and its venerable and somewhat narrow High Street, we find ourselves again confronted with houses and persons of an earlier era, and, consequently, we shall be able to dwell at greater length on the annals and anecdotes of which Kensington has been the scene. The Palace and the Church, of course, will form our central objects, to which, perhaps, we ought to add that old-world haunt of fashion, Kensington Square. The old town of Kensington consisted principally of one long street, extending about three-quarters of a mile in length, from the Gore to Earl's Terrace; but even that thoroughfare is of comparatively modern growth, for the only highway for travellers westward, in former times, was the old Roman (or present Uxbridge) Road, then bending southerly (as it still branches) to Turnham Green. Within the last century a number of small streets have been built on either side. Bowack, in his "History of Middlesex," thus describes the place in the middle of the last century:—"This town, standing in a wholesome air, not above three miles from London, has ever been resorted to by persons of quality and citizens, and for many years past honoured with several fine seats belonging to the Earls of Nottingham and Warwick. We cannot, indeed, find it was ever taken notice of in history, except for the great western road through it, nor hath anything occurred in it that might perpetuate its name, till his late Majesty, King William, was pleased to ennoble it with his court and royal presence. Since which time it has flourished even almost beyond belief, and is inhabited by gentry and persons of note; there is also abundance of shopkeepers, and all sorts of artificers in it, which makes it appear rather like part of London than a country village. It is, with its dependencies, about three times as big as Chelsea, in number of houses, and in summer time extremely filled with lodgers, for the pleasure of the air, walks, and gardens round it, to the great advantage of its inhabitants. The buildings are chiefly of brick, regular, and built into streets; the largest is that through which the road lies, reclining back from the Queen's House, a considerable way beyond the church. From the church runs a row of buildings towards the north, called Church Lane; but the most beautiful part of it is the Square, south of the road, which, for beauty of buildings, and worthy inhabitants, exceed several noted squares in London."

Kensington — "kingly Kensington," as Dean Swift called it—is not very frequently mentioned by Pepys, as that country village had not, in his days, become the "court suburb." He mentions, however, accompanying "my lord" (the Earl of Sandwich) to dine at Kensington with Lord Campden, at Campden House, and afterwards to call at Holland House. With two other trivial exceptions, this is all that we learn about Kensington from the old gossip's "Diary;" neither does the place figure in the "Memoirs of the Count de Gramont." It is on record that George II. admired the flat grounds of Kensington and Kew, as reminding him of "Yarmany." It is described by Bowack, in 1705, as being about three times as big as Chelsea. The manor of Abbots' Kensington, which occupies an area of about 1,140 acres in all, extends northwards so far as to include all the Gravel Pits and Notting Hill.

Although Kensington is so near London, and contains so many new buildings, the High Street has a considerable resemblance to that of a country town. The houses, for the most part, are of moderate size, and considerable variety is displayed in the style of building, so that the fronts of scarcely any two houses are alike. Faulkner, writing in 1820, remarks: "The town, being in the direct road for the western parts of England, is in a considerable bustle, and resembles the most populous streets in London, especially in an evening, when the mail-coaches are setting out for their various destinations." The chief coaching-inn and posting-house, at that time, was the "Red Lion," at the back of which is still to be seen a curious sun-dial, bearing the date 1713. Readers of Thackeray's "Esmond" will not have forgotten the picture he has given of the scene which might have been witnessed from the tavern at the corner of the old High Street, on the occasion of the accession of King George I. :—"Out of the window of the tavern, and looking over the garden wall, you can see the green before Kensington Palace, the palace gate (round which the ministers' coaches are standing), and the barrack building. As we were looking out from this window in gloomy distraction, we heard presently the trumpets blowing, and some of us ran to the window of the front room looking into the High Street, and saw a regiment of horse coming. 'It's Ormond's Guards,' says one. 'No, by G—; it's Argyle's old regiment!' says my general, clapping down his crutch. It was indeed Argyle's regiment that was brought up from Westminster, and that took the part of the regiment at Kensington." The sequel is soon told, and it shall here be told, in the words of "Esmond:"—"With some delays in procuring horses, we got to Hammersmith about four o'clock on Sunday morning, the 1st of August (1714), and half an hour after, it then being bright day, we rode by my Lady Warwick's house, and so down the street of Kensington. Early as the hour was, there was a bustle in the street, and many people moving to and fro. Round the gate leading to the palace, where the guard is, there was especially a great crowd; and the coach ahead of us stopped, and the bishop's man got down, to know what the concourse meant. Then presently came out from the gate horse-guards with their trumpets, and a company of heralds with their tabards. The trumpets blew, and the herald-at-arms came forward, and proclaimed 'George, by the grace of God, of Great Britain, France, and Ireland, King, Defender of the Faith.' And the people shouted 'God save the King!'" Thus was the first sovereign of the Hanoverian line proclaimed in the High Street of Kensington; and there, with the sound of King George's trumpets, were the last hopes of the Stuart line scattered to the winds of heaven. The spot where this proclamation took place is surely an object of historic interest to after ages.

Almost at the entrance of the High Street is the Palace Gate, with its sentinels on duty, and opposite to it stood, till recently, a good, moderate-sized house—a sort of undergrown mansion—which, as Leigh Hunt says, looked as if it "had been made for some rich old bachelor who chose to live alone, but liked to have everything about him strong and safe." Such was probably the case, for it was called Colby House, and was the abode of Sir Thomas Colby, of whom Dr. King tells us in his "Anecdotes of his Own Times," that being worth £200,000, and having no near relatives, he met with his death by getting up from his warm bed on a winter night to fetch the key of his cellar, which he had forgotten, for fear his servant might help himself to a bottle of wine. The house was inhabited, when Faulkner wrote his "History of Kensington," by one of the leading magistrates of the county. Its former eccentric owner was buried in the parish church. The house was standing till about 1872, when it was pulled down, along with the large red house, Kensington House, adjoining, to make a site for Baron Grant's mansion.

Kensington House, a dull and heavy building of red brick on the south side of the high road, nearly facing the Palace gates, was for some years inhabited by the notorious Duchess of Portsmouth, one of the many mistresses of Charles II. The house was long and low in proportion, and was screened from the road by a high wall. It is recorded that King Charles supped here the night before he was seized with the illness which proved his last. The house was afterwards turned into a school, kept by Elphinstone, who was known as the translator of Martial, and as a friend of Dr. Jortin, Benjamin Franklin, and Dr. Johnson. He was ludicrously caricatured by Smollett, in "Roderick Random," which was consequently a forbidden book in his school. At the outbreak of the first French Revolution the house was occupied by some French emigrant priests, members of the Jesuit Order, who kept here a college for the youth of the French and some of the English aristocracy, under the assumed name of "Les Pères de la Foi." The late Mr. Richard Lalor Sheil was sent here when a boy, and he tells us how the school was visited by "Monsieur"—as Charles X., afterwards King of France, was then called—in his brother's lifetime.

The building has been described as follows by Mr. Sheil*:—"I landed at Bristol, and with a French clergyman, the Abbé de Grimeau, who had been my tutor, I proceeded to London. The abbé informed me that I was to be sent to Kensington House, a college established by the Pères de la Foi—for so the French Jesuits settled in England at that time called themselves—and that he had directions to leave me there upon his way to Languedoc, from whence he had been exiled in the Revolution, and to which he had been driven by the *maladie de pays* to return. Accordingly, we set off for Kensington House, which is situated exactly opposite the avenue leading to the palace, and has the beautiful garden attached to it in front. A large iron gate, wrought into rustic flowers, and other fantastic forms, showed that the Jesuit school had once been the residence of some person of distinction. . . . It was a large old-fashioned house, with many remains of decayed splendour. In a beautiful walk of trees, which ran down from the rear of the building through the play-ground, I saw several French boys playing at swing-swang ; and the moment I entered, my ears were filled with the shrill vociferations of some hundreds of little emigrants, who were engaged in their various amusements, and babbled, screamed, laughed, and shouted, in all the velocity of their rapid and joyous language. I did not hear a word of English, and at once perceived that I was as much amongst Frenchmen as if I had been suddenly transferred to a Parisian college. Having got this peep at the gaiety of the school into which I was to be introduced, I was led, with my companion, to a chamber covered with faded gilding, and which had once been richly tapestried, where I found the head of the establishment, in the person of a French nobleman, Monsieur le Prince de Broglie."

Here, in 1821, whilst the house was still in the hands of the Jesuits, died—it is said, from the effects of tight lacing—Mrs. Inchbald, the authoress of the "Simple Story." She had resided in several other houses in Kensington before coming here. She had written many volumes, which she had by her in manuscript ; but on her death-bed, from some motive or other, she requested a friend to tear them to pieces before her eyes, not having the strength to perform the heroic deed of immolation with her own hands. Mr. and Mrs. Cosway, too, resided here for a short time, after leaving Stratford Place, and before settling down in the Edgware Road.

The building was subsequently turned into a private lunatic asylum, and was then popularly known as Old Kensington Bedlam. It was purchased in 1873 by "Baron" Albert Grant, who pulled it down and erected a modern Italian palace on its site. The cost of the building and grounds is stated to have exceeded one million sterling. The mansion contained a grand hall and staircase, built entirely of white marble, drawing-rooms, library, picture-gallery, three dining-rooms *en suite*, and a spacious ball-room. In the construction of the windows, numbering over a hundred, no less than three tons of stone were used. In the formation of the grounds, which are twelve acres in extent, Mr. Grant purchased an Irish colony situated in the rear of the Kensington High Street —formerly called the "Rookery" and "Jenning's Buildings"—both of which had been a nuisance to the parish for years past. These places were entirely demolished, and the ground was converted into a picturesque lake, three acres in extent, with two small islands in the centre. Baron Grant got into difficulties, and the house, after various efforts to secure a sale, in order that it might be converted into a club or hotel, was sold piecemeal as so much old materials, and finally pulled down in 1883 to make way for smaller houses.

Continuing our way westward, we come to the turning at Young Street, which leads into the square above alluded to. It is an old-fashioned, oblong enclosure, and bears the name of Ken-

---

* Quoted by Leigh Hunt, in "The Old Court Suburb."

sington Square. It was commenced in the reign of James II., and finished about 1698, as appeared by a date at one time affixed at the north-east corner. It is described by Bowack, in 1705, as "the most beautiful part of the parish south of the main road," and as "exceeding several noted squares in London for beauty of its buildings and (for) worthy inhabitants." While the Court was at Kensington, most of the houses were inhabited by

some of Montaigne's "Essays." It is said that, finding little or no information in the chapters as to the subjects their titles promised, he closed the book more confused than satisfied. "What think you of this famous French author?" said a gentleman present. "Think?" said he, smiling: "why, that a pair of manacles, or a stone doublet, would probably have been of some service to that author's infirmity." "Would you imprison a man

INTERIOR OF KENSINGTON CHURCH, 1850.

"persons of quality," ambassadors, gentry, and clergy; and at one time, as Faulkner tells us, upwards of forty carriages were kept by residents in and about the neighbourhood. In the reigns of William and Anne and the first two Georges, this square was the most fashionable spot in the suburbs; indeed, in the time of George II., the demand for lodgings here was so great, "that an ambassador, a bishop, and a physician have been known to occupy apartments in the same house." The celebrated Duchess de Mazarin appears to have resided here in 1692; and here she probably had among her visitors her "adoring old friend, Saint Evremond, with his white locks, little skull cap, and the great wen on his forehead." Here, too, Addison lodged for some time; and here it was that he read over

for singularity in writing?" "Why, let me tell you," replied Addison, "if he had been a horse he would have been pounded for straying; and why he ought to be more favoured because he is a man, I cannot understand." We shall have more, however, to say of Addison when we come to Holland House.

Somewhere about the south-west corner of the square lived, for several years, physician to King William III., and butt of all the wits of the time, Sir Richard Blackmore, the poet, of whom we have spoken in our account of Earl's Court. Hough, the good old Bishop of Winchester, lived here for many years; as also did Mawson, Bishop of Ely; and Dr. Herring, Bishop of Bangor, and afterwards Archbishop of Canterbury. Among other noted

OLD KENSINGTON CHURCH, ABOUT 1750.

OLD VIEW OF KENSINGTON, ABOUT 1750.

residents were the Rev. W. Beloe, the translator of Herodotus; and the Earl of Clanricarde.

Another resident in Kensington Square, during the early part of the present century, was Prince de Talleyrand, at one time Bishop of Autun, in France, and subsequently Ambassador-Extraordinary for that country to the Court of St. James's. Lord Palmerston used to declare that he was "exceedingly quiet and courteous, but he had a strange versatility not revealed to the world at large." When eighty years of age, and extremely lame, he still was fond of sharing the amusements of the young, and his smile was then so benign as quite to discredit the "sarcastic sneer" for which he was famous. "One night at the Duchess of Gramont's," writes Lady Clementina Davies, in her "Recollections of Society," "a game of forfeits was proposed. The duchess joined in the game, and lost her king. She asked how she could get it back. She was told she must ask some gentleman in the room to take a *tour de valse* with her, and she invited the lame and aged diplomatist to dance with her. He smiled, and instantly rose to comply. Several young men offered to take his place, but neither he nor the gay little duchess would allow of this, and Talleyrand seemed able to perform his share in the valse, and to be pleased with the exertion. He remained with his partner, and conversed with her in a style of brilliant animation. When Louis XVIII. was restored to the French throne, the sage minister said to him, 'Now, sir, as a king of the French people, you must learn to forget!' The Bourbons might have fared better could they have taken this wise counsel!"

Lady Clementina Davies, who lived on terms of intimacy with the Prince, declares that it is quite an error to suppose that he was a mere political hypocrite, or that he transferred his services from one sovereign to another with reckless indifference; but that, on the contrary, his only motive was a patriotic desire to advance the interests of his country. He was shamefully used by his parents on account of his club-foot; he was deprived of all his rights as the eldest son, and forced against his will to become a priest. In spite of his cynicism, the great diplomatist was a remarkably pleasant-tempered man, full of kindness to children, and possessing conversational powers of the highest orders.

Talleyrand, in the year 1831, is thus described by Macaulay among the guests he met at Holland House:—"He is certainly the greatest curiosity that I ever fell in with. His head is sunk down between two high shoulders. One of his feet is hideously distorted. His face is as pale as that of a corpse, and wrinkled to a frightful degree. His eyes have an odd glassy stare, quite peculiar to them. His hair, thickly powdered and pomatumed, hangs down his shoulders on each side as straight as a pound of tallow candles. His conversation, however, soon makes you forget his ugliness and infirmities. There is a poignancy without effort in all that he says, which reminds me a little of the character which the wits of Johnson's circle give of Beauclerk. . . . He told several stories about the political men of France, not of any great value in themselves; but his way of telling them was beyond all praise—concise, pointed, and delicately satirical. . . . I could not help breaking out into admiration of his talent for relating anecdotes. Lady Holland said that he had been considered for nearly forty years as the best teller of a story in Europe."

In this square, also, resided James Mill, the historian of British India, and father of Mr. John Stuart Mill, M.P., the political economist. He died in 1836, and was buried in the parish church. Here, too, lived for some years the Rev. J. R. Green, author of "The Making of England," and of other works. He died in 1883.

Part of the western side of the square is occupied by the front of the Kensington Proprietary Grammar School; and three or four of the largest mansions near the south-west angle form now the Convent of the Dames de Sacré Cœur, on whose garden a handsome Roman Catholic church, and also a convent chapel, have been built.

It is in Kensington Square that Thackeray, in his "Esmond," lays the scene which presents us with James Stuart, "the Prince" from Saint Germains, as lodging, and passing for the time as Lord Castlewood, holding himself in readiness for action when the death of Queen Anne was expected. He pictures the Prince walking restlessly upon "the Mall" at Kensington. The "little house in Kensington Square" figures from first to last in the above-mentioned work as the residence of Lady Castlewood and of Beatrix Esmond, and is the centre at once of love-making and of political plots, in the interest of the exiled Stuarts.

About the middle of the High Street stands Kensington Church, dedicated to St. Mary the Virgin. The present fabric dates only from the year 1869, having replaced an older structure. It was built from the designs of Sir Gilbert Scott, and has about it a degree of architectural dignity which befits the importance of the parish as the "Old Court Suburb," the abode of royalty, and a quarter inhabited by many wealthy and aristocratic families.

The style of design is that which was in vogue towards the close of the thirteenth century, and known as the Decorated, though it is freely adapted to present uses. It consists of a large nave and chancel, each with aisles, and additional aisles at the eastern part of the nave, which at that part, consequently, has double aisles on each side. The whole is of very lofty proportions, with clerestory both to nave and chancel. The tower and spire, which are on a considerable scale, are at the north-east angle, and connected with the chancel by an extra aisle, which contains the organ. The cost of the building was nearly £50,000, towards which Her Majesty the Queen gave £200, and the late vicar of the parish, Archdeacon Sinclair, made a donation of £1,000.

The old parish church of St. Mary's, though a plain and unpretending edifice, which Bishop Blomfield used to designate the ugliest in his diocese, was an interesting structure, not only on account of the numerous monuments which it contained, but far more on account of the historical reminiscences connected with it. What with partial rebuildings and wholesale repairs, it had been altered a dozen times in less than two centuries. It superseded a previous building of which little or nothing is recorded. It is more than probable that the ancient parish church of Kensington stood nearly on the spot in Holland Street now occupied by the church of the Carmelite Fathers, and opposite the vicarage. At all events, it stood a little to the north of the parish church of subsequent centuries, and not far from the Manor House, to which the vicarage is a successor; through there is a tradition, but unconfirmed, that the original parish church stood some distance to the north, near the Gravel Pits, and was removed hither at the time of the Conquest. The road, by its very narrowness and curvings, shows that it is an ancient way, and it is still traditionally called, or at all events was called within the memory of the present generation, the "Parson's Yard." It will not be a little singular if hereafter it should be discovered that the Carmelites have been building on the old foundations. The resolution to build this church was adopted by the vestry in 1696, and among the contributors were William III. and Queen Mary, as well as the Princess Anne. The king and queen not only subscribed to the building fund, but presented the reading-desk and pulpit, which had crowns carved upon them, with the initials "W." and "M. R." A pew, curtained round in the fashion of old times, was, in consequence, set apart for the royal family, and long continued to be occupied by residents in Kensington Palace,

amongst whom were the Duke and Duchess of Kent and the late Duke of Cambridge. It was in this church that the Duchess of Kent returned thanks after the birth of Queen Victoria.

Here were monuments to Edward, eighth Earl of Warwick and Holland, who died in 1759; and to "the three Colmans:" Francis Colman, some time British Minister to the Court of Florence; his son, George, "the Elder," and his grandson, George, "the Younger." The two latter wrote several comedies, and were proprietors of the Haymarket Theatre. Here also was buried one Sir Manhood Penruddock, who was "slain at Notting Wood, in fight, in the year 1608." At that time the nation was at peace; the "fight" which is recorded in the parish register probably means a "duel." Two interesting monuments by Chantrey, which were erected in the old parish church, have been replaced in the new edifice: the one in memory of a former vicar, Dr. T. Rennell; the other to a Peninsular officer, Colonel Hutchins, a native of Earl's Court.

Near one of the entrances to the church was a tablet recording a reputed donation of lands to the parish by Oliver Cromwell, of which Lysons states: "An anonymous benefactor, in 1652, gave some land at Kensington Gravel-pits, on which was formerly a malthouse. This is called Cromwell's gift, and a tradition has prevailed that is was given by Oliver Cromwell; but the parish have no evidence to ascertain it."

The peal of bells was cast by Janeway, of Chelsea, in 1772. In the parish books are several entries of sums paid for ringing the church bells on public occasions since the Revolution. The Battle of the Boyne, for instance, is thus recorded: "May 2, 1690.—Paid William Reynolds for the ringers on that day the news came of the victory gained by his Majesty at and near the Boyne, 12s." And again, the Battle of Blenheim is thus noted: "1704.—Paid Mr. Jackman for a barrel of beer for the victory over the French and Bavarians, 15s." Another entry runs as follows: "For Limerick's being taken, and 'twas false," (sic): on this occasion the ringers were contented with eighteen pence. Various sums are mentioned as having been paid on the arrival of King William and his Queen, such as became the royal parish, "kingly Kensington." In Murray's "Environs of London" it is stated that this church has had its "Vicar of Bray," in one Thomas Hodges, collated to the living by Archbishop Juxon. He kept his preferment during the Civil War and interregnum, by joining alternately with either party Although a frequent preacher before the Long Parliament, and one of the Assembly of Divines, he was made Dean of Hereford after the Restoration, but continued Vicar of Kensington.

Amongst the many interesting associations of the old church are several of the present century. Mr. Wilberforce, who, as we have stated, resided at Kensington Gore, is still remembered by many of the old inhabitants as sitting in the pew appropriated to the Holland House family. George Canning, who resided at Gloucester Lodge, might often be seen sitting in the royal pew; Coke, of Norfolk, the eminent agriculturist, had a pew here, which he regularly occupied. Professor Nassau W. Senior, the political economist, although living so far distant as Hyde Park Gate, might often be seen, in company with the late Mr. Thackeray, attending the early service; but neither of these eminent writers, it is said, rented a pew in the church. Lord Macaulay, too, whilst living at Holly Lodge, Campden Hill, regularly attended here during the last two summers of his life.

To the churchyard, in 1814, was added a new cemetery, where was previously an avenue of elms, through which ran the original approach from the town to Campden House. In the churchyard is a monument to Mrs. Elizabeth Inchbald, who is truthfully and touchingly described on it as "a beauty, a virtue, a player, and authoress of 'A Simple Story.'" She commenced her career as an actress in 1777, on the York circuit, but quitted the stage in 1789, continuing, however, for many years to entertain the public in the character of a dramatic author. Mrs. Inchbald died on the 1st of March, 1821, as we have stated above, at old Kensington House. The following instances of longevity are to be found in the registers of burials:—1786, Margaret Smart, aged 103; 1804, Jane Hartwell, from Methwold's Almshouses, aged 100; 1807, William Griffiths, of the Gravel-pits, aged 103. The present vicarage, built about 1774, superseded a humble structure little more than a cottage with latticed windows.

Returning again into the High Street, we notice, a few yards beyond the church, a curious-looking brick building, of two storeys, above which is a square tower, probably intended to hold a bell; this was the old Kensington Charity School, built by Sir John Vanbrugh. It is now a savings'-bank, with a new school-room by the side of it. Adjoining this building is the Vestry Hall, which has been recently erected in the Jacobean style. A new Town Hall adjoining it was built in 1879–80.

On the opposite side of the way, in a house which stood on the site of the Metropolitan Railway Station, lived for some years the celebrated political writer, William Cobbett, whom we have mentioned above. In a garden at the back of his house, and also at a farm which he possessed at the same time at Barn-Elms, Cobbett cultivated his Indian corn, his American forest-trees, his pigs, poultry, and butchers' meat, all which he pronounced to be the best that were ever beheld; but the aristocratic suburb, we are told, did not prove a congenial soil, and he quitted it a bankrupt. He entered Parliament as member for Oldham, but did not live long afterwards, dying in 1835.

Campden House—which stands on the western side of Church Street, in its own grounds—is mentioned in the "New View of London," published in 1708, among the noble palaces belonging to Her Majesty, Queen Anne, "for the Court to reside in at pleasure." But this statement is not quite true. The house never absolutely belonged to royalty. It was the residence of Baptist Hicks, Viscount Campden, after whom it was called, and who was the founder of Hicks's Hall, in Clerkenwell; * and it caused his name to be given to the neighbourhood as Campden Hill. The mansion, which underwent considerable alterations in its exterior at the beginning of the present century, was spacious and picturesque, with its bay windows and turrets; several of the rooms had ceilings richly worked in stucco, and chimney-cases much ornamented. It was built about the year 1612, for Sir Baptist Hicks, whose arms (with that date), and those of his sons-in-law, Edward Lord Noel and Sir Charles Morison, figured in one of the windows. In the great dining-room it is said that Charles II. more than once supped with Lord Campden. It has fine wainscoat panels, and the ceiling was divided into compartments, in which figured the arms of the family, and their alliances. The house was rented from the Noel family by the Princess of Denmark (afterwards Queen Anne), who resided there about five years with her son, the Duke of Gloucester; and about that time, according to Lysons, the adjoining house, afterwards the residence of Mrs. Pitt, is said to have been built for the accommodation of Her Majesty's household. The amusements and pursuits of the Duke of Gloucester, who died in early boyhood, were principally of a military cast, for he is said to have formed a regiment of his youthful companions, chiefly from Kensington, who seem to have been upon constant duty at Campden House. At the beginning of the eighteenth century Campden House was in the occupation of the Dowager Countess of Burlington and her son, Richard Boyle, afterwards Earl, famous for his taste in the

* See Vol. II., p. 322.

fine arts.　The house was afterwards held by the Noels, who parted with it to Nicholas Lechmere, the politician, who was created Lord Lechmere, and who resided here for several years.　His lordship, probably, is now best remembered by the place he occupies in Gay's (or Swift's) ballad, entitled "Duke upon Duke," where, having challenged one Sir John Guise to fight a duel, he contrives to give his foe the slip :—

> " Back in the dark, by Brompton Park,
> 　He turned up through the Gore ;
> So slunk to Campden House so high,
> 　All in his coach and four."

Towards the close of the last century the mansion became a boarding-school for ladies.　George Selwyn speaks of going there to see a *protégé* of his, Maria Fagniani, who was held to be a very lucky person, for he and his friend Lord March (afterwards Duke of Queensberry—"Old Q.") took themselves respectively for her father, and each of them left her a fortune.　She afterwards married the Marquis of Hertford.*　In the *Mirror* for 1840, we read : " There are two dogs, carved out of stone, on the end walls of the gate or entrance, leading to Campden House, near Campden Hill, Kensington ; they are pointer dogs, and very beautifully carved.　The boys in the neighbourhood have done them much damage by pelting them with stones for fun, but they have stood all their knocks well—their legs are nearly worn away. From these two dogs the entrance is generally called by the inhabitants 'The Dogs,' by way of distinction.　'The House,' the entrance-lane to which they guard, was formerly occupied by Queen Anne ; it is a plain substantial house, and now occupied as a ladies' school."　Later on it was again converted into a private residence.　It contained in all about thirty rooms, besides a private theatre, in which the Campden amateur artists used to perform for charitable objects.　The terrace steps and parapets were extremely massive and handsome, and in the garden, which was sheltered and sunny, the wild olive is said to have flourished.　A caper-tree long produced fruit here. The building was destroyed by fire in 1862, but was rebuilt immediately.

At Campden Hill was the observatory of Sir James South, one of the founders of the Royal Astronomical Society.　Among his working instruments here was a 7-feet transit instrument, a 4-feet transit circle, and one of the equatorials with which, between the years 1821 and 1823, he and Sir John Herschel made a catalogue of 380 double stars. It was about the year 1825 that Sir James settled

at Campden Hill ; but in the equipment of his observatory he appears to have been unfortunate, for one large equatorial instrument, constructed at great expense, which became the subject of a lawsuit, gave him such dissatisfaction that he ordered it to be broken up, and the parts sold by auction. Large printed placards were posted throughout the neighbourhood of Kensington, and advertisements also appeared in the daily papers, announcing that on such a day (named) a sale of an extraordinary nature would take place at the observatory.　These placards, from their singular character, attracted much attention.　The following is a copy :—

" Observatory, Campden Hill, Kensington.

" To shycock toy-makers, smoke-jack makers, mock-coin makers, dealers in old metals, collectors of and dealers in artificial curiosities, and to such Fellows of the Astronomical Society as, at the meeting of that most learned and equally upright body, on the 13th of May last, were enlightened by Mr. Airy's (the Astronomer Royal) profound *exposé* of the mechanical incapacity of English astronomical instrument-makers of the present day :—To be sold by hand, on the premises, by Mr. M'Lelland, on Wednesday, December 21, 1842, between eleven and twelve o'clock in the forenoon, several hundred-weight of brass, gun-metal, &c., being the metal of the great equatorial instrument made for the Kensington Observatory by Messrs. Troughton and Simms ; the wooden polar axis of which, by the same artists, and its botchings, cobbled up by their assistants (Mr. Airy and the Rev. R. Sheepshanks) were, in consequence of public advertisements, on the 8th of July, 1839, purchased by divers vendors of old clothes, and licensed dealers in dead cows and horses, &c., with the exception of a fragment of mahogany, specially reserved at the request of several distinguished philosophers, which, on account of the great anxiety expressed by foreign astronomers and foreign astronomical instrument-makers, to possess when converted into snuff-boxes as a *souvenir piquante* of the state of the art of astronomical instrument-making in England during the nineteenth century, will, at the conclusion of the sale, be disposed of at per pound."

At the hour appointed a number of marine-store dealers and other dealers in metal (some of whom had come in carts from town), with a sprinkling of astronomical instrument-makers, and scientific persons, were assembled outside Sir James South's residence, and were admitted into the grounds by a small door in the hedge close to the well-known circular building in which the equatorial instrument

---

* See Vol. IV., p. 287.

was at first placed. On entering the grounds, to the left appeared the wreck of the instrument which a few years ago excited the interest of men of science throughout the world, lying arranged in lots numbered from o to 14, lot 15 being the fragment of mahogany spoken of in the bill, and lot 16 a plaster bust of Professor Airy, which was mounted on the ledge of a window above the centre lot. On the right, on the spacious lawn,

tainly be futile. Even the portions of the enormous tube were bored with holes, and battered to attain that object. Sir James South, in answer to an inquiry by a gentleman present as to the cause of so much deterioration in the value of the property having been made, said he had been told that he should get only the value of old metal for it ; and knowing that those who purchased the material, had the parts been sold in a perfect state, would take

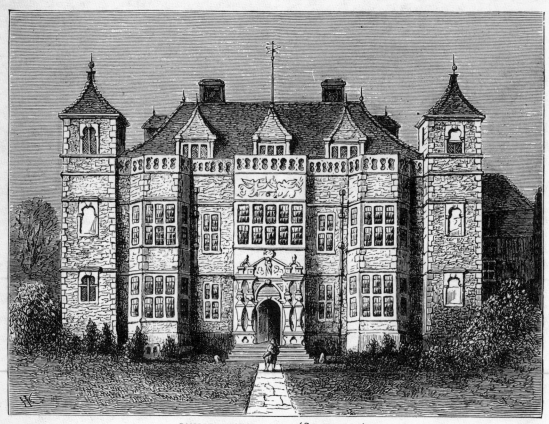

CAMPDEN HOUSE, 1720. (*See page* 130.)

was erected a large beam and scales, with weights for the purpose of ascertaining the weights of the different metals. Sir James South was present during the sale. He appeared in high spirits, and conversed with the company with his accustomed urbanity. The sale not being conducted by hammer, but by hand, was a very silent proceeding, and afforded no scope for either the eloquence or ingenuity of the auctioneer. The iron portion of the instrument, consisting of bolts, screws, &c., as well as the copper part, was unmutilated. The former fetched £3, and the latter 7d. per pound. The great equatorial instrument itself—viz., the tube, circle, &c., made of brass, had been broken into numerous pieces, which were divided into several lots, so that any attempt to reunite them would most cer-

them to the manufacturers, and from them receive a valuable consideration for them, he therefore determined to prevent its being devoted to any such ignoble purpose, and had mutilated it so that it should be of no value to any one beyond the intrinsic value of the metal. Notwithstanding these singular proceedings, one of Sir James's "equatorials" still remained mounted in his observatory, besides a few other instruments, including a transit circle, celebrated as having formerly belonged to Mr. Groombridge, and as having been the instrument with which the observations were made for the formation of the catalogue of circumpolar stars which bear his name. Sir James, whose contributions to scientific literature are well known, died here in 1867, at an advanced age. Kensington, of late years, has recovered some of its aristocratical character as a place of residence. Argyll Lodge, on Campden Hill, is the town-house of the Duke of Argyll, and Bedford Lodge, close by, was for many years the mansion of the Dowager Duchess of Bedford.

desired to have a list of the parochial charities, and a seat in the parish church. Although confined to the house by asthma during the winter, he was, as we have stated above, very regular in his attendance during the summer. A few days before his death, discussing the subject of church-

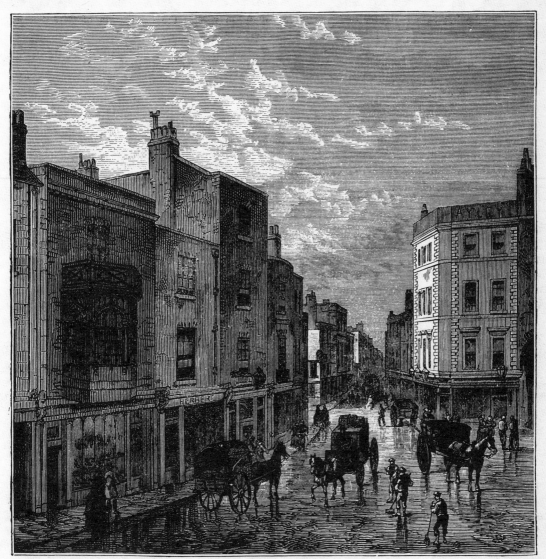

KENSINGTON HIGH STREET, IN 1860.

At Holly Lodge, Campden Hill, on the 28th of December, 1859, died Thomas Babington, Lord Macaulay, the essayist, orator, and historian, of whom we have already had occasion to speak in our accounts of the Albany and of Great Ormond Street.* When, after having been raised to the peerage, he went to reside at Holly Lodge, he

rates, he said, "Church-rates cannot last; and the proper substitute for them is a large subscription —I will give £100 as my share. I am not an exclusive, but of all Christian communions I consider the Church of England to be the best."

Lord Macaulay took great delight in his house and garden here; and he was never more pleased than when in his library, surrounded by his nephews and nieces.

* See Vol. IV., pp. 259, 562.

At a house in Orbell's Buildings, previously called Pitt's Buildings, on the south-east side of Campden Hill, died, March 20th, 1727, the great Sir Isaac Newton, at the age of eighty-five. His house seems to have had a back entrance in Church Street, where a gateway next the "George" Tavern is inscribed "Newton House." His estate at Kensington he left to a daughter of his nephew, Mr. Conduit, who married Lord Lymington, afterwards Earl of Portsmouth; and hence it is that the manuscripts of the great philosopher have been kept in the custody of the Wallop family.

A writer in the *Times* stated, in 1870, that the house actually occupied by Sir Isaac Newton was not the house named after him, but Bullingham House, where, he adds, "a slab put up in remembrance of him may still be seen in the garden wall."

The neighbourhood of Kensington Gravel Pits, by which name is understood a district of some extent bordering on the Uxbridge Road, has long been noted for salubrity of the air, and was a favourite residence of artists half a century ago. The high road through this district, known as High Street, Notting Hill, forms a kind of second Kensington High Street, being to the northern boundary of the suburb what the High Street, in the road to Hammersmith, is to Kensington proper.

Swift had lodgings in the Gravel Pits during the winter of 1712-13; and Lord Chatham's sister, Anne Pitt, is recorded to have died "at her house in Pitt Place, Kensington Gravel Pits," in 1780. To the south of the Gravel Pits was the Mall, which still exists as a street running at right angles to the Uxbridge Road.

Sheffield House, which stood between Church Street and Kensington Gravel Pits, owed its name to property possessed in this quarter by Sheffield, Duke of Buckingham, with the descendants of whose family it long remained. The house, however, has disappeared, and in its place have risen rows of houses overlooking Campden House Gardens and Palace Green.

Time was, and not so very long ago, when the artist body made their homes at Kentish and Camden Town, at Highgate, Hampstead, and St. John's Wood; but of late years they have flocked in far larger numbers to Kensington, no doubt on account of the convenience of access thence to all parts of the town, and of the good northern light which is secured to them by Kensington Gardens and the Park round Holland House. The Royal Academy Catalogue for 1876 shows that out of the total number of exhibitors, about a hundred lived in and around Kensington.

At his residence in the Mall, in 1844, died Sir Augustus Callcott, R.A., the eminent English landscape painter. Sir Augustus and his brother John W. Callcott, the musician, were the sons of a builder who resided near the "Gravel Pits," Kensington, where they were born in 1779 and 1766 respectively. At the time of the fire at Campden House, above mentioned, the adjoining mansion was in the occupation of Mr. Augustus Egg, a distinguished Royal Academician, and fears were entertained for the safety of his house and its valuable contents.

Sir David Wilkie was living in Kensington in 1834. Here he showed to his friends his picture of "John Knox preaching to his Congregation" before sending it in to the Academy. Mr. J. R. Planché, who was among the visitors, drew his attention to certain anachronisms in the armour, which the painter promised to alter; but time went on, the promise was never fulfilled, and the painting still exists to hand down a wilful blunder to posterity. Wilkie's first residence here was in Lower Phillimore Place, near the milestone; there he painted his "Chelsea Pensioners," his "Reading of the Will," his "Distraining for Rent," and his "Blind-man's Buff." He afterwards removed to Shaftesbury House, on the Terrace, and here the sunny hours of his life were spent. We get a glimpse of his daily habits in a letter which he wrote to his sister soon after settling here: "I dine, as formerly," he tells her, "at two o'clock, paint two hours in the forenoon and two hours in the afternoon, and take a short walk in the Park or through the fields twice a day." His last residence here, as Peter Cunningham tells us, was a detached mansion in Vicarage Place, at the head of Church Lane; there he took leave of his friends before his visit to the Holy Land, which shortly preceded his death.

At Kensington, John Evelyn, as he tells us in his "Diary," went to visit Dr. Tenison (afterwards Archbishop of Canterbury), "whither he had retired to refresh himself after he had been sick of the small-pox." This was just before the erection of the school in Leicester Square which bears Tenison's name. Kensington was the birthplace of Lord Chancellor Camden, who died in 1794, at the age of eighty. Sir John Fielding, the well-known magistrate, was also a resident here. Here, too, lived, and here died at an advanced age, Lady Margaret Macdonald, the mother of Chief Baron Macdonald, a lady who was visited by Dr. Johnson in his tour to the Hebrides. She was buried in the centre vault of the old church, close to the reading-desk, which was given to the parish by William III. It was her attendant and connection,

Flora Macdonald, who so heroically aided the escape of "Bonny Prince Charlie," after his defeat at Culloden.

Another Kensingtonian was Robert Nelson, the author of "Fasts and Festivals," and one of the founders of the Society for Promoting Christian Knowledge. He died in 1715, and was a man of such polished and courtly manners, that Dr. Johnson affirms him to have been the original whence Samuel Richardson drew his "Sir Charles Grandison."

It is worthy of note that the high road between London and Kensington was the first place where oil lamps with glazed lights were placed, for the convenience of the Court as they travelled backwards and forwards to St. James's and Whitehall. This was about the year 1694. The old method of lighting the thoroughfare with lanterns and wicks of cotton was then gradually laid aside. It does not appear, however, that the example of Kensington was at all speedily followed by the rest of the metropolis at the West End; for more than a quarter of a century later, in 1718, we find Lady Mary Wortley Montagu* contrasting the lighting of London at night with that of Paris in most unfavourable terms. If Chelsea, as Thackeray observes in his "Esmond," was even in Anne's time "distant from London, and the roads to it were bad, and infested by footpads," the same was true also of Kensington. Indeed, as a proof of the insecurity of the roads in the suburbs until after the introduction of gas and the establishment of a police force, we may be pardoned for informing our readers, on the authority of Walker's "Original," that, "at Kensington, within the memory of man, on Sunday evenings a bell used to be rung at intervals to muster the people returning to town. As soon as a band was assembled sufficiently numerous to ensure mutual protection, it set off, and so on till all had passed." So insecure was the state of the road—in fact, in spite of the patrol—that we read of a plot being concocted for the purpose of robbing Queen Anne as she returned from London to Kensington in her coach. Indeed, even as late as the end of the last century, a journey from London to the suburbs after night-fall was not accomplished without danger to purse and person too. Horace Walpole often travelled along this road in his carriage between Berkeley Square and Strawberry Hill. On one occasion, as he intimates in one of his letters to the Miss Berrys, he composed a long set of verses in praise of General Conway, then in chief command at the Horse Guards, whilst in his carriage, having "conceived and executed them between Hammersmith and Hyde Park Corner."

We learn from a private letter in the Record Office, descriptive of the Fire of London, that on that occasion a great quantity of the goods and property of the citizens was brought as far westward as Kensington for safety. The writer adds : "Had your lordship been at Kensington you would have thought for five days—for so long the fire lasted—that it had been Doomsday, and that the heavens themselves had been on fire ; and the fearful cries and howlings of undone people did much increase the resemblance. My walks and gardens were almost covered with the ashes of papers, linen, &c., and pieces of ceiling and plaster-work, blown thither by the tempest."

"In a curious little nook of the 'Court Suburb,' wherein the drama had furtively taken root," writes Mr. J. R. Planché, in his "Recollections," "I witnessed the performance of a piece entitled the 'Queen's Lover,' by a company of actors, all previously unknown to me, even by name, but who generally exhibited talent, and one, in my humble opinion, genius." Mr. Planché went thither in the company of Madame Vestris and Mr. Alfred Bunn, who at the time had succeeded to the united stage kingdom of Covent Garden and of Drury Lane. The person of "genius" was Henry Gaskell Denvil, in whom Bunn thought that he had found a second Kean. Instead, however, of encouraging him, he crushed his spirits and drove him out of life.

It would, perhaps, be a little singular if such an interesting "old-world" sort of place as Kensington should be without its "ghost-story ;" and it may be gratifying to find that it is not. Here is one, of no older date than the year 1868, which we quote from the newspaper reports at the time :—"In a small house, about twenty yards away from the main road, live an old lady, eighty-four years of age, and her daughter, with one servant. They have lived in the same house for nearly twenty years without any annoyance ; but for the last few months they are being constantly startled by a sharp loud knocking upon the panel of the street-door. Upon opening the door, however quickly, no sign of any one is to be discovered. No sooner are the ladies quietly settled again than rap-rap-rap ! comes upon the door. And this is repeated at irregular intervals through the evening. For some time it was attributed to some imps of school-boys, who are always ready for mischief, and but little notice was taken of it ; but the continuance of what was only annoying became at last a serious nuisance. The most nimble efforts were made, without success,

* Works, edited by Lord Wharncliffe, vol. ii., p. 118.

to 'catch' the offenders, but until a few nights ago the attacks were so arranged as never to take place in the presence of male visitors; consequently the ladies received much pity, but little sympathy, from their friends. After a time they became nervous, and at last really frightened. On Thursday evening a gentleman, the son of the old lady, called, and found them quite ill from nervous excitement, and was comforting them as well as he could, when a quick rap-rap-rap! at the front door made him jump up. In two seconds he was at the door, rushed out, looking in every direction without discovering a sound or a trace of any human being in any of the adjacent roads. Then, for the first time, he was able to understand from what his mother and sister had suffered, and set to work to examine the approaches to the door inside and out, and to solve the mystery, if possible. No sooner had he gone back to the little dining-room, and placed a chair in the open doorway, with a big stick handy to 'trounce' the perpetrator the next time, and begun to discuss what it was, than rap-rap-rap! sent him flying out into the street, to the astonishment of a passing cabman, who must have thought a madman had just escaped his keeper. This happened four or five times more; in fact, it only ceased about a quarter to eleven. He went round to the police-station, and had an officer put on special duty opposite the house for the next day, and spent the following morning in calling upon the neighbours, and carefully examining the gardens and walls which abutted upon the 'haunted' house. Not a mark of any sort was to be found, and he was quite convinced that the door could not have been reached from any point but right in front from the street, as there is no cellar or drain under the house. In the evening he took a friend down with him, and two more of his friends looked in later. The ladies were found in a painful state of nervous fright, as the nuisance had already been going on, and the maid-servant was crying. Altogether, it was a scene of misery. In the course of conversation the following facts came out :—It began on a Friday, the 18th of October, and has never missed a Friday since then. It has never been heard on Sunday, seldom on Saturday; never before the gas-lamps are lit, never after eleven. Just as all were talking at once, rap-rap-rap! In an instant all four gentlemen were in the front garden; the policeman was quietly standing opposite the door; the lady of the house opposite watching the door from her portico, and another gentleman from the leads. All declared that not a living creature had been near the house for at least a quarter of an hour. The whole thing seems inexplicable, and has created quite a sensation

in the neighbourhood." The mystery was afterwards solved, for it appeared that the servant-girl had caused the rapping by means of wires.

In Scarsdale Terrace, Wright's Lane, near the railway station, Kensington High Street, is the Crippled Boys' National Industrial Home. This charity was instituted in 1865, and was originally located in a house in the High Street. There are about fifty crippled boys in the Home, received from all parts of the kingdom, once destitute, neglected, or ill treated in their own dwellings, without any chance of rising, like other youths, to social independence by their own exertions, but now happily engaged for a term of three years in learning an industrial employment for this end. This charity has, notwithstanding its limited means, been of great service to many, the greater portion of whom are seen or heard of from time to time ; and it is astonishing to find how many crippled children there are throughout the country, whose anxious appeals to the committee for admission are very distressing.

Scarsdale House, a small mansion close by, was for many years a boarding-school, and as such, says Leigh Hunt, it must have been an eyesore to William Cobbett, the political writer, the back of whose premises in the High Street it overlooked. Scarsdale House, now no longer a boarding-school, appears to have returned to the occupation of the family who are understood to have built it, for its present inmate is the Hon. Edward Cecil Curzon, brother of the late Lord Zouche. It is conjectured that the house was built by the Earl of Scarsdale, whose family name was Leake, the Scarsdale celebrated by Pope for his love of the bottle—

"Each mortal has his pleasure ;—none deny
Scarsdale his bottle, Darty his ham-pie."

The short-lived Roman Catholic University College, which was formally inaugurated in 1874, stood on the site of Abingdon House, in Wright's Lane. The building, although comparatively small, was very complete in its arrangements, and comprised a theatre, lecture-rooms, a school of science, a discussion-room, and a chapel. A number of rooms were also set apart for the amusement or edification of the students in various ways. The college, which received the support and patronage of all the English Roman Catholic bishops, was founded mainly through the instrumentality of Monsignor Capel, who was appointed its first rector. It, however, failed after a brief career of usefulness, and, as its difficulties were found to be insurmountable, the institution was given up, and the buildings were pulled down about the year 1880. The site has since been built over.

Kensington always has had a large Irish element, and of late years, owing to the increasing population of the place, rapid strides have been made by the Roman Catholic body in augmenting their numbers.

The *London Review* of 1865 gives the following account of the progress of the Roman Catholic body of Kensington at that time :—" Formerly, for the accommodation of the whole of the Roman Catholics of this parish, there was but one small chapel near the High Street, which appeared amply sufficient for the members of that creed. But ten or twelve years ago a Roman Catholic builder purchased, at an enormous price, a plot of ground, about three acres in extent, beside the Church of the Holy Trinity, Brompton. For a time considerable mystery prevailed as to the uses it was to be applied to; but, shortly after the buildings were commenced, they were discovered to be the future residence and church of the Oratorian Fathers, removed to it from their former dwelling; and the chapel, a small and commodious erection, was opened for divine service. At first the congregation was of the scantiest description : even on Sundays at high mass, small as the chapel was, it was frequently only half filled; while on week days, at many of the services, it was no uncommon circumstance to find the attendance scarcely more numerous than the number of priests serving at the altar. By degrees the congregation increased, till the chapel was found too small for their accommodation, and extensive alterations were made to it; but these, again, were soon filled to overflowing, and further alterations had to be made, till at last the building was capable of holding, without difficulty, from 2,000 to 2,500 persons. It is now frequently so crowded at high mass that it is difficult for an individual entering it after the commencement of the service to find even standing room. In the meantime the monastery itself, if that is the proper term, was completed—a splendid appearance it presents—and we believe is fully occupied. The Roman Catholic population in the parish or mission, under the spiritual direction of the Fathers of the Oratory, now comprise between 7,000 and 8,000 souls. The average attendance at mass on Sunday is about 5,000, and the average number of communicants for the last two years has been about 45,000 annually. But in addition to this church, Kensington has three others—St. Mary's, Upper Holland Street; St. Simon Stock, belonging to the Carmelite Friars; and the Church of St. Francis Assisi, in Notting Hill. Of monasteries, or religious communities of men, it has the Oratorians before mentioned, and the Discalced Carmelites, in Vicarage Place. Of convents of ladies it has the Assumption, in Kensington Square ; the Poor Clares Convent, in Edmond Terrace ; the Franciscan Convent, in Portobello Road ; and the Sisters of Jesus, in Holland Villas. Of schools, the Roman Catholics possess, in the parish of Kensington, the Orphanage, in the Fulham Road ; the Industrial School of St. Vincent de Paul ; as well as the large Industrial School for Girls in the southern ward. All these schools are very numerously attended ; the gross number of pupils amounting to 1,200, those of the Oratory alone being 1,000. The kindness and consideration shown by the Roman Catholic teachers to the children of the poor is above all praise, not only in Kensington, but in all localities where they are under their charge ; and the love they receive from their pupils in return forms one of their most powerful engines in their system of proselytising."

The chapel of St. Mary's above mentioned, in Holland Street, is close to the principal street in Kensington, and is thus described in the " Catholic Hand-book," published in 1857 :—" It is a plain, unpretending edifice, the cross upon its front being the only feature to distinguish it from an ordinary Dissenting meeting-house. Its interior has a remarkable air of neatness. The building itself is an oblong square, built north and south, and capable of accommodating about 300 persons. It is lit by three windows at the northern end, and one window at the eastern and western sides. It is devoid of ornament, except at the south end, where the altar is raised between two pillars. The body of the chapel is fitted with low open seats, and at the northern end is a spacious gallery." Being superseded by other and larger ecclesiastical edifices, the old chapel is now used as a school-room. It was built about 1812 by the family of Mr. Wheble, the manufacturer of the celebrated Kensington candles, who began life with a small shop in High Street, but died worth a quarter of a million.

In Newland Terrace, on the south side of the main road, is the Church of Our Lady of Victories, which serves as a pro-cathedral, superseding the Church of St. Mary's, Moorfields. It is a lofty Gothic structure of the Early English type, with some details approaching more nearly to the Decorated style. It consists of a nave and side aisles, and a shallow chancel, in which is the throne of the archiepiscopal see of Westminster. The windows of the apse are filled with stained glass.

In the Kensington Road is the " Adam and Eve " public-house, where Sheridan, on his way to or from Holland House, regularly stopped for a dram ; and there he ran up a long bill, which, as we learn from Moore's diary, Lord Holland had to pay.

WEST FRONT OF KENSINGTON PALACE.

CHAPTER XII.

KENSINGTON PALACE.

"High o'er the neighbouring lands,
'Midst greens and sweets, a regal fabric stands."—*Tickell.*

Situation of Kensington Palace—Houses near it—Kensington Palace Gardens—The "King's Arms"—Henry VIII.'s Conduit—Palace Green—
The Kensington Volunteers—The Water Tower—Thackeray's House : his Death—Description of the Palace—The Chapel—The Principal
Pictures formerly shown here—Early History of the Building—William III. and Dr. Radcliffe—A "Scene" in the Royal Apartments—
Death of Queen Mary and William III.—Queen Anne and the Jacobites—"Scholar Dick," and his Fondness for the Bottle—Lax Manners
of the Court under the Early Georges—Death of George II.—The Princess Sophia—Caroline, Princess of Wales—Balls and Parties given
by her Royal Highness—An Undignified Act—The Duke of Sussex's Hospitality—Birth of the Princess Victoria—Her Baptism—Death of
William IV., and Accession of Queen Victoria—Her First Council—Death of the Duke of Sussex—The Duchess of Inverness—Other
Royal Inhabitants.

As in France, so also in England, nearly all the
palaces of royalty are located outside the city.
Greenwich, Eltham, Hatfield, Theobalds, Nonsuch,
Enfield, Havering-atte-Bower, Oatlands, Hampton
Court, Kew, Richmond, all in turn, as well as Kensington, have been chosen as residences for our
sovereigns. Kensington Palace, though actually
situated in the parish of St. Margaret, Westminster,
is named from the adjoining town, to which it would
more naturally seem to belong, and it stands in
grounds about 350 acres in extent.

Palace Gate House, a spacious mansion, with
ornamental elevation, standing on the north side
of the High Street, near the entrance to the

Palace, was long the residence of the late Mr.
John Forster, the historian, biographer, and critic,
and the friend of Charles Dickens. A broad roadway, leading from the High Street of Kensington
to the Bayswater Road, and known as Kensington
Palace Gardens, contains several costly mansions,
including one of German-Gothic design, built for
the Earl of Harrington in 1852.

In the High Street, close by the entrance to the
Palace, is the "King's Arms" Tavern, at which
Addison was a frequent visitor, when he took up
his abode in his adopted home at Holland House
as the husband of Lady Warwick.

On the west side of Palace Green, in what was

formerly called the King's Garden, Henry VIII. is said to have built a conduit, or bath, for the use of the Princess Elizabeth, when a child. It was a low building, with walls of great thickness, and the roof covered with bricks. The interior was in good preservation when Faulkner wrote his "History of Kensington," and afforded a favourable specimen of the brickwork of the period. It is clear, from an entry in the parish books, though unnoticed by Faulkner, that Queen Elizabeth, at least on one occasion subsequent to her childhood, stayed within the parish, for the parish officers are rebuked and punished for not ringing "when Her Majesty left Kensington." Probably this

the last century. In 1801 an engraving was published, showing the presentation of colours to the regiment; the original painting, together with the colours themselves—which were worked by the Duchess of Gloucester and her daughter, the Princess Sophia Matilda—are now in the Vestry Hall. In 1876 these colours were placed in front

KENSINGTON PALACE, FROM THE GARDENS.

entry refers to some visit which she paid to Holland House, where no doubt she was entertained as a guest by the then owner, the old Earl of Holland, or by Sir Walter Cope, who built the original mansion. On Palace Green are the barracks for foot-soldiers, who still regularly mount guard at the Palace. The Green, called in ancient documents the "Moor," was the military parade when the Court resided here, and the royal standard was hoisted on it daily.

Among the historical associations of this place must not be overlooked the Old Kensington Volunteers, which was formed towards the close of

of the Princess Louise, when she opened the New National Schools here, and the vicar of Kensington drew the attention of her Royal Highness to this work of her ancestors. Dr. Callcott, whom we have already mentioned as living near the Gravel Pits, was band-master in the above corps, which was disbanded at the Peace of Amiens, and also in the Kensington Corps of Volunteer Infantry, which was established in 1803.

On this green there stood formerly a water-tower of singular construction; it was built in the reign of Queen Anne, but had long ceased to be used when Faulkner wrote his "History of Kensington" in 1820. It was of red brick, and consisted of three storeys, surrounded by two heavy battlemented turrets; it is said to have been designed by Sir John Vanbrugh. The tower was removed in 1850.

In 1846, Thackeray removed from London to Kensington, taking up his abode at No. 13, Young Street, which connects the Square with the High Street, occupying also by day, for working purposes, chambers at 10, Crown Office Row, Temple. He afterwards removed to Onslow Square, Brompton; but about 1861, or the following year, he again removed to the more congenial neighbourhood of Kensington Palace, and took up his permanent abode in the "Old Court Suburb," about which Leigh Hunt has gossiped so pleasantly. He took on a long lease a somewhat dilapidated mansion, on the west side of Palace Gardens. His intention at first was to repair and improve it, but he finally resolved to pull it down, and build a new house in its place. This, a handsome, solid mansion of choice red brick, with stone facings, was built from his own designs, and he occupied it until his death. "It was," remarks Mr. James Hannay, "a dwelling worthy of one who really represented literature in the great world, and who, planting himself on his books, yet sustained the character of his profession with all the dignity of a gentleman." A friend who called on him there from Edinburgh, in the summer of 1862, knowing of old his love of the poet of Venusia, playfully reminded him what Horace says of those who, regardless of their death, employ themselves in building houses :—

> "Sepulchri
> Immemor struis domos."

"Nay," said he, "I am *memor sepulchri*, for this house will always let for so many hundreds "—mentioning the sum—"a year." Thackeray was always of opinion, that notwithstanding the somewhat costly proceeding of pulling down and re-erecting, he had achieved the result, rare for a private gentleman, of building for himself a house which,

HENRY VIII.'S CONDUIT. (*See page* 139.)

regarded as an investment of a portion of his fortune, left no cause for regret.

Mr. John Forster has told us, in his "Life of Charles Dickens," how the latter met Thackeray at the Athenæum Club, just a week before his death, and shook hands with him at parting, little thinking that it was for the last time. "There had been some estrangement between them since the autumn of 1858. . . . Thackeray, justly indignant at a published description of himself by a member of a club to which both he and Dickens belonged (the Garrick), referred the matter to the committee, who decided to expel the writer. Dickens, thinking expulsion too harsh a penalty for an offence thoughtlessly given, and, as far as might be, manfully atoned for by withdrawal and regret, interposed to avert the extremity. Thackeray resented the interference, and Dickens was justly hurt at the manner in which he did so. Neither," adds Mr. Forster, "was wholly in the right, nor was either altogether in the wrong." The affair, however, is scarcely worth being added as a fresh chapter to the "Quarrels of Authors." Thackeray had often suffered from serious illness, so that his daughter was not much alarmed at finding him in considerable pain and suffering on Wednesday, the 23rd of December, 1863. He complained of pain when his servant left his room, wishing him "good-night," and in the morning, on entering, the man-servant found him dead. He had passed away in the night from an effusion of blood on the brain.

Mr. Hannay wrote :—"Thackeray is dead; and the purest English prose writer of the nineteenth century, and the novelist with a greater knowledge of the human heart as it really is than any one—with the exception, perhaps, of Shakespeare and Balzac—is suddenly struck down in the midst of us. In the midst of us! No long illness, no lingering decay, no gradual suspension of power; almost pen in hand, like Kempenfelt, he went down. Well said the *Examiner*—' Whatever little feuds may have gathered about Mr. Thackeray's public life lay lightly on the surface of the minds that chanced to be in contest with him. They could be thrown off in a moment, at the first shock of the news that he was dead.' It seemed impossible to realise the fact. No other celebrity— be he writer, statesman, artist, actor—seemed so thoroughly a portion of London. That 'good grey head which all men knew' was as easy of recognition as his to whom the term applied, the Duke of Wellington. Scarcely a day passed without his being seen in the Pall-Mall districts; and a Londoner showing to 'country cousins' the wonders of the metropolis, generally knew how to arrange for them to get a sight of the great English writer."

The palace has been described as a "plain brick building, of no particular style or period, but containing a heterogeneous mass of dull apartments, halls, and galleries, presenting externally no single feature of architectural beauty; the united effect of its ill-proportioned divisions being irregular and disagreeable in the extreme." This criticism can hardly be considered too severe. Certain portions of the exterior, it is true, are admired as fine specimens of brickwork in their way; but it cannot be concealed that the general effect of the brick is mean and poor.

The following particulars of the interior of the palace, some of which stand good even at the present day, we glean from John Timbs' "Curiosities of London," published in 1855 :—" The great staircase, of black and white marble, and graceful ironwork (the walls painted by Kent with mythological subjects in chiaroscuro, and architectural and sculptural decoration), leads to the suite of twelve state apartments, some of which are hung with tapestry, and have painted ceilings. The 'Presence Chamber' has a chimney-piece richly sculptured by Gibbons, with flowers, fruits, and heads; the ceiling is diapered red, blue, and gold upon a white field, copied by Kent from Herculaneum; and the pier-glass is wreathed with flowers, by Jean Baptiste Monnoyer. The 'King's Gallery,' in the south front, has an elaborately painted allegorical ceiling, and a circular fresco of a Madonna, after Raphael. 'The Cube Room' is forty feet in height, and contains gilded statues and busts, and a marble bas-relief of a Roman marriage, by Rysbrack. The 'King's Great Drawing-room' was hung with the then new paper, in imitation of the old velvet flock. The 'Queen's Gallery,' in the rear of the eastern front, continued northwards, has above the doorway the monogram of William and Mary; and the pediment is enriched with fruits and flowers in high relief and wholly detached, probably carved by Gibbons. The 'Green Closet' was the private closet of William III., and contained his writing table and escritoire; and the 'Patchwork Closet' had its walls and chairs covered with tapestry worked by Queen Mary."

The palace contains a comfortable though far from splendid or tasteful suite of state apartments, the ceilings and staircases of which are ornamented with paintings by Kent. The grand staircase leads from the principal entrance to the palace, on the west, by a long corridor, the sides of which are painted to represent a gallery crowded with spectators on a Court day, in which the artist has introduced portraits of himself; of "Peter, the Wild Boy;" of Ulric, a Polish lad, page to George I.; and of the Turks Mahomet and Mustapha, two of his personal attendants, who were taken prisoners by the Imperialists in Hungary, and who, having become converts to Christianity, obtained posts at Court. Mahomet was extremely charitable, and Pope thus records his personal worth :—

"From peer or bishop 'tis no easy thing
    To draw the man who loves his God and king.
Alas ! I copy (or my draught would fail)
    From honest Mahomet or from Parson Hale."

The chapel royal is as plain and ordinary an apartment as a Scottish Presbyterian would wish to see; but it is remarkable for containing some fine communion plate. Divine service is performed here regularly by a chaplain to the household, and the public are admitted.

The fine collection of historical paintings which once adorned the walls of Kensington Palace is unrecorded in Dr. Waagen's "Art and Artists in England." The fact is that they have been, for the most part, dispersed, and many of them now are to be found at the Palace of Hampton Court, and other public buildings. Mr. George Scharf, F.S.A., in his "Notes on the Royal Picture Galleries," states that Kensington Palace, during the reign of George II., appears to have contained many, if not most, of the finest pictures. He especially notes Vandyck's pictures of King Charles and his Queen, Cupid and Psyche, and the same painter's "Three Children of Charles I.;" Queen Elizabeth in a Chinese dress, drawn when she was a prisoner at Woodstock; Kneller's portraits of King William and Queen Mary, in their coronation robes (Kneller was knighted for painting these pictures); Tintoretto's grand pictures of "Esther fainting before Ahasuerus," and "Apollo and the Nine Muses." It appears that about the time of the fire at Whitehall, the series of old heads and foreign portraits were transferred to Kensington, as Vertue—on the title to his engravings of them, in "Rapin," published in 1736—mentions them as being in the latter palace; and Walpole, in the first edition of his "Anecdotes" (1762), especially alludes to the early royal portraits at Kensington. He also speaks of a chamber of very ancient portraits—among them one of the Duke of Norfolk—as then existing in the Princess Dowager's house at Kew. A catalogue of these pictures was taken by Benjamin West, at the king's desire, in 1818. Unlike the portraits in most galleries, many of those at Kensington had no names attached to them; and thus, if we may judge from a complaint made by the unfortunate Princess Caroline of Wales, their interest was in a great measure destroyed. The fine collection of Holbein's original drawings and designs for the portraits of the leading personages in the Court of Henry VIII., now in the Royal Library at Windsor, was accidentally discovered by Queen Caroline in a bureau here, shortly after the accession of George II.

The palace has a character of its own among the other residences of the royal family. Leigh Hunt hits the right nail on the head when he speaks of it as possessing "a Dutch solidity." "It can be imagined full of English comfort," he adds; "it is quiet, in a good air, and, though it is a palace, no tragical history is connected with it; all which considerations give it a sort of homely, fireside character, which seems to represent the domestic side of royalty itself, and thus renders an interesting service to what is not always so well recommended by cost and splendour. Windsor Castle is a place to receive monarchs in; Buckingham Palace, to see fashion in; Kensington Palace seems a place to drink tea in; and this is by no means a state of things in which the idea of royalty comes least home to the good wishes of its subjects."

The original mansion was the suburban residence of Lord Chancellor Finch, afterwards Earl of Nottingham, and as such it bore the name of "Nottingham House," of which the lower portion of the present north wing is part. It was purchased for the sum of £20,000 from his successor by William III.; and, as Northouck writes, "for its convenience and healthful situation for the king to reside in during the sitting of Parliament." Shortly after its purchase by the Crown, the house was nearly destroyed by fire, and the king himself had a narrow escape from being burned in his bed. The building was at first, comparatively speaking, small, and the grounds only occupied a few acres. Evelyn, in his "Memoirs," under date February 25, 1690-1, says: "I went to Kensington, which King William has bought of Lord Nottingham,

and altered, but was yet a patched-up building, but with the gardens, however, it is a very neat villa." The king found its sequestered situation congenial with his moody and apathetic disposition, and therefore resolved to make it a royal residence superseding Whitehall. The palace was considerably enlarged by William III., at the suggestion of Queen Mary, from designs by Sir Christopher Wren, and surrounded by straight cut solitary lawns, and formal stately gardens, laid out with paths and flower-beds at right angles, after the stiffest Dutch fashion. Queen Anne added very largely to the size of the house, and also to the beauty of the gardens, such as that beauty may have been. The orangery, a fine detached building at a little distance on the north side, was built for her by Sir Christopher Wren. The eastern front of the palace itself was added by George I., from designs of Kent. The north-western angle was added by George II., in order to form a nursery for his children; and to his queen, Caroline of Anspach, we owe the introduction of the ornamental water into the gardens and pleasure-grounds. The house, which had been growing all this time in size, was finally brought to its present size or appearance by the Duke of Sussex, who added or rebuilt the rooms that form the angle on the south-west. The Duchess of Kent's apartments were in the south-east part of the palace, under the King's Gallery. A melancholy interest hangs about the irregular pile, for within its walls died William III. and his wife, Queen Mary; her sister, Queen Anne, and her consort, Prince George of Denmark, who was carried hence to his tomb in Westminster Abbey; George II.; and lastly, the Queen's favourite uncle, the Duke of Sussex.

Such, then, is a rough outline of the history of the once favourite residence of the House of Hanover. "In the metropolis of commerce," observes Macaulay, "the point of convergence is the Exchange; in the metropolis of fashion it is the Palace." This was eminently true, as we have seen, of the Palace at Whitehall in the days of the second Charles, who made his Court the centre of fashionable gaiety as well as of political intrigue. Under the first of our Hanoverian kings this centre was transferred to Kensington. But the centre had lost much of its attractiveness under them. "The Revolution," Macaulay writes, "gave us several kings, unfitted by their education and habits to be gracious and affable hosts. They had been born and bred upon the Continent. They never felt themselves at home on our island. If they spoke our language, they spoke it inelegantly and with effort. Our national character they never understood ; our national manners they hardly attempted to acquire. The most important part of their duty they performed better than any ruler that had preceded them : for they governed strictly according to law ; but they could not be the first gentlemen of the realm—the heads of polite society. If ever they unbent, it was in a very small circle, where hardly an English face was to be seen ; and they were never so happy as when they' could escape for a summer to their native land. They had, indeed, their days of reception for our nobility and gentry ; but the reception was a matter of form, and became at last as solemn a ceremony as a funeral." To the head-quarters of the Court at Kensington these remarks are to be applied quite literally.

William III. usually held his Courts at Kensington, and the decoration of the apartments of its palace was one of the chief amusements of his royal consort. And yet, fond as he was of Kensington, King William would often say that he preferred to be hunting on the shores of Guelderland rather than riding over the glades of this place or Hampton Court—a taste in which he was followed by George II. Indeed, with a natural love for his Dutch home, William made this palace and the gardens surrounding it look as much like his native country as he could.

Although William was not over-fond of his new subjects, and his Court, for the most part, was as gloomy as his gardens, yet there still might occasionally be seen here some of the liveliest wits and courtiers that have left a name in history. Here came the Earl of Dorset, Prior's friend, who had been one of the wits of the Court of Charles II. ; Prior himself, too, was there, and succeeded in obtaining an appointment as one of the " gentlemen of the king's bedchamber ;" Congreve, whose plays were admired by Queen Mary ; Halifax, who is spoken of as a "minor wit, but no mean statesman ;" Swift, and Sir William Temple ; Burnet, the gossiping historian, who afterwards became a bishop ; the Earl of Devonshire, "whose nobler zeal," as Leigh Hunt puts it, "had made him a duke, one of a family remarkable for their constant and happy combination of popular politics with all the graces of their rank." Among other visitors here at this period, too, were Lord Monmouth, afterwards Earl of Peterborough, "the friend of Swift and Pope, conqueror of Spain, and lover, at the age of seventy, of Lady Suffolk ;" Sheffield, afterwards Duke of Buckinghamshire, "a minor wit and poet, in love with (the rank of) the Princess Anne ;" and last not least, Peter the Great, the " semi-barbarian, the premature forcer of Russian pseudo-civilisation,

who came to England in order to import the art of shipbuilding into his dominions in his own proper mechanical person." Peter is stated to have frequently dined at Kensington Palace ; and it has been wondered how the two sovereigns got on so well together. Leigh Hunt tells a story how that one day the king took the Russian monarch to the House of Lords, when the latter, owing to a natural shyness, made the lords and the king himself laugh, by peeping strangely at them out of a window in the roof. He got the same kind of sight at the House of Commons ; and even at a ball at Kensington, on the Princess Anne's birthday, he contrived to be invisibly present in a closet prepared for him on purpose, where he could see without being seen.

Here, when William was ill with the dropsy, he called in the Court physician, Dr. Radcliffe, to pay him a professional visit. Showing him his swollen ankles, he exclaimed, " Doctor, what do you think of these ?" "Why, truly," answered Radcliffe, "I would not have your Majesty's two legs for your three kingdoms." With this ill-timed jest, though it passed unnoticed at the moment, it is needless to add that the doctor's attendance on the Court at Kensington ceased. It is true that in 1714 he was sent for by Queen Anne upon her death-bed ; but he was too ill to leave his house at Carshalton. His refusal, however, nearly exposed him to "lynch law," for the mob at the West End threatened to kill him if he came to London. The mob, however, was disappointed, for a few months later he died of the gout.

The following story, relating to a scene which happened in the royal apartments here, we tell in the words of Lord Sackville, as they stand recorded in the gossiping pages of Sir N. W. Wraxall :— " My father, having lost his own mother when very young, was brought up chiefly by the Dowager Countess of Northampton, his grandmother, who being particularly acceptable to Queen Mary, she commanded the countess always to bring her little grandson, Lord Buckhurst, to Kensington Palace, though at that time hardly four years of age ; and he was allowed to amuse himself with a child's cart in the gallery. King William, like almost all Dutchmen, never failed to attend the tea-table every evening. It happened that her Majesty having one afternoon, by his desire, made tea, and waiting for the king's arrival, who was engaged in business in his cabinet, at the other extremity of the gallery, the boy, hearing the queen express her impatience at the delay, ran away to the closet, dragging after him the cart. When he arrived at the door, he knocked, and the king asked, 'Who is there?' 'Lord Buck,' answered he. 'And what does Lord Buck want with me?' replied his Majesty. 'You must come to tea directly,' said he; 'the queen is waiting for you.' King William immediately laid down his pen, and opened the door; then taking the child in his arms, placed Lord Buckhurst in the cart, and seizing the pole, drew them both along the gallery, quite to the room

Queen Mary, consort of William III., died here of the small-pox, and the king's attachment to the palace is said to have increased, from the circumstance of its having been the scene of the last acts of the queen, who was justly entitled to his affection. It was here that the king also died, in consequence of an accident in riding at Hampton Court a few days previously. The readers of

QUEEN CAROLINE'S DRAWING-ROOM, KENSINGTON PALACE.

in which were seated the queen, Lady Northampton, and the company. But no sooner had he entered the apartment than, exhausted with the effort, which had forced the blood upon his lungs, and being naturally asthmatic, threw himself into a chair, and for some minutes was incapable of uttering a word, breathing with the utmost difficulty. The Countess of Northampton, shocked at the consequences of her grandson's indiscretion, which threw the whole circle into great consternation, would have punished him; but the king interposed in his behalf; and the story is chiefly interesting because (as serving to show how kindly he could behave to a troublesome child) it places that prince in a more amiable point of view than he is commonly represented in history."

Macaulay will not have forgotten the picture which he draws in the very last page of his history, when William, knowing that death was approaching, sent for his friends Albemarle, Auverquerque, and Bentinck, while Bishops Burnet and Tillotson read the last prayers by his bedside. After his Majesty's death, bracelets composed of the queen's hair were found upon his arm.

The Court at Kensington in Queen Anne's time was not much livelier than it had been in that of King William. Swift describes Anne, in a circle of twenty visitors, as sitting with her fan in her mouth, saying about three words once a minute to those that were near her, and then, upon hearing that dinner was ready, going out. Addison and Steele might have been occasionally seen at her

Kensington levees, among the Whigs; and Swift, Prior, and Bolingbroke among the Tories. Marlborough would be there also; his celebrated duchess, Sarah Jennings, had entered upon a court life at an early age as one of the companions of Anne during the princess's girlhood.

The last memorable interview between Queen Anne and the Duke of Marlborough took place here. When Queen Anne was lying in the agonies on Queen Anne, had their dinner here; and he tells us that Richard Steele liked the latter far better than his own chair at the former, "where there was less wine and more ceremony." Steele, who came to London in the suite of the Duke of Ormond, figures in the above work as "Scholar Dick;" he was one of the gentlemen ushers or members of the king's guard at Kensington.

When Esmond comes to England, after being

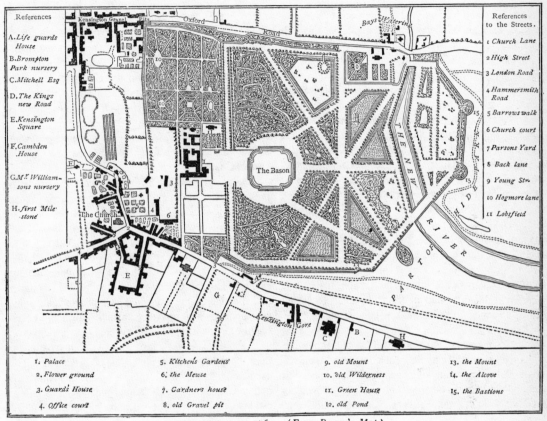

References

A. *Life guards House*
B. *Brompton Park nursery*
C. *Mitchell Esq*
D. *The Kings new Road*
E. *Kensington Square*
F. *Cambden House*
G. *Mr Williamsons nursery*
H. *first Mile stone*

References to the Streets.

1 *Church Lane*
2 *High Street*
3 *London Road*
4 *Hammersmith Road*
5 *Barrows walk*
6 *Church court*
7 *Parsons Yard*
8 *Back lane*
9 *Young Str*
10 *Hogmore lane*
11 *Lobsfield*

1. *Palace*	5. *Kitchens Gardens*	9. *old Mount*	13. *the Mount*
2. *Flower ground*	6. *the Mewse*	10. *old Wilderness*	14. *the Alcove*
3. *Guards House*	7. *Gardners house*	11. *Green House*	15. *the Bastions*
4. *Office court*	8. *old Gravel pit*	12. *old Pond*	

KENSINGTON IN 1764. (*From Rocque's Map.*)

of death, and the Jacobite party were correspondingly in the agonies of hope and expectation, two noblemen of the highest rank—John, Duke of Argyll, and the "proud" Duke of Somerset, who had been superseded in office at the time of the union with Scotland—suddenly, and unbidden, appeared at the council, and their unexpected presence is said to have stifled Lord Bolingbroke's designs, if he ever entertained any, of recalling the exiled Stuarts. On such slight events—accidents as we often call them—do the fates of dynasties, and indeed of whole nations, depend.

We learn from Thackeray's "Esmond" that while the royal guard had a very splendid table laid out for them at St. James's, the gentlemen ushers who waited on King William, and afterwards wounded at Blenheim, he finds Mrs. Beatrix installed as a lady-in-waiting at the palace, and thenceforth "all his hopes and desires lay within Kensington Park wall."

George I., whose additions to the palace were the cupola-room and the great staircase, frequently resided here, as also did his successor, George II. Here, free from the restraint caused by Sir Robert Walpole's presence, the latter king, when angry with his ministers or his attendants, would fly into furious rages, expending his anger even on his innocent wig; whilst his clever spouse, Queen Caroline, stood by, maintaining her dignity and self-possession, and, consequently, her ascendancy over him, and acting as a "conducting wire" between the sovereign and the premier. A good story is told by Horace Walpole, showing the lax and romping manners of the Court under the early Georges :—"There has been a great fracas at Kensington (he writes in 1742). One of the mesdames (the princesses) pulled the chair from under Countess Deloraine at cards, who, being provoked that her monarch was diverted with her disgrace, with the malice of a hobby-horse gave him just such another fall. But, alas! the monarch, like Louis XIV., is mortal in the part that touched the ground, and was so hurt and so angry, that the countess is disgraced, and her German rival remains in the sole and quiet possession of her royal master's favour." The Countess of Deloraine was governess to the young princesses, daughters of George II., and was a favourite with the king, with whom she generally played cards in the evenings in the princesses' apartments. Sir Robert Walpole considered her as a dangerous person about the Court, for she possessed, said the shrewd minister, "a weak head, a pretty face, a lying tongue, and a false heart." Lord Hervey, in his "Court Ballad," written in 1742, sarcastically styles her "*virtuous*, and *sober*, and *wise* Deloraine;" and in his "Memoirs," under date of 1735, he describes her as "one of the vainest as well as one of the simplest women that ever lived ; but to this wretched head," he adds, "there was certainly joined one of the prettiest faces that ever was formed, which, though she was now five-and-thirty, had a bloom upon it, too, that not one woman in ten thousand has at fifteen."

George II. died quite suddenly as he sat at breakfast in the palace, on Saturday, October 25, 1760. The building underwent considerable alterations during his reign, and he was the last monarch who resided here, George III. having chosen as his homes St. James's Palace, Kew Gardens, and Buckingham House.

The palace, too, was the home of the Princess Sophia, the poor blind daughter of George III. Miss Amelia Murray, in her "Recollections," speaks of having constantly spent an evening with her in her apartments here, and bears testimony to the goodness of her disposition, as "an example of patient and unmurmuring endurance such as can rarely be met with."

Here, too, the unfortunate Caroline, Princess of Wales, was living from 1810 down to 1814, when she removed to Connaught Place. Here she held, if we may so speak, her rival Court, and kept up a kind of triangular duel with her royal husband, and her wayward child, the Princess Charlotte, not at all to the edification of those around her, who were obliged to feel and to own that, injured as she undoubtedly was by one who had sworn to love and cherish her, she did but little to win the respect and regard of either the Court or the nation at large. The hangers-on of the Princess would seem to have been of the ordinary type of "summer friends." At all events, one of her ladies in waiting writes thus, with a vein of unconscious sarcasm : "These noblemen and their wives continued to visit her royal highness the Princess of Wales till the old king was declared too ill to reign, and the Prince became in fact regent ; then those ladies disappeared that moment from Kensington, and were never seen there more. It was the besom of expediency which swept them all away." It appears, however, that the Princess of Wales was well aware that her hangers-on were not very disinterested. At all events, she writes : "Unless I do show dem de knife and fork, no company has come to Kensington or Blackheath, and neither my purse nor my spirits can always afford to hang out de offer of 'an ordinary.'"

The friends of the Princess formed a circle by themselves. It included Lord and Lady Henry Fitz-Gerald, Lady C. Lindsay, Lord Rivers, Mr. H. (afterwards Lord) Brougham, Lord and Lady Abercorn, Sir Humphry Davy, Lady Anne Hamilton, Mr. (afterwards Sir William) Gell, Mr. Craven, Sir J. Mackintosh, Mr. R. Payne Knight, Mr. and Lady E. Whitbread, Lord and Lady Grey, and Lord Erskine—a most strange and heterogeneous medley. Very frequently the dinners at Kensington were exceedingly agreeable, the company well chosen, and sufficient liberty given to admit of their conversing with unrestrained freedom. This expression does not imply a licentious mode of conversation, although sometimes discretion and modesty were trenched upon in favour of wit. Still, that was by no means the general turn of the discourse.

One of the ladies of the Princess Caroline writes, under date of 1810 : "The Princess often does the most extraordinary things, apparently for no other purpose than to make her attendants stare. Very frequently she will take one of her ladies with her to walk in Kensington Gardens, who are accordingly dressed [it may be] in a costume very unsuited to the public highway ; and, all of a sudden, she will bolt out at one of the smaller gates, and walk all over Bayswater, and along the Paddington Canal, at the risk of being insulted, or, if known, mobbed, enjoying the terror of the unfortunate attendant who may be destined to walk after her. One day, her royal highness inquired at all the doors of Bayswater and its neighbourhood if there were any houses to be let, and went into many of them, till at last she came to one where some children of a friend of hers (Lord H. F.) were placed for change of air, and she was quite enchanted to be known by them, and to boast of her extraordinary mode of walking over the country."

Her royal highness gave plenty of balls and parties whilst residing here, and amused herself pretty well as she chose. In 1811 she is thus described by Lady Brownlow, in her "Reminiscences of a Septuagenarian:"—"I had scarcely ever seen the Princess, and hardly knew her by sight. At the time of which I speak, her figure was fat and somewhat shapeless; her face had probably been pretty in youth, for her nose was well formed, her complexion was good, and she had bright blue eyes; but their expression was bold—this, however, might be partly caused by the quantity of rouge which she wore. Her fair hair hung in masses of curls on each side of her throat, like a lion's mane. Everybody, before the peace with France, dressed much according to their individual taste; and her royal highness was of a showy turn: her gowns were generally ornamented with gold or silver spangles, and her satin boots were also embroidered with them. Sometimes she wore a scarlet mantle, with a gold trimming round it, hanging from her shoulders; and as she swam, so attired, down an English dance, with no regard to the figure, the effect was rather strange. . . . The princess's parties themselves," Lady Brownlow continues, "were marvellously heterogeneous in their composition. There were good people, and very bad ones, fine ladies and fine gentlemen, humdrums and clever people; among the latter the Rev. Sydney Smith, who, I thought, looked out of place there. . . . Her royal highness made rather a fuss with us, and we both always supped at her table. On one occasion I was much amused at seeing my father opposite to me, seated between the Duchess of Montrose and Lady Oxford. Sure never were there more incongruous supporters; and my father's countenance was irresistibly comic. 'Methought,' said he, as we drove home, 'that I was Hercules between Virtue and Vice.'"

The following anecdote of her royal highness shows how little of good sense or dignity she possessed:—"One day, the Princess set out to walk, accompanied by myself and one of her ladies, round Kensington Gardens. At last, being wearied, her royal highness sat down on a bench occupied by two old persons, and she conversed with them, to my infinite amusement, they being perfectly ignorant who she was. She asked them all manner of questions about herself, to which

they replied favourably; but her lady, I observed, was considerably alarmed, and was obliged to draw her veil over her face to prevent betraying herself; and every moment I was myself afraid that something not so favourable might be expressed by these good people. Fortunately, this was not the case, and her royal highness walked away undiscovered, having informed them that, if they would be at such a door at such an hour at the palace on any day, they would meet with the Princess of Wales, to see whom they expressed the strongest desire. This Haroun Al-Raschid expedition passed off happily, but I own I dreaded its repetition."

On another occasion her royal highness made a party to go to a small cottage in the neighbourhood of Bayswater, where she could feel herself unshackled by the restraints of royalty and etiquette; there she received a set of persons wholly unfit to be admitted to her society. It is true that, since the days of Mary of Scotland (when Rizzio sang in the Queen's closet), and in the old time before her, all royal persons have delighted in some small retired place or apartment, where they conceived themselves at liberty to cast off the cares of their high station, and descend from the pedestal of power and place to taste the sweets of private life. But in all similar cases, this attempt to be what they were not has only proved injurious to them: every station has its price—its penalty. By the Princess, especially, a more unwise or foolish course could not have been pursued, than this imitation of her unfortunate sister-queen of France. All the follies, though not the elegance and splendour, of Le Petit Trianon were aped in the rural retreat of Bayswater; and the Princess's foes were not backward at seizing upon this circumstance, and turning it (as well they might) to effect her downfall.

"Monk" Lewis, under date November, 1811, writes: "I have neither seen nor heard anything of the Princess since she removed to Blackheath, except a report that she is in future to reside at Hampton Court, because the Princess Charlotte wants the apartments at Kensington; but I cannot believe that the young princess, who has been always described to me as so partial to her mother, would endure to turn her out of her apartments, or suffer it to be done. I have also been positively assured, that the Prince has announced that the first exertion of his power will be to decide the fate of the Princess; and that Perceval, even though he demurred at endeavouring to bring about a divorce, gave it to be understood that he should have no objection to her being excluded from the coronation, and exiled to Holyrood House." Here the Princess was living in 1813, when she received the address of sympathy from the citizens of London— an address which was regarded by the Prince as the first step towards defying his authority.

The Duke of Sussex, whilst occupying apartments here, used to entertain his friends hospitably. Among others who dined here was Mr. Rush, ambassador from the United States in 1819-25, who gives us the following sketch :—

"The duke sat at the head of his table in true old English style, and was full of cordiality and conversation. . . . General principles of government coming to be spoken of, he expatiated on the blessings of free government, declaring that as all men, kings as well as others, were prone to abuse power when they got to possess it, the only safe course was to limit its exercise by the strictest constitutional rules. In the palace of kings, and from the son and brother of a king," adds the honest and sensible republican, " I should not have been prepared for this declaration, but that it was not the first time that I had heard him converse in the same way." The duke continued to reside in this palace till his death. He was very fond of the long room on the first floor, which he made his library, and where he received visitors. The interior of the room has been often engraved.

But that which invests Kensington Palace with the greatest interest is the fact that it was the residence of the late Duke and Duchess of Kent, in the year 1819, and consequently the birth-place of her present Majesty, who spent here nearly all her infancy, and the greater part of her youthful days. In the Gardens, as a child, the Princess Victoria used daily to take her walk, or ride in a goat or donkey carriage, attended by her nurses. Her most gracious Majesty was born at a quarter past four o'clock in the morning of the 24th of May, 1819, and on the 24th of the following month she was christened in the grand saloon of the palace by the name of Alexandrina Victoria. The reason of the choice of these two names is thus explained by the Hon. Amelia Murray, in her " Recollections :"—'It was believed that the Duke of Kent wished to name his child Elizabeth, that being a popular name with the English people. But the Prince Regent, who was not kind to his brothers, gave notice that he should stand in person as one godfather, and that the Emperor of Russia was to be another. At the baptism, when asked by the Archbishop of Canterbury to name the infant, the Prince Regent gave only the name of ' Alexandrina ;' but the duke requested that one other name might be added: ' Give her her mother's

also, then ; but,' he added, ' it cannot precede that of the Emperor.' The Queen, on her accession, commanded that she should be proclaimed as ' Victoria ' only."

We learn incidentally from Mr. Raikes' "Journal" that on the Princess Victoria coming of age, on the 24th of May, 1837, it was proposed by her uncle, the king, to form for her here an establishment of her own ; but that the idea was "combated by her mother, as it would have given the nomination of the appointments to the then Court party." The death of King William, however, which happened very shortly afterwards, put an end to the idea. On the 20th of June following, only a month after attaining her majority, as a girl of eighteen, she was waited upon here early in the morning by the Archbishop of Canterbury, and the then Lord Chamberlain, the Marquis of Conyngham, to receive the news that she was Queen of England !

For the following longer and more detailed account of the affair we are indebted to the " Diary of a Lady of Quality :"—" At Kensington Palace the Princess Victoria received the intelligence of the death of William IV., June, 1837. On the 20th, at 2 a.m., the scene closed, and in a very short time the Archbishop of Canterbury and Lord Conyngham, the Chamberlain, set out to announce the event to their young sovereign. They reached Kensington Palace about five ; they knocked, they rang, they thumped for a considerable time before they could rouse the porter at the gate ; they were again kept waiting in the court-yard ; they turned into one of the lower rooms, where they seemed forgotten by everybody. They rang the bell, desired that the attendant of the Princess Victoria might be sent to inform H.R.H. that they requested an audience on business of importance. After another delay, and another ringing to inquire the cause, the attendant was summoned, who stated that the *Princess* was in such a sweet sleep she could not venture to disturb her. Then they said, ' We are come to the *Queen* on business of state, and even her sleep must give way to that.' It did ; and, to prove that *she* did not keep them waiting, in a few minutes she came into the room in a loose white nightgown and shawl, her nightcap thrown off, and her hair falling upon her shoulders, her feet in slippers, tears in her eyes, but perfectly collected and dignified."

In this trying moment, though supported by her mother's presence, she gave vent to the feelings of her heart by bursting into a flood of tears as she thought of the responsibilities which had devolved upon her, and begged the Archbishop's prayers.

The story of Her Majesty's accession, and the

account of her first council, is thus told in the "Greville Memoirs :"—"1837, June 21. The King died at twenty minutes after two yesterday morning, and the young Queen met the council at Kensington Palace at eleven. Never was anything like the first impression she produced, or the chorus of praise and admiration which is raised about her manner and behaviour, and certainly not without justice. It was very extraordinary and far beyond what was looked for. Her extreme youth and inexperience, and the ignorance of the world concerning her, naturally excited intense curiosity to see how she would act on this trying occasion, and there was a considerable assemblage at the palace, notwithstanding the short notice that was given. The first thing that was to be done was to teach her her lesson, which, for this purpose, Melbourne had himself to learn. I gave him the council papers, and explained all that was to be done, and he went and explained all this to her. He asked her if she would enter the room accompanied by the great officers of state, but she said she would come in alone. When the lords were assembled, the Lord President informed them of the King's death, and suggested, as they were so numerous, that a few of them should repair to the presence of the Queen, and inform her of the event, and that their lordships were assembled in consequence ; and, accordingly, the two royal dukes, the two archbishops, the chancellor, and Melbourne, went with him. The Queen received them in the adjoining room alone. As soon as they had returned, the proclamation was read, and the usual order passed, when the doors were thrown open, and the Queen entered, accompanied by her two uncles, who advanced to meet her. She bowed to the lords, took her seat, and then read her speech in a clear, distinct, and audible voice, and without any appearance of fear or embarrassment. She was quite plainly dressed, and in mourning. After she had read her speech and taken and signed the oath for the security of the Church of Scotland, the Privy Councillors were sworn, the two royal dukes first by themselves ; and as these two old men, her uncles, knelt before her, swearing allegiance and kissing her hand, I saw her blush up to the eyes, as if she felt the contrast between their several and natural relations; and this was the only sign of emotion she evinced. Her manner to them was very graceful and engaging. She kissed them both, and moved towards the Duke of Sussex, who was furthest from her seat, and too infirm to reach her. She seemed rather bewildered at the multitude of men who were sworn, and who came one after another to kiss her hand ; but she did not speak to anybody, nor did she

make the slightest difference in her manner, or show any in her countenance to any individual of any rank, station, or party. I particularly watched her when Melbourne and her ministers, and the Duke of Wellington and Peel approached her. She went through the whole ceremony, occasionally looking at Melbourne for instructions when she had any doubt what to do, and with perfect calmness and self-possession, but, at the same time, with a modesty and propriety particularly interesting and ingratiating. When the business was done she retired as she had entered, and I could see that no one was in the adjoining room."

The scene at Kensington Palace on the above occasion is thus described by Mr. Rush, from the lips of the late Lord Clarendon, one of the Privy Councillors present at the time :—"Lord Lansdowne, the president, announced to the council that they had met on the occasion of the demise of the crown ; then with some others of the body, including the Premier, he left the council for a short time, when all returned with the Princess. She entered, leaning upon the arm of her uncle, the Duke of Sussex. The latter had not before been in the council-room, but resides in the same palace, and had been with the Princess in an adjoining apartment. He conducted her to a chair at the head of the council. A short time after she took her seat, she read the declaration which the sovereign makes on coming to the throne, and took the oath to govern the realm according to law, and cause justice to be executed in mercy. The members of the council then successively kneeled, one knee bending, and kissed the young queen's hand as she extended it to each —for now she was the veritable Queen of England. Lord Clarendon described the whole ceremony as performed in a very appropriate and graceful manner by the young lady. Some timidity was discernible at first, as she came into the room in the presence of the cabinet and privy councillors ; but it soon disappeared, and a becoming self-possession took its place. He noticed her discretion in not talking, except as the business of the ceremonial made it proper, and confining herself chiefly, when she spoke, to Lord Melbourne, as official head of the Ministry, and to her uncle, the Duke of Sussex."

The author of "The Diary of a Lady of Quality" thus describes the first meeting of the Privy Council of the youthful queen, which differs only in some slight particulars from the accounts given above : "The first act of the reign was, of course, the summoning of the council, and most of the summonses were not received till after the early hour fixed for its meeting. The Queen was, upon the opening of the doors, found sitting at the head of the table. She received first the homage of the Duke of Cumberland, who, I suppose, was not king of Hanover when he knelt to her; the Duke of Sussex rose to perform the same ceremony, but the Queen, with admirable grace, stood up, and preventing him from kneeling, kissed him on the forehead. The crowd was so great, the arrangements were so ill-made, that my brothers told me

Here, on the 21st of April, 1843, died, at the age of seventy, Augustus Frederick, Duke of Sussex. Mr. T. Raikes, in his "Journal," says of him: "He was a stout, coarse-looking man, of a free habit, plethoric, and subject to asthma. He lived at Kensington Palace, and was married to Lady Cecilia Gore, who had been made Duchess of Inverness by the Whigs. He had married previously, in 1793, Lady Augusta Murray; but that

THE ROUND POND, KENSINGTON GARDENS.

the scene of swearing allegiance to their young sovereign was more like that of the bidding at an auction than anything else."

The state document signed by the youthful sovereign is to be seen in the Record Office. Sir David Wilkie has painted the scene, but with a difference. The picture, it may be added, is well known to the public, thanks to the engraver's art. It may be a matter of wonder that the Lord Mayor of London (Alderman Kelly), should have figured in this picture; but on the sovereign's death the Lord Mayor is the only officer in the kingdom whose commission still holds good; and as such he takes his place, by virtue of his office, at the Privy Council board until the new sovereign is proclaimed.

marriage had been dissolved on the plea of the duke not obtaining his father's consent. He was always on bad terms with George IV., and under the weak government of William IV. he took the Radical line, courted the Whigs, and got the rangership of a royal park." He was buried at Kensal Green. His royal highness was, perhaps, the most popular of the sons of George III. He had a magnificent library at Kensington, including one of the finest collections of Bibles in the world, which was dispersed, soon after his death, under the hammer of the auctioneer. His widow, the Duchess of Inverness, was allowed to occupy his apartments until her death, in 1873. Under date of Sunday, 29th March, 1840, Mr. Raikes writes in his "Journal: "The Duke of Sussex claims from the Whig Ministry the public acknowledgment of his marriage with Lady Cecilia Underwood, and an addition of £6,000 a year to his income. This is the explanation: on the question of Prince Albert's precedence they first applied to the Duke of Sussex for his acquiescence, which he most

and professed to be the first to meet her wishes, but stipulating also that he expected a great favour for himself in return. This now proves to have been his object in view."

Shortly after the death of the duke, the following paragraph, headed "The late 'Duchess of Sussex,'"

SCOTCH FIRS, KENSINGTON GARDENS.

violently refused. They then went to the Duke of Cambridge with the same request, to which he made less difficulty, saying, that he wished to promote harmony in the family, and as it could not prevent him from being the son of his father, if the Duke of Sussex consented, he should not object. Lord Melbourne then returned to the latter, saying that the Duke of Cambridge had agreed at once; upon which Sussex, finding that he should lose all the merit of the concession, went straight to the Queen,

appeared in the *Times* newspaper: "As the fact is becoming a matter of general discussion, that in the event of the death of the King of Hanover, and of the Crown Prince, his son, the question of the title of Sir Augustus D'Este to the throne of that kingdom will create some controversy, the following letter from her royal highness (the Countess d'Ameland) to Sir S. J. Dillon, will not be uninteresting. It is dated so long since as December 16, 1811: 'My dear Sir,—I wished to have answered your last letter, but having mislaid your first, I did not know how to direct to you. I am sure you must believe that I am delighted with your pamphlet; but I must confess I do not think you have stated the fact quite exactly when you say (page 25) "that the question is at rest between me and the Duke of Sussex, because the connection has not only been declared illegal by sentence of the Ecclesiastical Court, but has been dissolved by consent—that I have agreed to abandon all claims to his name," &c. Now, my dear sir, had I believed the sentence of the Ecclesiastical Court to be anything but a stretch of power, my girl would not have been born. Lord Thurlow told me my marriage was good abroad—religion taught me it was good at home, and not one decree of any powerful enemy could make me believe otherwise, nor ever will. By refusing me a subsistence they forced me to take a name—not the Duke of Sussex's—but they have not made me believe that I had no right to his. My children and myself were to starve, or I was to obey; and I obeyed; but I am not convinced. Therefore, pray don't call this "an act of mutual consent," or say "the question is at rest." The moment my son wishes it, I am ready to declare that it was debt, imprisonment, arrestation, necessity (force like this, in short), which obliged me to seem to give up my claims, and not my conviction of their fallacy. When the banns were published in the most frequented church in London, and where all the town goes, is not that a permission asked? And why were they not forbid? I believe my marriage at Rome good; and I shall never feel "the question at rest" till this is acknowledged. Prince Augustus is now sent to Jersey, as Lieutenant D'Este, in the 7th Fusiliers. Before he went, he told his father he had no objection to go under any name they chose to make him take; but that he knew what he was, and the time, he trusted, would come when himself would see justice done to his mother and sister, and his own birth.'"

George III. having made St. James's and Buckingham Palace the head-quarters of royalty and the court, henceforward Kensington became the occasional or permanent residence of some of the younger branches of the royal family.

Kensington Palace, we need hardly add, is maintained at the cost of the nation; and, though no longer used actually as a royal residence, it is appropriated to the use of certain pensioned families, favoured by royalty, and a lady who is distantly connected with the highest court circles holds the envied and not very laborious post of housekeeper. It may safely be assumed, we think, that she is "at the top of her profession." The Right Hon. John Wilson Croker lived here for some time. The Duke and Duchess of Teck and the Marquis and Marchioness of Lorne have since occupied those apartments which formerly were inhabited by the distinguished personages mentioned above.

CHAPTER XIII.

KENSINGTON GARDENS.

"Where Kensington, luxuriant in her bowers,
Sees snow of blossoms, and a wild of flowers;
The dames of Britain oft in crowds repair
To gravel walks and unpolluted air :
Here, while the town in damps and darkness lies,
They breathe in sunshine and see azure skies;
Each walk, with robes of various dyes bespread,
Seems from afar a moving tulip-bed,
Where rich brocades and glossy damasks glow,
And chintz, the rival of the showery bow."—*Tickell.*

"Military" Appearance of the Gardens, as laid out by Wise and Loudon—Addison's Comments on the Horticultural Improvements of his Time—The Gardens as they appeared at the Beginning of the Last Century—Queen Anne's Banqueting House—Statue of Dr. Jenner—Bridgeman's Additions to the Gardens—The "Ha! ha!"—"Capability" Brown—The Gardens first opened to the Public—A Foreigner's Opinion of Kensington Gardens—"Tommy Hill" and John Poole—Introduction of Rare Plants and Shrubs—Scotch Pines and other Trees—A Friendly Flash of Lightning—The Reservoir and Fountains—Tickell, and his Poem on Kensington Gardens—Chateaubriand—Introduction of Hooped Petticoats—The Broad Walk becomes a Fashionable Promenade—Eccentricities in Costume—The Childhood of Queen Victoria, and her Early Intercourse with her Future Subjects—A Critical Review of the Gardens.

THE gardens attached to Kensington Palace, when purchased by William III., did not exceed twenty-six acres. They were immediately laid out according to the royal taste; and this being entirely military, the consequence was that closely-cropped yews, and prim holly hedges, were taught, under the auspices of Loudon and Wise, the royal gardeners, to imitate the lines, angles, bastions, scarps, and counter-scarps of regular fortifications. This curious upper garden, we are told, was long "the admiration of every lover of that kind of horticultural embellishment," and, indeed, influenced the general taste of the age; for Le Nautre, or Le Notre, who was gardener to the Tuileries, and had been personally favoured by Louis XIV., in conjunction with the royal gardeners, was employed by most of the nobility, during the reign of William, in laying out their gardens and grounds. Addison, in No. 477 of the *Spectator*, thus speaks of the horticultural improvements of this period :—"I think there are as many kinds of gardening as of poetry: your makers of pastures and flower-gardens are epigrammatists and sonneteers in this art; contrivers of bowers and grottoes, treillages and cascades, are romantic writers; Wise and Loudon are our heroic poets; and if, as a critic, I may single out any passage of their works to commend, I shall take notice of that part in the upper garden at Kensington which was at first nothing but a gravel-pit. It must have been a fine genius for gardening that could have thought of forming such an unsightly hollow into so beautiful an area, and to have hit the eye with so uncommon and agreeable a scene as that which it is now wrought into."

In 1691 these gardens are thus described :—"They are not great, nor abounding with fine plants. The orange, lemon, myrtle, and what other trees they had there in summer, were all removed to London, or to Mr. Wise's greenhouse at Brompton Park, a little mile from there. But the walks and grass were very fine, and they were digging up a plot of four or five acres to enlarge their gardens." Queen Anne added some thirty acres more, which were laid out by her gardener, Wise. Bowack, in 1705, describes here "a noble collection of foreign plants, and fine neat greens, which makes it pleasant all the year. . . . Her Majesty has been pleased lately to plant near thirty acres more to the north, separated from the rest only by a stately greenhouse, not yet finished." It appears from this passage that, previous to the above date, Kensington Gardens did not extend further to the north than the conservatory, which, as stated in the previous chapter, was originally built for a banqueting-house, and was frequently used as such by Queen Anne. This banqueting-house was completed in the year 1705, and is considered a fine specimen of brickwork. The south front has rusticated columns supporting a Doric pediment, and the ends have semi-circular recesses. "The interior, decorated with Corinthian columns," Mr. John Timbs tells us in his "Curiosities," "was fitted up as a drawing-room, music-room, and ball-room; and thither the queen was conveyed in her chair from the western end of the palace. Here were given full-dress *fêtes à la Watteau*, with a profusion of 'brocaded robes, hoops, fly-caps, and fans,' songs by the court lyrists, &c." When the Court left Kensington, this building was converted into an orangery and greenhouse.

Just within the boundary of the gardens at the south-eastern corner, on slightly rising ground, is the Albert Memorial, which we have already described,* and not far distant is the statue of Dr. Jenner, the originator of vaccination. This statue, which is of bronze, represents the venerable doctor in a sitting posture. It is the work of William Calder Marshall, and was originally set up in Trafalgar Square in 1858, but was removed hither about four years afterwards.

The eastern boundary of the gardens would seem to have been in Queen Anne's time nearly in the line of the broad walk which crosses them on the east side of the palace. The kitchen-gardens, which extended north of the palace, towards the gravel-pits, but are now occupied by some elegant villas and mansions, and the thirty acres lying north of the conservatory, added by Queen Anne to the pleasure-gardens, may have been the fifty-five acres "detached and severed from the park, lying in the north-west corner thereof," granted in the reign of Charles II. to Hamilton, the Ranger of Hyde Park, and Birch, the auditor of excise, "to be walled and planted with 'pippins and red-streaks,' on condition of their furnishing apples or cider for the king's use." This portion of the garden is thus mentioned in Tickell's poem :—

"That hollow space, where now, in living rows,
    Line above line, the yew's sad verdure grows,
Was, ere the planter's hand its beauty gave,
    A common pit, a rude unfashion'd cave.
The landscape, now so sweet, we well may praise;
    But far, far sweeter, in its ancient days—
Far sweeter was it when its peopled ground
    With fairy domes and dazzling towers was crown'd.
Where, in the midst, those verdant pillars spring,
    Rose the proud palace of the Elfin king;
For every hedge of vegetable green,
    In happier years, a crowded street was seen;
Nor all those leaves that now the prospect grace
    Could match the numbers of its pigmy race."

At the end of the avenue leading from the south part of the palace to the wall on the Kensington Road is an alcove built by Queen Anne's orders; so that the palace, in her reign, seems to have stood in the midst of fruit and pleasure gardens, with pleasant alcoves on the west and south, and

* See p. 38, *ante.*

the stately banqueting-house on the east, the whole confined between the Kensington and Uxbridge Roads on the north and south, with Palace Green on the west ; the line of demarcation on the east being the broad walk before the east front of the palace.

Bridgeman, who succeeded Wise as the fashionable designer of gardens, was employed by Queen Caroline, consort of George II., to plant and lay out, on a larger scale than had hitherto been attempted, the ground which had been added to the gardens by encroaching upon Hyde Park. Bridgeman's idea of the picturesque led him to abandon " verdant sculpture," and he succeeded in effecting a complete revolution in the formal and square precision of the foregoing age, although he adhered in parts to the formal Dutch style of straight walks and clipped hedges. A plan of the gardens, published in 1762, shows on the north-east side a low wall and fosse, reaching from the Uxbridge Road to the Serpentine, and effectually shutting in the gardens. Across the park, to the east of Queen Anne's Gardens, immediately in front of the palace, a reservoir was formed with the " round pond ; " thence, as from a centre, long vistas or avenues were carried through the wood that encircled the water—one as far as the head of the Serpentine ; another to the wall and fosse above mentioned, affording a view of the park ; a third avenue led to a mount on the south-east side, which was raised with the soil dug in the formation of the adjoining canal, and planted with evergreens by Queen Anne. This mount, which has since been levelled again, or, at all events, considerably reduced, had on the top a revolving "prospect house." There was also in the gardens a "hermitage :" a print of it is to be seen in the British Museum. The low wall and fosse was introduced by Bridgeman as a substitute for a high wall, which would shut out the view of the broad expanse of park as seen from the palace and gardens ; and it was deemed such a novelty that it obtained the name of a " Ha ! ha !" derived from the exclamation of surprise involuntarily uttered by disappointed pedestrians. At each angle of this wall and fosse, however, semicircular projections were formed, which were termed bastions, and in this particular the arrangement accorded with the prevailing military taste. Bridgeman's plan of gardening, however, embraced the beauties of flowers and lawns, together with a wilderness and open groves ; but the principal embellishments were entrusted to Mr. Kent, and subsequently carried out by a gentleman well known by the familiar appellation of " Capability " Brown. The gardens, it may be added, are still sufficiently

rural to make a home for the nightingale, whose voice is often heard in the summer nights, especially in the part nearest to Kensington Gore.

" Here England's daughter, darling of the land,
    Sometimes, surrounded with her virgin band,
    Gleams through the shades. She, towering o'er the rest,
    Stands fairest of the fairer kind confest ;
    Form'd to gain hearts that Brunswick's cause denied,
    And charm a people to her father's side.

" Long have these groves to royal guests been known,
    Nor Nassau, first, preferred them to a throne.
    Ere Norman banners waved in British air ;
    Ere lordly Hubba with the golden hair
    Pour'd in his Danes ; ere elder Julius came ;
    Or Dardan Brutus gave our isle a name ;
    A prince of Albion's lineage graced the wood,
    The scene of wars, and stained with lover's blood."

On King William taking up his abode in the palace, the neighbouring town of Kensington and the outskirts of Hyde Park became the abode of fashion and of the hangers-on at the Court, whilst the gardens themselves became the scene of a plot for assassinating William, and replacing James II. on the throne. The large gardens laid out by Queen Caroline were opened to the public on Saturdays, when the King and Court went to Richmond, and on these occasions all visitors were required to appear in full dress. When the Court ceased to reside here, the gardens were thrown open in the spring and summer ; they, nevertheless, long continued to retain much of their stately seclusion. The gardens are mentioned in the following terms by the poet Crabbe, in his " Diary :"—" Drove to Kensington Gardens : . . . effect new and striking. Kensington Gardens have a very peculiar effect ; not exhilarating, I think, yet alive [lively] and pleasant." It seems, however, that the public had not always access to this pleasant place ; for, in the " Historical Recollections of Hyde Park," by Thomas Smith, we find a notice of one Sarah Gray having had granted her a pension of £18 a year, as a compensation for the loss of her husband, who was " accidentally shot by one of the keepers while hunting a fox in Kensington Gardens."

According to Sir Richard Phillips, in " Modern London," published in 1804, the gardens were open to the public at that time only from spring to autumn ; and, curiously enough, servants in livery were excluded, as also were dogs. Thirty years later the gardens are described as being open " all the year round, to all respectably-dressed persons, from sunrise till sunset." About that time, when it happened that the hour for closing the gates was eight o'clock, the following lines, purporting to have been written " by a young lady aged nineteen," were discovered affixed to one of the seats :—

" Poor Adam and Eve were from Eden turned out,
    As a punishment due to their sin ;
But here after eight, if you loiter about,
    As a punishment you 'll be locked in."

It may be added that now, on stated days during the " London season," the scene in these gardens is enlivened by the exhilarating strains of military bands.   It is stated by Count de Melfort, in his " Impressions of England," published in the reign of William IV., that the Duke of St. Albans—we suppose, as Grand Falconer of England—is the only subject, except members of the royal family, who has the right of entering Kensington Palace Gardens in his carriage.   The fact may be true, but it wants verifying.

The author of an agreeable " Tour of a Foreigner in England," published in 1825, remarks :—" The Palais Royale gives a better idea of the London squares than any other part of Paris.   The public promenades are St. James's Park, Hyde Park, and Kensington Gardens, which communicate with each other.   I am sometimes tempted to prefer these parks to the gardens of the Luxembourg and the Tuileries, which, however, cannot give you any idea of them.   St. James's Park, Hyde Park, and Kensington Gardens are to me the Tuileries, the Champs Élysees, and the Jardin des Plantes united. On Sundays the crowd of carriages which repair thither, and the gentlemen of fashion who exhibit their horsemanship with admirable dexterity in the ride, remind me of Long Champs ; but hackney coaches are not allowed to enter here to destroy the fine spectacle which so many elegant carriages afford.   Sheep graze tranquilly in Hyde Park, where it is also pleasing to see the deer bounding about.   At Kensington Gardens you are obliged to leave your horse or carriage standing at the gate. Walking through its shady alleys I observed with pleasure that the fashionable ladies pay, in regard to dress, a just tribute to our fair countrywomen. Judging from the costumes of the ladies, you might sometimes fancy yourself walking under the chestnut trees of the Tuileries.   A line of Tasso may very well be applied to Kensington Gardens :—

' L'arte che tutto fa, nulla si scuopre.' "

Within the last half century these gardens have been greatly improved by drainage, relaying, and replanting.   Much of the surrounding walls, too, have been removed, and in their place handsome iron railings have been substituted.   The leading features of the gardens at the present time are the three avenues above mentioned, radiating from the east front of the palace, through dense masses of trees.   Immediately in front of the palace is a quaintly-designed flower garden, separated from the Kensington Road by some fine old elm-trees.   The broad walk, fifty feet in width, was once the fashionable promenade.   " Tommy Hill," and his friend John Poole, who made him his great character in *Paul Pry*, with " I hope I don't intrude," used to walk daily together here.   All the surrounding parts are filled in with stately groups of ancient trees ; and the total absence of anything that indicates the proximity of the town, renders this spot particularly pleasant and agreeable for a stroll on a summer's evening.   Keeping along the eastern margin of the gardens, and crossing the end of the broad avenue, the visitor soon reaches a new walk formed about the time of the first Great Exhibition.   Here will be found a large number of new and rarer kind of shrubs, with their popular and technical names all legibly inscribed.   Weale, in his work on London, published in 1851, says :— " It is in the introduction of these rarer plants that the idea of a ' garden ' is, perhaps, better sustained than in most of the other features of the place, which are those of a park.   The demand, indeed, for evergreens and undergrowth in these gardens is most urgent ; and if (which we greatly doubt) there exists a well-founded objection to the use of shrubs and bushes in tufts or in single plants, there certainly can be no reason why solitary specimens, or varied groups of the many kinds of thorn, pyrus, mespilus, laburnum, pine and fir, evergreen, oaks, hollies, yews, &c., should not be most extensively planted, and a large portion of the younger and smaller trees in the densest parts cut away to make room for them."   With reference to the trees in these gardens, a correspondent of the *Times* newspaper, in May, 1876, observes :—" The crowds who flock to Bushy Park or Kew do not see anything more fair than the tree-pictures now in Kensington Gardens, to which I beg to call the attention of all lovers of trees.   The hawthorns and horse-chestnuts are now in marvellous beauty, though one rarely sees anybody taking the least notice of them.   All the blaze of the autumnal ' bedding out ' is in point of beauty as nothing to what is now afforded here by a few kinds of ordinary hardy trees that cost little at first and take care of themselves afterwards. There is a little open lawn with a small lime-tree in its centre, quite near the ' Row ' corner of the gardens, around which there are several charming aspects of tree-beauty.   One hawthorn is about forty feet high.   Some of the central and unfrequented portions of the gardens are the most attractive.   Nobody can despair of growing flowering trees to his heart's content in London after seeing the mountains of horse-chestnut bloom and other masses of tree-flowers here. Let those interested see the old trees in the central parts as well as the newer plantations, which, however, are also beautiful."

At the north side, nearly facing Porchester Terrace, there are some fine trees, including Scotch pines, which, a few years ago, were a glory to the neighbourhood, and are duly celebrated by Mr. Matthew Arnold in his verses on Kensington

whether the branch can be removed without injury to the royal tree." "I accordingly wrote to my friend in the evening (Tuesday)," continues the author, "and on Thursday morning my friends discovered, to their infinite satisfaction, that the obtrusive branch had disappeared ; and, as a natural sequence, I came in for a warm benediction, and the Woods and Forests for their full share of praise as an exceptional department of the State, where

THE FLOWER WALKS, KENSINGTON GARDENS.

Gardens. Some of these, however, became so decayed that they were cut down by order of Her Majesty's Woods and Forests, in 1875.

The author of "Reminiscences of Fifty Years" tells an amusing story with reference to one of the trees in this part of the gardens. He was one day praising the charming view which some friends of his commanded from their drawing-room window overlooking the gardens. "Yes, the view would be perfect, if the branch of that large tree," to which they specially drew his attention, "did not interrupt it." "Well," remarked the other, "it is somewhat singular that I walked to your door with the nearest relative in London of the Chief Commissioner of Woods and Forests (the Right Hon. Mr. Milne), and I shall ask him to inquire

red tape was not used, and circumlocution unknown. The Chief Commissioner, on reading my note to his relative, gave orders on the Wednesday to the superintendent of Kensington Gardens to look at the tree, and if the branch could be taken off without serious prejudice, it was to be done. The superintendent reported at head-quarters on the Thursday that on visiting the tree at an early hour that morning he found the branch in question lying on the ground, having been struck off by lightning during the heavy storm of the previous night. The Chief Commissioner wrote an amusing letter on the occasion, alleging that I really must be one 'who could call spirits from the vasty deep,' and had evidently transferred my powers to Kensington Gardens, acting on the suggestion given in

Richard III., 'With lightning strike the murderer dead.' The same day," adds the author, "I visited the tree, which appeared, saving the amputation of the large branch, to have escaped all other injury. Had other trees not suffered severely in Kensington Gardens that night, it might have led to a special inquiry or inquest to ascertain whether it was lightning or a saw that I had employed in obliging my friends. I told them they owed everything

running between the basins, there is a larger fountain, of octagonal form. The end of the reservoir nearest the bridge forms an ornamental façade, enriched with vases of various patterns, filled with flowers. The centre of this façade has two draped female figures, seated, holding vases, from which flow streams; and between these two figures, but projecting forward, is another large fountain. The height of this balustraded façade is about eight feet

OUTFALL OF WESTBOURNE. 1850.

to the lightning; as I was much inclined to think that the Chief Commissioner, with every desire to meet their wishes, might possibly have deemed it his duty to postpone the consideration of the removal of so large and umbrageous a branch from the royal demesne to the Greek Calends."

Of the bridge over the Serpentine, at the northeast corner of the Gardens, we have already given an illustration.* At some distance on the west side of this bridge, as it leaves the Uxbridge Road, the Serpentine has been divided into a series of four large basins or reservoirs, of octangular form, each of which has a small fountain in the centre, encompassed with marble. In the central pathway,

above the water-level. At the other end of the reservoirs is an engine-house, containing engines for working the fountains. This building is of Italian design, and roofed with red Italian tiles. It stands just within the Gardens, at a short distance from the Bayswater Road.

Kensington Gardens have been celebrated by Tickell in the poem which bears their name, and from which we have quoted above; "verses," says Charles Knight, "full of fairies and their dwarfs, and Dryads and Naiads; verses made to order, and which have wholly perished as they deserve to perish." Tickell enjoyed the patronage of Addison, contributed papers to the *Spectator*, was contemporary with Pope, and published a translation of the "First Book of the Iliad," from his own pen, in

* See Vol. IV., p. 396.

apparent opposition to Pope's "Homer," of which the first part was published at the same time. As we read in Johnson's "Lives of the Poets," "Addison declared that the rival versions were both good, but Tickell's was the best. His poem on 'Kensington Gardens,' with the fairy tale introduced, is much admired; the versification is smooth and elegant. He is said to have been a man of gay conversation, but in his domestic relations without censure." Musical attractions were not wanting here in Tickell's time, if we may judge from the following couplet, which refers to Kensington Gardens :—

> "Nor the shrill corn-pipe, echoing loud to arms,
>   To rank and file reduce the straggling swarms."

Readers of the "Life of Chateaubriand" will remember that he was one of those who admired and enjoyed the repose of the leafy walks of these Gardens. Professor Robertson, in his "Lectures on Modern History and Biography," tells us how the venerable sage "would stroll under these beautiful trees, where in the days of his exile he used to meet his fellow-sufferers, the French priests, reciting their breviary—those trees under which he had indulged in many a reverie, under which he had breathed many a sigh for his home in La Belle France, under which he had finished 'Atala,' and had composed 'Réné.'"

Kensington Palace and its Gardens were the first places where the hooped petticoats of our great-grandmother's days were displayed by ladies of fashion and "quality." We do not purpose giving here a history of Englishwomen's dress; but it may be as well to record the fact that the hoop appears to have been the invention of a Mrs. Selby, whose novelty is made the subject of a pamphlet, published at Bath, under the title of "The Farthingale Reviewed; or, more Work for the Cooper : a Panegyrick on the late but most admirable invention of the Hooped Petticoat." The talented lady who invented it died in 1717, and is thus mentioned by a Mrs. Stone, in the "Chronicles of Fashion :" "How we yearn to know something more of Mrs. Selby, her personal appearance, her whereabouts, her habits, and her thoughts. Can no more be said of her, whose inventive genius influenced the empire for well-nigh a century, who, by the potency of a rib of whalebone, held the universal realm of fashion against the censures of the press, the admonitions of the pulpit, and the common sense of the whole nation? Mrs. Tempest, the milliner, had her portrait taken by Kent, and painted on the staircase of Kensington Palace ; and what was Mrs. Tempest that her lineaments should be preserved,

whilst those of Mrs. Selby, the inventor of the hoop, are suffered to fall into oblivion ?"

It was during the reign of George I. that the fashionable promenades in the Gardens became so popular, and the glittering skirts, which still lived in the recollection of our grandparents, would seem to have made their first appearance. Caroline of Anspach, the Prince of Wales's consort, probably introduced them, when she came with her bevy of maidens to Court. People would throng to see them ; the ladies would take the opportunity of showing themselves, like pea-hens, in the walks ; persons of fashion, privileged to enter the Gardens, would avail themselves of the privilege ; and at last the public would obtain admission, and the raree-show would be complete. The full-dress promenade, it seems, was at first confined to Saturdays ; it was afterwards changed to Sundays, and continued on that day till the custom went out with the closing days of George III.

In fact, during the last century the broad walk in Kensington Gardens had become almost as fashionable a promenade as the Mall in St. James's Park had been a century earlier, under Charles II. There might, probably, have been seen here, on one and the same day, during the portentous year 1791, Wilkes and Wilberforce ; George Rose and Mr. Holcroft ; Mr. Reeve and Mr. Godwin ; Burke, Warren Hastings, and Tom Paine ; Horace Walpole and Hannah More (whom he introduced to the Duke of Queensberry) ; Mary Wolstonecroft and Miss Burney (Madame d'Arblay), the latter avoiding the former with all her might ; the Countess of Albany (the widow of the Pretender) ; the Margravine of Anspach ; Mrs. Montagu ; Mrs. Barbauld ; Mrs. Trimmer ; Emma Harte (Lady Hamilton), accompanied by her adoring portrait-painter, Romney ; and poor Madame du Barry, mistress of Louis XV., come to look after some jewels of which she has been robbed, and little thinking she would return to be guillotined. The fashions of this half century, with the exception of an occasional broad-brimmed hat worn both by gentlemen and ladies, comprised the ugliest that ever were seen in the old Court suburb. Head-dresses became monstrous compounds of paste-board, flowers, feathers, and pomatum ; the hoop degenerated into little panniers ; and about the year 1770, a set of travelled fops came up, calling themselves Macaronis (from their intimacy with the Italian eatable so called), who wore ridiculously little hats, large pigtails, and tight-fitting clothes of striped colours. The lesser pigtail, long or curly, prevailed for a long time among elderly gentlemen, making a powdered semicircle between the shoulders; a plain cocked-hat adorned their heads; and, on a sudden, at the beginning of the new century, some of the ladies took to wearing turbans, surmounted with ostrich feathers, and bodies literally without a waist, the girdle coming directly under the arms. There was a song in those days, beginning—

"Shepherds, I have lost my love;
Have you seen my Anna?"

This song was parodied by one beginning—

"Shepherds, I have lost my waist;
Have you seen my body?"

Lady Brownlow, in her "Reminiscences of a Septuagenarian," tells us that after the Peace of Amiens, in 1802, she here met the celebrated Madame Recamier, who created a sensation at the West-end, partly by her beauty, but still more by her dress, which was vastly unlike the unsophisticated style and *poke* bonnets of the English ladies. "She appeared in Kensington Gardens *à l'antique*, a muslin gown clinging to her form like the folds of drapery on a statue; her hair in a plait at the back, and falling in small ringlets round her face, and greasy with *huile antique;* a large veil thrown over her head completed her attire, which not unnaturally caused her to be followed and stared at." No doubt, dressed in such a costume, and at such a period, Madame Recamier might well have been the "cynosure of neighbouring eyes."

During the early childhood of Her Majesty Queen Victoria, when living with her royal mother in Kensington Palace, the little princess was daily to be seen running about these gardens, or riding on her donkey about its walks; and her intercourse with the visitors there, we are assured by the author of an "Anecdotal Memoir of Her Majesty," was of a very interesting description. Some anecdotes upon this subject may be well introduced by the following remarks of a correspondent to the editor of a daily newspaper, when the princess was nearly three years old:—

"Passing accidentally through Kensington Gardens, a few days since, I observed at some distance a party, consisting of several ladies, a young child, and two men-servants, having in charge a donkey, gaily caparisoned with blue ribbons, and accoutred for the use of the infant. The appearance of the party, and the general attention they attracted, led me to suspect they might be the royal inhabitants of the palace; I soon learnt that my conjectures were well founded, and that her Royal Highness the Duchess of Kent was in maternal attendance, as is her daily custom, upon her august and interesting daughter, in the enjoyment of her healthful exercise. On approaching the royal party, the infant princess, observing my respectful recognition, nodded, and wished me a 'good morning' with much liveliness, as she skipped along between her mother and her sister, the Princess Feodore, holding a hand of each. Having passed on some paces, I stood a moment to observe the actions of the royal child, and was pleased to see that the gracious notice with which she honoured me was extended, in a greater or less degree, to almost every person she met: thus does this fair scion of our royal house, while yet an infant, daily make an impression on the hearts of many individuals which will not easily be forgotten. Her Royal Highness is remarkably beautiful, and her gay and animated countenance bespeaks perfect health and good temper. Her complexion is excessively fair, her eyes large and expressive, and her cheeks blooming. She bears a very striking resemblance to her late royal father, and, indeed, to every member of our reigning family; but the soft beauty, and (if I may be allowed the term) the dignity of her infantine countenance, peculiarly reminded me of our late beloved Princess Charlotte."

"This favourite donkey," we are further told by the above-mentioned authority, "a present from the Duke of York, bore his royal mistress daily round the gardens, to her great delight; so fond, indeed, was she of him, and of the exercise which he procured for her, that it was generally necessary to persuade her that the donkey was tired or hungry in order to induce her to alight. Even at this very early age, the princess took great pleasure in mixing with the people generally, and seldom passed anybody in the gardens, either when riding in her little carriage or upon her donkey, without accosting them with, 'How do you do?' or 'Good-morning, sir,' or 'lady;' and always seemed pleased to enter into conversation with strangers, returning their compliments or answering their questions in the most distinct and good-humoured manner. The young princess showed her womanly nature as a particular admirer of children, and rarely allowed an infant to pass her without requesting permission to inspect it and to take it in her arms. She expressed great delight at meeting a young ladies' school, and always had something to say to most of the children, but particularly to the younger ones. When a little older, she was remarkable for her activity, as, holding her sister Feodore in one hand, and the string of her little cart in the other, with a moss-rose fastened into her bosom, she would run with astonishing rapidity the whole length of the broad gravel walk, or up and down the green hills with which the gardens abound, her eyes sparkling with animation and glee, until the attendants, fearful of the effects of such violent exercise, were compelled to put a stop to it, much against the will of the little romp; and although a large assemblage of well-dressed ladies, gentlemen, and children would, on such occasions, form a semicircle round the scene of amusement, their presence never seemed in any way to disconcert the royal child, who would continue her play, occasionally speaking to the spectators as though they were partakers in her enjoyment, which, in very truth, they were. If, whilst amusing herself in the enclosed lawn, she observed, as sometimes happened, many persons collected round the green railings, she would walk close up to it, and curtsey and kiss her hand to the people, speaking to all who addressed her; and when her nurse led her away, she would again and again slip from her hand, and return to renew the mutual greetings between herself and her future subjects, who, as they contemplated with delight her bounding step and merry healthful countenance, the index of a heart full of innocence and joy, were ready unanimously to exclaim—

> " ' Long may it be ere royal state
>   That cherub smile shall dissipate;
>   Long ere that bright eye's peerless blue,
>   A sovereign's anxious tear bedew;
>   Ere that fair form of airy grace,
>   Assume the regal measured pace;
>   Or that young, open, cloudless brow,
>   With truth and joy that glitters now,
>   The imperial diadem shall wear
>   Beset with trouble, grief, and care.' "

In an article on Kensington Palace and Gardens, in the *Monthly Register* for September, 1802, the writer somewhat critically remarks:—"All the views from the south and east façades of the edifice suffer from the absurdity of the early inspectors of these grounds. The three vistas opening from the latter, without a single wave in the outline, without a clump or a few insulated trees to soften the glare of the champagne, or diminish the oppressive weight of the incumbent grove, are among the greatest deformities. The most exquisite view in the Gardens is near the north-east angle; at the ingress of the Serpentine river, which takes an easy wind towards the park, and is ornamented on either side by sloping banks, with scenery of a different character. To the left the wood presses boldly on the water, whose polished bosom seems timidly to recede from the dark intruder; to the right, a few truant foresters interrupt the uniformity of the parent grove, which rises at some distance on the more elevated part of the shore; and through the boles of the trees are discovered minute tracts of landscape, in which the eye of taste can observe sufficient variety of light and shade of vegetable and animal life to gratify the imagination, and disappoint the torpor, which the more sombre scenery to the east is accustomed to invite.

"The pencil of Claude and Poussin was employed on general landscape; and the transport inspired by their works is from the composition and general effect, not from the exact resemblance of objects, to which Swanevelt and Watteau were so scrupulously attentive. In the landscape of nature, as well as in the feeble imitations of the artist, individuals deserve some attention. The largest and most beautiful of all the productions of the earth is a tree. As the effulgent tints of the insect must yield to the elegance and proportion of the other orders of animals, when contemplated by our imperfect optics, so the gorgeous radiance of the flower must bend its coronal honours to this gigantic offspring of nature, whose ample foliage receives all the splendid effects of light and shade, and gives arrangement and composition to landscape. The trees that conduce to the sublime in scenery are the oak, the ash, the elm, and the beech. It is a defect in the gardens at Kensington that, excepting the elm, the whole of this beautiful fraternity is excluded, so that all the variety of tint in the spring and autumn is lost, and the gardens burst into the luxuriance of summer, and hasten to the disgrace of winter, without those gradations which indulgent Nature has contrived to moderate our transport on the approach of the one, and to soften our griefs on the appearance of the other. The dusky fir is the only melancholy companion the elm is here permitted to possess, who seems to raise his tall funereal head to insult his more lively associate with approaching decay. If in spring we have not here all the colours of the rainbow, in the forms of nascent existence; if in autumn the yellow of the elm, the orange of the beech, and the glowing brown of the oak do not blend their fading honours, it must be acknowledged that the elm is one of the noblest ornaments of the forest; it is the medium between the massive unyielding arm of the oak and the versatile pliancy of the ash; it out-tops the venerable parent of the grove, and seems to extend its mighty limbs towards heaven, in bold defiance of the awful monarch of the wood.

"Besides the disadvantage from the uniformity in the umbrageous furniture of these gardens, there is another, which we hardly know whether to attribute to design or accident. A tree rising like an artificial pillar from the smooth earth, without exposing any portion of the bold angles of its root, not only loses half its strength, but almost all its dignity. Pliny, endeavouring to give a grand idea of the Hercynian forest, describes the magnitude of the trees in that ancient domain of the Sylvani to be sufficient to admit mounted cavalry to pass beneath the huge radical curves. Whatever ornament Pliny's extravagance might attribute in this respect on the broad expanse of solitary Nature, this gigantic wildness would not be at all adapted to these pigmy haunts of man ; but some resemblance, some approach, should be attempted to the magnificence of her operations.

" ' ———A huge oak, dry and dead,
　　Still cull'd with relics of its trophies old,
　　Lifting to heaven its aged hoary head.'

" Such an object, with some of our readers, would be considered a venerable inmate of these gardens, and to us it would be infinitely preferable to the trim expedients of art. The insulated majesty of this ancient possessor of the soil would prevent the intrusion of the timid hand of man, and the character which this parent of the forest would impart to the general scenery would secure it from sacrilegious profanation."

CHAPTER XIV.

HOLLAND HOUSE, AND ITS HISTORICAL ASSOCIATIONS.

" Here Rogers sat, and here for ever dwell
With me those pleasures that he sang so well."—*Lord Holland.*

Earl's Court—John Hunter's House—Mrs. Inchbald—Edwardes Square—Warwick Road and Warwick Gardens—Addison Road—Holland House—An Antique Relic—The Pictures and Curiosities—The Library—The Rooms occupied by Addison, Charles Fox, Rogers, and Sheridan—Holland House under the Family of Rich—Theatrical Performances carried on by Stealth during the Commonwealth—Subsequent Owners of the Mansion—Oliver Goldsmith—Addison—The House purchased by Henry Fox, afterwards Lord Holland—The Story of Henry Fox's Elopement with the Daughter of the Duke of Richmond—Lady Sarah Lennox and the Private Theatricals—Charles James Fox—Henry Richard, third Lord Holland, and his Imperious Wife—Lord Macaulay, and other Distinguished Guests—"Who is Junius?"—Lord Holland and the Emperor Napoleon—Death of Lord Holland, and his Character, as written by a Friend—A Curious Custom—The Duel between Lord Camelford and Captain Best—Rogers' Grotto—The Gardens and Grounds—Canova's Bust of Napoleon—The Highland and Scottish Societies' Sports and Pastimes—A Tradition concerning Cromwell and Ireton—Little Holland House—The Residence of General Fox—The Nursery-grounds.

RETRACING our steps along the Kensington Road, we come to Earl's Court Road, a thoroughfare communicating with the western end of Cromwell Road, which comprises several highly respectable detached mansions. It probably owes its name to the Earls of Warwick and Holland, whose mansion faces it. Sir Richard Blackmore, the poet, appears to have had a residence here, for Pope writes, in his " Imitations of Horace "—

　" Blackmore himself, for any grave effort,
　　Would drink and doze at Tooting or Earl's Court."

In later times Earl's Court afforded a retirement to the eminent surgeon, John Hunter, who here made several experiments in natural history, and formed in the grounds surrounding his villa a menagerie of rare and valuable foreign animals. In the kitchen of Hunter's house the great surgeon literally boiled down the Irish giant, O'Brien, whose skeleton we have mentioned in our account of the Museum* in Lincoln's Inn Fields. Even the copper in which the operation was performed is religiously kept, and shown to curious visitors. After the death of Mr. Hunter, the house in which he resided was for some time occupied occasionally by the Duke of Richmond, who purchased the estate. The house, it may be added, has since been a *maison de santé*.

In Leonard's Place, and also in Earl's Court Terrace, Mrs. Inchbald resided for some time, in boarding-houses. At the back of Earl's Terrace is Edwardes Square, so called after the family name of Lord Kensington. This square is chiefly remarkable for the largeness as well as the cultivated look of the enclosure, which affords to the residents, and also to the inhabitants of the Terrace, who have the right of entry, the advantages of a larger kind of garden. Leigh Hunt mentions a tradition as current in Kensington that Coleridge once had lodgings in Edwardes Square ; but, he adds, " we do not find the circumstance in his biographies, though he once lived in the neighbouring village of Hammersmith."

Warwick Road and Warwick Gardens, which lie on the west side of Edwardes Square, are so named after the Earls of Warwick, the former owners of Holland House. In Warwick Gardens is a well-built Wesleyan chapel. Running parallel with Warwick Road, crossing by a bridge the Kensington Road, and continuing its course by Holland Road, is the West London Railway, and this we fix upon as the limits of our perambulations in the " far west." Addison Road, of course, is so named

* See Vol. III., p. 46.

after another and a distinguished occupant of Holland House, of which we shall presently speak ; and it forms a communication between the Kensington and Uxbridge Roads, skirting the west side of Holland Park. St. Barnabas Church, which stands in this road, and dates from about the year 1827, is built in the "late Perpendicular" style of Gothic architecture.

Having been built only in the early part of the

Cope, it was built, in the year 1607, from the designs of John Thorpe, the famous architect of several of the baronial mansions of England which were erected about that time. Although scarcely two miles distant from London, with its smoke, its din, and its crowded thoroughfares, Holland House still has its green meadows, its sloping lawns, and its refreshing trees; and the view of the quaint old pile which meets the wayfarer in passing along

EARL'S COURT HOUSE (FORMERLY JOHN HUNTER'S). (*See page* 161.)

seventeenth century, shortly after the death of Queen Elizabeth, Holland House has no history that carries us back beyond the first of the Stuarts ; nor, indeed, did the mansion become really celebrated till the reign of George I., when the widow of its owner, Rich, Earl of Holland and Warwick, married Addison, who died here. It afterwards came into the possession of the family of Fox, Lord Holland, firstly as tenants, and subsequently as owners of the freehold. The first Lord Holland and his lady were both persons of ability; and before the end of the reign of George II., Holland House had risen into a celebrity which it has never since lost.

The mansion takes its name from Henry Rich, Earl of Holland, by whose father-in-law, Sir Walter

the Kensington Road, on his road towards or from Hammersmith, is highly suggestive of rural solitude, and the effect is enhanced by the note of the nightingale, which is frequently heard in the grounds which surround the mansion. From Sir Walter Cope the property passed to his son-in-law, above mentioned, who much improved the house, and completed its internal decorations. The building follows the form so usually adopted at the era of its construction, and may be best described by saying that it resembles one-half of the letter H. The material is brick, with dressings and embellishments of stone and stucco. The projection in the central compartment of the principal division of the house forms at once a tower and porch. There is a building at each end of

OLD KENSINGTON.

1. Manor House.   2. Old Tavern.   3. Little Holland House.

the same division, with shingled and steep-roofed turrets, surmounted by a vane. A projecting arcade, terminated by a parapet of carved stone-work, ranges along the principal faces of the building; and the original court is bounded by a palisade. The present terrace in front of the house was raised about 1848, when the old foot-path, which ran immediately in front of its windows, was diverted from its course. The following are the particulars of the interior of this interesting mansion, as given in "Homes and Haunts of the Poets:"—"There is a fine entrance-hall, a library behind it, and another library extending the whole length of one of the wings and the house up-stairs, one hundred and fifty feet in length. The drawing-room over the entrance-hall, called the gilt-room, extends from front to back of the house, and commands views of the gardens both ways; those to the back are very beautiful." There was evidently a chapel attached to the house in former times, for there are some remnants of arches still existing, built into the walls of rooms which now serve a very different purpose. The old bronze font, or "stoup," for holy water, too, stands by the staircase in the inner hall, supported by a comparatively modern tripod of the same material. It appears to have been made in the year 1484, by a Fleming, named Cassel, or Caselli; "around it, far interspersed with odd old Scriptural and armorial devices, is written, in Gothic letters, an abbreviated rendering of the passage in the Psalm, so familiar to Catholic ears: 'Asperges me hyssopo, et mundabor; lavabis me, et super nivem dealbabor.'" Many of the pictures which adorn the walls are by some of the best masters. One apartment, called "The Sir Joshua Room," con-tains several of Reynolds's works, the best of which are considered "Muscipula," a child holding up a mouse in a cage, with puss looking wistfully on from below; a portrait of Baretti, author of the Italian Dictionary, who was tried for murder,* but received favourable testimony from Dr. Johnson, Burke, and Garrick, and was acquitted; and the beautiful Lady Sarah Lennox, whom George III. noticed with admiration when a little girl in Ken-sington Gardens. His Majesty, it is related, requested to see her again in later years, and, in fact, wished much to marry her when she had grown into a young lady. She was one of the bridesmaids at his wedding, when, if report be true, he kept his eyes steadily fixed on her during the ceremony of his own marriage with Charlotte of Mecklenburg. This room contains also Murillo's

"Vision of St. Antony of Padua." The gilt-room —which has lost some of its former glories, in the shape of frescoes on the chimney-piece, supposed to represent the Aldobrandini Marriage, and which are presumed to be buried underneath a coating of plaster — was prepared by the first Earl of Holland of the line of Rich for the purpose of giving a ball to Prince Charles on the occasion of his marriage with Henrietta Maria of France; the ball, however, for some unexplained reason, never came off. This apartment is now said to be tenanted by the solitary ghost of its first lord, who, according to tradition, "issues forth at mid-night from behind a secret door, and walks slowly through the scenes of former triumphs, with his head in his hand." This, however, is not the only "ghost story" connected with Holland House, for credulous old Aubrey tells us: "The beautiful Lady Diana Rich, as she was walking in her father's garden at Kensington, to take the fresh air before dinner, about eleven o'clock, being then very well, met with her own apparition, habit, and every thing, as in a looking-glass. About a month after, she died of the small-pox. And it is said that her sister, the Lady Elizabeth Thynne, saw the like of herself before she died. This account," he adds, "I had from a person of honour."

Among the most noticeable pictures which abound in the map-room and the picture-room, are some by Watts, who is considered by many one of the greatest of contemporary English artists. In the latter room mass was said daily during the brief stay of Marie Amélie, the late Queen of the French, in the house in 1862. In the print-room are some specimens of the Italian, German, Dutch, Flemish, French, Spanish, and English schools; the Rembrandts being the most worthy of note. Hogarth is represented in the next room. Here, among the portraits, are those of Tom Moore, by Shee, and of Rogers, by Hoffner; there are also some fine Dutch sea-pieces. The library, a very handsome long room, contains, besides its literary treasures, among other relics, a table used by Addison at the Temple. There is a glowing notice of this room by Macaulay, too long for quotation. In the yellow drawing-room there is "a pair of candlesticks in Byzantine ware, which belonged to Mary Queen of Scots. They were in her posses-sion at Fotheringay Castle, and thus were witnesses to the last hours of her life's tragedy." There is, too, "an ancient poison-ring," with a death's head in carbuncle, supposed to have been sent to the same unfortunate queen. Here are also numerous relics of the great Napoleon: among them is a locket, containing some of his hair, a ring, and a

---

* See Vol. IV., p. 220.

cross worn by him in his island prison at St. Helena. The miniature-room, it need scarcely be added, has its treasures; as have also "Lady Holland's private rooms" and the "blue-room." The former had a narrow escape from destruction by fire a few years ago. Among the remaining curiosities and works of art preserved here, is an interesting collection of fans, some of which are very beautifully painted. "One of these," as the Princess Marie Lichstenstein informs us in her account of Holland House, "is historically interesting, having been painted by a daughter of George III., before the union of Ireland with England. It bears the rose and the thistle, but no shamrock; and the motto, 'Health is restored to one, happiness to millions,' seems to indicate the occasion for which it was painted." Autographs, too, and manuscripts of famous characters, are not wanting: among them are those of Catherine, Empress of Russia; Napoleon I., Voltaire, Addison, Petrarch, letters of Philip II., III., and IV. of Spain; and music by Pergolese, copied by Rousseau.

"The library," says Leigh Hunt, in his "Old Court Suburb," "must originally have been a greenhouse or conservatory; for, in its first condition, it appears to have been scarcely anything but windows, and it is upwards of ninety feet long, by only seventeen feet four inches wide, and fourteen feet seven inches in height. The moment one enters it, one looks at the two ends, and thinks of the tradition about Addison's pacings in it to and fro. It represents him as meditating his 'Spectators' between two bottles of wine, and comforting his ethics by taking a glass of each as he arrived at each end of the room. The regularity of this procedure is, of course, a jest; but the main circumstance is not improbable, though Lord Holland seems to have thought otherwise. He says (for the words in Faulkner's 'Kensington' are evidently his):—'Fancy may trace the exquisite humour which enlivens his papers to the mirth inspired by wine; but there is too much sober good sense in all his lucubrations, even when he indulges more in pleasantry, to allow us to give implicit credit to a tradition invented, probably, as excuse for intemperance by such as can empty two bottles of wine, but never produce a 'Spectator' or a 'Freeholder.'" Of other apartments which have any particular interest attached to them, is the chamber in which Addison died; the bed-room occupied by Charles Fox; that of Rogers, the poet, who was a frequent visitor here; and also that of Sheridan, "in the next room to which," as Leigh Hunt informs us "a servant was regularly in attendance all night, partly to furnish, we believe, a bottle of champagne to the thirsty orator, in case he should happen to call for one betwixt his slumbers (at least, we heard so a long while ago, and it was quite in keeping with his noble host's hospitality; but we forgot to verify the anecdote on this occasion), and partly—of which there is no doubt—to secure the bed-curtains from being set on fire by his candle."

In a previous chapter we have narrated the descent of the manor of Kensington from the time of the Conquest, when it was held by the De Veres, down to the present day. Sir Walter Cope, the purchaser of the Vere property in Kensington, was a master of the Court of Wards in the time of James I., and one of the Chamberlains of the Exchequer. He built the centre of the house and the turrets, and bequeathed it, as already stated, to Sir Henry Rich, the husband of his daughter and heiress, Isabel. Not long afterwards, Sir Henry was raised to the peerage, when he assumed his title of nobility from his wife's inheritance—that of Lord Kensington. The wings and arcades were added by this nobleman, who also completed the internal decorations. His lordship was a courtier, and had the honour of being employed to negotiate a marriage between Prince Charles and the Infanta of Spain; but the negotiation proved abortive. Lord Kensington's services were, nevertheless, appreciated and rewarded by an earl's coronet and the insignia of the Garter. The new title chosen by his lordship was Holland, and thence the manor house of Kensington received its present appellation. This Earl of Holland was a younger son of Robert Rich, first Earl of Warwick, by his marriage with Penelope, daughter of Queen Elizabeth's favourite, the Earl of Essex, and the "Stella" of Sir Philip Sidney. He was a favourite with King James's "Steenie," Duke of Buckingham, whom he almost rivalled in coxcombry. During the prosperous portion of Rich's career, Holland House, no doubt, was the centre of rank and fashion. The name of Bassompierre, the French ambassador, figures among the guests here at that time. The earl was a political waverer in the "troublous times" of Charles I. He was twice made a prisoner in the house: first by Charles, in 1633, upon the occasion of his challenging Lord Weston, and a second time by command of the Parliament, after the unsuccessful issue of his attempt to restore the king, in 1648. In the following year he lost his life on the scaffold in Palace Yard, Westminster; foppish to the last, he is reported to have died in a white satin waistcoat or doublet, and a cap made of the same material, trimmed with silver lace. Within a few months of the earl's execution, Holland House became the head-quarters of the Parliamentary army, General Fairfax becoming its occupant. In the *Perfect Diurnal*, a journal of the day, is this entry:—"The Lord-General (Fairfax) is removed from Queen Street to the late Earl of Holland's house at Kensington, where he intends to reside." The mansion, however, was soon restored to the earl's widow and children; and it remained quietly in the possession of the family almost as long as they lasted.

It is well known that throughout the gloomy reign of Puritanism, under Oliver Cromwell, the dramatic profession was utterly proscribed. We are told that during this period the actors, who had been great loyalists, contrived to perform secretly and by stealth at noblemen's houses, where purses were collected for the benefit of "the poor players." In the "Historia Histrionica," published in 1699, it is stated that, "In Oliver's time they [the players] used to act privately, three or four miles or more out of town, now here, now there, sometimes in noblemen's houses, in particular, Holland House at Kensington, where the nobility and gentry who met (but in no great numbers) used to make a sum for them, each giving a broad piece, or the like."

From the Restoration to the time of the Georges, Holland House appears to have been let by the noble owners on short leases to a variety of persons, and sometimes even in apartments to lodgers. Leigh Hunt, in his work already quoted, mentions the names of several who, in this manner, resided here: among them, Arthur Annesley, the first Earl of Anglesey; Sir John Chardin, the traveller; Catherine Darnley, Duchess of Buckinghamshire; William Penn, the founder of Pennsylvania; and Shippen, the famous Jacobite, whom Pope has immortalised for his sincerity and honesty. Robert Rich, the son and successor of the first Earl of Holland, succeeded his cousin as Earl of Warwick, in consequence of failure of the elder branch, and thus united the two coronets of his family. He was the father of Edward Rich, Earl of Warwick and Holland, whose widow, Charlotte, daughter of Sir Thomas Myddleton, of Chirk Castle, Denbighshire, married, in 1716, the Right Honourable Joseph Addison, and thus, "by linking with the associations of Kensington the memory of that illustrious man, has invested with a classic halo the groves and shades of Holland House." Edward Henry, the next earl—to whom, as we have stated, there is a monument in Kensington Church—was succeeded by his kinsman, Edward Rich; and the daughter and only child

of this nobleman dying unmarried, the earldom became extinct in the middle of the last century. Holland House then came into the possession of the youthful earl's first cousin, William Edwardes (a Welsh gentleman, who was created a Peer of Ireland, as Baron Kensington), and was eventually sold to the Right Honourable Henry Fox, the distinguished politician of the time of George II., who, on being created a peer, adopted the title of Holland, and with his descendants the mansion has continued ever since.

To the literary circle, of which this house was the centre, it is impossible to say how many poets, essayists, and other writers have owed their first celebrity. It is said that even Goldsmith's charming novel, "The Vicar of Wakefield," here found its earliest admirer. This beautiful little work remained unnoticed, and was attacked by the reviews, until Lord Holland, who had been ill, sent to his bookseller for some amusing book. This was supplied, and he was so pleased that he spoke of it in the highest terms to a large company who dined with him a few days after. The consequence was that the whole impression was sold off in a few days.

It has been said that Addison obtained an introduction to his future wife in the capacity of tutor to her son, the young Earl of Warwick; but this supposition appears to be negatived by two letters written by Addison to the earl, when a boy, wherein the writer evinces an entire ignorance of the advances which his correspondent might have made in classical attainment. The letters are dated 1708. Addison had been appointed Under-Secretary of State two years previously, and it seems improbable that he should have undertaken the office of tutor at a subsequent period. His courtship of the countess, however, is said to have been marked by tedious formalities; and it is further asserted that her ladyship at first encouraged his overtures with a view of extracting amusement from the diffidence and singularity of his character. From the following anecdote, which is told respecting Addison's courtship, there would seem to be a show of truth in the story. The tenor of this anecdote is that "he endeavoured to fathom her sentiments by reading to her an article in a newspaper (which he himself had caused to be inserted), stating the probability of a marriage taking place between the reader and the auditress! From a comparison of dates, and a further examination of internal evidence," adds the narrative, "there is reason to suppose that Addison meant as a playful description of his own courtship that of Sir Roger de Coverley to the widow with a white hand; and, if so, how highly is the world indebted to the warm fancy of the one party, and the want of determination in the other !" It was, in all probability, at this period of his life that Addison had a cottage at Fulham ; at all events, he figures in " Esmond," as walking thither from Kensington at night-time. " When the time came to take leave, Esmond marched homewards to his lodgings, and met Mr. Addison on the road, walking to a cottage which he had at Fulham, the moon shining on his handsome serene face. 'What cheer, brother !' says Addison, laughing ; 'I thought it was a foot-pad advancing in the dark, and, behold, it is an old friend ! We may shake hands, colonel, in the dark, 'tis better than fighting by daylight. Why should we quarrel because I am a Whig and thou art a Tory ? Turn thy steps and walk with me to Fulham, where there is a nightingale still singing in the garden, and a cool bottle in a cave I know of. You shall drink to the Pretender, if you like ; I will drink my liquor in my own way !'"

The growing renown of Addison—perhaps his fame as a writer, or, more probably, his accession of political importance—assisted in persuading the countess to become his wife. But the marriage was productive of little comfort ; and this unfortunate marriage is said to have been the cause of his indulging to excess in drink. Be that as it may, Addison himself wrote vehemently against cowardice seeking strength "in the bottle ;" yet it is asserted that he often withdrew from the bickerings of his Countess to the coffee-house or the tavern. His favourite places of resort are said to have been the White Horse Inn, at the bottom of Holland House Lane, and Button's Coffee-house, in Russell Street, Covent Garden, where we have already made his acquaintance.* The fruit of this unpropitious union was one daughter, who died, at an advanced age, at Bilton, an estate in Warwickshire which Addison had purchased some years previously. Addison himself died at the end of three years after his marriage. The story of his death-bed here has been often told, but very probably it is a little apocryphal in its details. Lord Warwick was a young man of very irregular life, and of loose opinions. Addison, for whom he did not want respect, had very diligently endeavoured to reclaim him ; but his arguments and expostulations had no effect. One experiment, however, remained to be tried. When he found his life near its end, he directed the young lord to be called, and told him, " I have sent for you that you may see how a Christian can die."

It was to this young nobleman that Somerville addressed his " Elegiac Lines on the Death of Mr. Addison," wherein occur the lines having reference to his burial in Westminster Abbey :—

"Can I forget the dismal night that gave
My soul's best part for ever to the grave ?
How silent did his old companions tread,
By midnight lamps, the mansions of the dead,
Thro' breathing statues, then unheeded things,
Thro' rows of warriors, and thro' walks of kings !
What awe did the slow, solemn knell inspire,
The pealing organ, and the pausing choir ;
The duties by the lawn-rob'd prelate paid,
And the last words, that dust to dust convey'd !"

A short time before his death, Addison sent to request a visit from the poet Gay, and told him, on their meeting, that he had once done him an injury, but that if he survived his present affliction he would endeavour to repair it. Gay did not know the nature of the injury which had been inflicted, but supposed that he might have lost some appointment through the intervention of Addison.

" Addison," writes Leigh Hunt, " it must be owned, did not shine during his occupation of Holland House. He married, and was not happy ; he was made Secretary of State, and was not a good one ; he was in Parliament, and could not speak in it ; he quarrelled with, and even treated contemptuously, his old friend and associate, Steele, who declined to return the injury. Yet there, in Holland House, he lived and wrote, nevertheless, with a literary glory about his name, which never can desert the place ; and to Holland House, while he resided in it, must have come all the distinguished men of the day, for, though a Whig, he was personally 'well in,' as the phrase is, with the majority of all parties. He was in communication with Swift, who was a Tory, and with Pope, who was neither Tory nor Whig. It was now that the house and its owners began to appear in verse. Rowe addressed stanzas to Addison's bride ; and Tickell, after his death, touchingly apostrophizes the place—

" 'Thou hill, whose brow the antique structures grace,
Rear'd by bold chiefs of Warwick's noble race ;
Why, once so loved, whene'er thy bower appears,
O'er my dim eyeballs glance the sudden tears ?'

*   *   *   *   *   *

" It seems to have been in Holland House (for he died shortly afterwards) that Addison was visited by Milton's daughter, when he had requested her to bring him some evidences of her birth. The moment he beheld her, he exclaimed, ' Madame, you need no other voucher ; your face is a sufficient testimonial whose daughter you are.

It must have been very pleasing to Addison to befriend Milton's daughter; for he had been the first to popularise the great poet by his critiques on 'Paradise Lost,' in the *Spectator*."

After the death of Addison, Holland House remained in the possession of the Warwick family,

Anne. After having had a numerous offspring by one wife, Sir Stephen married another at the age of seventy-six, and had three more children, two of whom founded the noble families of Holland and Ilchester. It was reported that Stephen Fox had been a singing-boy in one of our English cathedrals;

ROGERS' SEAT AND INIGO JONES' GATEWAY, HOLLAND HOUSE.

and of their heir, Lord Kensington, until, as we have stated above, it was purchased by Henry Fox, who subsequently became a lord himself, and took his title from the mansion. This was towards the close of the reign of George II.

Henry Fox, the first Lord Holland of the new creation, was the youngest son of Sir Stephen Fox, a distinguished politician during the reigns of Charles II., James II., William III., and Queen

Walpole says he was a footman; and the late Lord Holland, who was a man of too noble a nature to affect ignorance of such traditions, candidly owns that he was a man of "very humble origin." Henry Fox was the political opponent of the first William Pitt, afterwards Earl of Chatham. The chief transactions of his lordship's public life are all duly recorded in the pages of history. Leigh Hunt, in his own lively manner, writes thus of

HOLLAND HOUSE.

him :—" Fox had begun life as a partisan of Sir Robert Walpole ; and in the course of his career held lucrative offices under Government—that of Paymaster of the Forces, for one—in which he enriched himself to a degree which incurred a great deal of suspicion." A good story is told concerning Fox whilst he held the above-mentioned office ; it is one which will bear repeating here. After Admiral Byron's engagement in the West Indies, there arose a great clamour about the badness of the ammunition served out. Soon afterwards, Mr. Fox fought a duel with a Mr. Adam. The former received his adversary's ball, which, happily, made but a very slight impression. " Egad, sir !" observed Fox, " it would have been all over with me if we had not charged our pistols with Government powder."

Fox, however, was latterly denounced, in a City address, as the " defaulter of unaccounted millions." " Public accounts, in those times, were strangely neglected ; and the family have said that his were in no worse condition than those of others; but they do not deny that he was a jobber. Fox, however, for a long time did not care. The joyousness of his temperament, together with some very lax notions of morality, enabled him to be at ease with himself as long as his blood spun so well. He jobbed and prospered ; ran away with a duke's daughter ; contrived to reconcile himself with the family (that of Richmond) ; got his wife made a baroness ; was made a lord himself—Baron Holland, of Foxley ; was a husband, notwithstanding his jobbing, loving and beloved ; was an indulgent father ; a gay and social friend—in short, had as happy a life of it as health and spirits could make, till, unfortunately, health and spirits failed, and then there seems to have been a remnant of his father's better portion within him, which did not allow him to be so well satisfied with himself in his decline." The story of Henry Fox's elopement with the Duke of Richmond's daughter, Lady Georgiana Caroline Lennox, is thus told in the " Old Court Suburb :"—" The duke was a grandson of Charles II., and both he and the duchess had declined to favour the suit of Mr. Fox, the son of the equivocal Sir Stephen. They reckoned on her marrying another man, and an evening was appointed on which the suitor in question was to be formally introduced to her. Lady Caroline, whose affections the dashing statesman had secretly engaged, was at her wits' end to know how to baffle this interview. She had evaded the choice of the family as long as possible, but this appointment looked like a crisis. The gentleman is to come in the evening ; the lady is to prepare for

his reception by a more than ordinary attention to her toilet. This gives her the cue to what is to be done. The more than ordinary attention is paid ; but it is in a way that renders the interview impossible. She has cut off her eyebrows. How can she be seen by anybody in such a trim ? The indignation of the duke and duchess is great ; but the thing is manifestly impossible. She is accordingly left to herself for the night ; she has perfected her plan, in expectation of the result ; and the consequence is, that when next her parents inquire for her, she has gone. Nobody can find her. She is off for Mr. Fox." This runaway marriage took place in the Fleet Prison, in the year 1744. In January, 1761, two years before the elevation of Mr. Fox to the peerage, Horace Walpole was present at a performance of private theatricals at Holland House—a sight which greatly entertained him. The play selected to be performed by children and very young ladies was *Jane Shore*, Lady Sarah Lennox, a sister of Lady Georgiana Fox, enacting the heroine ; while the boy afterwards eminent as Charles James Fox played the part of " Hastings," and his brother, Henry Edward, then six years old, enacted the " Bishop of Ely," dressed in lawn sleeves, and with a square cap (this little boy died a general in the army in 1811). Walpole praises the acting of the performers, but particularly that of Lady Sarah Lennox, who, he says, " was more beautiful than you can conceive, . . . in white, with her hair about her ears, and on the ground ; no Magdalen by Correggio was half so lovely and expressive." The charms of this lovely person had already made an impression on the heart of George III., then newly come to the throne at two-and-twenty. There seems no reason to doubt that the young monarch formed the design of raising his lovely cousin (for such she was, in a certain sense) to a share of the throne. The following story concerning the pair we quote from Timbs' " Romance of London : "—" Early in the winter of 1760-1, the king took an opportunity of speaking to Lady Sarah's cousin, Lady Susan Strangways, expressing a hope at the drawing-room that her ladyship was not soon to leave town. She said that she should be leaving soon. ' But,' said the king, ' you will return in summer for the coronation.' Lady Susan answered that ' she did not know—she hoped so.' ' But,' said the king again, ' they talk of a wedding. There have been many proposals ; but I think an English match would do better than a foreign one. Pray, tell Lady Sarah Lennox I say so.' Here was a sufficiently broad hint to inflame the hopes of a family, and to raise the head of a blooming girl of sixteen to the fifth heavens. It happened, however, that Lady Sarah had already allowed her heart to be pre-occupied, having formed a girlish attachment for the young Lord Newbottle, grandson of the Marquis of Lothian. She did not, therefore, enter into the views of her family with all the alacrity which they desired. According to the narrative of Mr. Grenville, she went the next drawing-room to St. James's, and stated to the king, in as few words as she could, the inconveniences and difficulties in which such a step would involve him. He said that was his business; he would stand them all; his part was taken, and he wished to hear hers was likewise. In this state it continued, whilst she, by the advice of her friends, broke off with Lord Newbottle, very reluctantly, on her part. She went into the country for a few days, and by a fall from her horse broke her leg. The absence which this occasioned gave time and opportunities for her enemies to work; they instilled jealousy into the king's mind upon the subject of Lord Newbottle, telling him that Lady Sarah Lennox still continued her intercourse with him; and immediately the marriage with the Princess of Strelitz was set on foot; and at Lady Sarah's return from the country, she found herself deprived of her crown and her lover, Lord Newbottle, who complained as much of her as she did of the king. While this was in agitation, Lady Sarah used to meet the king in his rides early in the morning, driving a little chaise with Lady Susan Strangways; and once, it is said, that, wanting to speak to him, she went dressed like a servant-maid, and stood amongst the crowd in the guard-room, to say a few words to him as he passed by." Walpole also relates that Lady Sarah would sometimes appear as a haymaker in the park at Holland House, in order to attract the attention of the king as he rode past; but the opportunity was lost. The gossiping chronicler adds also, that his Majesty blushed scarlet red at his wedding-service when allusion was made to "Abraham and *Sarah*." The lady survived her disappointment, and became the mother of the gallant Napiers.

Three children were the fruit of Lord Holland's marriage with Lady Georgiana Lennox, and he proved the fondest of parents. When his lordship was dangerously ill, he was informed that George Selwyn had called at his door to inquire after him. Selwyn, as is well known, was notorious for his passion for "being in at the death" of all his acquaintances, and for attending, more especially, every execution that took place. "Be so good," said his lordship, "in case Mr. Selwyn calls again, to show him up without fail; for if I am alive, I shall be delighted to see him, and if I am dead, I am sure he will be very pleased to see me.'

Of Stephen, second Lord Holland, we have nothing to say, beyond that he was good-natured and whimsical, and that he died before reaching his thirtieth year. His brother, the celebrated Charles James Fox, the "man of the people," is not much associated with Holland House, except as a name. Here, it is true, he passed his boyhood and part of his youth, during which period he was allowed to have pretty much his own way; in fact, he was what is generally styled a "spoilt child." His father is said never to have thwarted his will in anything. Thus, the boy expressing a desire one day to "smash a watch," the father, after ascertaining that the little gentleman did positively feel such a desire, and was not disposed to give it up, said, " Well, if you must, I suppose you must;" and the watch was at once smashed. On another occasion, his father, having resolved to take down the wall before Holland House, and to have an iron railing put up in its stead, found it necessary to use gunpowder to facilitate the work. He had promised his son, Charles James, that he should be present whenever the explosion took place. Finding that the labourers had blasted the brickwork in his absence, he ordered the wall to be rebuilt; and, when it was thoroughly cemented, had it blown up again for the gratification of his favourite boy; at the same time advising those about him never, on any account, to break a promise with children.

Henry Richard Fox, the third lord, who came to the title before he was a year old, lived to rescue the mansion from the ruin which at one time threatened it, and may be said to have resided in it during the whole of his life, in the enjoyment of his books, and dispensing his hospitalities to wits and worthies of all parties. His lordship married Elizabeth, the daughter and heiress of Mr. Richard Vassall, whose name he afterwards assumed; his children retaining the name of Fox. It is, perhaps, to this nobleman, with the exception of Addison, that Holland House owes most of its celebrity and its literary interest. Among the visitors round its hospitable board, Macaulay mentions the name of Prince Talleyrand, Lord Lansdowne, Lord John Russell, Lord Melbourne, the Marchioness of Clanricarde (Canning's daughter, who for many years did not forget to take vengeance on the colleagues and political opponents who had killed her father); Lord King, the bishop-hater; Wilberforce, the philanthropist; Lord Radnor, Charles Grant, and Mackintosh. Byron and Campbell, too, were guests here; and the name of Lord Holland is embalmed by the former in his dedication of "The Bride of Abydos," and by the latter in that of "Gertrude of Wyoming."

It is evident from Macaulay, Tom Moore, and the other members of the Holland House clique, that, though they were nominally the guests of Lord Holland, their real entertainer was her ladyship, in whom was illustrated the proverb which declares that "the grey mare is often the better horse." In fact, she was not only lady paramount in the house, but often insolently imperious towards her guests, whom, as one man wittily remarked, she treated like her *vassals*, though she was only a *Vassall* herself, alluding, of course, to her maiden name. "The centurion," it has been remarked, "did not keep his soldiers in better order than she keeps her guests. It is to one, 'Go,' and he goeth; and to another, 'Do this,' and it is done. 'Ring the bell, Mr. Macaulay.' 'Lay down the screen, Lord Russell; you will spoil it.' 'Mr. Allen, take a candle, and show Mr. Cradock the pictures of Buonaparte.'" Lord Holland was, on the other hand, all kindness, simplicity, and vivacity. One of the occasional visitors here, Mr. Granville Penn, said about her ladyship a good thing, which, while it helped to establish his credit as a wit, excluded him from its hospitable doors for ever. "Holland House," a friend remarked to him, "is really a most pleasant place; and in Lord Holland's company you might imagine yourself inside the home of Socrates." "It certainly always seemed so to me; for I often seemed to hear Xanthippe talking rather loud in the adjoining room," was Mr. Penn's reply. In fact, Lady Holland herself, who presided at the *réunions* of Holland House, was most arbitrary and domineering in her manner, and, consequently, made herself unpopular with some of her guests. When she heard that Sir Henry Holland was about to be made a baronet, she expressed herself vexed that there would be "two Lady Hollands." But that could not be helped. Ugo Foscolo, in spite of having obtained the *entrée* of Holland House, could not help regarding her with aversion, and once said, with a strong emphasis, that, "though he could go anywhere"—even to a certain place, which shall be nameless—"with his lordship, he should be sorry to go to heaven with Lady Holland."

Macaulay did not find an *entrée* here till after he had made his mark in Parliament. Lady Holland on one occasion took him into her own drawing-room to see her pictures, which included thirty by Stothard, all on subjects from Lord Byron's poems. "Yes," said her ladyship, "poor Lord Byron sent them to me a short time before the separation. I sent them back, and told him that, if he gave them away, he ought to give them to Lady Byron. But he said that he would not, and that if I did not take them the bailiffs would, and that they would be lost in the wreck." Samuel Rogers promised to be there to meet Macaulay, "in order to give him an insight into the ways of that house," and of its imperious mistress, whose pride and rudeness must have been simply intolerable to ordinary mortals. Rogers was the great oracle of the Holland House circle—a sort of non-resident premier. To some members of the literary world who had not the privilege of joining in the charming circle at Holland House, the sense of their exclusion seemed to find vent in some shape or form. Theodore Hook would appear to be one of these, for about the year 1819, among other experiments, he tried to set up a tiny magazine of his own—the *Arcadian*—published, we believe, at a shilling; but we know not how many numbers of it were issued before the publisher lost heart. One number contained a lengthy ballad of provoking pungency, satirising Holland House in very severe terms.

Some excellent remarks *àpropos* of Holland House gatherings and its associations may here be abridged from Mr. J. Fisher Murray's "Environs of London," in which a scholar who had the *entrée* of that hospitable mansion writes, at once prophetically and pathetically, as follows:—"Yet a few years, and these shades and these structures may follow their illustrious masters. The wonderful city which, ancient and gigantic as it is, still continues to grow, as a young town of logwood by a water-privilege in Michigan, may soon dispense with those turrets and gardens which are associated with so much that is interesting and noble; with the courtly magnificence of Rich, with the loves of Ormond, with the councils of Cromwell, with the death of Addison. The time is coming when, perhaps, a few old men, the last survivors of our generation, will seek in vain, amid new streets and squares, and railway stations, for the site of that dwelling which in their youth was the favourite resort of wits and beauties, of painters and poets, of scholars, philosophers, and statesmen; they will remember, with strange tenderness, many objects familiar to them—the avenue and terrace, the busts and the paintings, the carvings, the grotesque gilding, and the enigmatical mottoes. With peculiar tenderness they will recall that venerable chamber in which all the antique gravity of a college library was so singularly blended with all that female grace and wit could devise to embellish a drawing-room. They will recollect, not unmoved, those shelves loaded with the varied learning of many lands and many ages; those portraits in which were preserved the features of the best and wisest Englishmen of two generations. They will recollect how many men who have guided the politics of Europe, who have moved great assemblies by reason and eloquence, who have put life into bronze or canvas, or who have left to posterity things so written that society will not willingly let them die, were there mixed with all that was lovely and gayest in the society of the most splendid of modern capitals. . . . They will remember the singular character, too, which belonged to that circle; in which every talent and accomplishment, every art and science, had its place. They will remember how the last Parliamentary debate was discussed in one corner, and the last comedy of Scribe in another; while Wilkie gazed in admiration on Reynolds's 'Baretti;' while Mackintosh turned over Thomas Aquinas to verify a quotation; while Talleyrand related his conversation with Barras at the Luxembourg, or his ride with Lannes over the field of Austerlitz. They will remember, above all, the grace and the kindness—far more admirable than grace—with which the princely hospitality of that ancient mansion was dispensed; they will remember the venerable and benignant countenance of him who bade them welcome there; they will remember that temper which thirty years of sickness, of lameness, and of confinement served only to make sweeter; and, above all, that frank politeness which at once relieved all the embarrassment of the most timid author or artist who found himself for the first time among ambassadors and earls. They will remember, finally, that in the last lines which he traced he expressed his joy that he had done nothing unworthy of the friend of Fox and of Grey; and they will have reason to feel a similar joy if, in looking back on many troubled years of life, they cannot accuse themselves of having done anything unworthy of men who were honoured by the friendship of Lord Holland."

Mr. Rush, in his "Court of London," tells us a good story of a little incident which happened in the drawing-room here after dinner. Advancing towards Sir Philip Francis, Mr. Rogers asked permission to put a question to him. Francis, no doubt, guessed what was coming, for everybody at the time was asking, "Who is Junius?" and many persons were even then more than disposed to identify him with the author of the "Letters" which were published under that signature, and were exciting the nation. Francis, who was an irritable man, shut him fairly up with the words, "At your peril, sir!" On this, Rogers quietly turned away, observing that if Francis was not "Junius," at all

events he was "Brutus." It is not a little singular, if the letters were not written by Francis, that they ceased to appear after the very day on which Francis quitted the shores of England for India, and that Garrick, who was in the secret, prophesied a day or two before that they were about to cease.

On the death of his uncle, Charles James Fox, Lord Holland was introduced into the Cabinet as Lord Privy Seal; but the strength of the Whig portion of the Government had then departed, and the only measure worthy of notice in which his lordship co-operated after his accession to office was the Bill for the Abolition of the Slave Trade. He took an active part in the multifarious debates upon the Catholic question, the Regency Bill, &c.; and when the Bill to legalise the detention of Napoleon as a prisoner of war was before the House of Lords, Lord Holland raised his voice against it, and, until death relieved the prisoner, he never ceased to deprecate what he deemed the unwarrantable conduct towards him of the British Government and its agents.

Lord Holland died in October, 1840, after an illness of only two days' duration. Mr. T. Raikes, in notifying the occurrence in his "Diary," remarks:—"Flahault had been staying at Holland House while he was in England, and left him in good health on Tuesday. He arrived here yesterday morning, and to-day receives the account of his death. Lord Holland was in the Cabinet, and held the lucrative post of Chancellor of the Duchy of Lancaster; he was sixty-seven. When I went to Eton he was the head of the school, and was the first prepositor that gave me my liberty. He was a mild, amiable man, ruled by his wife. She was a Miss Vassall, with a large fortune, who eloped with him from her first husband, Sir Godfrey Webster; she is a great politician, and affects the *esprit fort*. They kept a hospitable house, and received all the wits of the day." The following lines were written by Lord Holland on the morning of the day when his last illness commenced, and were found after his death on his dressing-room table:—

"Nephew of Fox and friend of Grey,
Sufficient for my fame,
If those who knew me best shall say
I tarnished neither name."

Mr. Raikes also adds:—"Mrs. Damer writes me that the new Lord Holland inherits an estate of £6,000 per annum, on which there is an enormous debt. Holland House is left to Lady Holland, who will not live there." "Lord Holland," says Mr. Peter Cunningham, "called on Lord Lansdowne a little before his death, and showed him his epitaph of his own composing. 'Here lies Henry Vassall Fox, Lord Holland, &c., who was drowned while sitting in his elbow-chair.' He died in this house, in his elbow-chair, of water in the chest."

The following is a character of Lord Holland, written by a friend :—" The benignant, the accomplished Lord Holland is no more ; the last and best of the Whigs of the old school, the long-tried friend of civil and religious liberty, has closed a life which

to have a hearing for every argument, lest a truth should be shut out from his mind. The charm of his conversation will never be forgotten by those who have enjoyed it. His mind was full of anecdote, which was always introduced with the most felicitous appositeness, and exquisitely narrated.

"Lord Holland had lived with all the most distinguished and eminent men of the last forty years ; but his knowledge of the greatest, the most eloquent,

HOLLAND HOUSE, FROM THE NORTH.

has been an ornament and a bulwark of the Liberal cause. He was one of England's worthies in the pristine sense of the word ; and a more finished example of the steady statesman, the urbane gentleman, and the accomplished scholar, never existed. Lord Holland's was a fine mind, and a fine mind in perpetual exercise of the most healthful kind. It was observed of him that he was never found without a good book in his hand. His understanding was thoroughly masculine, his taste of a delicacy approaching perhaps to a fault. His opinions he maintained earnestly and energetically, but with a rare, a beautiful candour. Nothing was proscribed with him. As of old, the meanest wayfarers used to be received hospitably, lest angels should be turned away ; so Lord Holland seemed

the most witty, or the most learned, had not indisposed him to appreciate merits and talents of a less great order. He was a friend of merit wherever it could be found, and knew how to value and to encourage it in all its degrees.

"None ever enjoyed life more than Lord Holland, or enjoyed it more intellectually, and none contributed more largely to the enjoyment of others. He possessed the sunshine of the breast, and no one could approach him without feeling its genial influence. Lord Holland was a wit, without a particle of ill nature, and a man of learning, without a taint of pedantry. His apprehension of anything good was unfailing ; nothing worth observing and remarking ever escaped him. The void which Lord Holland has left will never be filled ; a golden link with the genius of the last age is broken and gone. The fine intellect, whose light burned at the shrine of freedom, is extinguished. An influence the most propitious to the peace, so precious to the world's best interests, is lost when the need of it is great indeed."

streets and villas between Kensington and Notting Hill. In the above year, however, this feeling was quieted by the rumour that Lady Holland, the widow of the last lord, had disposed of the reversion of the house, by sale, to the Earl of Ilchester, who, it was stated, had expressed his intention of

GRAND STAIRCASE, HOLLAND HOUSE.

Lord Holland was succeeded in his title and estates by his only son, Henry Edward, who was some time the British Minister at the Court of Tuscany. He died at Naples in 1859, when the barony became extinct. From that time, down to the year 1874, it was always a matter of apprehension that a day would sooner or later come when, as prophesied by Sir Walter Scott, Holland House must become a thing of the past, and be swept away in order to make room for new lines of

keeping the mansion in its integrity. Lord Ilchester's name is Fox-Strangways, and it is the latter name that has been assumed by his branch of the family, the first Lord Holland and the first Lord Ilchester, as stated above, having been brothers. Lord Macaulay, in writing of Holland House, says it "can boast of a greater number of inmates distinguished in political and literary history than any other private dwelling in England." In the lifetime of the third Lord Holland it was the meeting-place of the Whig party ; and his liberal hospitality made it, as Lord Brougham tells us, "the resort not only of the most interesting persons composing English society, literary, philosophical, and political, but also to all belonging to those classes who ever visited this country from abroad."

With the death of the third Lord Holland, the glories of Holland House may be said to have passed away, although the building has been occupied as an occasional residence by the widow of the last lord since his death in 1859 ; and an air of solitude seems indeed to have gathered round the old mansion. A custom was observed for many years, till a recent date, of firing off a cannon at eleven o'clock every night ; this custom originated, we believe, through a burglary which was once attempted here.

Several spots in the grounds round the house have acquired celebrity in connection with some name or circumstance. Of these we may note the part lying to the west, towards the Addison Road, which formerly went by the name of "the Moats," where the duel between Captain Best and the notorious Lord Camelford took place, early in the present century. The exact spot is supposed to have been the site of the older mansion belonging to the De Veres. The quarrel between Lord Camelford and Mr. Best, of which we have spoken in our accounts of New Bond Street and Conduit Street,* was on account of a friend of Lord Camelford, a lady of the name of Symons, and it occurred at the "Prince of Wales's" coffee-house in Conduit Street. The duel was fought on the following day (March 7, 1804), and Lord Camelford was killed. Although there really was no adequate cause for a quarrel, the eccentric nobleman would persist in fighting Mr. Best, because the latter was deemed the best shot in England, and that "to have made an apology would have exposed his lordship's courage to suspicion." The parties met on the ground about eight o'clock in the morning, and having taken up their position, Lord Camelford gave the first shot, which missed his antagonist, when Mr. Best fired, and lodged the contents of his weapon in his lordship's body. He immediately fell, and calling his adversary to him, seized him by the hand, and exclaimed, "I am a dead man ! you have killed me ; but I freely forgive you." He repeated several times that he was the sole aggressor. He was conveyed to a house close at hand, and a surgeon soon arrived from Kensington, and immediately pronounced the wound mortal. Upon the spot where the duel was fought the late

Lord Holland set up an "expiatory classical altar," which, however, was removed a few years ago. With the passion for eccentricity which had characterised him, Lord Camelford had directed that he should be buried in a lonely spot on an island in Switzerland, which had interested him during his travels ; his wishes, however, were not complied with, for his body was interred in the vaults of St. Anne's Church, Soho, where it still remains.* "This very spot," the Princess Marie Lichstenstein tells us, "was, a few years ago, the scene of merry parties, where the Duke and Duchess d'Aumale used to fish with the late Lord Holland." At the back of the mansion is a broad expanse of greensward, dotted here and there with stately elms ; and here, in an alcove facing the west, is inscribed the couplet that we have given as a motto to this chapter, and which was put up by the late Lord Holland in honour of Mr. Rogers. Here is also a copy of verses by Mr. Luttrell, expressing his inability to emulate the poet. The undulating grounds on this side of the house are terminated by a row of mansions built on the fringe of the estate ; and the eastern side is bounded by a rustic lane, in part overhung with trees. Close by the western side of the house are small gardens, laid out in both the ancient and modern styles, the work of the late Lady Holland, the former of them being a fitting accompaniment to the old house. Here are evergreens clipped into all sorts of fantastic forms, together with fountains and terraces befitting the associations of the place. In one of these gardens, says Leigh Hunt, was raised the first specimen of the dahlia, which the late Lord Holland is understood to have brought from Spain ; in another, on a pedestal, is a colossal bust of Napoleon, by a pupil of Canova. Engraved on the pedestal is a quotation from Homer's "Odyssey," which may be thus rendered in English :—

> " The hero is not dead, but breathes the air
>   In lands beyond the deep :
> Some island sea-begirded, where
>   Harsh men the prisoner keep."

The Highland and Scottish Societies' gatherings, with their characteristic sports and pastimes, were held in these grounds for many years.

The grounds around the house are rich in oaks, plane-trees, and stately cedars, whose dark foliage sets off the features of the old mansion. Of the grounds in front of the house, there is a tradition that Cromwell and Ireton conferred there, "as a place in which they could not be overheard." Leigh Hunt, in his "Old Court Suburb," observes

---

* See Vol. IV., pp. 302, 323.

* See Vol. III., p. 182.

that, "whatever the subject of their conference may have been, they could not have objected to being seen, for there were neither walls, nor even trees, we believe, at that time in front of the house, as there are now; and," he adds, "we may fancy royalists riding by, on their road to Brentford, where the king's forces were defeated, and trembling to see the two grim republicans laying their heads together."

Near Holland House, in Nightingale Lane, stands a small mansion, called Little Holland House, where Mrs. Inchbald once spent a few days with its occupant, a Mrs. Bubb; here, too, lived and died Miss Fox, sister of the late Lord Holland.

Facing the Uxbridge Road at the extreme end, at the north-west corner of the grounds of Holland House, there was a smaller mansion, with a "pleasaunce" garden and lawn, of about seven acres, which for many years was owned and tenanted by a natural son of Lord Holland— General Fox, the celebrated numismatist, some

time M.P. for Stroud, and Secretary to the Ordnance Board, who married Lady Mary Fitzclarence. The grounds, however, were sold in 1875 for building purposes, and the house was soon after pulled down.

At the western extremity of the parish of Kensington, on the road towards Hammersmith, were the nursery-grounds of Messrs. Lee. These grounds, says Leigh Hunt, "have been known in the parish books, under the title of the Vineyard, ever since the time of William the Conqueror. Wine, described as a sort of burgundy, was actually made and sold in them as late as the middle of the last century. James Lee, the founder of the present firm who own the grounds, was the author of one of the earliest treatises on botany, and a correspondent of Linnæus." In Faulkner's "History of Kensington," published in 1820, we read that the nursery-grounds round this neighbourhood covered no less than 124 acres, and that they belonged to eight different proprietors.

CHAPTER XV.

NOTTING HILL AND BAYSWATER.

The Old Turnpike Gate—Derivation of the Name of Notting Hill—The Manor of Notting or Nutting Barns—Present Aspect of Notting Hill—Old Inns and Taverns—Gallows Close—The Road where Lord Holland drew up his Forces previous to the Battle of Brentford—Kensington Gravel Pits—Tradesmen's Tokens—A Favourite Locality for Artists and Laundresses—Appearance of the District at the Beginning of the Present Century—Reservoirs of the Grand Junction Waterworks Company—Ladbroke Square and Grove—Kensington Park Gardens—St John's Church—Notting Hill Farm—Norland Square—Orme Square—Bayswater House, the Residence of Fauntleroy, the Forger—St. Petersburgh Place—The Hippodrome—St. Stephen's Church—Portobello Farm—The Convent of the Little Sisters of the Poor—Bayswater—The Cultivation of Watercresses—An Ancient Conduit—Public Tea Gardens—Sir John Hill, the Botanist—Craven House—Craven Road, and Craven Hill Gardens—The Pest-house Fields—Upton Farm—The Toxophilite Society—Westbourne Grove and Terrace—The Residence of John Sadleir, the Fraudulent M.P.—Lancaster Gate—The Pioneer of Tramways—Queen Charlotte's Lying-in Hospital—Death of Dr. Adam Clarke—The Burial-ground of St. George's, Hanover Square.

As soon as ever we quit the precincts of Kensington proper, and cross the Uxbridge Road, we become painfully conscious of a change. We have left the "Old Court Suburb," and find ourselves in one that is neither "old" nor "court-like." The roadway, with its small shops on either side, is narrow and unattractive, and the dwellings are not old enough to have a history or to afford shelter for an anecdote. About the centre of this thoroughfare, at the spot whence omnibuses are continually starting on the journey eastward towards the City, stood, till about the year 1860, a small and rather picturesque turnpike-gate, which commanded not only the road towards Notting Hill and Shepherd's Bush, but also that which branches off to the north and north-east in the direction of the Grove of Westbourne. What rural ideas and pictures arise before our mental eye as we mention Notting —possibly Nutting—Hill, and the Shepherd's Bush

and Westbourne Grove! We fear that the nuts, and the shepherds, and the nightingales which, so lately as the reign of William IV., sang sweetly here in the summer nights, are now, each and all, things of the past.

Notting Hill is said to derive its name from a manor in Kensington called "Knotting-Bernes," or "Knutting-Barnes," sometimes written "Notting," or "Nutting-barns"—so, at least, writes Lysons, in his "Environs of London." He adds that the property belonged formerly to the De Veres, Earls of Oxford (which would naturally be the case, as it formed part of Kensington parish and manor); and subsequently to Lord Burleigh, who, as we have already seen, lived at Brompton Hall, not very far from the neighbourhood of Kensington. In Robins' "History of Paddington," we read that the "manor of Noting barons, *alia* Kensington, then 'Nutting Barns,' afterwards called

'Knotting-barns,' in Stockdale's new map of the country round London, 1790; 'Knolton Barn,' now 'Notting-barns,' was carved out of the original manor of 'Chenesitun.'" From an inquisition taken at Westminster, in the reign of Henry VIII., it appears that "the manor called Notingbarons, *alias* Kensington, in the parish of Paddington, was held of the Abbot of Westminster as of his manor of Paddington by fealty and twenty-two shillings rent;" but since the time of the Reformation "Notting-barns" seems to have been considered a part of Kensington. Notting Barns Manor was held successively by the De Veres, and by Robert Fenroper, Alderman of London, who exchanged with King Henry VIII. It was afterwards granted to Pawlet, Earl of Wiltshire, from whom it passed to Lord Burghley. The manor was next held by the Copes, Andersons, and Darbys, and in 1820 it was owned by Sir William Talbot. Down to a very recent period, much of the district through which we are about to pass bore rather a bad character for thieves and housebreakers, and was somewhat noted for its piggeries and potteries; but these have all been swept away by the advancing tide of bricks and mortar. The "potteries" are still kept in remembrance by Pottery Lane, in which is the Roman Catholic Church of St. Francis of Assisi, referred to in a previous chapter. The ground about Notting Hill lies high, and the soil is a stiff clay, while that of Kensington proper is chiefly sand and gravel; but in reality, Notting Hill forms part and parcel of Kensington itself, which stretches away some distance northward in the direction of Kensal Green. "The principal street," writes Faulkner, in 1820, "runs along the high road for about three furlongs. The village enjoys an excellent air and beautiful prospects on the north, and lying in the direct road for Uxbridge and Oxford, it is enlivened every hour by the passage of mail-coaches, stages, and wagons."

The neighbourhood has become, of late years, a favourite residence for artists and sculptors, among whom may be reckoned Mr. J. Philip, Mr. Watts, Mr. Holman Hunt, and also Mr. William Theed. On either side of a narrow lane leading from Campden Hill towards Holland House is a nest of mansions, each standing in its own grounds, known as the "Dukery." Among its present and late occupants are the Dukes of Argyll and Rutland, the Dowager Duchess of Bedford, and Lords Airlie and Macaulay.

Cornelius Wood, a celebrated soldier of fortune, characterised in the *Tatler* under the name of "Silvio," died here in 1711. As in most of the suburbs of London which lay along the main roads, so here the various inns and taverns would appear to have shown by their signs a tendency to the sports of the road, for within a short distance we find "The Black Lion," "The Swan," "The Feathers," "The Nag's Head," "The Horse and Groom," and "The Coach and Horses," many of which, no doubt, were, half a century ago, the resorts of highwaymen when they had done a little bit of business on the Uxbridge or the Harrow Road, and which, if their mute walls could speak, might tell many a tale of coaches robbed, and the plunder shared between the "knights of the road" and obliging landlords.

The parish extends along the Uxbridge Road as far as Shepherd's Bush. On the left of the road was a piece of waste ground, known till recently as "Gallows Close," so called from the fact of two men having been executed here for a highway robbery in 1748. The gallows, or part of it, remained till about 1800. The ancient highway from London to Turnham Green is said by Faulkner, in his "History of Kensington" (1820), to have passed by Tyburn to the Gravel Pits, and to have branched off to the left at Shepherd's Bush, through a field, at the western extremity of which (he adds) the road is still visible, though now entirely impassable from the overhanging branches of the trees on both sides of the road, and from having become a deep slough in the neighbourhood of Pallenswick Green. This was the road where the Earl of Holland drew up his forces previous to the Battle of Brentford, as related in "Clarendon's History of the Rebellion." But we must not travel too far afield.

We have already spoken of Kensington Gravel Pits. This must be understood as a vague name for an undefined district, lying partly to the north and partly to the south of the Uxbridge Road; indeed, the greater part was on the north side: this is evident from the fact that the house belonging to Lord Craven, at Craven Hill, which was borrowed by Queen Anne as a nursery for her children, is mentioned by contemporary writers as being "situated at Kensington Gravel Pits." Several local tradesmen's tokens, dated in 1660-70, at the Gravel Pits, are engraved by Faulkner. Since the disappearance of the actual gravel pits, their name seems to have been superseded by the joint influence of the new streets on Notting Hill and in Bayswater. Leigh Hunt, in his "Old Court Suburb," says:—"Readers may call to mind a remnant of one of the pits, existing but a few years ago, to the north of the Palace in Kensington Gardens, and adding greatly to their picturesque look thereabouts. A pleasant poetical tradition was connected with it, of which we shall have something further to say.

Now, the Gravel Pits were the fashionable suburb resort of invalids, from the times of William and Anne to the close of the last century. Their 'country air,' as it was called, seems to have been preferred, not only to that of Essex, but to that of Kent. Garth, in his 'Dispensary,' makes an apothecary say that sooner than a change shall take place, from making the poor pay for medicine to giving it them gratis—

> " ' Alps shall sink to vales,
> And leeches in our glasses turn to whales ;
> Alleys at Wapping furnish us with new modes,
> And Monmouth Street Versailles' riding hoods ;
> The rich to th' Hundreds in pale crowds repair,
> And change "the Gravel Pits" for Kentish air.' "

The spot, in fact, has long been held in high repute for the salubrity of the air, and in the last generation it had become a noted place for the residence of artists. The neighbourhood, too, has long been a favourite haunt and home of laundresses ; and no wonder, for Faulkner, in his "History of Kensington," speaks of an overflowing spring on the Norland House Estate as "peculiarly soft, and adapted to washing," the same water being "leased to three persons, who pay each seven shillings a week for it, and retail it about the neighbourhood at a halfpenny a pail."

These were really gravel pits half a century ago, and the inequality of the surface bore testimony to the fact. Sir A. Calcott's house was in a hollow, artificially made, and his garden was commanded from above by that of his next-door neighbour, Mr. Thomas Webster, then a rising artist, but who retired from the Royal Academy in 1876. Faulkner thus writes in his "History of Kensington," published in 1820 :—"The valley on the north is laid down with grass, and the whole of this district appears to have undergone but little alteration, in respect to culture and division of the land, for several ages. Although the distance from London is scarcely three miles, yet the traveller might imagine himself to be embosomed in the most sequestered parts of the country, for nothing is heard to interrupt the course of his meditations but the notes of the lark, the linnet, or the nightingale. In the midst of these meadows stands the Manor House of Notting Barns, now occupied by William Smith, Esq., of Hammersmith. It is an ancient brick building, surrounded by spacious barns and other out-houses ; the public road to Kensal Green passes through the farm-yard." How altered the appearance of the neighbourhood at the end of half a century !

It is much to be lamented by the lovers of rural scenery that here, as indeed on every side of London, acres which, only half a century ago, were still nursery-grounds and market-gardens, have been forced to give place to railways and their approaches, and to the building of suburban towns. To use the words of a writer in the *Cornhill Magazine* in 1866 :—"The growth of London has gradually pushed the market-gardener into the country; and now, instead of sending up his produce by his own wagon, he trusts it to the railway, and is often thrown into a market fever by a late delivery. To compensate him, however, for the altered state of the times, he often sells his crops, like a merchant upon 'Change, without the trouble of bringing more than a few hand-samples in his pockets. He is nearly seventy years of age, though he looks scarce fifty, and can remember the time when there were 10,000 acres of ground under cultivation for vegetables within four miles of Charing Cross, besides about 3,000 more acres planted with fruit to supply the London consumption. He has lived to see the Deptford and Bermondsey gardens sadly curtailed ; the Hoxton and Hackney gardens covered with houses ; the Essex plantations pushed further off; and the Brompton and Kensington nurseries—the home of vegetables for centuries—dug up, and sown with International Exhibition temples, and Italian Gardens, that will never grow a pea or send a single cauliflower to market. He has lived to see Guernsey and Jersey, Cornwall, the Scilly Isles, Holland, Belgium, and even Portugal, with many other still more distant places, competing with the remote outskirts of London, and has been staggered by seeing the market supplied with choice early peas from such an unexpected quarter as French Algeria."

Building operations would seem to have commenced about this neighbourhood, on either side of the main road, in the early part of the present century. Much later, about the year 1857, a portion of the north margin of Holland Park, abutting upon the roadway, and extending from Holland Lane to Addison Road, was cut off and laid out for building purposes, and two rows of mansions, with large gardens before them, have been erected.

Close by, on the top of Campden Hill, but separated from the main road by Notting Hill Square and Grove, are the reservoirs and engine-house of the Grand Junction Waterworks Company. The chief works in connection with this company are situated on the north bank of the Thames, a little above Kew Bridge. The water is taken by a large conduit pipe from the middle of the river to the works on the shore, where it is pumped into filtering reservoirs, &c., and then supplied to the town. In connection with the works at Kew is a stand-pipe, upwards of 200 feet in height, by which the water is conveyed through the main pipes into the districts to be supplied. The main which brings the water to Campden Hill is between six and seven miles in length, and the reservoir here is capable of containing 6,000,000 gallons. The tall brick shaft of the works here forms a conspicuous object on every side of Notting Hill. In 1811 a company was formed, who availed themselves of the powers granted by a clause in the Grand Junction Canal Company's Act, for supplying water brought by the canal from the rivers Colne and Brent, and from a large reservoir supplied by land drainage in the north-western part of Middlesex. These waters were represented to

called Tower Crecy, erected by Mr. Page, the architect of Westminster Bridge, in honour of the Black Prince, whose emblems adorn the exterior in all its stages. It is said that the holder of the lease of the house is bound to hoist on its summit a flag on the anniversary of the Battle of Crecy. Between Holland Park and the Waterworks are

HOUSE AT CRAVEN HILL IN 1760.

be much superior to that of the Thames; but experience disappointed the hopes of the projectors: the water was found not only to be bad in quality, but deficient in quantity also; and after various vain expedients to remedy the evils, the company, which had taken the name of the "Grand Junction Waterworks Company," resorted to the Thames, taking their supply from a point near Chelsea Hospital. Adjoining the Waterworks is a lofty castellated building in the Gothic style,

some detached mansions—Aubrey House and others. One of these was the site of some medicinal wells which were of repute in the last century.

On the north side of Notting Hill is Ladbroke Square—so called after the name of the family who took it on a building lease—and which, for style in the houses and the general appearance of the central enclosure, falls but little short of some of the more aristocratic squares of the West-end. The west end of the Square is crossed by Ladbroke Grove, which extends northward as far as Kensal New Town. On the north side of the Square are Kensington Park Gardens, a name given to a goodly row of houses overlooking the Square. The handsome modern Gothic, or Early English, church of St. John, not far off, in Lansdowne Crescent, dates from the year 1845. It is cruciform in plan, with an elegant spire rising from the intersection of the nave and chancel. This church stands on what was "Notting Hill Farm," when Faulkner wrote in 1820, a lonely hill commanding extensive views, owing to the absence of woods.

erected about 1815, called St. Petersburg Place, Moscow Road, Coburg Place, &c. These names commemorate the visit of the Allied Sovereigns, in 1814. In the centre of Petersburg Place, Mr. Orme erected in 1818 a private chapel, to serve as a chapel of ease to Paddington. It appears to have been the first private speculation of the kind in the suburbs, and not to have been built till the growth of the population rendered it necessary.

NOTTING BARN FARM, 1830.

Norland Square perpetuates the name of Norland House, a small but well-wooded estate, which, in the reign of William IV., belonged to one of the Drummonds, the bankers, of Charing Cross. Many of the new streets about Notting Hill were built between the years 1850 and 1860.

Orme Square, which abuts upon the Uxbridge Road, overlooking Kensington Gardens, is named after a Mr. Orme, formerly a printseller in Bond Street, who purchased a considerable space of ground lying to the west of Craven Hill, upon which the Square is built. Bayswater House, an isolated mansion in the Bayswater Road, between Lancaster Gate and Orme Square, was the residence of Fauntleroy, the forger. A new range of buildings, to the north-east of Orme Square, was

Much of the ground about this neighbourhood, before it was cut up into streets, terraces, crescents, &c.—indeed, as lately as the time when Queen Victoria ascended the throne—was the scene of an establishment which enjoyed some popularity while it lasted—namely, the Hippodrome; but so brief is fame, that although it was flourishing at the above period, it had become almost forgotten after a lapse of twenty years, and its site clean blotted out. For much of the following sketch of the Hippodrome in all its novelty and pride, we are indebted to the *Sporting Magazine* for 1837:— "Making the *cours aristocratique* of Routine (*alias* Rotten) Row, you pass out at Cumberland Gate, and then trot on to Bayswater. Thence you arrive at the Kensington Gravel Pits, and descending where on the left stands the terrace of Notting Hill, find opposite the large wooden gates of a recent structure. Entering these, I was by no means prepared for what opened upon me. Here, without figure of speech, was the most perfect race-course that I had ever seen. Conceive, almost within the bills of mortality, an enclosure some two miles and a half in circuit, commanding from its centre a view as spacious and enchanting as that from Richmond Hill (?), and where almost the only thing that you can *not* see is London. Around this, on the extreme circle, next to the lofty fence by which it is protected, ... is constructed, or rather laid out—for the leaps are natural fences—the steeplechase course of two miles and a quarter. Within this, divided by a slight trench, and from the space appropriated to carriages and equestrians by strong and handsome posts all the way round, is the race-course, less probably than a furlong in circuit. Then comes the enclosure for those who ride or drive as aforesaid ; and lastly, the middle, occupied by a hill, from which every yard of the running is commanded, besides miles of country on every side beyond it, and exclusively reserved for foot people. I could hardly credit what I saw. Here was, almost at our doors, a racing emporium more extensive and attractive than Ascot or Epsom, with ten times the accommodation of either, and where carriages are charged for admission at three-fourths less. This great national undertaking is the sole result of individual enterprise, being effected by the industry and liberality of a gentleman by the name of Whyte. . . . This is an enterprise which must prosper; it is without a competitor, and it is open to the fertilization of many sources of profit. As a site for horse exercise, can any riding-house compare with it ? For females, it is without the danger or exposure of the parks ; as a training-ground for the turf or the field it cannot be exceeded ; and its character cannot be better summed up than by describing it as a necessary of London life, of the absolute need of which we were not aware until the possession of it taught us its permanent value."

The earliest mention of the Hippodrome in the *Racing Calendar* is to be found in the volume for 1837, when two races were run, the one for fifty and the other for a hundred sovereigns—three horses starting for one, and four for the other.

"At the close of the reign of William IV.," says Mr. Blaine, in his " Rural Sports," "an attempt was made to establish a regular series of race meetings, and also a training locality within two miles of the metropolis. To this intent a large portion of land was treated for and engaged close to Notting Hill. Here were erected stabling and boxes for about seventy-five race-horses, with every convenience for a training establishment ; a very good race-course also was formed, and numerous stakes were run for on it in 1838. But, unfortunately, the proprietors overlooked one circumstance at once fatal to the Hippodrome, as the establishment was named : the soil was a deep, strong clay, so that the training-ground could be used by horses only at particular periods of the year. This was a difficulty not to be got over, and as a race-course the Hippodrome soon closed its short career, doubtless with a heavy loss to the proprietors."

It would appear, from other channels of sporting information, that the first public day was given on Saturday, the 3rd of June, 1837, and that it naturally drew together as brilliant an assembly as ever met together in London. "On account of its vicinity to town, every refreshment was provided at a rate for which those who had been used to the terrible extortions elsewhere would hardly have been prepared. Splendid equipages occupied the circle allotted to them, while gay marquees, with all their flaunting accompaniments, covered the hall, filled with all the good things of this life, and iced champagne, which can hardly be called a mortal beverage. The racing was for plates of fifty and 100 sovereigns, with moderate entrances, given by the proprietors. The £100 plate was won by Mr. Wickham's ' Pincher,' and the steeplechase by Mr. Elmore's ' Lottery,' ridden by Mason. There was a second meeting appointed for Monday and Tuesday, the 19th and 20th of the same month, but the former day alone ' came off,' the other day's racing being postponed on account of the death of King William."

A writer in the *Sporting Magazine*, who signs himself " Juan," remarks :—" As a place of fashionable resort, it certainly opened under promising auspices, the stewards being Lord Chesterfield and Count D'Orsay. Another year, I cannot doubt, is destined to see it rank among the most favourite and favoured of all the metropolitan rendezvous, both for public and for private recreation. Unquestionably, of the varieties of the present season none has put forward such a claim to popularity and patronage as the ' Hippodrome.' " But the defect, which we have already mentioned, in the subsoil was irremediable ; and after four years of a very chequered and struggling career, its last public meeting was held in June, 1841. At this date the land along its southern and eastern sides was beginning to be in demand for building purposes, and so pieces were sliced off to form those streets and thoroughfares which lie to the north of Westbourne Grove and south of the Great Western Railway. A large portion of the riding ground, however, was still kept laid down in turf—rather of a coarse kind, it must be owned; and some hedges were preserved, over which dashing young ladies would ride their chargers as lately as the year 1852. But in the course of the next five or six years the green sward, and the green trees, and the green hedges were all swept away, and on the spot selected by the "Di Vernons" and "pretty horse-breakers" for their trial-jumps now stands St. Stephen's Church.

Portobello Farm was marked in the maps of the neighbourhood as lately as 1830: it was named by its then owner at the time of the capture of that city by Admiral Vernon. It then stood in the midst of open fields, in which the cows and sheep grazed and pigs were fed. In what is now Portobello Road, skirting the eastern end of Ladbroke Square, stands a convent of the Little Sisters of the Poor. The "sisters" themselves feed off the scraps left by the paupers whom they support by going round to the doors of London houses for broken victuals. Upwards of a hundred poor persons are daily supported by the "sisters" in this benevolent manner. The head-quarters of this charity are at Hammersmith, where the chief institution will be described in its proper place. There was a pretty walk this way across to Kensal Green till about 1850-60.

The splendid new town of Bayswater, close by, which has joined North Kensington and Shepherd's Bush on to London, had no existence during the first few years of Queen Victoria, when "Hopwood's Nursery Ground" and the Victoria Gardens —so famed for running-matches and other sporting meetings—faced the dull brick wall which effectually shut out the green glades and leafy avenues of Kensington Gardens from the view of passengers along the Bayswater Road. Bayswater is a vague name for the district extending from the Gravel Pits to the north-west corner of Hyde Park. Lord Chesterfield, in one of his poems, has praised the healthiness of the situation, though, probably, he was too fond of the town to walk often so far in the direction of the open country. The whole district of streets, squares, terraces, and crescents sprung into existence in the course of about ten years—between 1839 and 1849. Bayswater was noted of old for its springs, reservoirs, and conduits, supplying the greater part of the City of London with water. With regard to the origin of the name of Bayswater, the following particulars from the disclosures made in a trial at Westminster, as summarised by a writer in the first volume of *Notes and Queries*,

help to elucidate the question :—"The Dean and Chapter of Westminster are possessed of the manor of Westbourne Green, in the parish of Paddington, parcel of the possessions of the extinct Abbey of Westminster. It must have belonged to the Abbey when *Domesday* was compiled; for, although neither Westbourne nor Knightsbridge (also a manor of the same house) is specially named in that survey, yet we know, from a later record of the time of Edward I., that both of those manors were members, or constituent hamlets, of the *ville* of Westminster, which is mentioned in *Domesday* among the lands of the Abbey. The most considerable tenant under the abbot in this *ville* was *Bainiardus*, probably the same Norman associate of the Conqueror who is called Baignardus and Bainardus in other parts of the survey, and who gave his name to Baynard's Castle. The descent of the land held by him under the abbot cannot be clearly traced, but his name long remained attached to part of it; and as late as the year 1653 a parliamentary grant of the Abbey or Chapter lands to Foxcrafte and another, describes 'the common field at Paddington' as being 'near to a place commonly called *Baynard's Watering*.' In 1720, the lands of the Dean and Chapter in the same common field are described, in a terrier of the Chapter, to be in the occupation of Alexander Bond, of *Bear's Watering*, in the same parish of Paddington. The common field referred to is the well-known piece of garden-ground lying between Craven Hill and the Uxbridge Road, called also *Bayswater Field*. We may, therefore, fairly conclude that this portion of ground, always remarkable for its springs of excellent water, once supplied water to Baynard, his household, or his cattle; that the memory of his name was preserved in the neighbourhood for six centuries; and that his 'watering-place' now figures on the outside of certain omnibuses, in the streets of London, under the modern name of 'Bayswater.'"

The running streams and gravelly soil of this neighbourhood were at one time highly favourable for the growth of watercress, of which, as lately as the year 1825, there were several cultivators here, as in other places in the vicinity of London. The cultivation of watercress is said to have been first attempted, at the commencement of the present century, by a Mr. Bradbury, near Gravesend. Gerarde, the herbalist, says that eating watercresses restores the "wonted bloom to the cheeks of young ladies." Perhaps that is one reason why that plant is so popular.

On a slanting grassy bank, about a hundred yards from the back of the line of dwelling-houses now bearing the name of Craven Hill, stood, down to about the year 1820, an ancient stone-built conduit-house, whence the water-supply was conveyed by pipes underground into the City. Conduit Passage and Spring Street, both near at hand, thence derive their designation. The conduit was constructed and kept up by the Corporation of London, "to preserve a large spring of pure water, which rose at the spot, and was formerly conveyed by leaden pipes (cast in Holland) to Cheapside and Cornhill." "It was," says a writer in the *City Press*, "one of the most ancient springs in the vicinity of London, and, being situate in a manor once belonging to the Sanford family, and subsequently to the Earl of Craven, was granted to the citizens by one Gilbert Sanford in the twenty-first year of the reign of Henry III., A.D. 1236." Some reference is made to it in Lysons' "Environs of London," where it is stated that the water, "conveyed by brick drains, supplies the houses in and about Bond Street, which stand upon the City lands." Lysons further states that "the springs at this place lie near the surface, and the water is very fine." One of the principal reservoirs here, of which the Serpentine received the overplus, was situated where Trinity Church now stands, at the corner of Gloucester Gardens, Bishop's Road, not far from the "Royal Oak" tavern. In the *Saturday Magazine* for May 18th, 1844, there is an illustration of the Conduit-head at Bayswater, and in the article which accompanies it, the writer thus observes:—"The sources of the various conduits of London, formerly kept with so much care, have for the most part entirely disappeared. That at Paddington, however, still exists, though probably not in its original form ; and Mr. Matthews says that, up to a recent period, it afforded a plentiful supply of water to some houses in Oxford Street. The conduit, or spring, is situate in a garden about half a mile to the west of the Edgware Road, and at the same distance from Bayswater, within two hundred or three hundred yards of the Grand Junction Water Company's reservoirs. It is covered by a circular building in good condition, and some of the pipes continue in a sound state, although several centuries have elapsed since they were laid down. From the same source, about a century ago, the palace at Kensington received a part of its supply, which was effected by the aid of a water-wheel placed at Bayswater Bridge ; but on the establishment of the Chelsea Waterworks, it became useless, and was removed."

There is also in the illustrated edition of Pennant's "London," in the British Museum, a print of this conduit as it appeared in the year 1798, of which a copy is given on page 186. The aqueduct itself was "round, and cased thick with stone, and in the upper spiral part they lapped over each other, tile-like, and were fastened together with iron cramps to the brickwork, thick within. It was of a regular circumference, from the pediment or base about eight feet, and then spread up to the point, and was capped with a ball. Its height, about twenty feet, had four airlets, resembling windows, with a door next the garden, plated with iron plates, over which, in an oblong square, was cut, 'REP. ANNO 1632'; in another part were the City arms, with the date, 1782." The water, we are told, was constantly issuing from under the door, through a wooden pipe, at the rate of thirty gallons an hour, and took its course under the bridge into Kensington Gardens. When this water was let to the proprietors of Chelsea Waterworks, a stipulation was made that the basin therein should be kept full. This spring also supplied the basin in Hyde Park, whence, as we have already seen, it was conveyed by a water-wheel, "at Hyde Park wall, near Knightsbridge chapel," on to the Thames at Pimlico. It also took a subterraneous course into the City, "whose name and arms it bore," and whose property it was, and to whom now, no doubt, the land belongs all round about whereupon it was built. The water-course to the City was formerly denoted by stones above ground, laid along through the fields; and in the burying-ground of St. George, Hanover Square, which abuts upon the Bayswater Road, was once a brick well and several stones, marked with the City arms, and the date of 1773. There was also a well against the shop, 254, Oxford Street, with the City arms, inscribed "1772." In the centre of the "conduit-field" there was a very curious antique stone, much mutilated, which pointed out the rise of the spring. There were also two other mark-stones, almost hid in the earth, near to the conduit. When the Craven Hill estate was parcelled out for building purposes, the stone conduit-house was pulled down, and the stream was led either into the main sewer or into the river Serpentine, which rises much farther up in a north-easterly direction, and now rushes, occasionally with great impetus, under the centre of the roadway in Kensington Garden Terrace, and, crossing the Bayswater Road, enters Kensington Gardens where the fountains are.

Apropos of the ancient streams in this locality, it may be added that it is said there was in the olden days very good fishing in the trout stream which ran from Notting Hill Manor towards Hay

Hill, Berkeley Square, taking its course through Brook Street, Grosvenor Square, which was built on the high banks of the said stream, where it ceased to blend with the Tye. We know that as early as the reign of Henry III. there were six fountains in this locality from which water was supplied to the City by means of pipes.

In Lambert's "London and its Environs," published in 1805, we read :—"Bayswater is a hamlet to Paddington, about a mile from London, on the Uxbridge Road. Its public tea-gardens formerly belonged to the celebrated Sir John Hill, who here cultivated the medicinal plants from which he prepared his essences, tinctures, &c." Sir John Hill was the son of a clergyman, born about 1716, and bred as an apothecary. He was employed by Lord Petre and the Duke of Richmond in the arrangement of their botanic gardens in Essex and Sussex; and by their assistance he executed a scheme of travelling over several parts of the kingdom, to collect the most rare plants, accounts of which he published by subscription. But this proved a failure, and showed that he was in advance of his time. His "Vegetable System" extends over twenty-six folio volumes! and for this he was rewarded by a Swedish order of knighthood from the king of that country. It appears that, for a time at least, Sir John Hill, though little better than a charlatan and an empiric, enjoyed the reputation of a great and learned botanist. He was at one time a second-rate actor, and he made an unsuccessful attempt to obtain admission into the Royal Society. Garrick's epigram on him is well known, and has often been quoted :—

> " For physic and farces his equal there scarce is ;
>   His farces are physic ; his physic a farce is."

Among the medicines produced by Sir John Hill were his "Water-dock Essence" and his "Balm of Honey." These gardens are now covered by the long range of mansions called Lancaster Gate. They were originally known as the "Physic Garden," and were opened as a place of amusement towards the close of the last century. They were still in existence as gardens as late as 1854, though no longer frequented by pleasure-seekers of the upper classes. It is not a little singular that the gardens at Bayswater are not even mentioned by name, in the article on "Old Suburban Tea Gardens," in Chambers' "Book of Days." Faulkner, writing in 1820, says that within the last few years Bayswater has increased to a "popular neighbourhood."

Craven House, which gave its name to Craven Hill, above mentioned, became the residence of Lord Craven's family some time before 1700, on their removal from Drury Lane. It was borrowed

(as stated above) by Queen Anne, as a nursery for her son, the little Duke of Gloucester, before she engaged Campden House, where we have already seen her.

Craven Hill is now called Craven Road, the inequality of it having been levelled by filling up the low ground where a small brook once crossed it from north to south. The houses in Craven Road and Craven Hill Gardens stand on the site of a field which was given about the year 1720 in exchange for the "Pest-field," near Golden Square, already mentioned ; and it may be the reverse of comforting to the inhabitants to know that, under an old agreement between Lord Craven and the parochial authorities, the plot of ground in question may be taken for the purpose of a burial-ground, in case London should ever again be visited with the plague ; unless, indeed, this liability has been done away with by the Act which enforces extra-mural interments. This land was not used during the cholera of 1849; and at the present time, as we have shown above, a grand London square, called Craven Gardens, alone indicates the site of the Pest-house fields. The property, which belonged in former times to one Jane Upton, and was called Upton Farm, was purchased by the trustees of this charity-estate for £1,570.

In 1821 the Toxophilite Society rented about four acres of ground here, between Sussex Gardens and the Bayswater Road, just opposite the point where Hyde Park and Kensington Gardens meet ; they formed then part of quite a rural district, the ground shelving down somewhat steeply on the west to a little brook. A pavilion was erected here for the use of the members, and we are told that "there was space for three pairs of targets, with a range of about 200 yards." The Society held these grounds until 1834, when they removed to their present gardens in the Regent's Park. The exact site of these grounds is preserved in the name of the Archery Tavern in Bathurst Street, leading to Sussex Square.

In the fields a little to the north of Craven Hill, towards Westbourne Green, was the cottage (see page 147) where the Princess of Wales used to throw off the restraints of royal etiquette in the company of her intimate friends.

The district lying between Kensington Gardens and Paddington, a little to the north of Bayswater, was known, till the reign of George IV., as West bourne Green, and was quite a leafy retreat at the time of that king's accession. That portion of the district lying to the north of Westbourne Grove and Bishop's Road will be best dealt with in our chapter on Paddington ; but with regard to Westbourne Grove itself, we may state that, as lately as 1852, this thoroughfare, which now consists almost entirely of attractive shops, was a quiet street, consisting of detached cottages, with gardens in front. At the end nearest Paddington was an open nursery garden, rich in dahlias, geraniums, &c.

Oxford Square and Norfolk Square, may be rapidly passed over. Each and all of these places can boast of goodly mansions, interspersed with gardens and enclosures filled with trees and shrubs; but the whole district is of too modern growth to have a history.

THE BAYSWATER CONDUIT IN 1798. (*From Pennant.*)

Westbourne Terrace, which unites Bishop's Road with Craven Road, is so called from the West Bourne, a small brook running from Kilburn between Paddington and Bayswater, and passing into the Serpentine. It was built in 1847–52.

Sussex Gardens and Sussex Square, Pembridge Square and Crescent, Talbot and Leinster Squares, Hyde Park Gardens and Hyde Park Square, Cleveland Square and Queen's Road and Gardens,

Southwick Crescent and Place are named after Southwick Park, Hampshire, the property of the Thistlethwayte family, formerly joint-lessees of the Paddington Manor.

In Gloucester Square, Westbourne Terrace, at No. 11, lived John Sadleir, the fraudulent M.P., who committed suicide on Hampstead Heath in February, 1856.

A splendid new city of palaces, Lancaster Gate,

NOTTING HILL IN 1750.

&c., sprung up between 1860 and 1870, on the site of Hopwood's Nursery Grounds and the Victoria Tea Gardens, which we have mentioned above.

About the year 1861, we may here remark, a novelty, in the way of street railways, was introduced in the Bayswater Road, by Mr. George F. Train, who was at least the pioneer of a useful invention. Permission had been given by the Commissioners of Highways for Mr. Train to lay down the rails for his new conveyance, and the event was inaugurated by a public banquet at St. James's Hall. Notwithstanding the coldness with which the project was at first received,· the plan has since been carried out in various parts of London in the tramways.

In the autumn of 1832, when the cholera was spreading death far and wide throughout the land, Dr. Adam Clarke, the author of a well-known Commentary on the Bible, here fell a victim to that fatal malady. He was engaged to preach at Bayswater on Sunday, the 26th of August, and on the Saturday before he was conveyed there in a friend's chaise. He was cheerful on the road, but was tired with his journey and listless in the evening ; and when a gentleman asked him to preach a charity sermon for him and fix the day, he replied, "I am not well; I cannot fix a time ; I must first see what God is about to do with me." He retired to bed early, not without some of those symptoms that indicated the approach of this awful disease, but which do not appear to have excited any suspicions in himself or in his friends. He rose in the morning ill, and wanting to get home ; but before arrangements could be made for his removal, he had sunk into his chair —that icy coldness, by which the complaint is

characterised, had come on, and when the medical men arrived, they pronounced it a clear case of cholera. His wife and most of his children, short as the summons was, gathered about him—he had ever been the most affectionate of husbands and parents—and his looks indicated great satisfaction when he saw them ; but he was now nearly speechless. "Am I blue ? " however, he said to his son—a question indicating his knowledge of the malady under which he was sinking ; and without any effort of nature to rally, he breathed his last.

On the north side of the Bayswater Road, about a quarter of a mile from the site of Tyburn Turnpike, is a dreary burial-ground, of about an acre, with a chapel of the plainest description, belonging to the parish of St. George, Hanover Square. In this burial-ground was deposited, in 1768, the body of Laurence Sterne, the author of " Tristram Shandy," who had died in poverty at his lodgings in Bond Street, as we have already stated. But the body was afterwards taken up by some of the "resurrection men," and sent to Cambridge to the professor of anatomy for dissection. Such, at all events, is the story told by Sir J. Prior, in his " Life of Malone." His grave here is marked by a plain upright stone, with an epitaph clumsily expressed, "a perpetual memorial of the bad taste of his brother masons."

Among other eminent persons buried here were Mr. J. T. Smith, the author of " The Book for a Rainy Day," and many other antiquarian works on London ; Mrs. Radcliffe, the author of " The Mysteries of Udolpho ; " and last, not least, General Sir Thomas Picton, who fell at Waterloo ; but in 1859 his body was removed, and re-interred in St. Paul's Cathedral.

CHAPTER XVI.

TYBURN AND TYBURNIA.

"The three-square stilt at Tyburn."—*Old Saying.*

Derivation of the Name of Tyburn—Earliest Executions on this Spot—Sir Roger Bolinbroke, the Conjuror—Elizabeth Barton, the "Holy Maid of Kent"—Execution of Roman Catholics—Morocco Men—Mrs. Turner, the Poisoner, and Inventor of the Yellow Starched Ruffs and Cuffs— Resuscitation of a Criminal after Execution—Colonel Blood—Jack Sheppard and Jonathan Wild—Mrs. Catherine Hayes—"Clever Tom Clinch"—"Execution Day"—The Execution of Lord Ferrers—The Rev. Mr. Hackman—Dr. Dodd—The Last Act of a Highwayman's Life —"Sixteen-string Jack"—McLean, the "Fashionable Highwayman"—Claude Duval—John Twyn, an Offending Printer—John Haynes, and his Resuscitation after Hanging—Ryland, the Forger—An Unlucky Jest—"Jack Ketch"—Tyburn Tickets—Hogarth's "Tom Idle"— The Gallows and its Surroundings—The Story of the Penance of Queen Henrietta Maria—An Anecdote about George III.—The Site of Tyburn Tree—The Tyburn Pew-opener—Tyburnia—Connaught Place—The Princess Charlotte and the Prince of Orange—The Residence of Mr. T. Assheton-Smith, and of Haydon the Painter.

TYBURNIA, which of late years has become almost, if not quite, as fashionable and aristocratic as Belgravia, is the district lying between Edgware Road and Westbourne and Gloucester Terrace and

Craven Hill, the south side of which is bounded by the Bayswater Road, and may be said to have sprung into existence only since the reign of William IV.

The little river Tyburn, or Tybourn, whence the district derives its name, consisted of two arms, one of which, as already stated, crossed Oxford Street, near Stratford Place; while the other, further to the west, followed nearly the course of the present Westbourne Terrace and the Serpentine. Five hundred years ago, or less, it was a pleasant brook enough, with rows of elms growing on its banks. These trees were a place of execution in those days; and Roger de Mortimer, the paramour of Queen Eleanor, widow of Edward II., was dragged thither on a hurdle, and hung and quartered, his body being exposed there for several days. Elm's Lane, Bayswater, now swept away, preserved down to our own time the memory of these fatal elms, which are to be regarded as the original "Tyburn Trees." It was at a subsequent time that the place of execution was removed nearer to London, the corner of the Edgware Road. Here it became a fixture for centuries; here many notable and many notorious persons have "died in their shoes," to use a favourite cant expression. Here suffered the "Holy Maid of Kent;" Mrs. Turner, the poisoner, and the inventor of the starched ruff which adorns so many portraits of fair ladies of other days; Felton, the assassin of the Duke of Buckingham; a batch of the parliamentary regicides; some dozens of Roman Catholic priests, condemned as "traitors;" a long line of illustrious highwaymen, such as Jack Sheppard and Jonathan Wild; Lord Ferrers, the murderer of his steward; Dr. Dodd, for forgery; and last, not least, Mother Brownrigg, the same

"Who whipped three female 'prentices to death,
And hid them in the coal-hole."

An absurd derivation of the name has been suggested, as though it was from the words "tie" and "burn," though some countenance is given to the derivation by the fact that traitors were strung or "tied" up first, and afterwards "burnt." But the real origin is from the little brook, or burn, which ran by the spot, as above mentioned.

The gallows were removed hither (as we have seen) from opposite to St. Giles's Pound; but there had been occasional executions here earlier: for instance, it is upon record that Judge Tressilian and Nicholas Brembre, or Brambre, were hung here in A.D. 1388. Mr. Dobré was at great pains to discover the record of an earlier execution here, but failed.

The complete history of the neighbourhood of "Tyburn Tree" has still to be written, though the materials are far from scanty; for between the Reformation and the reign of George III., few years elapsed in which Roman Catholic priests, and even laymen, were not sent thither to suffer, nominally as "traitors," but in reality because they were the adherents of a proscribed and persecuted faith, and refused, at the bidding of an earthly sovereign, to abandon their belief in the Pope as the spiritual head of Christendom. Here, too, during the same period, almost as many men of a different stamp paid the last penalty of the law for violating other enactments—highwaymen, robbers, forgers, and murderers. The highwaymen generally went to the scaffold merrily and jauntily, as men who had all their lives faced the chance of a violent death, and were not afraid to meet it at Tyburn. As they passed along the streets in the fatal cart, gaily dressed in their best clothes, young women in the crowd would present them with nosegays, and in the eyes of the assembled multitudes their deaths were regarded as almost as glorious as those of the Roman Catholic "confessors" were esteemed by their co-religionists.

Our readers will not, of course, forget the lines in the song of "Macheath," in the *Beggar's Opera*, which thus refer to Tyburn:—

"Since laws were made for every degree,
To curb vice in others as well as in me,
I wonder we ha'nt better company
'Neath Tyburn Tree."

One of the earliest executions on this spot was that of "Sir Roger Bolinbroke, the conjuror" (A.D. 1440), who suffered for high treason, in conjunction with the Duchess of Gloucester, as recorded by Shakespeare.* From the Harleian MSS., No. 585, we learn his fate in detail. On the same day on which he was condemned at Guildhall, he was drawn from the Tower to Tyburn, and there hanged, beheaded, and quartered, his head being set up on London Bridge, and his four quarters being disposed of in like manner at Hereford, Oxford, York, and Cambridge.

Here was executed, in the fifteenth century, Fisher, a skinner, already mentioned† by us as the man who released Sir John Oldcastle when a prisoner in the Tower.

Here, in 1534, were executed Elizabeth Barton, the so-called "Holy Maid of Kent," who had prophesied the speedy death of Henry VIII.; several of her supporters suffered with her.

Here, too, a few years later, suffered Sir Thomas Percy, Aske, D'Arcy, Bigod, Sir John Bulmer, and the Abbot of Jewaux, for the share they had taken in a foreign pilgrimage and in a last desperate effort to restore the Catholic religion in England.

* See *Henry VI.*, part ii., act 1, sc. 2.   † See Vol. II., p. 65.

Tyburn is mentioned by Holinshed, who writes of a certain "false servant" that, being convicted of felony in court of assize, he was judged to be hanged, "and so *was at Tyburn*."

To enumerate the names of all who suffered the "extreme penalty of the law" at Tyburn would be a difficult, and, indeed, a needless task. Among those who went thither to end their days, however, were not only murderers, highwaymen, and traitors, but also housebreakers, sheep-stealers, and forgers; the penalty of death, however, was not confined to them, but was made to include even some of the loose and disreputable hangers-on of the demoralising State lottery-offices, known as "Morocco men," for going about the country with red morocco pocket-books, in which they entered the names of the victims whom they gulled.

Here was executed Mrs. Turner, the poisoner, for complicity with the Countess of Somerset in the murder of Sir Thomas Overbury, an event which formed one of the episodes in the corrupt reign of James I. "Mrs. Turner's execution," says John Timbs, in his "Romance of London," "excited immense interest. She was a woman of great beauty, and had much affected the fashion of the day. Her sentence was to be 'hang'd at Tiburn in her yellow Tinny Ruff and Cuff, she being the first inventor and wearer of that horrid garb.' The ruff and cuff were got up with *yellow starch*, and in passing her sentence, Lord Chief Justice Coke told her that she had been guilty of all the seven deadly sins, and declared that as she was the inventor of the yellow-starched ruffs and cuffs, so he hoped that she would be the last by whom they would be worn. He accordingly ordered that she should be hanged in the gear she had made so fashionable. The execution attracted an immense crowd to Tyburn, and many persons of quality, ladies as well as gentlemen, in their coaches. Mrs. Turner had dressed herself specially for her execution: her face was highly rouged, and she wore a cobweb lawn ruff, yellow-starched. An account, printed next day, states that 'her hands were bound with a black silk ribbon, as she desired; and a black veil, which she wore upon her head, being pulled over her face by the executioners, the cart was driven away, and she left hanging, in whom there was no motion at all perceived.' She made a very penitent end. As if to ensure the condemnation of yellow starch, the hangman had his hands and cuffs of yellow, 'which,' says Sir S. D'Ewes, 'made many after that day, of either sex, to forbear the use of that coloured starch, till it at last grew generally to be detested and disused.'"

Following in the wake of Mrs. Turner, came

Southwell, the "sweet versifier;" Felton, the assassin of the Duke of Buckingham; and John Smith, the burglar, of Queen Anne's time. In connection with this last-named execution, even the gallows may be said to have its romantic side; for we read in Chambers' "Book of Days" that a reprieve came after Smith had been suspended for a quarter of an hour. He was taken down, bled, and *revived*.

We have already mentioned Colonel Blood's bold attempt to seize the Duke of Ormonde in St. James's Street.* He also endeavoured to complete his act of highway violence by hanging his victim by open force at Tyburn; but, happily for the duke, he did not succeed in the attempt.

We next come to the names of two others who have become famous through the agency of cheap literature—Jack Sheppard, the notorious housebreaker, and Jonathan Wild, the "thief and thief-taker." Of the early life of the first-named culprit we have already spoken in our account of Wych Street, St. Clement Danes;† and for his various exploits in Newgate we must refer our readers to our account of that prison.‡ The whole career of crime as practised by this vagabond carpenter has been strikingly told by Mr. Harrison Ainsworth, in his romance of "Jack Sheppard;" and his portrait, as he appeared in the condemned cell at Newgate, was painted by Sir James Thornhill, and sold by thousands as a mezzo-tint engraving. Jonathan Wild's particular sphere of action lay in the trade of the restoration of stolen property, which he carried on for many years through a secret confederacy with all the regular thieves, burglars, and highwaymen of the metropolis, whose depredations he prompted and directed. His success received some check by an Act of Parliament passed in 1717, by which persons convicted of receiving or buying goods, knowing them to have been stolen, were made liable to a long term of transportation. Wild, however, managed to elude this new law; but he was at last convicted, under a clause which had been enacted with a particular view to Wild's proceedings—such as trafficking in stolen goods, and dividing the money with felons. His execution took place at Tyburn, in May, 1725. At his trial he had a printed paper handed to the jury, entitled, "A list of persons discovered, apprehended, and convicted of several robberies on the highway, and also for burglary and housebreaking, and also for returning from transportation: by Jonathan Wild." It contained the names of thirty-five robbers, twenty-two housebreakers, and ten

* See Vol. IV., p. 166.   † See Vol. III., p. 34.   ‡ See Vol. II., p. 459.

returned convicts, whom he had been instrumental in getting hanged before he found the tables turned against himself.

Among the hundreds of murderers hung at Tyburn, few were more notorious than Catharine Hayes, who was executed in 1726. She and her husband lived in Tyburn Road, now called Oxford Street, but, not being contented with her spouse, she engaged two assassins, Wood and Billings, to make him drunk, and then aid her in dispatching him. They did so, and chopped up the body, carrying the head in a pail to the Horseferry at Westminster, where they threw it into the Thames, the other portion being secreted about a pond in Marylebone Fields. The head being found and identified, search was made for the rest of the body, and this being discovered, the other murderers were hung near the spot where Upper Wimpole Street now stands. Mrs. Hayes was reserved to suffer at Tyburn, blazing fagots being placed under her. The murder, as might be imagined, caused a great sensation when it became known, and is constantly mentioned in the publications of the time.

The following lines, from Swift's "Tom Clinch going to be Hanged," give a picture of the grim cavalcade wending its way from Newgate to Tyburn, in 1727:—

"As clever Tom Clinch, while the rabble was bawling,
Rode stately through Holborn to die in his calling,
He stopped at the 'George' for a bottle of sack,
And promised to pay for it—when he came back.
His waistcoat, and stockings, and breeches were white,
His cap had a new cherry-ribbon to tie 't;
And the maids to the doors and the balconies ran,
And cried 'Lack-a-day! he's a proper young man!'"

"Execution-day," as it was termed, must have been a carnival of frequent occurrence. Horace Walpole says that in the year 1752 no less than seventeen persons were executed at Tyburn in a batch. One of the most memorable executions that took place here was on the 5th of May, 1760, when that eccentric nobleman, Lawrence, third Earl Ferrers, met his fate for the murder of his steward, a Mr. John Johnson. The scene of the tragedy was his lordship's seat of Staunton Harold, near Ashby-de-la-Zouche, and the deed itself was deliberately planned and carried out. The career of Lord Ferrers for many years previously had been one of the grossest dissipation, and had resulted in his estates becoming seriously involved. The Court of Chancery ordered that the rents due to him should be paid to a receiver, the nomination of the said receiver being left to his lordship, who hoped to find in that person a pliant tool, who would take things easily and let him have his own way. The person whom Lord Ferrers so appointed was none other than Mr. Johnson, who had been in the service of his lordship's family, as steward, for many years. But he soon found out that he had got a different man to deal with than he had expected; and, accordingly, from that time, he conceived an inveterate hatred towards him, on account of the opposition which he offered to his desires and whims, and he finally resolved to "move heaven and earth" to obtain his revenge. Lord Ferrers' household at that time consisted of a Mrs. C——, who acted as housekeeper, her four daughters, and five domestic servants; and Mr. Johnson's farm-house, the Mount, was about a mile distant from the mansion, across the park. On Sunday, the 13th of January, in the year 1760, Lord Ferrers called on Mr. Johnson, and, after some discourse, arranged for another meeting, to take place at Staunton on the following Friday, at three o'clock. The Friday came round, and Johnson was true to his appointment. Shortly before that hour, his lordship had desired Mrs. C—— to take the children out for a walk, and the two men-servants he had contrived to get out of the way on different pretexts, so that when Johnson arrived there was no one in the house except his lordship and the three maidservants. On the arrival of Mr. Johnson he was at once admitted into his lordship's private sitting-room. "They had sat together, talking on various matters, for some ten minutes or more, when the earl got up, walked to the door, and locked it. He next desired Johnson at once to settle some disputed account; then, rising higher in his demands, ordered him, as he valued his life, to sign a paper which he had drawn up, and which was a confession of his (Johnson's) villany. Johnson expostulated and refused, as an honest man would refuse, to sign his name to any such document. The earl then drew from his pocket a loaded pistol, and bade him kneel down, for that his last hour was come. Johnson bent one knee, but the earl insisted on his kneeling on both his knees. He did so, and Lord Ferrers at once fired. The ball entered his body below the rib, but it did not do its fell work instantaneously. Though mortally wounded, the poor fellow had strength to rise and to call loudly for assistance. The earl at first coolly prepared as though he would discharge the other pistol, so as to put his victim out of misery; but, suddenly moved with remorse, he unlocked the door and called for the servants, who, on hearing the discharge of the pistol, had run, in fear and trembling, to the wash-house, not knowing whether his lordship would not take it into his head to send a bullet through their bodies also. He called them once and again, desired one to fetch a surgeon, and another to help the wounded man into a bed. It was clear, however, that Johnson had not many hours to live; and, as he desired to see his children before he died, the earl ordered that they should be summoned from the farm. Miss Johnson came speedily, and found

for trial at the bar of the House of Peers. His trial lasted nearly three days, and resulted in his being sentenced to be "hanged by the neck until he was dead;" but, "in consideration of his rank," a few days' extension of time was allowed before the sentence was carried into effect, and also he was permitted to be hanged with a silken instead of a hempen rope. Lord Ferrers, to use the slang expression of the sporting world, "died game."

THE PLACE OF EXECUTION, TYBURN, IN 1750.

her father apparently in the agonies of death, and Lord Ferrers standing by the bedside, and attempting to stanch the blood that flowed from the wound." During the night, by a clever *ruse*, Johnson was removed to his own house, where he lingered only a few hours, dying early the next morning. The coroner's jury returned a verdict of "wilful murder" against Lord Ferrers, who was at once lodged in Leicester Gaol. About a fortnight afterwards, we are told, he was brought up to London in his own landau, drawn by six horses, under a strong guard, and he was "dressed like a jockey, in a close riding frock, jacked boots and cap, and a plain shirt." Arraigned before the House of Lords, he was at once committed to the Tower, and two months later was again brought up

To the last he had respect to his rank, and, declining to journey to Tyburn in a cart, went slowly and stately thither in his own landau, again drawn by six horses. In this, dressed in his wedding suit, he rode as calmly to the gallows as the handsomest highwayman of his day, and went through the performance there with as little unnecessary affectation as though, like many a "gentleman of the road," he had looked to such an end as "the appropriate and inevitable conclusion of his career." It may be added that the landau in which Lord Ferrers rode to Tyburn was never used again, but was left to rot away and fall to pieces in a coach-house at Acton. His lordship's body found a grave at old St. Pancras Church.

In our account of Covent Garden, in a previous

volume,* we have spoken at some length of the murder of Miss Reay by the Rev. Mr. Hackman. Boswell was present at Hackman's trial at the Old Bailey, and further, after his condemnation and sentence, attended him in his coach to Tyburn, in company with a sheriff's officer. Selwyn, who, like Boswell, was fond of seeing executions, was not present on this occasion; but his friend, the Earl of Carlisle, attended, in order "to give some

The two were drawn in an open cart from Newgate to Tyburn, the execution being attended by an immense crowd. In apprehension of an attempt to rescue the criminal, twenty thousand men were ordered to be reviewed in Hyde Park during the execution, which, however, "though attended by an unequalled concourse of people, passed off with the utmost tranquillity." "Upon the whole," writes a friend of George Selwyn, who was present, "the

EXECUTION OF LORD FERRERS AT TYBURN.   (*From an Old Print of the Period.*)

account of Hackman's behaviour." This he did, to the following effect :—" The poor man behaved with great fortitude ; no appearances of fear were to be perceived, but very evident signs of contrition and repentance. He was long at his prayers ; and when he flung down his handkerchief as the sign for the cart to move on, Jack Ketch, instead of instantly whipping on the horse, jumped on the other side of him to snatch up the handkerchief, lest he should lose his rights. He then returned to the head of the cart, and Jehu'd him out of the world."

In 1777, Dr. Dodd, in company with another felon, made his exit from the world at Tyburn Tree.

piece was not very full of events. The doctor, to all appearance, was rendered perfectly stupid from despair. His hat was flapped all round and pulled over his eyes, which were never directed to any object around, nor ever raised, except now and then lifted up in the course of his prayers. He came in a coach, and a very heavy shower of rain fell just upon his entering the cart, and another just at his putting on his nightcap. During the shower an umbrella was held over his head, which Gilly Williams, who was present, observed was quite unnecessary, as the doctor was going to a place where he might be dried. . . . The executioner took both the doctor's hat and wig off at the same time. Why he put on his wig again I do not know, but he did ; and the doctor took off his wig a second time, and tied on a nightcap, which did not fit him ; but whether he stretched that or took another, I could not perceive. He then put on his nightcap himself, and upon his taking it, he certainly had a smile on his countenance ; and very soon afterwards there was an end of all his hopes and fears on this side of the grave. He never moved from the place he first took in the cart ; seemed absorbed in prayer, and utterly dejected, without any other signs of animation but in praying. I stayed till he was cut down and put into the hearse. The body was hurried to the house of Davies, an undertaker in Goodge Street, Tottenham Court Road, where it was placed in a hot bath, and every exertion made to restore life, but in vain." We have already given some particulars of the life of Dr. Dodd, and of the crime for which he suffered ; * it only remains to add that Dr. Johnson made eloquent and strenuous exertions with his pen to get the capital sentence remitted, but in vain. " The malevolence of men and their good nature," wrote Horace Walpole, " displayed themselves in their different characters against Dodd. His character appeared so bad to Dr. Newton, Bishop of Bristol, that he said, ' I am sorry for Dr. Dodd.' Being asked why, he replied, ' Because he is to be hanged for the least crime he ever committed.' "

The fondness which many minds feel (or rather felt) for these melancholy sights is thus discussed by Boswell and Dr. Johnson :—" I mentioned to him that I had seen the execution of several convicts at Tyburn† two days before, and that none of them seemed to be under any concern. *Johnson :* ' Most of them, sir, have never thought at all.' *Boswell :* ' But is not the fear of death natural to man ?' *Johnson :* ' So much so, sir, that the whole of life is but keeping away the thoughts of it.' He then, in a low and earnest tone, talked of his meditating upon the awful hour of his own dissolution, and in what manner he should conduct himself upon that occasion. ' I know not,' said he, ' whether I should wish to have a friend by me, or have it all between God and myself.'

" Talking of our feeling for the distresses of others —*Johnson :* ' Why, sir, there is much noise made about it, but it is greatly exaggerated. No, sir, we have a certain degree of feeling to prompt us to do good ; more than that Providence does not intend. It would be misery to no purpose.' *Boswell :* ' But

suppose now, sir, that one of your intimate friends were apprehended for an offence for which he might be hanged.' *Johnson :* ' I should do what I could to bail him, and give him any other assistance ; but if he were once fairly hanged, I should not suffer.' *Boswell :* ' Would you eat your dinner that day, sir ?' *Johnson :* ' Yes, sir ; and eat it as if he were eating with me. Why, there's Baretti, who is to be tried for his life to-morrow ; friends have risen up for him on every side, yet if he should be hanged, none of them would eat a slice of pudding the less. Sir, that sympathetic feeling goes a very little way in depressing the mind.' " ‡

Tyburn Tree was the usual end of the " highwayman," as people in the days of Queen Anne and the Georges euphemistically called the robber and assassin of the king's high road. " Alas ! " writes Thackeray, " there always came a day in the life of that warrior when it was the fashion to accompany him as he passed, without his black mask, and with a nosegay in his hand, accompanied by halberdiers, and attended by the sheriff, in a carriage without springs, and a clergyman jolting beside him, to a spot close by Cumberland Gate and the Marble Arch, where a stone still records that ' here Tyburn turnpike stood.' What a change in a century ; nay, in a few years ! Within a few yards of that gate the fields began : the fields of his exploits, behind the hedges of which he lurked and robbed. A great and wealthy city has grown over those meadows. Were a man brought to die thereon, the windows would be closed, and the inhabitants would keep their houses in sickening horror. A hundred years ago people crowded there to see the last act of a highwayman's life, and made jokes on it. Swift laughed at him, grimly advising him to provide a holland shirt and white cap, crowned with a crimson or black ribbon, for his exit, to mount the cart cheerfully, shake hands with the hangman, and so farewell ; or Gay wrote the most delightful ballads, and then made merry over his hero."

Among those who suffered here the penalty of their crimes as highwaymen was the notorious " Sixteen-string Jack," who is said by Dr. Johnson to have " towered above the common mark " in his own line as much as Gray did in poetry. He was remarkable for foppery in his dress, and, as Boswell tells us, derived his name from a bunch of sixteen strings which he wore at the knees of his breeches. John Rann, for such was this malefactor's real name, was executed here in November, 1774, for robbing Dr. Bell, the chaplain to the Princess Amelia, in Gunnersbury Lane.

---

* See page 47, *ante.*

† Six unhappy men were executed at Tyburn on Wednesday, the 18th (*one* day before). It was one of the irregularities of Mr. Boswell's mind to be passionately fond of seeing these melancholy spectacles. Indeed, he avows and defends it (in the *Hypochondriac,* No. 68, *London Mag.,* 1783) as a *natural* and irresistible impulse.—CROKER.

---

‡ Boswell's "Life of Johnson."

" Rann was a smart fellow, and a great favourite with a certain description of ladies ; he had been coachman to the Earl of Sandwich, when his lordship resided in the south-east corner house of Bedford Row. It was pretty generally reported that the *sixteen strings* worn by this freebooter at his knees were in allusion to the number of times he had been tried and acquitted. However, he was caught at last ; and J. T. Smith records his being led, when a boy, by his father's playfellow, Joseph Nollekens, to the end of John Street, to see the notorious terror of the king's highway, Rann, pass on his way to execution. The malefactor's coat was a bright pea-green ; he had an immense nosegay, which he had received from the hand of one of the frail sisterhood, whose practice it was in those days to present flowers to their favourites from the steps of St. Sepulchre's Church, as the last token of what they called their attachment to the condemned, whose worldly accounts were generally brought to a close at Tyburn, in consequence of their associating with abandoned characters. Such is Mr. Smith's account of the procession of the hero to Tyburn ; and Nollekens assured Smith, had his father-in-law, Mr. Justice Welsch, been high constable, they could have walked all the way to Tyburn by the side of the cart." The " sixteen strings " which this freebooter wore at his knees were, in reality, to the initiated at least, a covert allusion to the number of times that he had been tried and acquitted. Fortunately for the Boswell illustrators, there is an etched portrait of " Sixteen-string Jack ; " for, thief though he was, he had the honour of being recorded by Dr. Johnson. A correspondent of Hone's " Year-Book," published in 1832, states that he well remembered seeing " Sixteen-string Jack " taken in the cart to Tyburn.

It was, in fact, at Tyburn that most of the highwaymen of the last century—of whom Captain Macheath was another example, and whose exploits were so well known on Hounslow Heath, at Finchley, and on the Great North Road—closed their career.

" The species of gentleman highwayman," observes Mr. James Hannay, " no longer exists to frighten the traveller, and does no greater harm than put you to sleep in the pages of a novel. A gentleman can now roll through the country in his travelling-carriage without any fear of being robbed by a gallant horseman, summoning him to surrender with the air of a courtier, and pocketing his money with a quotation from Horace. The last of these heroes long ago died on that greatest of all ' trees of liberty,' the tree of Tyburn ; and his only representative now-a-days is the common footpad—a vulgar fellow—who knocks you down, and rifles you when you are insensible."

Another notorious character who was hanged here about the middle of the last century was McLean, the " fashionable highwayman," of whom Walpole thus writes :—" One night, in the beginning of November, 1749, as I was returning from Holland House by moonlight, about ten o'clock, I was attacked by two highwaymen in Hyde Park, and the pistol of one of them going off accidentally, raised the skin under my eye, left some marks of shot in my face, and stunned me. The ball went through the top of the chariot, and if I had sat an inch nearer to the left side, must have gone through my head." One of these highwaymen was McLean. He also attacked and robbed Lord Eglinton, Sir Thomas Robinson, Mrs. Talbot, and many others. He carried off a blunderbuss belonging to the old Scotch earl. McLean was at one time a grocer in Welbeck Street, but having the misfortune to lose his wife, he gave up business and took to the road, having as a companion, one Plunket, a journeyman apothecary. McLean was captured in the autumn of 1750, by selling a laced waistcoat to a pawnbroker in Monmouth Street, who happened to carry it to the very man who had just sold the lace Walpole tells us " there were a wardrobe of clothes, three-and-twenty purses, and the celebrated blunderbuss found at his lodgings, besides a famous kept mistress." Soame Jenyns, in his poem entitled " The Modern Fine Lady," written in the year this " fashionable highwayman " came to grief, writes—

" She weeps if but a handsome thief is hung."

To which is appended this note :—" Some of the brightest eyes were at this time in tears for one McLean, condemned for robbery on the highway."

Even a cursory account of Tyburn would be incomplete without mention of one more highwayman, who here paid the penalty of his offences on the triangular gallows. This was Claude Duval, who was, perhaps, even more famous than McLean. He made Holloway the chief scene of predatory exploits. In Lower Holloway his name was long kept in remembrance by Duval's Lane, which, curiously enough, as John Timbs tells us in his " Romance of London," " was previously called Devil's Lane, and more anciently Tolentone Lane." Macaulay, in his " History of England," says that Claude Duval " took to the road, and became captain of a formidable gang ; " adding that " it is related how, at the head of his troop, he stopped a lady's coach, in which there was a booty of four hundred pounds ; how he took only one hundred, and suffered the fair owner to ransom the rest by dancing a coranto with him on the heath." This celebrated exploit has been made the subject of one of Mr. Frith's remarkable pictures, and has been engraved. Duval was arrested at the "Hole-in-the-Wall," a noted house near Covent Garden, and he was executed in January, 1669, in the twenty-seventh year of his age. It is on record how that, "after *lying in state* at the Tangier Tavern, in St. Giles's, he was buried in the middle aisle of St. Paul's, Covent Garden, his funeral being attended with flambeaux and a numerous train of mourners, 'to the great grief of the women.'"

Tyburn, it may be added, has also some other associations, being connected with the history of newspapers and the liberty of the press. At the Restoration the latter had almost ceased to exist, and the press had not only to make itself heard through the small voice of a "Licencer," but to regulate its proceedings by Act of Parliament. In 1663 a Tyburn audience was assembled to witness the execution of a troublesome printer. He was named John Twyn, and had carried on his business in Cloth Fair, near to Milton's hiding-place, when he had "fall'n on evil days." Twyn was accused of having printed some seditious work bearing on the arguments often urged against the Commonwealth, "that the execution of judgment and justice is as well the people's as the magistrates' duty; and if the magistrates pervert judgment, the people are bound by the law of God to execute judgment without them and upon them." Roger L'Estrange was the "licencer" who had hunted up this offending printer; and Chief Justice Hyde sentenced him to be "drawn on a hurdle to Tyburn, and there hanged by the neck;" and, being alive, that he should be cut down, and his body mutilated in a way which decency forbids the mention of; that his entrails should afterwards be taken out, "and, you still living, the same to be burnt before your eyes; your head to be cut off, and your head and quarters to be disposed of at the pleasure of the King's Majesty." It is fortunate for the law, as well as for offenders, that such merciful and upright judges have ceased to exist.

In 1782, the year preceding that which witnessed the last executions at Tyburn, the dead body of one John Haynes, a professional thief and housebreaker, who, in consequence, had finished here his career, was taken, as a "subject" for dissection, to the residence of Sir William Blizard. The body, we are told, showed signs of life, and Sir William perfected its recovery. Anxious to know the sensations which John Haynes had experienced at the moment of his suspension, the surgeon questioned the thief

earnestly upon the subject. The only answer he could obtain was as follows :—"The last thing I recollect was going up Holborn Hill in a cart. I thought then that I was in a beautiful green field; and that is all I remember till I found myself in your honour's dissecting-room." It is worthy of record that the last criminal executed here was one Ryland, who was hung for forgery in 1783; after which the gallows were taken down about London in order to concentrate the executions at Newgate and Horsemonger Lane.

Many good stories are told about Tyburn; among others, the following :—"A celebrated wit one evening was walking along a lane near Oxford Road, as it was then called, when he was accosted by a shabby-looking fellow, who asked him the way to Tyburn. The gentleman, being fond of a jest, answered, 'Why, you have only to rob the first person you meet, and you will find the way there easily.' The fellow thanked him, and pulled out and presented a pistol, threatening to blow his brains out if he did not give up his purse. The wit was forced to comply, and lost his money and his jest at once."

Before leaving the subject of the "gallows," a word or two about "Jack Ketch" and his office may not be out of place. The origin of the name "Jack Ketch," as applied to the public executioner, is thus explained in Lloyd's MS. Collection of English Pedigrees in the British Museum. We give it for what it is worth. "The Manor of Tyburn," writes Mr. Lloyd, "where felons were for a long time executed, was formerly held by Richard Jacquett, from whence we have the name Jack Ketch as a corruption." But the work of the executioner was sufficiently artistic to admit of degrees of skill. Thus Dryden remarks :—"A man may be capable (as Jack Ketch's wife said of her servant) of a plain piece of work, a bare hanging; but to make a malefactor die sweetly was only belonging to her husband."

The earliest hangman whose name has descended to us, if we may trust the authority of that accomplished antiquary, the late Dr. Rimbault, is one Bull, who is mentioned in his public capacity in Gabriel Harvey's tract against Nash, called "Pierce's Supererogation" (1593). Bull was succeeded by the more celebrated Derrick, who cut off the head of the unfortunate Earl of Essex in 1601. In Dekker's "Bellman of London," printed in 1608, under the article "Prigging Law," are the following notices of this worthy :—"For he rides his circuit with the devil, and Derrick must be his host, and Tiburne the land at which he will light." "At the gallows, where I leave them, as to the haven at which they must all cast anchor, if Derrick's cables do but hold." Again, at the end of his "Wonderful Year," is this passage :— " But by these tricks imagining that many thousands have been turned wrongfully off the ladder of life ; and praying that Derrick or his successors may live to do those a good turn that have done so to others. *Hic finis Priami!* Here is an end of an old song." Derrick held his unenviable post for nearly half a century ; and from him was named the temporary crane formed on board ship for unloading and general hoisting purposes, by lashing one spar to another, gibbet fashion. The next hangman was the notorious Gregory Brandon, who, as the story goes, by a *ruse* played upon Garter King-at-Arms, had a grant of arms confirmed to him, and was thereby "made a gentleman," which the mob in a joke soon elevated into esquire, "a title by which he was known for the rest of his life, and which was afterwards transferred to his successors in office." He had frequently acted as a substitute for Derrick ; and had become so popular that the gallows was sometimes called by his Christian name, as may be seen in the following lines :—

> " This trembles under the Black Rod, and he
> Doth fear his fate from the *Gregorian* tree."

Gregory Brandon was succeeded by his son Richard, who seems to have claimed the gallows by inheritance. This Richard Brandon, as we have shown in a previous volume, has the credit of being the executioner of Charles I.* " Squire" Dun was the next common hangman, and he in turn was succeeded by the veritable Jack Ketch, who was the executioner of Lord William Russell and the Duke of Monmouth. Macaulay, in his account of the death of the latter, says : " He then accosted John Ketch, the executioner, a wretch who had butchered many brave and noble victims, and whose name has, during a century and a half, been vulgarly given to all who have succeeded him in his odious office. ' Here,' said the duke, ' are six guineas for you. Do not hack me as you did my Lord Russell. I have heard that you struck him three or four times. My servant will give you some gold if you do the work well.' " This notable functionary does not seem to have had a very easy time of it ; at all events, in 1678, a broadside was published, entitled " The Plotter's Ballad : being Jack Ketch's incomparable receipt for the cure of traytorous recusants." In the same year appeared a quarto tract : " The Tyburn Ghost ; or, Strange Downfal of the Gallows : a most true Relation how the famous Triple Tree, near Paddington, was pluckt

up by the roots, and demolisht by certain Evil Spirits ; with Jack Ketch's Lamentation for the Loss of his Shop, 1678." In the next year was produced " Squire Ketch's Declaration concerning his late Confinement in the Queen's Bench and Marshalsea, whereby his hopeful harvest was liked to have been blasted." Two years later we find him at Oxford : —" Aug. 31, 1681. Wednesday, at 11, Stephen College suffered death by hanging in the Castle Yard, Oxon, and when he hanged about half an hour was cut down by *Catch*, or *Ketch*, and quartered under the gallows." † The name of Ketch is often mentioned, in the lampoons of the day, along with that of the infamous Judge Jeffreys, as his brother in crime. One poet writes :—

" While Jeffreys on the bench, Ketch on the gibbet sits."

He is also mentioned by D'Urfey, in his humorous poem, entitled " Butler's Ghost," published in 1682 ; and in the following year he is thus mentioned in the epilogue to Dryden and Lee's " Duke of Guise : "—

> " Lenitives, he says, suit best with our condition ;
> Jack Ketch, says I, 's an excellent physician."

For the following scrap of antiquarian lore respecting the interesting locality of which we treat, our readers are indebted to " honest " John Timbs : —" Formerly, when a person prosecuted another for any offence, and the prisoner was executed at Tyburn, the prosecutor was presented with a ' Tyburn Ticket,' which exempted him and its future holders from having to serve on juries. This privilege was not repealed till the sixth year of the reign of George IV."

The following is said to be the reason why Tyburn was chosen as the place of execution and burial of traitors :—The parishioners of St. Sepulchre's, near Newgate, were not over-well pleased that the bodies of those malefactors who had suffered the last penalty of the law should be buried amongst them ; in proof, it may be mentioned, on the authority of a letter from Fleetwood to Lord Burghley, that they " would not suffer a traytor's corpes to be layed in the earthe where theire parents, wyeffs, chyldren, kynred, maisters, and old naighboures did rest : and so his carcas was returned to the buryall ground neere to Tyborne."

The gallows at Tyburn was triangular in plan, having three legs to stand on, and appears to have been a permanent erection. From the number of criminals hanged there, it would indeed seem to have been useless to have taken it down after each execution. We may learn, from a sermon preached

---

* See Vol. III., p. 350.　　　　　　　　† " A'Wood's Life," by Dr. Bliss, 1848.

by good Bishop Horne, towards the close of the eighteenth century, that it was no uncommon thing to see scores of felons executed here. Taylor, the Water Poet, in "The Praise and Virtue of a Jayle and Jaylers" (1623), gives these lines :—

> "I have heard sundry men ofttimes dispute,
> Of trees that in one yeare will twice beare fruit ;
> But if a man note Tyburn, 'twill appeare
> That that's a tree that bears twelve times a yeare."

cart, riding up Holborn in a two-wheeled chariot, with a guard of halberdiers. 'There goes a proper fellow,' says one ; 'Good people, pray for me.' Now I'm at the three wooden stilts. Hey ! now I feel my toes hang i' the cart ; now 'tis drawn away ; now, now, now !—I'm gone !"

At Tyburn, upon the restoration of monarchy, was performed the farce of dragging Sir Henry Mildmay, Wallop, and some other members of the

CONNAUGHT PLACE.

Again, in Dr. Johnson's "London" (a poem), we read :—

> "Scarce can our fields—such crowds at Tyburn die—
> With hemp the gallows and the fleet supply."

Then there is a parody on Gray's "Elegy," in which we read—

> "Yet e'en these humble vices to correct,
> Old Tyburn lifts his triple front on high."

In Shirley's play of *The Wedding*, published in 1629, an execution at Tyburn is thus depicted :—"*Rawbone:* I do imagine myself apprehended already ; now the constable is carrying me to Newgate ; now, now, I'm in the Sessions House, in the dock ; now I'm called ; 'Not guilty, my lord.' The jury has found the indictment, *billa vera.* Now, now, comes my sentence. Now I'm in the

regicide party, to the fatal tree, with halters round their necks. Miles Corbet, the regicide also, having been arrested on the Continent, was brought to London, dragged through the streets hither, and executed.

Evelyn, in his "Diary," under date January 30, 1661, the first anniversary of the murder of Charles I. since the Restoration, writes :—"The carcases of those rebels, Cromwell, Bradshaw, the judge who condemned his Majesty, and Ireton (son-in-law to the Usurper), were dragged out of their superb tombs in Westminster among the kings to Tyburn, and hanged on the gallows there from nine in the morning till six at night, and then buried under that fatal and ignominious monument in a deep pit, thousands who had seen

The IDLE PRENTICE Executed at Tyburn.

Proverbs CHAP: I. Vers: 27, 28.
When feare cometh as desolation, and their
destruction cometh as a Whirlewind: when
distress cometh upon them. Then they shall
call upon God, but he will not answer.

THE IDLE APPRENTICE EXECUTED AT TYBURN   (After Hogarth's Print.)

them in all their pride being spectators." How far this "deep pit" can be regarded as really the last resting-place of Cromwell's body may be inferred from what we have already written on the subject, in our account of Red Lion Square, Holborn.*

In the "New View of London," published in 1708, no mention is made of either Oxford or Uxbridge Road, but the thoroughfare is entered as Tyburn Road. It is thus described as lying "between St. Giles' Pound, east, and the lane leading to the Gallows, west, 350 yards in length." The writer adds:—"This street has its name as being the next street to Tyburn, the place for execution of all such malefactors, generally speaking, as have committed acts worthy of death within the City and Liberties of London and County of Middlesex. I have known, he continues, "nineteen executed at one sessions, though these are held about eight times a year; but this is near twenty years ago." He then congratulates the nation on the decrease in the number of executions of late, which he ascribes to improvements in the law, and to the efforts of societies for the reformation of manners; and ends by telling a story of a man who revived, after being cut down off the gallows, in 1705.

Tyburn, it need scarcely be added, figures constantly in the caricatures of Hogarth. Thus, in his "Industry and Idleness," "Tom Idle" goes to Tyburn in a cart with a coffin in it, whilst the other apprentice, Francis Goodchild, drives to the Mansion House, as Lord Mayor of London, with footmen and sword-bearer, the King and the Court looking on from a balcony in St. Paul's Churchyard, and smiling approval. In Hogarth's print of Tyburn Tree, the hangman is represented coolly smoking his pipe, as he reclines by the gibbet, in full view of the hills of Hampstead and Highgate. "Could Tom Idle's ghost have made its appearance in 1847," asks Thackeray, in his "Humourists," "what changes would have been remarked by that astonished escaped criminal! Over that road which the hangman used to travel constantly, and the Oxford stage twice a week, go ten thousand carriages every day; over yonder road, by which Dick Turpin fled to Windsor, and Squire Western journeyed into town, when he came to take up his quarters at the Hercules Pillars on the outskirts of London, what a rush of civilisation and order flows now! What armies of gentlemen with umbrellas march to banks, and chambers, and counting-houses! What regiments of nursery-maids and pretty infantry; what peaceful processions of

policemen; what light broughams and what gay carriages; what swarms of busy apprentices and artificers, riding on omnibus-roofs, pass daily and hourly! Tom Idle's times are quite changed; many of the institutions are gone into disuse which were admired in his day. There's more pity and kindness, and a better chance for poor Tom's successors now than at that simpler period, when Fielding hanged him and Hogarth drew him."

Tyburn also figures in one of Hogarth's pictures of "Marriage à la Mode," where Counsellor Silvertongue pays the last penalty of the law for sending a certain noble earl out of the world before his time. In Hogarth's hands, no doubt, Tyburn was usefully employed, both

"To point a moral and adorn a tale."

But Tyburn has witnessed other scenes besides those of which we have spoken above. The story of Queen Henrietta Maria doing penance here is thus told by Mr. S. W. Gardiner, in his "History of England under the Duke of Buckingham and Charles I.:"—"It was after a long day spent in attendance on the devotions of her Church at the Chapel at St. James's that the young queen of Charles I. strolled out, with her ladies, to breathe the fresh evening air in St. James's Park. By-and-by she found her way into Hyde Park, and by accident or design directed her steps towards Tyburn. In her position it was quite natural that she should bethink herself of those who had suffered there as martyrs for the faith which she had come to England to support. What wonder if her heart beat more quickly, and if some prayer for strength to bear her weary lot rose to her lips? A week or two probably passed away before the tale reached Charles, exaggerated in its passage through the mouths of men. . . . The Queen of England, he was told, had been conducted on a pilgrimage to offer prayer to dead traitors, who had suffered the just reward of their crimes. The cup of his displeasure was now full; . . . those who had brought her to this should no longer remain in England. . . . On July 31 the king and queen dined together at Whitehall. After dinner he conducted her to his private apartments, locked the door on her attendants, and told her that her servants must go." Meanwhile, Conway was taking measures for the removal of her ladies to Somerset House. "As soon as the young queen perceived what was being done she flew to the window and dashed to pieces the glass, that her voice might be heard by those who were bidding her adieu for the last time; and Charles, it is said, dragged her back into the room, with her hands

---

* See Vol. IV., p. 546.

bleeding from the energy with which she clung to the bars." As we have already stated, in our account of Somerset House,* no time was lost in sending off the queen's French attendants to their native country.

It is more probable that the act on the part of her Majesty was a voluntary one; for, although pious and devout, the queen was not at all a person to be led blindly at the will of any confessor. However, in the illustrated edition of Pennant's "London," in the British Museum, there is to be seen a copy of a rare German print, purporting to be a representation of the scene. At a short distance off is the confessor's carriage, drawn by six horses; in the coach is seated the confessor himself, and a page, with a lighted candle or torch, is standing at the door. The fact is certainly recorded in a cotemporary document published in the first series of "Original Letters," edited by Sir Henry Ellis; but as the language used is of the most rabid and foul-mouthed kind—the confessor being styled "Luciferian," and the details of the affair styled "ridiculous," "absurd," "beggarly"—we may reasonably entertain a doubt whether it was not a "mare's-nest." In all probability the story was concocted by some Titus Oates of the day. The letter in question, which purports to be "from Mr. Pory to Mr. Joseph Mead," contains the following expressions :—" No longer agone then upon St. James *his day last*, those hypocritical dogges made the pore Queen to walke a foot (some add bare-foot) from her house at St. James to the gallowes at Tyborne, *thereby to honour the Saint of the day* in visiting that holy place where so many martyrs (forsooth) had shed their bloud in defense of the Catholique cause. . . . Yea, they have made her to go barefoot, to spin, to eat her meat out of tryne (wooden) dishes, to waite at the table and serve her servants, with many other ridiculous and absurd penances. It was, certainly, 'high time' that this French train should be dismissed; and packed off they were ·('contumaciously refusing to go') in coaches, carts, and barges, to Gravesend."

If it be true that old George III. took such an interest in the welfare of those condemned to die upon the gallows as he is represented to have done in an anecdote which was at one time freely circulated, his time must have been pretty well occupied by devotional exercises. The anecdote in question, albeit highly honourable to his sense of public duty, is mentioned on the authority of Stevenson, the American envoy in London. Some extraordinary occurrence having called a French

statesman to the palace as late as two o'clock in the morning, he found the king in his cabinet, examining the case of a prisoner condemned to execution. The envoy afterwards ascertained that the king keeps a register, recording the name of every person capitally condemned, the decision, and its reasons. Frequently, in the still hours of the night, he performs the task of investigating those cases, and adds to the record the circumstances which had influenced his decision. The envoy probably did not know that the great and good George III. had pursued nearly the same practice fifty years before, weighed the evidence with the deepest anxiety, and generally shut himself up in his cabinet at Windsor (it was presumed in prayer) during the hour appointed for the execution in London.

The exact spot on which the fatal Tyburn Tree was erected has been often discussed by antiquaries. It would appear, however, to be identified with the site of the house in the south-east corner of Connaught Square, formerly numbered 49; for in the lease granted by the Bishop of London, to whom the property belongs, this fact is particularly mentioned. A writer in *The Antiquary*, in October, 1873, says, with reference to this subject :—" I was born within 100 yards of the exact spot on which the gallows stood, and my uncle took up the stones on which the uprights were placed. The following is his statement to me, and the circumstance of his telling it :—In 1810, when Connaught Place was being built, he was employed on the works, and for many years lived at the corner of Bryanston Street and the Edgware Road, nearly opposite Connaught Mews. My father, a master carpenter, worked for several years in Connaught Place, and on one occasion he employed his brother, I think in the year 1834; at all events, we had just left No. 6, the residence of Sir Charles Coote. It was at this time I said to my uncle, 'Now you are here, tell me where the gallows stood;' to which he replied, 'Opposite here, where the staves are.' I thereupon crossed over, and drove a brass-headed nail into the exact spot he indicated. On reaching home, I told my mother of the occurrence, and asked if it were correct. She said it was so, for she remembered the posts standing when she was a child. This might be about the year 1800; and, as she was born in Bryanston Street, I believe she stated what she knew to be a fact. I well remember Connaught Square being built, and I also recollect a low house standing at the corner of the Uxbridge Road, close to No. 1, Connaught Place (Arklow House), and that, on the removal of this house,

---

* See Vol. III., p. 91.

quantities of human bones were found. I saw them carted away by Mr. Nicholls, contractor, of Adams' Mews. He removed Tyburn toll-house in 1829. From what I have been told by old inhabitants that were born in the neighbourhood, probably about 1750, I have every reason to believe that the space from the toll-house to Frederick Mews was used as a place of execution, and the bodies buried adjacent, for I have seen the remains disinterred when the square and adjoining streets were being built."

Smith, in his "History of St. Marylebone," states that "the gallows were for many years a standing fixture on a small eminence at the corner of the Edgware Road, near the turnpike, on the identical spot where a toll-house was subsequently erected by the Uxbridge Road Trust. Beneath this place are supposed to lie the bones of Bradshaw, Ireton, and other regicides, which were taken from their graves after the Restoration, and buried under the gallows. The gallows itself subsequently consisted of two uprights and a cross-beam, erected on the morning of execution across the Edgware Road, opposite the house at the corner of Upper Bryanston Street and the Edgware Road, wherein the gallows was deposited after being used; this house had curious iron balconies to the windows of the first and second floors, where the sheriffs sat to witness the executions. After the place of execution was changed to Newgate, in 1783, the gallows was bought by a carpenter, and made into stands for beer-butts in the cellars of the 'Carpenters' Arms' public-house, hard by."

"Around the gibbet," says Mr. Timbs, in his "Curiosities of London," "were erected open galleries, like a race-course stand, wherein seats were let to spectators at executions: the key of one of them was kept by Mammy Douglas, 'the Tyburn pew-opener.' In 1758, when Dr. Henesey was to have been executed for treason, the prices of seats rose to 2s. and 2s. 6d.; but the doctor being 'most provokingly reprieved,' a riot ensued, and most of the seats were destroyed."

The name of "Tyburn," thus mixed up with the saddest portions of our national history, and associated with ideas of villany and crime, very naturally smelt anything but sweet in the nose of the metropolis; and it was not until the city grew in bulk so tremendously that it threatened to burst its swathing bands, that the region around the old gallows, now known as "Tyburnia," came to be built upon, and inhabited by the upper classes of society.

It is recorded by Mr. Percy Fitzgerald, in his sketch of Charles Townshend, that his eccentric mother, Audrey, Lady Townshend, who so long "entertained" at her house in Whitehall, was one day rallied by her friends on taking a short lease of "a villa at Tyburn." "Oh," replied the witty woman, "you see it is a neighbourhood of which I could never tire, for my neighbours are being hanged every week; so we are always changing!" It was this same lady who, on being asked if it was true that Whitfield had recanted, answered, "No, madam; but I know he has canted;" and who sarcastically remarked of the royal family, who took a fancy to go to all public shows and suppers, that it was "the cheapest family to see, and the dearest to keep, of any that had ever been seen."

Mr. G. A. Sala hits the right nail on the head, in his "Gaslight and Daylight," when he remarks that while the region of the Grosvenors is the place for the "swells of the peerage, those of blue blood and the strawberry-leaves," Tyburnia suits admirably "the nobility of yesterday, your mushroom aristocrats, millionaires, ex-lord mayors, and people of that sort;" and he also pithily adds, "Tyburn is gone: I am not such an old fogey as to remember *that*, nor so staunch a conservative as to regret it now that it is gone."

"Tyburnia" proper, as we may call the city which sprang up between the Edgware Road and Westbourne Terrace, in the reign of William IV., consists of squares, terraces, and rows of stately mansions, which now rival in elegance her more southern sister, "Belgravia." Oxford and Cambridge Terraces, which run from the Edgware Road to the southern end of Westbourne Terrace, with Oxford and Cambridge Squares to the south of them, will long keep in remembrance the munificence of Lady Margaret, Countess of Richmond, as the founder of divinity professorships in our two great and ancient universities.

The Rev. J. Richardson, referring to the days of the Regency, writes thus in his "Recollections," published in 1856 :—"The northern boundary of the old metropolis, then called Oxford Road, terminated abruptly at the entrance of the Park, where now stands the triumphal arch lately removed from Buckingham Palace. The now fashionable district which forms one side of the Bayswater Road, and occupies the angle between that road and Paddington, was, in the eyes of all respectable people, a locality to be avoided. Ragged fields stretched over scores of acres of ground; and the ominous name of Tyburn frightened, not, indeed, those whom it ought to have deterred, but those who either assumed a character for decency, or really possessed one. In fact, this part was a blank in the improvements of London for years after other suburbs had been built upon; and it was not until comparatively a recent date that the tea-gardens, and other similar low haunts of debauchery, gave way to the elegant and stately buildings with which it is now covered." It is impossible not to recognise these places of amusement in the portrait which Charles Dickens gives us, in his "Sketches by Boz," of the typical London tea-gardens, with their snug boxes and alcoves; the men and women, boys and girls, sweethearts and married folk, babies in arms and children in chaises, the pipes and the shrimps, the cigars and the periwinkles, the tea and tobacco, are each and all described with a skill almost equal to that of a photographer. To the particular "Sketch" entitled "London Recreations" we must refer our readers for all further details. As we have shown in the preceding chapter, the last of the tea-gardens—covering what is now Lancaster Gate—did not disappear until about 1855.

At Connaught House, Connaught Place, close by the Edgware Road, the unfortunate Caroline, Princess of Wales, took up her residence when banished from the Palace; and hither came the Princess Charlotte in a hackney-coach, when she quarrelled with her father and left Warwick House, as we have stated in our account of that place.* The young princess, as she advanced towards womanhood, became more and more intractable and wilful. In the end, the Regent and his Ministers thought the best step would be to find her a husband; and the youthful Prince of Orange was suggested as the most eligible. He was by birth a Protestant; he had been educated at Oxford, and had served in Spain with credit; but the self-willed young lady refused him—in a word, "turned up her nose" at him. Every opportunity was given to him to make himself agreeable to the future heiress of the English throne; but either his capacities and acquirements were of a low order, or the princess had proposed to herself quite another standard of excellence as her *beau ideal*. She simply said "she did not like Oranges in any shape;" and though her royal papa stormed, and bishops reasoned with her, her resolution remained unshaken. The public admired her pluck and firmness, and her refusal to be sold into matrimony like a common chattel. She was a princess, but she was also a true-hearted woman, and she felt that she must really love the man whom she should

wed, if she would escape the unhappiness which had darkened the married life of her parents. The fortunate individual who pleased her taste was not long in appearing; and her marriage with Prince Leopold of Saxe-Coburg was solemnised, ere long, with her father's consent, and with the hearty good wishes of the people. The Prince himself, then a humble cadet of a petty German house, was travelling in England; he met the Princess Charlotte at one of the many mansions of the aristocracy, and he soon obtained an interest in her affections, and also the consent of the Prince Regent, who was probably glad enough to get his intractable daughter off his hands at any price. Leopold at that time was one of the noblest-looking young princes in Europe. Tall and princely in his bearing, and fascinating in his manners, a brave soldier, and an accomplished courtier, he was worthy to win such a prize. They were married on May 2nd, 1816. Alas! within a little more than a year the great bell of St. Paul's was tolled to announce to a sorrowing people the death of the princess in giving birth to a dead infant!

The sale of the effects of the Princess of Wales, at Connaught House, took place in October, 1814. The name of the mansion was at a later date changed to Arklow House; the latter, like the former, being one of the titles inherent in the royal family. The late Duke of Sussex was also Baron of Arklow. Sir Augustus D'Este, son of the Duke of Sussex, lived here for some time subsequently. It is now the town residence of Mr. A. Beresford-Hope.

At No. 13 in Hyde Park Square, lived that specimen of a fine old English gentleman, Mr. T. Assheton-Smith, whose name is so well known among Masters of Hounds. A glass apartment on the roof of this house, after his death, was magnified, by the fears of the servant-girls in the neighbourhood, into the abode of a ghost; and the ghost—or, at all events, the alarm—was only suppressed by editors "writing it down" in the London newspapers.

In concluding this chapter, we may remark that the whole neighbourhood is of too recent a growth to have many historical reminiscences. Haydon, the painter, it is true, lived for some time in Burwood Place, close by Connaught Square, and there he died by his own hand in 1846. We shall have more to say about him when we come to Paddington.

* See Vol. IV., p. 82.